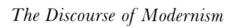

The Discourse of Modernism

The Discourse
of Modernism

TIMOTHY J. REISS

Cornell University Press

Ithaca and London

First published 1982 by Cornell University Press.
Published in the United Kingdom by Cornell University Press Ltd.,
Ely House, 37 Dover Street, London W1X 4HQ.

International Standard Book Number 0-8014-1464-4
Library of Congress Catalog Card Number 81-15212
Printed in the United States of America
Librarians: Library of Congress cataloging information appears on the last page of the book.

The paper in this book is acid-free, and meets the guidelines for permanence and durability of the Committee on Production Guidelines for Book Longevity of the Council on Library Resources.

For Jean

(and all the waiting)

and in memory of my mother,
1909–1981

Contents

I was young then and did not know how difficult it is for Western man to understand the dream-heavy classical soul. They are so far apart. The god of superlative shape has been replaced by the god of superlative force and between the two conceptions there is all space.

—Eric Ambler, *Journey into Fear*

Expressing their thoughts in words of which they are not the masters, enclosing them in verbal forms whose historical dimensions they are unaware of, men believe that their speech is their servant and do not realize that they are submitting themselves to its demands.

—Michel Foucault, *Les mots et les choses*

It may always be asserted that determinant paths *must* exist between the slave system characteristic of Greek society and the miracle of geometry, that the appearance of the applied sciences from the neoclassical era on *must* be conditioned in various ways by the mercantile economy of modern Europe, and so on. It can be asserted. It is correct to do so. That does not change the fact that the outline of these paths, the detailed description of such conditions is nonexistent. The matter has perhaps been logically demonstrated, it has not been shown.

—Michel Serres, "Les sciences"

Preface

The present work examines aspects of the emergence and development, of the consolidation and growth to dominance, of modern Western discourse—or, as I will be calling it, the "analytico-referential." The book sets up a model to describe how one dominant discourse gives way to another. In particular, it shows the creation and development of the various elements fundamental to analytico-referential discourse, and it demonstrates at the same time the necessary occultation of other elements whose visible presence in discourse would subvert its overt aims (though such occultations are not "intentional"). The basic claim is that the kind of epistemic development seen in the early seventeenth century, preceded by at least a century of crisis and followed by a half century of consolidation, is being echoed in our own time and is leading to a similarly significant and complete conceptual change. I also claim that the change of our own time can be understood only in the light of the earlier one, and that it is urgent to understand just what kind of arguments and assertions were necessary to the establishment of the "discursive class" now being placed in question. The principal corpus I use in establishing these claims is composed of science fictions and utopias drawn from the critical historical moment of the European Renaissance and Neoclassicism. These brief assertions require some immediate explanation and clarification.

The term "discourse" refers to the way in which the material embodying sign processes is organized. Discourse can thus be characterized as the visible and describable praxis of what is called "thinking." For thinking is nothing but the organization of signs as an ongoing process. Signs themselves may be 'defined' provisionally as the nondiscrete 'elements' composing the process toward meaningfulness that itself is both defined by and defining of what signs are. So

9

cumbersome a turn of phrase is necessary for the moment, in order to avoid such simplifying definitions as: signs are mediators between concepts and things, or concepts and other concepts; or signs are discrete units of signifying systems (usually taking natural languages as exemplary cases) that in combination with other signs of the same system refer to other such units or to nonsignificant objects outside the system; or, more simply, a sign is a unit of meaning (undefined) that stands for some other meaningful or nonmeaningful unit.

All such definitions as these last refer the idea of the sign to a particular order of conceptualization, to what used to be called a particular *Weltanschauung.* The excessively cumbersome 'definition' offered above implies that the only evidence whatsoever not only for thinking but for *all* human knowing and doing, without exception, is our common use of signs. We may therefore say that such use *is* human action, and that it is *all* human action of whatever kind. No doubt such action (process, exchange, production, or whatever) is not definable *only* in such terms, but no matter in what additional terms one may wish to define it, it is specifically *human* action only to the extent that *we* can make it meaningful. That is the sense in which such action may be considered first and foremost a matter of the production and movement of signs.

The definition is cumbersome in particular because I wish to indicate that the use and definition of signs themselves change as the discursive process moves along. Precisely the why, how, and wherefore of such change are what this book seeks to explore in the context of a specific historical period in the West: such change, too, is the reason for the provisional nature of the 'definition.' By the end of the volume it will be found impossible to give any universally valid definition of the sign, of meaningfulness, or of their associated terms, because such concepts will be clearly seen as inseparably bound up in the constant development of discourses. With this proviso, one might well parody the beginning of Wittgenstein's *Tractatus* and affirm that our use of signs is all that is the case. A similar view is expressed by C. S. Peirce and M. M. Bakhtin: all human action, all human mental life, and indeed the universe as a whole, insofar as it relates to things human, are a matter of the production, interpretation, and interrelating of signs.

Signs are not disembodied ideas, therefore. They are available only in specific material and in specific processes. Such material and such processes are themselves caught within a network of contextual relations, within a definable if exceedingly complex environment, from which they are inseparable. They are the stuff of history, of society in movement, of conceptual processes in flux, of economic and political forces in motion, of developing artistic forms, and so on. Actual processes of material production, for example, are as much systems of meaning as are natural languages—and only so are they available to us as knowledge and action (though the processes through which they come to be meaningful are obviously not those of language). What I will be calling "discursive classes"—the particular network of relations ordered by given practices of signifying systems (to some degree what Michel Foucault has called *epistemes*)—are therefore specific to a time, a place, and a society, though it is such discursive class in turn that permits these three to be defined.

I use the singular "class" here because I will be arguing that, generally speaking, one discursive class is dominant at any given time and place—barring specifiable moments of transition. That is to say that one such class provides the conceptual tools that make the majority of human practices meaningful: meaningful in the sense that they may be analyzed into their manner, nature, and purpose, and may be related to one another as defining the 'human.' Yet where one class is dominant, there may well be others that are contemporaneous with it. Indeed, I will suggest that the dominant theoretical model is apparently invariably accompanied by a dominant occulted practice. This is composed of widespread activities (though the phrase is awkward) that escape analysis by the dominant model, that do not acquire 'meaningfulness' in its terms, that are therefore in the strictest sense *unthinkable*.

When elements from such occulted practice start to become tools for analysis, then the previously dominant model is gradually rendered inoperative, and there is a passage to new dominances, making use both of quite new elements and of already emergent ones, and accompanied by residual elements that only slowly pass out of sight and mind. Such a passage occurs when internal contradictions of the dominant model begin to prevent its effective functioning, when it begins to produce strong alternative elements of discourse (as we will see in Kepler, for example), and when the dominant occulted practice begins to become conceptually useful. This assertion implies, of course, that what was just said about signs as being the whole case applies absolutely only insofar as such practices are grasped in their historicity: that is, as *already* meaningful for us looking 'back' at them. Only as past activities can *all* human practices be considered to be discursive. This argument is akin to Peirce's constant assumption that something can be done about a set of facts only if that set conforms to a (previously known) generalization.

The practice "occulted" for us in our time escapes signification by very definition. Nonetheless, it may be hoped that this way of conceptualizing what I am calling discursive practices can enable us to grasp the nature of such practice, its place, and its manner of functioning.

All this is extremely abstract, and the first two chapters will make the matter somewhat more concrete. The Middle Ages may thus be characterized as ruled by a dominant theocratico-theological model, accompanied by an occulted feudal practice ("occulted" in the simple sense that it is not generally used to explain and analyze most human—and nonhuman—practices). Notably in Machiavelli certain of these feudal relations begin to provide elements for what will become a "capitalist" analytic, leading directly to the dominance of what I call analytico-referential discourse—a term clarified in Chapter 1 but whose development is the object of this entire volume. It is accompanied, I suggest, by occulted relations of socioeconomic production. In the nineteenth century Marx will play the role Machiavelli played in the sixteenth, and while this book is mainly concerned with the emergence and growth to dominance of analytico-referential discourse, it will also pay some attention, as I say, to the crisis and limits *ad quem* of that discourse (brought on in part by the accession to meaningfulness of the previously occulted socioeconomic relations of production).

Such a theoretical model allows for both continuity and change, for moments of stability and passages of discontinuity. It also allows for some 'explanation' of how and why such moments and passages alternate. In a single volume one cannot hope to cover all discursive domains, all kinds of discourse, for it is clear that in order to show the working of such a model and such processes of change and development some close analysis of punctual examples of the use of sign systems is essential: the corpus must be precise, relatively homogeneous, and sufficiently complex to avoid oversimplification; it must make use of an unsimplified signifying material (natural languages being clearly exemplary); and it must be open enough to the overall discursive environment to make contextualization fairly easy. For an initial study, therefore, the corpus of utopias and science fictions already indicated seems almost ideal. It provides precision and homogeneity. It admits of facility neither in its elaboration nor in its signifying material. It furnishes a clear meeting ground for political and scientific theory, for economic and philosophical elaboration, not to mention for explorations in 'linguistics' and 'psychology,' literature and aesthetics.

The claims of the book therefore exceed rather considerably what might seem to be suggested by the apparently narrow corpus explored in Chapters 3 to 11. The book tries to show the emergence and development of elements fundamental to the discourse variously called "positivist," "capitalist," "experimentalist," "historicist," "modern," and so on—depending on which particular type of discourse is the object of the description. The critical method and many of its assumptions are derived principally from the work of Michel Foucault, though not uncritically: certain of their aspects are further developed here, the notion of epistemic "rupture" (recently pasted over by Foucault himself) is replaced with the attempt, already explained in brief, to show how one episteme (or "discursive class," as I call it) in fact develops out of another, and other aspects are provided with the added precision afforded by the use of a rather narrowly defined textual corpus—even if I do not always stick to it.

This theoretical basis, its present application, and its epistemological ramifications and implications are explored in the first two chapters. Here is justified the hypothesis that the European seventeenth century saw the rise to dominance of a new class of discourse, the analytico-referential, and the gradual occultation of others that might have been available as alternative modes for human thought and action. The chief of these for the period immediately preceding is that of "patterning," a class of discourse whose functioning is explored briefly by reference to such as Paracelsus, Rabelais, Cusanus, Agricola, Bruno, and to the contemporary work of Claude Lévi-Strauss, Gérard Simon, and Ian Hacking, among others. This is also opposed in Chapter 2 both to the Greek experience and to that of the Middle Ages. The following nine chapters are composed of close analyses of the texts of my literary corpus, these texts being constantly referred to parallel developments in philosophy, political theory, and science, as illustrated most notably by Kepler himself, Bruno, Descartes, Galileo, Bacon, Hobbes. The analyses are at once an investigation of the ordering principles of the texts studied and a demonstration of the general epistemic development that is the volume's hypothesis.

The conclusions explored in Chapter 12 essentially suggest (1) that these developments are indeed general discursive ones, and situated quite precisely in a specific historical moment, and (2) that such notions as those of truth and valid experiment (in science), of referential language and representation (in all types of discourse), of possessive individualism (in political and economic theory), of contract (in sociopolitical and legal theory), of taste (in aesthetic theory), of common sense and the corresponding notion of concept (in philosophy) are, in fact, hypostatizations of a particular discursive system. It is also suggested throughout the book, suggestion that culminates in a brief proposal for an analysis of the controlling discursive constraints of Freudian theory and practice, that the series of necessary occultations and traps accompanying this development have now been brought back to the surface of discourse and are responsible for a contemporary crisis—at the same time that they propose suggestions for its solution.

The debts I have incurred over the years are numerous. I thank first of all the students who participated in seminars at Yale University and at the universities of Montreal, Toronto, and British Columbia—some concerned with this material, all with the underlying theoretical matrix. Without the stimulation they provided, this volume might not have seen the light of day, certainly not in its present form. I owe thanks as well to Jacques Neefs and the students in his seminar at the Université de Paris VIII (Vincennes) in 1971–72, who, by inviting me to present the ideas in what are now the three chapters centered on Cyrano, enabled me to profit from their responses and questions.

It is impossible to name all the colleagues, friends, and acquaintances who have commented upon versions of parts of the volume, and all the others who, in one way or another, have provided encouragement and occasions for fruitful exchanges of ideas. Nonetheless, it is a pleasure to record those to whom I feel most indebted: Pierre Beaudry, Michel De Certeau, Robert Elbaz, Françoise Gaillard, Pierre Gravel, Claude Imbert, Wladimir Krysinski, Louis Marin, Georges May, Christie V. McDonald, Walter Moser, Patricia Parker, Chantal Saint-Jarre, Michel Serres, Paul Zumthor. The general debt to Michel Foucault is self-evident. I also thank Nancy S. Struever, William J. Kennedy, and especially Peter Haidu, whose admirably attentive readings of earlier versions of the complete text enabled me to make essential corrections and improvements. Eugene Vance gave most generously of his time and knowledge of the Middle Ages in reading the penultimate version of Chapter 2, allowing me at once to avoid egregious errors and to avail myself of texts that provide more thorough support for what, in so short a space, must still remain little better than a series of rather contentious assertions.

One further acknowledgment of this nature is a necessary pleasure here. Only subsequent to his reading of Chapter 2 did I learn from my colleague Gené Vance of the existence of a remarkable series of unpublished papers by F. Edward Cranz of Connecticut College, dealing with the Middle Ages and early Renaissance and with their intellectual relations both with Antiquity and with our own time. Upon reading them, I was both astonished by the proximity of our positions (and sometimes their expression) concerning the probable impossibility of our ever fully 'understanding' Antiquity, and disconcerted by the fact that he, along with others, placed the conceptual break with which I am here concerned with Anselm and Abelard around 1100 A.D., whereas I insist it comes much later. My Chapter 2 argues that while 'emergent' discursive elements may be found long before the sixteenth century, it is not possible to maintain that anything like our modern episteme begins to develop prior to that time. On the other hand, I do think it is possible to allow for the development of a new episteme around 1100 that is itself replaced during the sixteenth century: the disagreement is thus less considerable than I had at first thought. The fact remains (I argue) that at least one vital element of *our* episteme is lacking until very much later than the twelfth century. In any case, the existence of these important papers needed mention, and I am grateful to Gene Vance for making the first of them available to me and to F. Edward Cranz for sending additional ones and permitting me to use them in my text and bibliography. I would also like to acknowledge the care taken by Bernhard Kendler and Kay Scheuer in shepherding this book to publication, and the excellent copy editing achieved by Jane Reverand.

A few paragraphs of Chapter 1 and much of Chapter 5, though in very different form, appeared in *Yale French Studies,* no. 49 (1973). Chapter 3, again in a quite different version, appeared in *Sub-Stance* no. 8. (Winter 1974). I thank the editors of these journals for permitting me to use much of this material again. The research of which this book is one result (another being my recently published *Tragedy and Truth,* written, so to speak, 'inside' the present work, and now forming something of a footnote to it: the demonstration of a special case) was begun in 1971–72, during my tenure of a Morse Fellowship from Yale University. I owe a deep debt of gratitude to the previous year's Morse Fellowship Committee of Yale College, and I am happy to record it. I am also grateful to the administration of the Université de Montréal, who, by granting me a sabbatical leave in 1977–78, made it possible to complete the research. A Canada Council Leave Fellowship in 1978, though granted for the writing of *Tragedy and Truth,* also allowed me the possibility of working in libraries of the first rank, from which this book has greatly benefited.

Our children have had to put up with a lot of absence, unavailability, and preoccupation, and I am grateful to them for not complaining overmuch. But finally, the main gratitude is due Jean Reiss, whose forbearance is beyond words, marital pact, or the reckoning of amity.

Timothy J. Reiss

Montreal

A Note on Punctuation

In what follows, double quotation marks indicate citations of other authors, terms used in a commonly accepted sense to which I am referring as quotations (though no particular source may be provided), or, in some few cases, phrases cited from earlier parts of my book. Single marks, except when they indicate a quotation within a quotation, are used for other emphases—most often either to indicate the inappropriateness of some habitually used term or to signal that a term taken from one discursive logic (or class of discourse, as it will be called hereafter) is being unavoidably but unsuitably applied to a different such logic.

The Discourse of Modernism

1 · On Method, Discursive Logics, and Epistemology

What a piece of work is man! how noble in reason! how infinite in faculty! in form, in moving, how express and admirable! in action how like an angel! in apprehension how like a god! the beauty of the world! the paragon of animals! And yet, to me, what is this quintessence of dust? man delights not me.
                                        —William Shakespeare, *Hamlet*

Mark all mathematical heads, which be only and wholly bent to those sciences, how solitary they be themselves, how unfit to live with others, and how unapt to serve in the world.
                                        —Roger Ascham, *The Scholemaster*

"For almost two centuries, the European mind has put forward an unprecedented effort to explain the world, so as to conquer and transform it."[1] Only recently has this European mind—at least commonly—become aware that something may be amiss in this desire for conquest, dominion, and possession. Yielding in part before the growing evidence of its own impotence, we are beginning to realize that the expression and implementation of this desire is the mark of a particular epistemological inflection that is far from the only one possible, or even available. Forms of thought and the desires accompanying them are open to study and to the clarification of what they may seek to hide. They can be changed. Generally speaking, whatever may be the modalities of action with which we endow it, we place the moment of our particular inflection somewhere within the period in the West termed the "Renaissance."

Anchoring itself principally, though not only, in the close consideration of a "literary" corpus, the following study will be concerned with that moment when two separate modes of conceptualization

---

1. Mircea Eliade, *Forgerons et alchimistes* (Paris, 1956), p. 12.

21

become visible. It will seek to follow the production of what I will call one *"class"* of discourse from within another. It will attempt to describe the gradual domination of the earlier by the later, to show how the separation itself becomes functional in discourse, how it is elaborated, and how the domination occurs. It will try to reveal some of the necessary ramifications and consequences of that domination.

Such a project is clearly a highly motivated one. I will be tending to reduce the episteme preceding that with whose rise to dominance I am chiefly concerned to the rule of a single class of discourse. I will not try to argue that such a move is anything but a heuristic tactic, and one that conduces, I confess, to telescoping a thousand years of complex development and to flattening out the enormously rich variety expressed especially by the thinkers of the eleventh–thirteenth centuries (though this variety itself, I argue, occurs under the sway of a single discursive dominance). It is indeed perfectly possible that several classes of discourse coexist in the Middle Ages: difficulties and slowness of communication, the separation of the educated clerical stratum from that of the politically dominant feudal aristocracy, and of both from the popular or village culture, seem to ensure that such would be the case. But that there may be several classes of discourse vying, so to speak, for power is not the main point here. Such struggle will doubtless always exist, but what the present essay aims to show is the accession to dominance for our modernity of a single discursive class. That dominance replaces another, and the fact that other discursive relationships may blur the transition must remain for my purposes a secondary consideration, as must also the possibility that a prior break of some kind may have occurred around the eleventh century—though both matters will be discussed briefly and my choice justified in Chapter 2.[2]

2. This is not really such a simplification as it may appear. Certainly the 'clear' existence of the division into three orders is the result of a long and complex development whose stabilization can really be argued only for the eleventh century and thereafter. Its existence seems undoubted in the later Middle Ages. One may invoke the evidence of a diversity of historians, social and economic, from Henri Pirenne to Carlo Cipolla, from Marc Bloch to M. M. Postan and many others, however various their views as to the details of the development. Georges Duby, in particular, has shown that such a division would be hard to argue for the seventh and eighth centuries—but in any case the dearth of documents precludes a discursive analysis of that period. One also needs to distinguish between a theoretical model that grows over a long period of time (from Augustine to Aquinas, say, or from Charlemagne to Saint Louis) and concrete practices that only gradually consolidate and become fully articulated with such theory (if ever). Still, in the later period, for example, the fact that the standard of living of the lowest-level knight may have been more or less identical with that of his peasant support group does not affect his belonging to a separate order. In Chapter 2, I distinguish in this regard between a theory and a practice,

I will argue that a discourse of 'resemblance' produces from within itself a certain kind of analytical system. When this becomes a conscious process viewed as promising a 'truly objective' knowledge of the 'real order' of things, then it is seen as superior to the earlier structure that bore it. An initial displacement is therefore speedily followed, as an essential part of the same process, by a complete replacement. What I will call an "analytico-referential" class of discourse becomes the single *dominant* structure and the necessary form taken by thought, by knowledge, by cultural and social practices of all kinds. This dominance still exists today, and I would suggest that it is only by revealing the occultations, the repressions, the willingly accepted 'traps' of the newly dominant discourse that we can hope to understand fully its consequences for ourselves. Only by studying the specific discursive response to what was viewed (by such as Galileo, Bacon, Descartes, and Hobbes) as a particular crisis of discourse can we ourselves hope to respond to what is perhaps a similar crisis in our time.

Three events of considerable symbolic significance lie at the doorway of what Alfred North Whitehead called "the first century of modern science." The first, in 1600, was the burning of Giordano Bruno, the thinker who in so many ways represents an effort to combine two different modes of thought, two classes of discourse:

---

between a theologico-theocratic model and feudal and corporative practices (which distinction makes it possible to speak of Augustine as though he were not separated from Aquinas by some eight centuries, inasmuch as his writings are a part of the composition of the theory: however much that, too, may develop). I suggest that the medieval episteme must be considered as an articulation of both, and that in a sense the articulation subsumes the division of the three orders into 'patterns of meaningfulness' that make of them a single epistemic phenomenon (both for us and for them). For the historical development, reference to certain works of Georges Duby is perhaps sufficient: *The Early Growth of the European Economy: Warriors and Peasants from the Seventh to the Twelfth Century*, tr. Howard B. Clarke (London, 1974); *Les trois ordres, ou l'imaginaire du féodalisme* (Paris, 1978). Extensive bibliographical references concerning monetary theory and economic practices in the Middle Ages can be found, among other places, in the notes to Timothy J. Reiss and Roger H. Hinderliter, "Money and Value in the Sixteenth Century: The *Monete cudende ratio* of Nicholas Copernicus," *Journal of the History of Ideas*, 40 (1979), 293–313. My present argument is based on the assumption that the obvious diversity and complexity of the thousand-year-long "Middle Ages" need not prevent us from *understanding* them as an epistemic totality. I assume that such understanding need not in itself be a simplification, provided one views "episteme" as a process of development and of meaningful articulation, not merely as a static and unchanging *Weltanschauung* or ideology characterizing for a time a given culture and society. Do I need to make it clear here, therefore, that by the term "episteme" I mean *a way of knowing* a particular order of reality, not simply the 'object' of such knowledge? The concept of episteme is a means for us to grasp concrete processes occurring *somewhere* over *some* period of time: to refer to those processes as themselves 'the' episteme is simply a useful shorthand.

"In his execution there was an unconscious symbolism: for the subsequent tone of scientific thought has contained distrust of his type of general speculativeness."[3] By the time he was sent to the stake, Bruno was a figure known throughout Europe, both by his writings and by his extensive travels.

During the same year occurred another event of great importance, though it lacked the striking impact of Bruno's death or the massive symbolic significance of the third event. Sometime in the course of 1600 William Gilbert published in London his *De magnete*. P. Fleury Mottelay writes that "the work created a powerful impression at the time," though less in England than on the Continent, where Galileo among others seems to have greeted its appearance with enthusiasm. Richard Foster Jones has somewhat modified that estimation by remarking that though Gilbert's "reputation was high with those who were qualified to appreciate his work," it was otherwise "never widely noticed."[4] Be that as it may, the work explained an instrument, the compass, that not only possessed some symbolic value by virtue of its obvious connection with the voyages of discovery (with which it was often credited), but that was also one of the three 'inventions,' along with gunpowder and the printing press, which writers of the age constantly urged as evidence of superiority against those who would disparage the moderns. Indeed, the immediate significance of the book lay more in the strong stance it took against the ancients and in its concrete practical demonstration of an efficacious experimentalism than it did in the discoveries in electricity and magnetism recorded there. Certainly the *De magnete* had been preceded years earlier by the experimental anatomical work of Vesalius, and was very soon to be joined by that of Harvey. Gilbert, however, happened to publish at a particularly auspicious conjuncture.

Still, whatever the importance of the Englishman's work from this point of view, it was not to produce the same shock as the third event: the publication, just a decade later, of an even more celebrated work, as much polemical pamphlet as record of 'scientific' observations. In the latter half of 1609 modern technological thinking was provided with its most eloquent metaphor, as Galileo interposed the distance of the telescope between the human mind and the material world before it, the object of its attentive gaze. It goes

3. Alfred North Whitehead, *Science and the Modern World* (1925; rpt. New York, 1967), p. 1.
4. William Gilbert, *De magnete*, tr. P. Fleury Mottelay (1893; rpt. New York, 1958), p. xii; Richard Foster Jones, *Ancients and Moderns: A Study of the Rise of the Scientific Movement in Seventeenth-Century England*, 2d ed. (St. Louis, Mo., 1961), p. 20.

without saying that the interposition and the space are both simultaneous creations of the metaphor: the one presupposes the other. They will become the transparent instrumentality of a supposedly 'neutral' and 'objective' scientific discourse. The metaphor is itself the mark therefore of a particular epistemology created by the discursive activity into which it is inserted. The metaphor was to become distinctly literary and haunt, directly or indirectly, much of the imaginative writing of the following century once the scientist had written it down and published it as the *Sidereus nuncius* in 1610.

The reaction to the appearance of this text was, as Gérard Simon has recently remarked, a general one "of curiosity, incredulity and stupefaction."[5] Yet Galileo's telescope only confirms a visual distancing whose entrance into consciousness is especially marked by this metaphor. At least since the considerations of Nicolaus Cusanus and others upon perspective, the abstractions of a continuous *interpretation* of the material signs ('signs' and 'objects' being taken as ontologically equal) were reduced by a certain visualization. What Father Ong has been able to write of Ramus's 'reduction' of the linguistic order to visual image, Jean Paris and Michel Beaujour could claim as already the case in Rabelais's writing.[6] Nancy Struever can show how Cusanus opposes, in his very writing, the figural to the abstract as the "radical" to the "traditional." At first this corresponds to a replacement of a kind of potential 'wholeness' of knowledge (concluded in the divine Word) by a perspectival and incomplete process of knowing. It opposes an "infinite essence" to a finite semiotic process: an opposition that is the mark of an incommensurability viewed by Cusa "as the proper foundation of all inquiry: 'finiti ad infinitum nulla est proportio.'"[7] We will see this opposition at work in precise manner in More's *Utopia*.

Cusanus, Rabelais, and others represent, as we will also see shortly, a critical moment of passage. But this passage is soon countered and replaced by a new certainty. Once the telescope metaphor becomes generalized, it increasingly comes to preempt other possible forms of sign-functioning. A passage in Frege concerning conception and

5. Gérard Simon, *Kepler astronome astrologue* (Paris, 1979), p. 397.

6. Walter J. Ong, S.J., *Ramus, Method, and the Decay of Dialogue* (Cambridge, Mass., 1958); Jean Paris, *Rabelais au futur* (Paris, 1970); Michel Beaujour, *Le jeu de Rabelais* (Paris, 1969): "It is by a transformation of sight, and a promotion of the visual faculties, that the abstract structures of medieval thought will be *turned*" (p. 29).

7. Nancy S. Struever, "Metaphoric Morals: Ethical Implications of Cusanus' Use of Figure," in *L'archéologie du signe*, ed. Lucie Brind'amour and Eugene Vance (Toronto, 1982). I am grateful to my colleague Gene Vance for having communicated to me the texts of this collection prior to its publication.

meaning, in which the telescope aimed at the moon is used as an extended illustrative simile, helps to confirm the importance and implications of the metaphor for the modern episteme and as a symbol for the functioning of signs in its discourse. For the metaphor is thereby demystified, and at a moment (the late nineteenth century) perhaps as critical for the by then long-dominant discourse of analysis and reference it symbolized as the sixteenth century had been for its inception. At almost exactly the same moment, as we will see especially in my concluding chapter, Freud hypostasizes and 'internalizes' the metaphor as a true description of the psyche's relation with the external world and as a means of understanding real mental functioning. In a sense, Galileo, Frege, and Freud symbolize the limits *a quo* and *ad quem* of analytico-referential discourse: a leitmotiv that will recur in this study and be considered more fully, as I say, in Chapter 12. The first represents the moment when what had been the scattered elements of crisis congeal unmistakably into a potentially precise discursive direction. The second two mark a moment when the dominance of that discourse had been cast into ineradicable doubt, even though it maintains to this day a considerable vivacity.[8]

The telescope may therefore be taken as a fair representation of what happened to the linguistic sign itself, increasingly able to be defined as an arbitrarily selected transparent instrument placed between concept and object. This 'fact' is of particular interest to the present study because it is chiefly concerned with 'literary' texts, and because it is widely assumed that literary discourse, in some sense and degree, emphasizes its own status as a linguistic operation. It is indeed precisely in writing a "baroque" rhetoric/poetic that Emanuale Tesauro, a mere fifty years after the *Sidereus nuncius*, reverses Galileo's metaphor, though quite without any historical effect.

The conceit of the very title of Tesauro's treatise, *Il cannocchiale aristotelico* (1654), is that metaphor is itself a telescope (*cannocchiale*). The presence of *ingegno*, writes Tesauro, is the mark of all superior literary texts. Its constituents are clever conceits and subtle metaphors: which are really all forms of metaphor in general. And this is

8. For an analysis of the generalization in question, see Reiss, "Espaces de la pensée discursive: Le cas Galilée et la science classique," *Revue de synthèse*, no. 85–86 (Jan.–July 1977), pp. 5–47. The passage in Frege is to be found in "On Sense and Reference" [*Ueber Sinn und Bedeutung*], in *Translations from the Philosophical Writings of Gottlob Frege*, ed. and tr. Peter Geach and Max Black (Oxford, 1952), p. 60. Some further implications have been discussed in Reiss, "Peirce and Frege: In the Matter of Truth," *Canadian Journal of Research in Semiotics*, 4, no. 2 (Winter 1976–77), 5–39; see esp. pp. 14, 18–19.

to be divided into two aspects: *perspicacia* and *versabilità*. "Perspicacity," he affirms, "penetrates the farthest and most minute circumstances of every subject." At the same time, "versatility [but also "reversibility"] speedily compares all these circumstances among themselves and with the subject: it connects and separates them; increases or diminishes them; derives one from the other; outlines the one with the other or with marvellous dexterity puts one in place of the other as the juggler does his stones."[9]

Tesauro emphasizes that what is called 'truth' is therefore in its essence a 'lie': for what is 'known' of any object is but the consequence of these activities of mind. The telescope is nothing but metaphor. An object may be unambiguous inasmuch as it is but an object to be observed, but as soon as it becomes a *suggetto* of understanding it is, precisely, subject not object. As Ezio Raimondi has remarked, the meaning given to the object of such activities is entirely contingent upon the whim of the operator and the power of the metaphor: "The result of such a view of things becomes, like the human body of which the first pages of the *Cannocchiale* speak, 'a page always ready to receive new characters and to erase them': a great encyclopedia of images and ideas [*nozioni*; also, meanings], which, embellished with the inventions of art, arouses 'wit's lust.'"[10]

Only fifty years later, then, the metaphor of the telescope was powerful enough to withstand being stood on its head. Tesauro's treatise is a commentary on a discourse which, I claim, has by that time become hegemonous, and it is rapidly relegated to the ranks of the unread. One of the (minor) indications of that hegemony is the fact that until very recently indeed Tesauro's seven-hundred-page treatise was considered worthy of little more than the passing footnote, if that, even in the most extensive literary histories published in Italy. Its existence and the silence which rapidly enveloped it are both indications that it is the mark of a certain passage: a passage from one discursive space to another.

In what follows, the name *discourse* will refer to a rather large and somewhat ill-delimited definitional field taken over, at least partially, from the studies of Michel Foucault. Firstly, *discourse*—here—is a coherent set of linguistic facts organized by some enunciating entity.

Such a statement elicits at least two comments. In the first place it is clear that by the use of the term *discourse* must be meant *any*

9. Emanuale Tesauro, *Il cannocchiale aristotelico*, ed. and intro. August Buck (Bad Homburg, [1968]; reprint of 1670 Turin edition), p. 51.
10. Ezio Raimondi, *Letteratura baroca: Studi sui seicento italiano* (Florence, 1961), p. 21.

semiotic system as practiced, not necessarily a simply 'linguistic' one in any narrow sense (as the term has been generally used). I assert that such a broader definition is essential: language, in other words, is but one of the possible materials through and in which discursive order manifests itself. The narrower statement simply refers to the corpus studied here. It enables me to avail myself of certain simplifications—for it is clear that other signifying material and processes cannot necessarily be analyzed in the same way. In the second place the term *entity* may seem an odd way of talking about the production of sense and in need of some explanation.

I dare not write some such phrase as 'enunciating subject' because that immediately implies a particular *class* of discourse: a class based on the assumption of the identity of an *I*, the discursive order I will be calling the "analytico-referential." It has yet to be shown that such a class of discourse is universal, and what follows disputes any such a priori assumption. The term *entity* should be relatively 'safe,' in part because of its very strangeness. It does not, of course, mean to indicate any incontrovertible *origin* of discourse. It merely supposes that the practice of discourse, any discourse, appears to depend on a supposition of *ens*, of 'being,' even though such 'being' is of necessity itself produced by discourse. *Entity* is taken here as a meaning produced by all discourse, *a meaning which is at the same time the producer of discourse*. It is, if you will, an empty metaphor marking the production of discourse (at once produced and producing). The telescope, for example, is one particular way of filling that 'emptiness.' Once given specificity (as an *I*, for example, in the case of the telescope metaphor), the mark becomes a mask, sign of an occultation as well as the form the occultation takes: the *I* of a *cogito* for which the mark of the seizure of knowledge (con*cept*; con*cipere*; be*griff*) becomes a neutral, transparent sign. It becomes the index of a discursive class that conceals the necessity, as Foucault puts it, of conceiving "discourse as a violence that we do to things, or, at all events, as a practice we impose upon them": a practice, he continues, in which "the events of discourse find the principle of their regularity."[11]

In all discourse not only are the linguistic (semiotic) facts, the signifying elements, organized by some entity, but we may assume that they are not aimless. They *show* some goal. Ernst Cassirer would have it that they are always a mediation between *I* and the world, but such a view takes the separation of *I* and the world as an a priori and reduces all discourse to the same intentionality. Such a view is there-

11. Michel Foucault, *The Discourse on Language*, printed as an appendix to *The Archaeology of Knowledge*, tr. A. M. Sheridan Smith (New York, 1976), p. 229.

fore entirely indicative of the particular discursive hegemony which the following study will seek to elucidate.

Secondly, then, if discourse speaks *of* phenomena (no matter what precise inflection one may wish to give to the word 'phenomena'), it orders them. By this is meant simply that discourse and the material in which it is manifest are never the elements of what might be taken as a neutral mediation. That is so even assuming that discourse may, according to its "class," serve a *primary function* as mediation *of* things, for example, as opposed to mediation *between* enunciators. Foucault remarks in this connection that it is not a matter of "treating discourses as groups of signs (signifying elements referring to contents of representations) but as practices that systematically form the objects of which they speak. Of course, discourses are composed of signs; but what they do is more than use these signs to designate things. It is this *more* that renders them irreducible to the language [*langue*] and to speech."[12]

Third, elaborated discourse therefore always has a 'reference' of some kind, even if it may only be 'apparent' to a 'reader' accustomed to a different discursive class. Such would necessarily be the case for a discourse whose own elaboration is its reference. (Is this what is being sought by a Jacques Derrida? or by a Roland Barthes—in his last writings?) In one sense, because reference is always the creation of discourse, such is always the case. But the analytico-referential at any rate assumes an exterior and marks that assumption in its own elaboration. Indeed, this reference is always in some sense *grasped* by discourse. It is—and I insist on the ambiguity of the word because it enables us to use it of discourse in general—it is the *relation* of discourse. This *relation*, what Foucault calls the *more* of language, will have to be given a status 'beyond' the language which is but one of its possible materials. This *relation* is the way in which semiotic systems are used, organized (though it goes without saying that such systems can only be studied in that use and organization: they do not preexist).

The relation of which I am speaking varies, and that variation makes it possible to speak of different classes of discourse. Two such variations immediately come to mind, partly because both have been studied at some length and partly because they appear to correspond to the epistemic change this study aims to describe in some detail. I am thinking of a relation of narration, assuming some commented exterior whose existence as a knowable reality is taken as

12. Foucault, *Archaeology of Knowledge*, p. 49.

prior to that of discourse (the discourse of analysis and reference, of historicism, of experimentalism), and of a relation of the 'formation of patterns' (the placing of things by their resemblances, by their similarities, for example—though such notions themselves need to be made precise). Lévi-Strauss has suggested that the discourse of the modern natural sciences (a 'type' within my analytico-referential) is an ordering of the world by the mind, while what he calls "mythical thought" is an ordering of the mind 'by' the world (*bricolage*).[13]

The first of these two, narration, is a 'telling' (relating) of exterior things and events. It is thus that in the *De augmentis scientiarum* (especially book II, chapters 1–3) Sir Francis Bacon calls the individual sciences "histories" (and we still speak, of course, following his practice, of "natural history"). The second of Lévi-Strauss's two discourses is a kind of patterning which refuses the ontological and epistemological distinction made in the first between an interior and an exterior, which assumes therefore that all 'objects' are 'signs,' all signs objects (though the distinction is obviously not one it can make). It assumes that discourse is a part of the 'world' and not distinct from it. It gives no special privilege either to the enunciator of discourse or to the act of enunciation.

Gérard Simon, in his recent study of the conceptual foundations of Kepler's thought (as he terms it), remarks that what gave rise to his researches was the striking similarity between the episteme of resemblance (what I will be calling the "discourse of patterning") and what Lévi-Strauss calls "the savage mind." He comments of astrology that it operates, once it has been constituted as a form of knowledge, as a "system of transformations" whose function is to "guarantee an ideal convertibility between the celestial and the terrestrial (meteorology), the universal and the individual (genethlialogy), nature and history (universal apotelesmatics)."[14] I am struck by the same similarity: indeed, my own textual analyses and the fundamental theoretical schema to be set forward here were completed well before Simon's researches were available. My argument then will be that there is a gradual disappearance of a class of discursive activity, a passage from what one might call a discursive *exchange within* the world to the expression of knowledge as a reasoning *practice upon* the world. This last initially emerges simply as a new and perhaps unfamiliar element within a still dominant class of discourse. Over a period of time other elements gather around this 'first' one and come to form a discursive order capable of producing meaningful constructs that

13. Claude Lévi-Strauss, *The Savage Mind* (Chicago, 1966), ch. 1, pp. 1–33.
14. Simon, *Kepler*, pp. 103–4.

are quite new. Such consolidation eventually results in the dominance of what has now become a different discursive class.

Analytico-referential discourse, in the sense I use the phrase here, seems largely the creation of the European sixteenth century. (Chapter 2 will deal with the question of whether such a discursive class existed earlier.) Its name is composed from what may be seen as the fundamental scheme of its functioning, the basic process through which it enables thought and action to occur. During the period of which I will be speaking, a discursive order is achieved on the premise that the 'syntactic' order of semiotic systems (particularly language) is coincident both with the logical ordering of 'reason' and with the structural organization of a world given as exterior to both these orders. This relation is not taken to be simply one of analogy, but one of identity. Its exemplary formal statement is *cogito—ergo—sum* (reason—semiotic mediating system—world), but it is to be found no less in the new discursive "instauration" worked out by Bacon (to be considered in Chapter 6). Its principal metaphors will be those of the telescope (eye—instrument—world) and of the voyage of discovery (self-possessed port of departure—sea journey—country claimed as legitimate possession of the discoverer).

Simultaneously with this claim of logical identity, various devices are elaborated enabling a claim for the adequacy of concepts to represent objects in the world and for that of words to represent those concepts. The outcome is that the properly organized sentence (a concern dominant among grammarians of the second half of the century) provides in its very syntax a correct *analysis* of both the rational and material orders, using elements that *refer* adequately through concepts to the true, objective nature of the world. Such is the basic ordering process of analytico-referential discourse.

What appears to have been initially important is that the awareness of the sign's *arbitrary* nature grows to a point where that arbitrariness becomes conceptually 'usable.' It will be possible to assign a 'signification' independent of the object but which, in its denotative percision, allows a belief in its referential adequacy—or, rather, allows a claim for such adequacy to be developed. When the word was felt to inhere in some way in the thing, it was possible to gloss it endlessly. Indeed, no other kind of knowledge was possible. To accumulate bits and pieces of meaning, a variety of *nozioni,* was to approach understanding of the thing, of its place and that of the glosser in some divine plan—or world soul, as it became in the early European Renaissance. The greater the accumulation of such meanings, the nearer the approach to a wisdom conceived as knowing participation in a totality (as we will see with respect to Paracelsus and Kepler himself).

Between the 'new' word and the object to which it is applied there is now no 'give'—indeed, no give and take. The thing is frozen in its name. The very arbitrariness of the word permits the assimilation of the phenomenon it denotes to a mental order, to a discursive system in which it can be assigned a position and within whose symbolizations and relationships it may be *known*.[15] It allows the world of phenomena and of concepts (*any* phenomena and concepts supposed as outside the discourse being used to denote them) to be serialized into a grammar, and to be analyzed by virtue of the signification given to each element in that grammar. Such an operation is impossible when noun (name) and object are perceived as essentially inseparable (as is the case, we will see, in the discourse of patterning, of resemblance). Paracelsus will be able to say that it is by the inherent signs (signatures) that "one may know another—what there is in him." One must understand that all things have "true and genuine names."[16]

In such a discourse name and object are themselves part of an order of which the enunciator is also a part. Paracelsus will call such an enunciator the "signator," of whom there are three different levels: "Man, Archeus, and the Stars." The names they 'give' are not in the least bit arbitrary, and he writes, for example: "it should be remarked that the signs signed by man carry with them perfect knowledge and judgment of occult things, as well as acquaintance with their powers and hidden faculties." It is Adam himself, "the Protoplast," who was the originator of all "skill in the science of signatures."[17] Such a class of discourse places the enunciator within the same structure as englobes name and object as well. Its elements may thus be available to a continuous interpretation, but they cannot be grasped as a whole from within and thereby known in the same sense as they may be by a discourse based on a practice of difference and alterity. The patterns of such a discourse suggest an *essence* that escapes its enunciator as a whole must its parts. That may explain why, at the very moment of the changing discursive practice, Ramus criticizes Platonic 'Forms,' themselves suggestive of just such an es-

15. On this see Reiss, "The *concevoir* Motif in Descartes," in *La cohérence intérieure: Etudes sur la littérature française du xviie siècle, présentées en hommage à Judd D. Hubert,* ed. J. Van Baelen and David L. Rubin (Paris, 1977), pp. 203–22.

16. Paracelsus the Great (Aureolus Philippus Theophrastus Bombast von Hohenheim), *The Hermetic and Alchemical Writings,* ed. Arthur Edward Waite, 2 vols. (1894; rpt. Berkeley, 1976), II.304, I.188.

17. Ibid., I.171, 188.

sence, with the remark that by Idea "nothing else was meant in Plato but logic."[18] The essence in question becomes but the product of discourse. The remark indicates an attempt to reduce one class of discourse to the norms of another.

Ramus, indeed, views Platonic discourse as one of resemblance or of patterning. He criticizes Plato precisely for his assumptions concerning the identity of things, forms, and the words which relate them. It is in such terms that he opposes Plato to Aristotle: Aristotle, "says that the mind of man has not made present in our bodies, as Socrates has sometimes argued, a knowledge of all things but rather the faculty and power of knowing them, just as our eyes do not bring with them from our mother's womb the species of color but only the power of seeing them."[19] Interpretation, which is alone possible in the class of discourse Ramus intends here to criticize, cannot be equated with what we now term 'knowledge' or, more precisely, 'scientific knowledge.' That is indicated, for example, by the four stages of medieval criticism, terminating as they do in the anagogic, pertaining to the unknowable Truth, Essence, Idea, Logos, or, as it becomes for such as Paracelsus or Kepler, World Soul. This question of medieval patterns will, as I say, be discussed at greater length in Chapter 2. For the present I want to deal more particularly with the emergence of a new dominant discourse and with what appears to have immediately preceded it during the European Renaissance.

I have suggested that the reductive metaphor of the telescope was of considerable importance: it stood for the emergence of a new kind of conceptualizing practice. Nonetheless, like Tesauro later, Galileo himself always recognized that signs (whether mathematical or linguistic) fall in between what is taken as the conceptualizing mind and a world of objects. They fall, to keep the metaphor, in the space of the telescope itself. They can be identified neither with the mind nor with the world, but they are subject to the organization of the former. Such a division of elements is essential to our modern episteme. It is the order of the *cogito—ergo—sum*: mind—signs—world. But Galileo himself always emphasizes that knowledge is a sign-manipulating activity. This is why he argues that a star seen through the telescope is not the same object as the star seen with the naked eye, or that changing the length of the telescope gives us a

---

18. Pierre de la Ramée [Petrus Ramus], *Dialectique (1555)*, ed. and intro. Michel Dassonville (Geneva, 1964): "ne fut entendu autre chose en Platon que le genre logicien" (p. 93).

19. Ibid., p. 100.

different instrument and therefore yet again a different object.[20] The terms used by Galileo to describe the scientist's acquisition of knowledge are always those of violence.[21]

For Galileo discourse represents not the object itself but the *distance* between the object and the mind *perceiving* and then *conceiving* it. For a similar point of view, though Bacon and Descartes both remain ambiguous on the matter, we have to jump (once again) to the late nineteenth century and the discussions of Helmholtz and Hertz—in the context of a crisis in the very discourse Galileo's work helps to install. The grave problems of representation that such an idea of knowledge poses is squarely faced by Galileo: for we cannot, he affirms, translate into discourse a conception that is an individual, and therefore unusable, representation of a thing perceived as though it were the thing, as Bacon calls it, "in itself." That assumes as a consequence that the scientific knowledge of objects is nought but the result of sign-manipulation, and that their 'truth' is merely their *utility* for the betterment of men's lives. One might say that this awareness within discourse of the individual's 'enunciative responsibility' is an indication that the analytico-referential discourse is as yet but emergent, and still far from dominance. It will in fact take Locke's discussions about private and public concepts and private and public language before the 'objectivity' of such discourse can be finally and formally 'justified,' before the presence in discourse of enunciative responsibility can be dispensed with.

In Bacon the solution to the epistemological problem thus posed (for a science wishing to be 'objective') is sought in what he terms "a gradual and unbroken ascent"—in effect, an endless chain of reasoning. Experimental discourse is not at first an attempt to describe the thing itself so much as a description of the human *sighting* of the thing, of a particular *discursive* relationship (Bacon) between an object clearly defined in space and time and the mind perceiving it under the same restrictions. There is always the tacit implication that these restrictions are themselves a product of the discourse (mind) that inscribes the description in question. Discourse stands for distance, and it is just that distance that poses the problem. It is largely 'overcome' by Descartes.

There is no question but that Descartes, from the *Regulae* on, is far

20. The first example is from the *Discourse on Comets* (1619), ostensibly written by Mario Guiducci but known to have been dictated by Galileo; the second is from *The Assayer*. Both are in *The Controversy of the Comets of 1618*, tr. Stillman Drake and C. D. O'Malley (Philadelphia, 1960), pp. 44, 223.

21. For greater precision on these matters, see Reiss, "Espaces de la pensée discursive."

more radical than this. He chooses to reject ocular evidence altogether, or we should rather say, perhaps, ocular propositions. He prefers to reconstruct them from 'first principles,' as he does in the *Monde* and in the *Traité de l'homme*. The effect ultimately is to impose an intellectual structure upon the perceived world. Like Bacon, Galileo, and Hobbes, Descartes's avowed aim is possession and utility. That this is a stage in the development suggested as already underway in Rabelais's writing seems clear. There, for instance, the Picrocholine war, started by a minor quarrel between buyers and sellers, expands by a kind of discursive *naming* process into an immense conquest of empire. Past, present, and future merge in the deliberations of Picrochole and his lieutenants into a vast nomination of possessions—the entire world: after France, Spain, North Africa, and the Mediterranean basin, "it will be better for you first to conquer Asia Minor, Caria, Lycia, Pamphilia, Cicilia, Lydia, Phrygia, Mysia, Bythinia, Charazia, Adalia, Samagaria, Castamena, Luga, and Sebaste, all as far as the Euphrates." As the conversation proceeds the invasion and conquest of the rest of Europe and Asia Minor will be, is being, has already been, achieved. The troops are now waiting at Constantinople. Jean Paris remarks with justice: "To name is the wondrous equivalent of possession. To enumerate provokes a kind of hypnosis whereby the distance between the real and the fictional evaporates."[22]

The systematic discourse that names and enumerates becomes, replaces, the order of the world that it is taken as representing. In Rabelais's text, however, the discursive practice remains ambiguous, because the enumeration is a simple accumulation of adjectives, of substantives, of verbs and adverbs: and that simple accumulation prevents the use of a syntax as the analysis of that to which it would refer. In a sense the 'real' here becomes a fiction. And whether Rabelais is here parodying a certain discourse or not makes no difference: such a parody would still indicate the existence of what is being parodied. Faced with this kind of discursive practice, our own is likely to find itself at a loss. This syntactically 'unrestrained' accumulation is quite foreign to us. Terence Cave has thus recently commented that Rabelais's writing confronts us with "a narrative so plural that no commentary can control it."[23] 'Pieces' of the real, so to speak, are seized within a process whose discursivity is not only not

22. François Rabelais, *Gargantua and Pantagruel*, tr. J. M. Cohen (Harmondsworth, 1955), p. 111; Jean Paris, *Rabelais*, p. 107.

23. Terence Cave, *The Cornucopian Text: Problems of Writing in the French Renaissance* (Oxford, 1979), p. 213. The entire volume is an important examination of problems of writing and meaning in the Renaissance.

concealed but is indeed emphasized as a system of transformations. The similarity with Paracelsus's signatures is evident. One would be tempted to argue on the other hand that in later Cartesianism, if not in Descartes himself, a 'fictional' system becomes the *real* (that is indeed what happens in the *Monde*). And if this opposition between the two modes corresponds to that made by Lévi-Strauss between mythical thought and scientific thought it is obviously not accidental.

The Galilean trinity of mind/discourse/phenomena, which opens up various distances within the order of which Rabelais's text is still to some extent representative, is reduced by later Cartesianism to a dichotomy. Language reveals thought, and inasmuch as that thought can be taken as referring directly to objects (in perception) language can operate as a perfect stand-in for both. To be sure, it is not the object itself, but it is a sufficiently accurate representation for the purposes of discourse, into whose analytical process it can be inserted. When the Port-Royal theories of language and thought argue that the verb is an affirmation of things rather than a simple statement of perception, they are arguing that grammatically speaking (and for them, epistemologically) the affirmation of things *contains* the statement of perception and subsumes it. This is because the signified (concept/percept) is seen as congruent, if not in fact identical, with the referent (percept/thing). Port-Royal has already traveled some way from the still ambiguous practice of Descartes himself to the certainty of Cartesianism. Word and thing are brought to coincide in the sense that the former is a completely adequate and transparent representation of the latter. Possession by and in the discourse of analysis and referentiality is made possible.[24]

Instead of an 'ideal' exchange between the scientist's encoding of nature and his perception of it, which would call for a constant readapting of the codifying practice, of discourse (such as Galileo appears to seek), the Cartesians, and the empiricists likewise, will assert their possession of the domain to which any given discourse

24. Much has been written to show this operation in the *Grammar* and *Logic* of Port-Royal. See, e.g., Noam Chomsky, *Cartesian Linguistics* (New York and London, 1966), pp. 33–46; Michel Foucault, *Les mots et les choses* (Paris, 1966), pp. 72–78, 92–136; Roland Donzé, *La grammaire générale et raisonnée de Port-Royal* (Berne, 1967); Jean-Claude Chevalier, *Histoire de la syntaxe: Naissance de la notion de complément dans la grammaire française (1530–1750)* (Geneva, 1968), pp. 483–539; Louis Marin, *Critique du discours: Sur la "Logique de Port-Royal" et les "Pensées" de Pascal* (Paris, 1975); Reiss, "Du système de la critique classique," *XVIIe Siècle*, 116 (1977), 3–16; Reiss, "Sailing to Byzantium: Classical Discourse and Its Self-Absorption," *Diacritics*, 8, no. 2 (Summer 1978), 34–46; and Reiss, "Cartesian Discourse and Classical Ideology," *Diacritics*, 6, no. 4 (Winter 1976), 19–27.

refers. This was achieved thanks to the establishment of a discursive class (to which such given 'types' of discourse belong) determined as true, objective, and the permanent manifestation of universal common sense. This marks a denial, an occultation, of the acknowledgment that the human view of the world is necessarily a 'perspectival' one. It marks the assertion of such a view as absolute. To be sure, the problems raised are not immediately simple of resolution. The silence of Cyrano's narrator at the end of the *Voyage dans le soleil* might well be interpreted as a recognition of his inability to resolve the manifold questions he has raised (see Chapter 9). But by the beginning of the eighteenth century things will have solidified to such a degree that even a critique of the now-dominant discourse will fall within the same limits.

It is only at the end of the nineteenth century that the analytico-referential discourse of assertion and possession, of permanent and universal human reason, and of absolute objective truth comes to be opposed by another. Michel Foucault is able to remark, for example, that in the analysis of finitude then undertaken, discourse will once again be marked by its own discursive nature. 'Knowledge' will be the process of enunciation itself, not the object of that enunciation: "To be finite, then, would simply be to be trapped in the laws of a perspective which, while allowing a certain apprehension—of the type of perception or understanding—prevents it from ever being universal and definitive intellection."[25]

The accession to dominance of a single discursive order is naturally visible in all the discursive practices of the age, though some, no doubt, are more exemplary than others. A good case is that of the development of probability theory. As Ian Hacking has observed, this is an important example of such effects as those being discussed.[26] It assumes the possibility of the direct application of an abstract mathematical calculus to concrete phenomena in the world, and it assumes at the same time that a single structure of order is common

25. Michel Foucault, *The Order of Things* (tr. of *Les mots et les choses*; New York, 1973), p. 372. A little later he writes: "this is why the analysis of finitude never ceases to use, as a weapon against historicism, the part of itself that historicism has neglected: its aim is to reveal, at the foundation of all the positivities and before them, the finitude that makes them possible; where historicism fought for the possibility and justification of concrete relations between limited totalities, whose mode of being was predetermined by life, or by social forms, or by the significations of language, the analytic of finitude tries to question this relation of a human being to the being which, by designating finitude, renders the positivities possible in their concrete mode of being" (p. 373).

26. Ian Hacking, *The Emergence of Probability: A Philosophical Study of Early Ideas About Probability, Induction, and Statistical Inference* (Cambridge, 1975).

to an unlimited number of such phenomena. In the literary discursive development to be followed in this volume it is by no means indifferent, therefore, that such a 'theory' should become an important element in Cyrano's novels. (Though I will only discuss it with regard to the *Voyage dans la lune*, probability seems to be behind the changing form of the 'tree people,' for example, in the *Voyage dans le soleil.*) It is quite possible, indeed, that its appearance in Cyrano's novels preceded its more formal elaboration by Hobbes, Pascal, and the later seventeenth century. The possibility of elaborating a theory of probability is axiomatic in the analytico-referential discourse of representation. Though in a nonmathematical form, it will have become central to epistemology and to the very concept of the human by the time of Locke's *Essay Concerning Human Understanding* in 1690: a probabilistic theory of knowledge and human action based upon the statistical reliability of the accumulation of particulars.

Such, too, is the case for the linear narration of causality, the very model, no doubt, of analysis for this discursive class. Its most simple and schematic literary form will become that of the modern detective novel: as I will suggest later with regard to Cyrano and Defoe, this is really but a simplification of earlier novel forms as it is also an almost programmatic fulfillment of the structure of experimentalism. Literary 'effects' of this kind are by no means marginal or mere digressions. They are exemplary of the elements fundamental to the institution of the dominant discourse of analysis and reference. Their presence in 'literary discourse,' however, is especially significant: it is worth reminding ourselves that the very concept of 'literature' in the sense it has today is not simply a growth of the new order, but is also one of its ideological foundations.[27] In this connection, one example of the effect of this discursive elaboration is of particular interest, and I will glance at it briefly: that of literary criticism.

The very priorities I have been underscoring seem apparent in the 'Malherbian' systematization of a literary code (for example) that seeks to provide an adequate representation of a (human) nature claimed as permanently one with itself, the same everywhere, and objectively knowable. That systematization was to be carried out with a vengeance in the second half of the seventeenth century by such as La Mesnardière, d'Aubignac, de Pure, Rapin, Dacier, Valincour, and

27. I have explored this at some length in "The Environment of Literature and the Imperatives of Criticism," *Europa*, 4 (1981), to appear. But see also various works by Raymond Williams: in particular, *The Country and the City* (London, 1973), *Culture and Society 1780–1950* (London, 1958), *The Long Revolution* (London, 1961), and *Marxism and Literature* (Oxford, 1977). My own long discussion of this last may be useful: "The Trouble with Literary Criticism," *Europa*, 3 (1980), 223–40.

Boileau in France, by such as Dryden, Rymer, Dennis, Pope and Addison in England. Yet it is perhaps of more interest to know that it was simultaneously with the scientific and philosophical work of Galileo, Bacon, and Descartes that the need was felt in France for a word that would express the 'inexpressible' as an objective, describable *something*. The very fact of discourse, which for Galileo expresses the *exchange* between mind and matter (once that division has been asserted), should make such a need irrelevant. Yet E. B. O. Borgerhoff was able to note a first substantival use of the phrase *je ne sais quoi* in 1628.[28] This will be consecrated in the second half of the century as the object of discussions on the *sublime*, which will become in turn the foundation of discussions on taste and of the new science of aesthetics in the eighteenth century.

All discourse is now a descriptive instrument capable of being regularized into geometrical, algebraic, and even, perhaps, *précieux* forms. Literature, it will be argued, is at once an order identical to that of the world (both human and natural) and an exact representation of that world. Hence the attraction of critics to literary rules (initially undermined somewhat by the concept of the sublime, which was itself however to become the object of a scientific discourse) whose possible analogy with an experimental discourse proves so attractive to the eighteenth century. This is clear from Hobbes, and becomes even more so in a critic of the late seventeenth century such as Thomas Rymer, who can write of Aristotle:

> The truth is, what Aristotle writes on this Subject [tragedy], are not the dictates of his own magisterial will, or dry deductions of his Metaphysicks: But the poets were his Masters, and what was their practice, he reduced to principles. Nor would the *modern Poets* blindly resign to this practice of the *Ancients*, were not the Reasons convincing and clear as any demonstration in *Mathematicks*. 'Tis only needful that we understand them, for our consent to the truth of them.[29]

This position will be taken to its logical extreme in the course of the following century: as an object for critical study, literary discourse will be equated rigorously with the natural (and ethical) order insofar as its status regarding veracity, actuality, and reality is concerned. The metalanguages that deal with it (grammar, poetics,

28. E. B. O. Borgerhoff, *The Freedom of French Classicism* (Princeton, 1950), p. 190: the use occurs in Ogier's *Apologie pour Monsieur de Balzac*.

29. Thomas Rymer, "The Preface of the Translator" to Rapin's *Reflections on Aristotle's Treatise of Poesie*, in *The Critical Works of Thomas Rymer*, ed. Curt A. Zimansky (New Haven, 1956), pp. 2–3.

rhetoric, aesthetics) will thus become the sciences which progressively reveal the knowledge contained in the (discursive) order of literature. In this way, just as Newton was able "to trace out a series of truths bound each to the next" and thus to establish a true physical science by the observation of nature, so too for every other metadiscourse:

> Just as good grammars and good poetics were composed only after there had been good prose and verse writers, so it happened that the art of reasoning was known only in proportion as we had good minds which reasoned well in diverse manners. You may suppose by this that this art has made its greatest progress during the 17th and 18th centuries. Indeed, the true method is due to these two centuries. It was first known in the sciences, where ideas are formed naturally, and determined almost without difficulty. Mathematics are the proof. . . . If the Tartars wanted to form a poetics, you may be sure it would be a bad one, because they do not have any good poets. The same is true of logics composed before the seventeenth century. There was then only one way of learning to reason: that was to consider the sciences in their origin and progress.[30]

Scientific discourse was destined to remain the model and exemplar of all discourses of truth—of all *knowledge*—with few doubts until the last third of the nineteenth century and even, though with increasing attacks, to the present.

Hobbes sought to apply Galileo's method to moral and political philosophy and to criticism. The Cartesian cast of Rymer's affirmation is apparent and quite typical of such efforts to demonstrate the identity of the functioning of the laws of nature and of "these fundamental Rules and Laws of" literature.[31] This, too, is the significance of the appearance of the so-called *normative* grammars toward the end of the seventeenth century. Leonard Bloomfield dismisses the grammarians responsible as contradicting linguistic principles,[32] but it is clear that any correspondence between the discourse and an order taken as outside discourse could have no meaning if the linguistic side of the equation could not be fixed. That fact would seem to be behind, for example, Boileau's criticism of pastoral on the grounds

30. [Etienne Bonnot de] Condillac, *Cours d'étude pour l'institution du Prince de Parme: Histoire moderne*, ed. G. Le Roy (Paris, 1948), II.221, 229.

31. Rymer, "Preface," p. 4. I have dealt more extensively with this discourse of literary criticism in my *Tragedy and Truth: Studies in the Development of a Renaissance and Neoclassical Discourse* (New Haven and London, 1980), ch. 1, pt. 1.

32. Leonard Bloomfield, *Language* (1933; rpt. London, 1970), pp. 6–7, 496–97, and passim.

that it used words in such a way as to multiply their meanings and so to make them incomprehensible—a practice which Tesauro had seen as essential to all great literature: for Tesauro the danger was not incomprehensibility but the belief in objective representation. As Foucault puts it: "It is thus part of the very nature of grammar to be prescriptive, not by any means because it is an attempt to impose the norms of a beautiful language obedient to the rules of taste, but because it refers the radical possibility of speech to the ordering system of representation."[33]

A practice of discourse that *uses* words as though they are in some way essential and inherent in the object can do with a relatively loose verbal structure. It can undermine its own syntactic forms. It can play with grammar. This kind of discourse is manifest in Rabelais's test. *Utopia,* we will see, strives in vain to reach a practice of this sort through rather different techniques. Things have a structure of their own: a material manifestation of the 'divine soul of the world,' they may be subject to the interrogation of human discourse, but they cannot be organized by it. Rather, they 'organize' it. The new practice requires a tight discursive system because things otherwise become incoherent. For the mind that works in this way, writes Gaston Bachelard (from the vantage point of analytico-referential discourse), "every phenomenon is a moment in the theoretical mind, a stage of discursive thinking, a *prepared-for* result."[34] Bachelard calls it the "formal imagination." He opposes it to the "material imagination," a mode of thinking that uses the immediate images of things as its code: those very experiences that Galileo scorns as utterly useless. It is what Lévi-Strauss refers to as mythical thought, what I will be calling the "discourse of patterning."

Analytico-referential discourse assumes that the world, as it can be and is to be known, represents a fixed object of analysis quite separate from the forms of discourse by which men speak of it and by which they represent their thoughts. This is the case whether the difficulties of analysis then be posed in terms of the world which is to be seized (idealism) or in those of its representation (empiricism). This assumption is basic to all the discourses of neoclassicism. Equally basic is the assumption that the proper *use* of language will not only *give* us this object in a gradual accumulation of detail (referentiality), but will also *analyze* it in the very form of its syntactic organization. Moreover that syntax not only analyzes the world but also

33. Foucault, *Order of Things*, p. 87.
34. Gaston Bachelard, *La formation de l'esprit scientifique: Contribution à une psychanalyse de la connaissance objective*, 7th ed. (Paris, 1970), p. 102.

presents (performs, even, according to Port-Royal) the mental judgment taken to be coincident with that process of analysis in syntax.
The assumption of this coincidence of universal reason and general
grammar was essential.

After its installation neoclassical discourse does not include within
its functioning, within its practice, what we may call *the responsibility of
enunciation*. The assumption of objectivity and the consequent exclusion of whatever cannot be brought to fit its order are necessarily
accompanied by the occultation of the enunciating subject *as discursive activity* and, therefore, of its responsibility for the status of the
objects of which it speaks: Galileo's *I* becomes Descartes's *we* and the
objectivity of "common speech" from Locke to Lavoisier. It is not
simply the formal ordering of language, obviously common to all
discursive practice, that is in question. It is the fact that after the
Renaissance such ordering is taken as isomorphic with the (unique)
order of phenomena, whether natural, social, or ethical, and so able
to *provide* (not invent or create) an adequate and even precise knowledge of that order.

It may be that this analytical discourse is only a particular twist in a
dialectical discursive search (as Lévi-Strauss calls it) for some form
of pragmatic knowledge that does go back to ancient Greece. Husserl argues this way when he affirms that what he calls Western
"thinking" since the *Aufklärung* is an aberration.[35] The present study
will question such an interpretation and such a claim. The evidence
seems convincing that before the modern advent of analytico-referential discourse some other class of discourse was dominant, that its
mode of functioning was quite different from our own, and that it
was from within that functioning that the discourse of analysis and
reference was produced.

When the linguistic sign was felt to inhere in the thing or to be
coextensive with it, it was at once the subject and the object of an
interpretative reading of the *signatura rerum*. Paracelsus (1493–1541)
can claim, for example, to be teaching a science "in which there are
two kinds of operation, one produced by nature itself, in which

---

35. Edmund Husserl, "Die Krisis des europäischen Menschentums und die Philosophie," tr. in his *Phenomenology and the Crisis of Philosophy*, tr. Quentin Lauer (New
York, 1965), pp. 149–92. For these remarks see pp. 179ff. Husserl is speaking about
the period that runs from the beginning of the seventeenth century (roughly) through
the end of the nineteenth. Lévi-Strauss adds that our culture since Descartes is a
"virus" within the body of "flesh and blood" civilizations: *Anthropologie structurale deux*
(Paris, 1973), p. 333. Jacques Derrida adds his voice to this fashionably pessimistic
clamor in *De la grammatologie* (Paris, 1967), pp. 145–48, while Colin Morris remarks
rather more mildly of what he refers to as Western individualism that "one might
almost regard it as an eccentricity among cultures" (*The Discovery of the Individual,
1050–1200* [New York, 1972], p. 2).

there is a selected man through which nature works and transmits her influence for good or evil, and one in which she works through other things, as in pictures, stones, herbs, words, or when she makes comets, similitudes, halos or other unnatural products of the heavens."[36] Here man is at once a part of 'nature' and an intermediary for the effecting of nature's 'influence.' Words and all other signs are in just the same situation: they can be read, while at the same time they produce the reading. "Form and essence," writes Paracelsus, "are one thing": "Whatever anything is useful for, to that it is assumed and adapted. So if Nature makes a man, it adapts him to its design. And here our foundation is laid. For everything that is duly signed its own place should properly be left; for nature adapts everything to its duty." And this is how the signature is provided, "which has to do with the signs to be taken into consideration, whereby one may know another—what there is in him. There is nothing hidden which Nature has not revealed and plainly put forward."[37] As Ian Hacking observes of the series of signs quoted just previously, the members of the set mentioned by Paracelsus are no longer for us "a 'natural kind,' namely a collection between which there are manifest family resemblances. The resemblances between words and stones, herbs and comets, are now lost to us."[38]

The case is exactly similar for our and Kepler's different conceptions of the planet Mars, which nonetheless remains for each of us unambiguously the same object inasmuch as it is 'something' we can observe in the sky. Gérard Simon notes that "what has changed is the manner of *classifying* it." Indeed, he remarks later that for Kepler the medical theories advanced by Paracelsus were at the same level of progress as the reformed religion and Copernican astronomy. And Kepler viewed that last as inseparable from astrology.[39] The scientist has no doubt whatsoever that the earth is endowed with a soul whose existence is proved by "the generation of metals, the conservation of terrestrial heat, the exuding of vapors intended to give birth to rivers, rain, and other meteorological effects. All these things prove that its form is not simply conservative, as is the case for the stars, but well and truly vegetative."[40] He therefore argues that all things participate in a whole (the earth itself being part of a

36. Quoted by Hacking (*Emergence*, p. 39) from the *Sämtliche Werke*, ed. K. Sudkoff, 14 vols. (Munich, 1922–23), XII.460. Cf. *Hermetic and Alchemical Writings*, I.189–90.
37. Paracelsus, *Hermetic and Alchemical Writings*, II.304.
38. Hacking, *Emergence*, p. 40.
39. Simon, *Kepler*, pp. 12, 49 n. 1.
40. Johannes Kepler, *De fundamentis astrologiae certioribus*, 1602; quoted by Simon, *Kepler*, p. 47.

greater vital harmony: hence his faith in astrology) and that all things are signs of the same totality. All reasoning from cause to effect is, under such circumstances, only a special case of analogical reasoning, as metonymy can be read as a special case of metaphor. Given this participation in a whole, reasoning can only be the search for resemblances, the accumulation of patterns: thus the need for men who "have had experience in the art of signature" and who can discover the "genuine names" and natures of things.[41]

In Paracelsus, as elsewhere in what Hacking terms the "low sciences" of the age (astrology, medicine, alchemy, mining), no distinction is to be made between a verbal sign and any other kind of sign in nature. All are equally valid manifestations of the relation between man and nature, between the universal and the individual, between the natural and the supernatural: their organization into patterns of resemblance allows these aspects to be transformed into one another. Paracelsus is able to affirm that Nature "indicates the age of a stag by the ends of his antlers and it indicates the influence of the stars by their names." Once again Hacking remarks, "in our conceptual scheme the names of the stars are arbitrary and the points of the antlers are not. For Paracelsus both are signs and there are true, real, names of things." And lest we should be tempted to take Paracelsus for an extreme case, we are wise to turn to a work with less universal pretensions—say, Georgius Agricola's *De re metallica* (1556). There, too, the very same scheme is found: "Agricola is telling us how to read aright, and how to find the Sentences on the earth's surface that say what minerals are down below."[42] Here again Paracelsus has his say:

> None can deny, then, that by means of chiromancy all minerals and metallic bodies of mines, which lie hid in secret places of the earth, may be known from their external signs. That is the chiromancy of mines, veins, and lodes, by which not only those things which are hidden within are brought forth, but also the exact depth and richness of the mine and yield of metal are made manifest.

Even when we meet with an author whose concerns seem immediately practical (but what, after all, are Agricola's?), the assertions are at least ambiguous. In Vannoccio Biringuccio's *Pirotechnia*, for example, considered the first treatise on metallurgy, we seem to meet

41. Paracelsus, *Hermetic and Alchemical Writings*, I.177, 189.
42. Hacking, *Emergence*, pp. 42–43. The Paracelsus quotation is from the *Sämtliche Werke*, XIII.376.

only with natural signs indicative of the presence of various kinds of ore, but which are very different from Paracelsus's signatures (not only natural and human, but also given by the Archeus and by the stars). And Biringuccio remarks that he finds the reading of signatures "a fabulous thing." Yet he hastens to add that though he has "never heard that it is practised," such a method may in fact be a true means to reach the earth's mineral secrets.[43] Still, *Pirotechnia* appeared in 1540, the year before Paracelsus's death and only three before Copernicus's. The latter's death was simultaneous with the publication of his *De revolutionibus orbium coelestium,* and in the same year, 1543, Vesalius published his seven books on the human body— a work that very clearly heralded a quite different and experimentally oriented way of inferring knowledge from 'signs.'

We may then be forgiven for viewing Biringuccio's attitude as a harbinger of a new discourse, as an indication that texts like those of Paracelsus are already residual—despite the fact that Kepler is still to come, who presents even more clearly, as we will see, a moment of change. In spite of himself, it is the Imperial Mathematician who will finally undermine the dominance of the discourse of patterning, but in Biringuccio it already appears as something of a dying whimsy. Already we catch a glimpse of Bacon, who, in *The New Organon,* clearly distinguishes between "the Idols of the human mind and the Ideas of the divine. That is to say, between certain empty dogmas, and the true signatures and marks set upon the works of creation as they are found in nature" (book I, aphorism xix).

Despite his vocabulary here, Bacon is distinguishing between genuine "ideas," which signify for us the 'objective meaning' of things, and those "idols" which are the unjustified and unfounded figments of the human imagination (unfounded, that is to say, in "particulars" and "works"). Bacon is of course writing more than three-quarters of a century later, after the blurring of the period of Biringuccio, Copernicus, and Vesalius has been much clarified. This clarification was not simply the consequence of theorizing by a Galileo or Bacon himself, but followed upon such experimental achievements as those recorded in Gilbert's *De magnete* in 1600, or in the Lumleian lectures that William Harvey started giving in 1616, due to culminate in the *De motu cordis* of 1628, after Bacon's death. This publication was "universally acknowledged," write the translators of the lectures, "to be the first brilliant demonstration of modern scientific method."

43. Paracelsus, *Hermetic and Alchemical Writings,* I.182; Vannoccio Biringuccio, *Pirotechnia,* tr. Cyril Stanley Smith and Martha Teach Gnudi (1942; rpt. Cambridge, Mass., 1966), p. 14.

Like others, Harvey had started out a "confirmed Aristotelian," and the Lumleian lectures, created in 1582 and from the first distinguished by their obligatory inclusion of human dissection, were nonetheless always supposed to be based on the authority of the ancients.[44] Medical practice in England remained for a long time behind what could be found in certain Continental centers, so it is not astonishing that we can remark in Harvey's lecture notes from 1616 on a gradual passage from the old to the new, as though he were heeding Bacon's rousing (and as yet unpublished) call to strip the mind bare and erect a new logical construction. Texts such as those of Harvey and Kepler show in their very elaboration a moment of change (though it will not be consolidated for many a year). Still, the potential for and the necessity of that coming change is already apparent in Biringuccio, Copernicus, and Vesalius.

Like Gérard Simon, I will affirm that the discursive practice analyzed by Lévi-Strauss in its manifestation through the material called *myth* (itself revealed in the latter's work only in linguistic formations) is the same relation as that indicated here by the references to Paracelsus, Agricola, Rabelais, and Kepler. In Lévi-Strauss's analysis "mythical thought" is not a content but a way of ordering content. That leads to a potential confusion that I will try to avoid: 'mythical discourse' as a relation is not to be confused with 'myth' as the material of that relation. This is why I am calling the relation one of "patterning." It is nonetheless the case that various studies of the discourse in which myth appears as such material may help us to an understanding of this relation.

And we can do with all the help we can get. For our discourse is the serial one of analytico-referentiality, while that of patterning depends on the operation of an entirely different ordering process. One may perhaps call it, with intentional ambiguity, an order of the formation of complexes, and it is a seemingly nonconceptualized ordering (by definition, if such a term may be applied at all, because it does not seek to separate concept and object). We are confronted therefore with an obvious difficulty: the analysis of such an order, of such a patterning, will tend to endow it with the *meaning* of a different type of discourse. The analysis will necessarily formulate it in terms of our own discursive order. The difficulty is not easily avoided, for we cannot so simply escape the bounds of our own order: and our *study* of the change will be a form of *knowing*, a product of

44. William Harvey, *Lectures on the Whole of Anatomy*, an annotated translation of *Prelectiones anatomiae universalis* by C. D. O'Malley, F. N. L. Poynter, and K. F. Russell (Berkeley and Los Angeles, 1961), pp. 11, 3–7.

the analytical method. That is a risk one cannot really avoid. If the distinction made by Nietzsche, for example, with regard to an 'original' split between the Apollonian and the Dionysiac (which seems to bear comparison with what we are here discussing) seems often unclear and 'mystical,' this is certainly partly because the second is quite simply closed to the first.

Any *definition* of the one in terms of the other is probably impossible, and if, for purposes of exposition—and only very tentatively—the one may on occasion be represented in a two-dimensional model as functioning at right angles to the other (following the example of Lévi-Strauss and others), such a representation pretends at best only to the status of a metaphor. In that sense, it might appear that Lévi-Strauss has allowed himself to be taken in by the metaphor of the two-dimensional model, seeing in it a precise reflection of common patterns of human thinking. In *Mythologiques,* for example, the anthropologist seeks to apply to mythical thinking the general grammar/universal reason equation of the Cartesians by making various different myths into the various speech acts of a common and general human language, which in turn corresponds to the universal workings of the mind. Although one might not wish to deny the generality of the patterns, the conclusions as to their meaning appear problematic and make of them almost a variant of the analytico-referential in respect of their operating principles.[45]

In a rather similar way, Gérard Simon in his study of what he considers from the first to be Kepler's entirely alien conceptual space claims to be able to study the "internal norms of a functioning of thought" without the interference of "any projection of our own."[46] Yet that very claim to objectivity is based on a rationality whose absoluteness both Simon himself and the mere existence of a work like Kepler's deny. Such 'objectivity' is therefore relative only to the functioning of that rationality and to certain of its conceptual exclusions. The mere use of the notion is therefore already an interference with the internal norms of Kepler's discourse, for the concept of 'objective analysis' is itself oriented by the particular classificatory grid which succeeded that earlier class of discourse.

One cannot escape *in this way* the objective fact that one is oneself inserted in a particular episteme: that *fact* must needs be fully ac-

45. This was no doubt not the case at first in Lévi-Strauss's work, but by the conclusion of *Mythologiques* such patterns seem to be emerging. In this regard, Jonathan Culler has advanced some useful criticisms: *Structuralist Poetics: Structuralism, Linguistics, and the Study of Literature* (London, 1975), e.g., pp. 48–49.
46. Simon, *Kepler,* p. 14.

cepted before there can be the slightest hope of deflecting a condition which is after all our life situation. That is why, when I take over for strictly demonstrative purposes a descriptive model, a grid whose application to the Oedipus myth Lévi-Strauss himself claimed as no more than heuristic, I will not ascribe to it any value other than that it permits the demonstration of a difference. But it will serve to indicate that that difference is a fundamental one between two different classes of discourse. It will also help us to illustrate a development in their relationship. Still, such differences can only be shown, they cannot be told. Such is the case no matter into what detail we may seek to go in order to show the functioning of a different discursive space. The detail accumulated by a Lévi-Strauss or by a Simon still only shows a difference.

As soon as one seeks to analyze the specific ordering, the specific 'conceptual basis' of that detail inasmuch as it reveals a different discursive ordering process, our analysis itself necessarily denies all our efforts to do what Simon claims to be able to do: to deny the projection of the internal norms of our own practice of thought. However, though one must needs be aware of it, this does not seem to me a particularly uncomfortable restriction on our knowledge of 'past' modes of thought. We are, after all, seeking to recapture them for the light they may throw on the limits, the exclusions, and the capacities of our own, though it cannot, of course, give us any 'solution' to those limits. It is not some impossible comprehension of a past structure of thought 'in its own terms' which matters, but the fact of its demonstrable *difference.*

The risk we face, therefore, is one of diverting the structures of a different discursive class to the forms of our discourse. It is a difficulty akin to what is suggested by Wittgenstein's luminous and amusing remark, "If a lion could talk we could not understand him."[47] With this proviso in mind, I will use the suggestions made by various analyzers of mythical discourse concerning specific alternative ways of *structuring* and *using* discourse. My use, in the study of Kepler's *Somnium,* of Jung's explorations into the so-called pseudo-sciences of alchemy and astrology is by no means arbitrary; nor is it the result of a confusion arising from different meanings of the word 'myth,' as used, for example, by Jung and various historians of religion on the one hand, and by anthropologists on the other. In any case, both refer thereby to a similar kind of discursive material even though their handling of it is utterly at odds.

47. Ludwig Wittgenstein, *Philosophical Investigations* (1953; rpt. Oxford, 1972), II.xi.223.

The point is that astrology—with its analogical reasoning, with its assumption of a sympathy between all things as the sign of a universal vitalism, with its reading and interpretation of signs organized by resemblance, in patterns—is for Kepler an overarching structure. Or at least, taken together with a Pythagorean mathematics, a reasoning from geometrical proportionality, and a musical harmony, it is such a structure. Within this structure Kepler can hope to reach a 'comprehension' of a universal whole: adopting a process close to the medieval notion of reading through the traces of the divine creation to God's will. Chapter 2 will show this more clearly. Kepler's *ars combinatoria,* which Simon suggests leaves us with an impression of "bric-a-brac" (thinking perhaps of Lévi-Strauss's *bricolage*), is precisely what will be dominated by the powerful instrument of analysis: the effort to *comprehend* by placing signs/things into a pattern of resemblances will be replaced by the effort to make things usable. The function of the Keplerian patterning is "to make the world say what it has to say both through its motions and through its proportions."[48] That is a concept of 'comprehension' virtually beyond our concrete understanding. It is clear that such words as 'comprehension,' 'knowledge,' 'meaning,' 'sense' are to acquire an altogether different meaning. Jung's studies are useful not because they tell us how Kepler's discourse functions but because they supply material which serves to indicate its difference. But if Jung's researches can supply us with some of the material, it is those of Lévi-Strauss which must supply us with the principal model.

For the discourse of patterning must be taken first of all as a system of transformations organizing a comprehension of society and the individual, of nature and culture, of the 'natural' and the 'supernatural.' It provides a tool that makes it possible to deal with what would otherwise appear as unresolvable differences and contradictions (and which do so once the discourse of patterning is no longer operative as the dominant class of discourse). In Lévi-Strauss's analysis the significant elements of 'mythical thought' are not the themes which Jung and his followers equate each with a specific meaning, or which Cassirer, with his avowed neo-Kantianism, views as the evidence of a particular way of organizing the primary and permanent categories of the human mind—Space, Time, and Number.[49] The material of myth simply provides a space in which certain relational possibilities may be elaborated. This has nothing to do

48. Simon, *Kepler,* pp. 56, 65.
49. Ernst Cassirer, *The Philosophy of Symbolic Forms,* tr. Ralph Manheim, 3 vols. (1955; rpt. New Haven and London, 1968), II.73–151.

with the simple one-to-one signifier/signified dichotomy such as that established by Jung: "The true constituent units of myth are not the isolated relations but *bundles of such relations,* and it is only as bundles that these relations can be put to use and combined so as to produce a meaning." These bundles are composed, writes Lévi-Strauss elsewhere, of the "remains and debris of events seized in the concrete world."[50]

It goes without saying that our readings of such discourse are in a sense merely an accumulation of different meanings, for us. We compose a set of parallel readings, interpretations, all equally 'possible' just because they are an ordering of one class of discourse in terms of another. This is, in fact, precisely what Kepler does with respect to his own text of the *Somnium.* Georges Dumézil has given us an analysis of the 'story' of the Horatii in which he seeks to show a passage from a discourse of patterning to one of analysis in just these terms. He shows how what was originally a kind of patterning was absorbed into the 'history' of Rome by such commentators as Livy and Florus, and how this results in its adjustment to a kind of linearization: since the patterning cannot be 'understood' in accordance with a 'serial logic' it is adjusted to that logic and thereby understood in terms of a particular social, psychological, political, ethical, and juridical 'knowledge.'[51]

In the passage from patterning to analysis as Dumézil traces it in respect to the Horatii relation, the second emerges as a kind of interpretative reading of the first. What happens is that (1) the episodes are clearly differentiated in terms of their 'proper' meaning, (2) they are given a reference (to a sociopolitical code whose fabric they help *explain* and in whose terms *they* can in turn be explained), and (3) an order of causality is installed. In this reading, the various Horatius 'mythemes' which had been variants of a single relation, juxtaposing and ordering perhaps war and peace, unity and multiplicity, life and death, simply become a series of successive episodes in the analytical historical discourse relating the establishment of the nation of Rome. They help to formulate a particular system of morality and a code of military and individual ethics.

The best-known brief attempt to show how a discourse of patterning may function and which implies the possibility of a passage to

50. Claude Lévi-Strauss, "The Structural Study of Myth," in *Structural Anthropology,* tr. Claire Jacobson and Brooke Grundfest Schoepf (New York and London, 1963), p. 211; *The Savage Mind,* p. 22.

51. Georges Dumézil, "Lecture de Tite-Live," *Cahiers pour l'analyse,* no. 7 (March–April 1967): *Du mythe au roman,* pp. 5–31. This text was originally published as ch. 4 of *Horace et les Curiaces* (Paris, 1942).

linear narration is, I suppose, Lévi-Strauss's examination of the Oedipus myth.[52] There is no need to repeat it in full here. For my purpose it will suffice to recall the main lines of that reading, in which the various elements (episodes) of the Oedipus story are reduced to four vertical columns. In each of these are placed "several relations belonging to the same bundle." The relations in a given column have a discoverable feature in common, thus: the "over-rating of blood relations," "the underrating of blood relations," "the denial of the autochthonous origin of man," "the persistence of the autochthonous origin of man." The pattern "provides a kind of logical tool which relates the original problem—born from one or born from two?—to the derivative problem: born from different or born from same?" (for the culture believes that humans are autoch-thonous but knows also that they are born from the union of man and woman). The discourse of patterning provides an ordering which absorbs, for example, causality and difference. It is synchronic and tends not to resolve apparent conceptual contradictions, but places them in a relational context that allows them to be 'coped with.'

All of this is similar (not surprisingly) to what Simon has shown with regard to Kepler. He is able to enumerate certain of the elements which function within the discourse: sensible qualities treated as logical classifiers, analogical relations admitted as criteria of truth rather than 'rational' ones, the absence of the causal imperative, in which one may see the first clause of the credo of rationality. Simon can also show how the privilege accorded by Kepler to a certain kind of causal explanation remains nonetheless subservient to and in the service of a belief that the universe is full of signs composing a meaning which it is the specialist's task to decipher. Here, indeed, we can see at work the growth of future dominance from within the very structure of the earlier discourse.

For the functioning of the causality in question appears to depend on certain constants which are similar to those that order our own concept of causality, but its logical operators and its relational vari-ables, Simon shows, are quite different. The operators and variables in question, available to a particular structure of order, enter into a scheme of meaningfulness of which that order is itself only one aspect: it is not constitutive of that scheme, but one of the bits and pieces which compose it. For Kepler, such structures of thought (though they may provide a point of access *for us* to the scheme) are

52. "The Structural Study of Myth," pp. 213–19.

themselves merely a part of the overarching order. For Kepler, causality could never be universalized. It is a heuristic and methodological bridge helping only to provide access to a system of transformations. It helps us to the comprehension of a divine order whose nature is ultimately ineffable, and in whose ineffability the very system of transformations itself, as a part of that order, must ultimately participate. Only with all of that in mind can the four-column grid suggested by Lévi-Strauss be usefully manipulated: it will be indicative of a discursive difference, not 'objectively' descriptive of a discursive reality.

From Cusanus to Bruno, from Rabelais to Campanella, from Paracelsus to Kepler, from Boehme even to Galileo with his great book of nature, this conceptual space remains to a greater or lesser extent the one occupied by writers of all kinds—even if, in the last case especially, we are already, as it were, in transit. It is perfectly true that such writers as Paracelsus and Agricola remain exemplary references for researchers as late as the "Puritan scientists" of the interregnum in England, as Charles Webster has written at considerable length. He notes that their work, particularly in their preferred categories of "communications, education, medicine, technology, economic planning and agriculture," was essential to the advancement of modern science, and observes that one of the reasons why Bacon was thought of by them "as the authentic guide to intellectual regeneration" was precisely his own ties to such conceptualization.[53] That, of course, also ties Bacon to Kepler.

This blurring of the passage from patterning to analytico-referentiality is a consequence of the very growth of the latter from within the former. In the more general terms of a study in the history of ideas, Hiram Haydn long ago described such a blurring.[54] It is why the lines of discursive development toward dominance need to be made clear: not merely as a sociohistorical phenomenon, but as a discourse whose consequences remain with us. The scientific development as such cannot be 'understood' without an awareness of its grounding within what is now to us a quite unfamiliar discursive space, as both Webster and Simon have observed. My argument will concern the nature of the discourse which comes to dominate those discursive practices "which have subsequently been discarded" and the manner in which it does so from within those very practices. The

53. Charles Webster, *The Great Instauration: Science, Medicine, and Reform, 1626–1660* (London, 1975), pp. 31, 12 (but the entire volume is in some sense concerned with the influence of Bacon and "baconianism").
54. Hiram Haydn, *The Counter Renaissance* (New York, 1950).

manner of the gradual occultation of the "general conceptual framework" which gave birth to analytico-referential discourse and some
of the consequences of that occultation are what the following analyses will seek to show.[55]

In this connection Gérard Simon argues that the way Kepler conceives of the application of quantitative arguments to matters of
celestial motion marks a moment of transition: "an application of the
schemas of analogical thought to the field of quantity." This is the
obverse of the appearance of a causal order in his discourse. What is
new derives from what preceded it: "the Keplerian sphere symbolizes the appearance, in the heart of an episteme of similitude and
with the help of elements it provides, of new requirements produced
by the concern for a quantified causal explanation constituting the
World in Nature." The same author notes a further precise analogy
in Kepler with what we have already seen in Paracelsus. Kepler views
such notions as the world soul, light and fire, magnetism and attraction, physical force, as members of a single paradigm, whereas we
can only view them as belonging to different sets:

> Far from renewing the norms implied by his predecessors' knowledge
> [*savoirs*], it is just because he pursues their logic to its limit that new
> observations lead him to question what had been inferred from that
> logic until then. One could amuse oneself with a parody of Marx: a style
> of discourse never disappears before all the forms of knowledge it is
> capable of organizing have been developed, and new and higher rela-
> tions of enunciation are never substituted for it before the theoretical
> conditions for the existence of those relations have unfolded from
> within the very heart of the old *savoirs*.[56]

For Kepler, as for Paracelsus and the later English Puritans, the
world, the universe, has its soul. The functioning of that soul is
revealed by all things, living and insensible, vital and material, natural, supernatural, and artificial, conceptual and sensual, imaginary
and real. All things without exception are equally signs available for
interpretation and diverse kinds of use. Webster writes thus of the
appeal of Paracelsan medicine to Puritan thought: "all things had a
part in a single world soul by virtue of their common origin."[57] In a
similar way, the fact that for a Kepler analytical reading is but a part
of analogical reasoning is why Simon can call him "one of the founders of modern science whom it is nonetheless strictly impossible to

55. The quotations are from Webster, *The Great Instauration*, p. xv.
56. Simon, *Kepler*, pp. 134–36, 350.
57. Webster, *The Great Instauration*, p. 285.

reduce to the norms of our modernity." To read Kepler, then, from the perspective of the Enlightenment's reading of Newton (whose own 'mystical' undertakings are nowadays also familiar) is simply to appropriate bits and pieces of "a ruined whole," and what we miss in such an undertaking is an awareness of "a radical cultural heterogeneity."[58]

The metaphor of the telescope with which I began this introductory chapter can teach us something about this heterogeneity. As we learn from Tesauro, it is the mark of a change in discourse. The word, the very concept of sign, passed down the telescope with the image, so to speak, until it was conceived of as a simple mental creation, possessing a quite arbitrary relationship with the thing. The sign had been in all ways the equal of the thing. Now the word has become as it were a means of visualizing the object. It has become the mark of, but also a bridge over, a new space between the intellect and the world. It is now possible to turn an abstract system into a true knowledge of a real world, one taken as *not* ordered by man.

After discussing *Utopia* in Chapter 3, one of the points my reading of Kepler's *Somnium* will seek to make in Chapter 4 is that *for us* the heterogeneity in question to some extent masks itself: just because the new is produced from the old. It is already 'on the move.' It is already producing out of itself a system that will prove a more powerful instrument than the discursive organization out of which it comes. Doubtless one should rather affirm that the sociocultural conditions with which it combines (made by and making them) will cause it to become a more powerful instrument. That that is so is partly on account of its power for the production of what Bacon calls "works" and partly because what one might call its 'instrumental will' for effecting 'development' ('progress,' as it will shortly be termed) in the human and natural world corresponds with and becomes a part of the gradual accession to economic and bureaucratic power of a mercantile and juridical class whose past was a complete blank so far as the dominant theological-feudal ideology of an earlier power structure was concerned.

58. Simon, *Kepler*, pp. 8–9.

2 · Questions of Medieval Discursive Practice

> Now, seeing that all creatures, even those that are devoid of reason, are directed to God as their last end, and that all reach this end in so far as they have some share of a likeness to Him, the intellectual creature attains to Him in a special way, namely, through its proper operation, by understanding Him. Consequently this must be the end of the intellectual creature, namely, to understand God.
> —Thomas Aquinas, *Summa contra Gentiles*

Though the preceding chapter has quite clearly stated the hypothesis underlying this study and provided a justification of its methodology, it will perhaps have seemed insufficiently attentive to matters of chronology. I am very aware that the selection of such figures as Paracelsus, Agricola, Rabelais, Kepler, and others as my heuristic starting point may well be interpreted as a means of avoiding any consideration of the formidable conceptual machinery mounted by the Middle Ages. In this regard two possible objections need to be confronted immediately, a third being included with them. It is indeed the case that all are of a historical cast, and while their dismissal may not be essential to the analyses to come (inasmuch as these analyses themselves will ultimately have to validate the hypothesis), they cannot be left to simmer unseen.

The first objection concerns the various claims according to which an analytico-referential discourse was installed by Aristotle and his successors, from Boethius (and indeed Augustine) to Abelard, from Aquinas (and Averroës) to Marsilius, from Anselm to Ockham—and thence to Descartes and the modern era. This may be referred to as the argument that analytico-referentiality is hegemonous ever since the golden age of Athens, or the argument of long continuity. As far as the present study is concerned, it carries with it the evident corollary that the dominant discursive class of the Middle Ages is the same as that of neoclassicism. This corollary is often separated from its principal: it then becomes the argument that even if the assertion of long continuity is impossible, there is nonetheless a 'short continuity' between the Middle Ages and our modernity in consequence of a radical conceptual break situated somewhere at the beginning of the twelfth century. From Anselm and Abelard, the argument then runs, we can follow the installation of forms of thought of which, for example, Descartes is the direct inheritor.

The third principal objection is to the effect that no form of patterning discourse (or any other that is not analytico-referential) was any longer current during the Middle Ages. Since hegemony by no means supposes unicity, this objection is not a necessary consequence of either of the first two objections—though it is often treated as if it were. On the surface any of these would seem to weaken my basic argument, though the separate textual studies hereafter will have to resolve the matter in the end.

Space does not permit nor the present purpose require that any of these questions be dealt with in depth. It will suffice if I can show why the traditional dating of Renaissance developments remains imperative, even though my conception of their manner may be different.[1] I need to show (1) why it is not possible to accept recent arguments, by Husserl, Gusdorf, Derrida, and many others, that the discursive and conceptual changes go back at least to Aristotle and

1. The *locus classicus* of the tradition remains, of course, Jacob Burckhardt, *The Civilization of the Renaissance in Italy*, tr. S. G. C. Middlemore, 2 vols. (New York, 1958; 1st German edition, 1860). This had been preceded by Jules Michelet's *La Renaissance* (Paris, 1855), and was to be followed by cultural criticism from Walter Pater (1873) on. It is the case that Michelet views Abelard, Dante, and a few others as precursors, mysteriously three hundred years ahead of their time, while Pater considers Abelard and certain aspects of the Middle Ages in a similar way, and a writer as late as Winckelmann (1717–68) as still belonging to the Renaissance—but by and large as dates were clear and limited. The concept was first contested in depth, perhaps, by C. H. Haskins, *The Renaissance of the Twelfth Century* (Cambridge, Mass., 1927), and the controversy has not settled since. Like Haskins, Etienne Gilson tended to place the origins of modern thought in the Middle Ages, the succession being more or less continuous despite subtleties of argumentation. Others have gone further: the view of Western thought and culture as presenting a single continuous phenomenon, the manifestation of an essentially permanent and basically unchanging human spirit, is advanced, for example, by Ernst Robert Curtius, *European Literature and the Latin Middle Ages*, tr. Willard R. Trask (1953; rpt. New York and Evanston, 1963). Fundamentally, this is also the judgment proposed by Erich Auerbach, *Mimesis: The Representation of Reality in Western Literature*, tr. Willard R. Trask (Princeton, 1953). Other recent scholars, such as Paul Oskar Kristeller, in his *Renaissance Thought: The Classic, Scholastic, and Humanist Strains* (New York, 1961), esp. pp. 3–11, and Erwin Panofsky, in his *Renaissance and Renascences in Western Art* (1960; rpt. New York and Evanston, 1969), esp. pp. 1–41, have returned to Burckhardt's view—in the main, at least. Panofsky, in particular, argues for a combination of a quite new "physiognomy" and the continuity of certain disparate elements as fundamental to what may be called the "Renaissance" (pp. 4, 37). Though my terms will be very different, the basic historical view is similar.

possibly to Plato: a discussion that will lead us to the assertion that we cannot even understand the ancient Greeks in anything like 'their own terms,' let alone follow them. I need to show (2) that these changes do not even go as far back as the Middle Ages, though we may be led to accept some idea of a break around 1100, and even to find some scattered elements of a future discourse that may be viewed as emerging (a fact that would be very far from undermining my hypothesis: the break of the twelfth century itself will be seen rather as installing a class of discourse that is becoming inoperative by the Renaissance). I need to suggest (3) the presence during the Middle Ages of dominant discursive practices that are other than analytico-referential. (I will need a measure of goodwill as far as this last is concerned, because only the later textual analyses will provide some detail of the functioning of analytico-referential discourse.)

These objections really need only two, not three, kinds of refutation. It if can be shown, for example, that 'Aristotelian discourse' lacks an element essential to the analytico-referential, then the first objection falls. Provided it is essential, the absence of only one such element is enough. It does not, however, resolve the 'corollary' to this first objection, since it is evidently possible to set aside any idea of continuity with the Greeks and still maintain, like Colin Morris, Walter Ullmann, F. Edward Cranz, Etienne Gilson, and others, that medieval rationality continues unbroken into neoclassicism. The tactic must change, therefore, and the second refutation will have to be positive rather than negative. I will have to show strong evidence of the dominant presence of another class or other classes of discourse during the Middle Ages (a one or ones that will not be important in the Renaissance, so that we may allow for some kind of conceptual 'break' between Antiquity and the Middle Ages, around 1100 say, without having to assume that it therefore leads directly into our modernity).

If these arguments can be convincingly made then the objection of 'short continuity' falls and, possibly, the objection concerning the absence of patterning—assuming I can suggest in this case that such a discourse was importantly present during the Middle Ages. Again, for my present purpose it will suffice if the mere possibility of its presence can be affirmed. The necessarily long full demonstration is obviously out of the question in a study whose principal concerns are with a later moment of discursive history.

The first objection, then, is that something closely akin to analytico-referential systematizing discourse has ruled Western thought without any significant break ever since the Greek fourth century. Let us admit immediately that there is no question but that some kind of analogous split did occur between the sixth and fourth centuries B.C. Such an affirmation does not, however, permit us to assume that it resulted in the rule of a discourse identical to that which may have been dominant in the Middle Ages or to one which became dominant from the European Renaissance on ("dominant" in the sense that its organizing elements controlled the analysis and understanding of the majority of human practices). I will propose in a moment a single suggestion as prolegomenon to a more complete refutation than can be advanced here, on the grounds (as I have said) that the absence of one element essential to the analytico-referential discourse is sufficient evidence of the absence of such an episteme. But this sufficiency rests on the assumption that an episteme is a complete network of relations together composing some sort of whole. Only thus does the absence of a single element imply a quite distinct total configuration. Such an assumption needs perhaps some introductory evidence (though I hope the second half of this chapter will provide conclusive evidence, at least for the Middle Ages).

For our episteme it would seem apparent that in the demarcation of mind and matter, of the conceptualizing faculty and its external referent such as we perceive in analytico-referential discourse, the concept of *will*—indeed of *individual will*—in some form or another must be of prime importance.[2] Yet one can readily follow a considerable change in the way it is conceptualized from the Greeks to the modern period. For our modernity, after the Renaissance, *will* has become associated with an entirely human *reason* of which it is the guide and efficient cause (how this was achieved will be part and parcel of the analyses set forth in later chapters). In medieval theory, basically ruled in this matter by Augustine, *will* could only be associated with the 'passions' and opposed to a rational understanding tending toward knowledge of God: untrammeled human 'will,' assuming it thinkable, could only lead to error and falsehood. The second half of the present chapter will explore this question in rather more detail. For the Greeks the situation is again quite different.

Before discussing the question of *will* with some precision, it is necessary to take a quick glance at the more general contexts, con-

---

2. A considerable bibliography could be constituted on this subject, but for brevity I refer to two previously mentioned articles: Reiss, "Espaces de la pensée discursive: Le cas Galilée et la science classique," *Revue de synthèse*, no. 85–86 (Jan.–July 1977), pp. 5–47, and "Cartesian Discourse and Classical Ideology," *Diacritics*, 6, no. 4 (Winter 1976), 19–27.

ceptual networks of which *will* is but one element. For *will* in the modern sense is very clearly a central aspect of some idea of self-identity. F. Edward Cranz has remarked that the mere absence of any self-identity as a center of knowing (and doing) is one of the several characteristics that make it difficult if not impossible for us to 'understand' the Ancients. He notes, too, that there is no fundamental dichotomy for the Greeks between the world of thought and that of things—something we saw as essential for analytico-referential discourse and which is clearly of a part with a concept of self-identity. For the Greeks, language and thought, he writes, were essentially *conjunctive*: from Plato to Augustine one sought knowledge by following a path inward through the "soul" to the imprinted universal. The immense difference Cranz sees in Anselm and Abelard at the beginning of the twelfth century is that knowledge becomes *disjunctive*.[3] Cranz does not discuss the matter in these terms, but such disjunction is still not yet concerned with a 'modern' notion of individual *will*.

When speaking of elements of knowledge and action, of being and human praxis as discursive characteristics of an episteme, we need to remain always aware of their whole context and orientation. Such texts as the *Peri hermeneias* and the *Analytica posteriora seem* to proffer theoretical attitudes toward speech and language, reason and judgment not far removed from what we find as well in the Renaissance and seventeenth century (for example): the separation of words and things, the notion of words as signs of concepts, verbal definition as necessary to any referential use of terms, the conventional nature of language, and so on. We seem to be concerned, that is to say, with those very matters of difference and distance, of separation and arbitrariness, of which I spoke in Chapter 1 as an essential part of the emerging new discourse. For the seventeenth century, however, such aspects of language and discourse are ineluctably bound up with a particular characterization of reason, will, human action, and knowledge—with being itself. The nature of the characterizations is specific to a particular 'conceptual' (or discursive) network. It may be necessary for a formal treatment of such matters to deal with them

3. I refer here to a number of unpublished papers by Professor Cranz (see the Bibliography), and in particular to "New Dimensions of Thought in Anselm and Abelard as against Augustine and Boethius" (1971). I am grateful to their author for allowing me to make reference to his papers, and to my colleague Gene Vance for having made them available to me. I would like to express again my deep appreciation to Gene Vance, who freely availed me especially of his knowledge of St. Augustine and referred me to a number of the Saint's writings to which I would otherwise have remained inattentive.

separately, as Aristotle does in his various treatises. But it is as a whole network that they become epistemically meaningful, and a fundamental difference in any one of these basic constituents as they appear in diverse cultures and times will imply a different episteme (though this is not to exclude the presence of emerging elements, the process of gradual change within an episteme).

Like the texts of the *Organon*, Augustine's early *De magistro* appears to teach us about the arbitrary and conventional nature of verbal signs, about the relation of distance between signs and things signified or signifiable, between signs and other signs. And that would seem to lead this discussion into a claim of continuity well up through the Middle Ages, for, as Steven Ozment has recently remarked: "Augustine was to the intellectual history of the Middle Ages what classical civilization was to its political and cultural history: a creative source, whose recovery and study spurred new directions of thought and controversy down through the Reformation of the sixteenth century."[4] Reading a text like the *De magistro*, however (and even more the *De Trinitate*, as we will see), one becomes rapidly aware of a profound contextual difference between the Augustinian considerations just mentioned and those of a "Cartesian" or of a post-Saussurian linguistics.

For the Bishop of Hippo, all such signs serve a *commemorative* function. Speaking is reminding, understanding is remembering: "Regarding, however, all those things which we understand, it is not a speaker who utters sounds exteriorly whom we consult, but it is truth that resides within, over the mind itself." Words remind us of this, so that we come to *re*discover, in truth, "He who is said to *dwell in the inner man*, He it is who teaches—Christ—that is, *the unchangeable Power of God and everlasting Wisdom*." Thus Augustine can add that a man is taught not by mere words, verbal signs, "but by the realities themselves made manifest to him by God revealing them to his inner self." The "arbitrariness" of words needs to be understood as a function of this commemorative operation. Teachers (all speakers) "teach" by bringing their pupils (all listeners) to gaze "attentively at that interior truth," potentially able to be "unveiled" in anyone through the release of memory.[5]

While this is evidently as far from our own order of thought as are the classifications of Paracelsus, it is close to Plato and perhaps cer-

---

4. Steven E. Ozment, *The Age of Reform, 1250–1550: An Intellectual and Religious History of Late Medieval and Reformation Europe* (New Haven and London, 1980), p. 2.

5. St. Augustine, *De magistro*, in *The Greatness of the Soul; The Teacher*, tr. and ed. Joseph M. Colleran (1950; rpt. Westminster, Md., 1964), pp. 177, 179, 185.

tain aspects of Aristotle. The *Posterior Analytics* begin as an effort to rid themselves of the Platonic dilemma as recorded in the *Meno*: "either a man will learn nothing or [he will learn] what he already knows." Aristotle's answer is to assert that the arguments to be presented in the *Posterior Analytics,* arguments presented as enabling us to discover the first principles of a true scientific knowledge, are such as will permit us to find in ourselves "pre-existent knowledge." The first example of this given was destined to become an exemplary cliché of Western arguments about the nature of thought: that the angles of a triangle equal two right angles. Aristotle responds to Plato therefore by asserting that the knower "*knows* not without qualification but only in the sense that he *knows* universally." In this sense the premises of such demonstrable knowledge "must be true, primary, immediate, better known than and prior to the conclusion." Indeed, in themselves they "must be primary and indemonstrable."[6]

That this is a response to Plato ignored by Augustine seems clear: but is it Descartes? Are these the "clear and distinct ideas" discovered by the willful reason of the later new man? It would seem absolutely not. As the discussion of the *De anima* tells us, these elements of knowledge are imprinted in the mind insofar as mind is embodied in corporality, but they are not imprinted in the mind as "pure" mind (that is, independently of "actual knowledge," which depends upon its concrete embodiment). In some way, therefore, the primary and indemonstrable premises are a potential contained in "universal mind" prior to its actual embodiment. We are not perhaps so far from the Platonic *Idea* as is sometimes claimed:

> Actual knowledge is identical with its object: in the individual, potential knowledge is in time prior to actual knowledge, but in the universe as a whole it is not prior even in time. Mind is not at one time knowing and at another not. When mind is set free from its present conditions it appears as just what it is and nothing more: this alone is immortal and eternal (we do not, however, remember its former activity because, while mind in this sense is impassible, mind as passive is destructible), and without it nothing thinks.[7]

Embodied mind is passive. It is definable as that which receives whatever is able to be thought: among such things, presumably, the

6. Aristotle, *Analytica posteriora*, 71a–b, in *The Basic Works*, ed. Richard McKeon (New York, 1941), pp. 111–12.

7. Aristotle, *De anima*, III.5.430a, *Basic Works*, p. 592. This is a profoundly disputed passage, but it is worth noting here precisely because it is so indicative of a quite unfamiliar manner of thinking.

true, primary, and immediate premises of all particular knowledge.[8] However one interprets this not always very clear discussion of the *De anima* and balances it with such texts as the *Analytica posteriora*, that they produce a very different configuration from what is implied by the term "Cartesian" is apparent. Within that configuration it will be useful to explore in detail one element as definitive evidence of the dominance of a different discursive class. If I take the concept of *will* as an exemplary case, it is certainly in part because it is just such a fundamental element. It is also, however, because the concept has been discussed at length and the material is readily accessible for an argument that seeks, as here, to be indicative rather than exhaustive.

Jean-Pierre Vernant has observed that the notion of a personal will in the modern sense of a reasoned intellectual process toward (possessive) action cannot be enunciated in ancient Greek. It is, he remarks, no more isolated in Aristotle's moral thinking than it is in the vocabulary available to him. Nor was it available earlier (Vernant's discussion starts with Aeschylus). The word *hekōn*, usually translated as "voluntarily" or "by an act of will," merely means "willingly" or even "wittingly," in opposition to *akōn*, "in spite of oneself" or "unwittingly." It applies to *any* action that is not externally imposed or entirely contingent upon circumstances. An animal, too, can act *hekōn*. Gerald Else has arrived, quite independently of Vernant, at very similar conclusions with regard to Aristotle's *Poetics*, when he discusses the distinction to be made between acts that are *hekousia* and those that are *akousia*.[9]

---

8. *De anima*, III.4.429a–430a, *Basic Works*, pp. 589–91. On the soul (and passive mind) as embodiment, see *De anima*, II.1.412a: "the soul must be a substance in the sense of the form of a natural body having life potentially within it" (*Basic Works*, p. 555). Cranz has recently sought to explore in its own terms the mental configuration in question: "Two Debates about the Intellect: 1, Alexander of Aphrodisias and the Greeks; 2, Nifo and the Renaissance Philosophers" (lecture, December 1979).

9. Jean-Pierre Vernant, "Ebauches de la volonté dans la tragédie grecque," in Vernant and Pierre Vidal-Naquet, *Mythe et tragédie en Grèce ancienne* (Paris, 1972), pp. 48–54 (Vernant notes that he is here following the commentary of Gauthier and Jolif on the *Nichomachean Ethics*); Gerald F. Else, *Aristotle's Poetics: The Argument* (Cambridge, Mass., 1963), p. 380. Else refers especially to the *Nichomachean Ethics* (bk. III), to *Rhetoric* (I.13.1347b4–10), and to *Ethics* (V.20.1135a15–1136a9). The question has received extensive treatment at the hands of Anthony Kenny: first, and rather briefly so far as Aristotle is concerned, in his *Will, Freedom, and Power* (Oxford, 1975), esp. pp. 15–19; second, in his more recent *Aristotle's Theory of the Will* (New Haven, 1979). In his *Pour une logique du sujet tragique: Sophocle* (Montreal, 1980), Pierre Gravel has argued that what is essentially revealed in Sophocles' tragedies is the inability to constitute anything like a 'subject.' I have myself sought to show among other things how Renaissance tragedy, on the contrary, achieves just exactly the constitution of such a subject: *Tragedy and Truth: Studies in the Development of a Renaissance and Neoclassical Discourse* (New Haven and London, 1980).

The point being made by Vernant and Else is not at all that which Anthony Kenny has dismissed, at the outset of a recent book on the subject, as "a commonplace of Aristotelian scholarship": namely, "that Aristotle had no theory of the will." On the contrary, their point is, precisely, that he *does* have a theory of the will but that it is different from ours. Kenny points out that the terminological pairs "voluntary" and "involuntary," "voluntarily" and "involuntarily," by which the above words are usually translated into English, owe more to the Latin terms *voluntarium* and *involuntarium* "used in the medieval translations of Aristotle" (a fact whose significance will be seen a little later in the present chapter) than they do to the original Greek vocabulary, to which they are more or less inadequate. He observes, too, that so central a term as *prohairesis* can only be translated clumsily as "purposive choice"—the clumsiness reflecting "the fact that no natural English concept corresponds to Aristotle's." In this context, he observes, "many of the traditional English expressions for Aristotelian concepts are misleading." In fact, Kenny's diverse references to French and German commentators would allow him to assert this to be the case for modern European languages in general.[10]

What such commentaries indicate is not that Aristotle has no concept of the will, but that it fits into a quite different general conception of human action from our own. There is indeed no active and separate intellectual *will* common only to men and qualitatively different from the generalized faculty allowing of any action ("embodied mind," argues the *De anima*, is by definition "*passive*"). Vernant suggests that the idea of "free will" is not really fixed in the vocabulary until some time between Diodorus Siculus (first century B.C.) and Epictetus (first century A.D.).[11] By that time the entire notion is on the verge of being absorbed into a Christian theological problematic and the discussions of neo-Platonism. There we have to deal, as I will suggest shortly, with a different class of discourse altogether.

Inasmuch as I am concerned here with the 'chronology' of discourses it is perhaps worth recalling, as P. O. Kristeller remarks, that the Aristotelian corpus remained relatively out of sight after his death. It was kept in the library of his school and was there available only to its own teachers. The corpus was published between the first century B.C. and the first century A.D. (dates that are doubtless not coincidental as regards those just mentioned), and "until the second century A.D., outside the circle of scholars trained in the Aristotelian

---

10. Kenny, *Aristotle's Theory of the Will*, pp. vii, 27, 69 n. 1, 111.
11. Vernant, "Ebauches de la volonté," p. 53 n. 20.

school, the systematic writings of Aristotle [as opposed to the more popular, literary ones, now no longer extant] exercised little or no influence upon the development of ancient thought, and it would be anachronistic to assume such an influence as a major factor in the Platonic Academy, in Stoicism, Epicureanism, or Skepticism, in Philo or in the early Christian thinkers." There was no doubt a certain circulation of ideas first propounded by the Stagirite, thanks to his successors at the school, from Theophrastus to Alexander of Aphrodisias (c. 200 A.D.), but the dominant strain in Greek thought was to be neo-Platonism, which reigned supreme from the third to the sixth century A.D.[12] Quite apart from the almost anecdotal corroboration this brings to Vernant's analysis of the development of a Greek term semantically akin to our own "free will" (since it would doubtless have been in Aristotle if anywhere that such a concept would have been developed), such a situation tends to imply that discourse was so fragmented throughout this period that it is scarcely possible to speak of a single one as hegemonous. Slowness and difficulties of communication together with the dispersion of centers of learning would almost seem to guarantee such a situation.

So far as a particular concept of *will* is concerned, Vernant adds that the opposition *akōn/hekōn* was in actuality a juridical one. It was not at all "based in its principle upon the distinction between the voluntary and the involuntary. It rests upon the distinction made by the social conscience, under specific historical conditions, between totally reprehensible action and excusable action, which, beside legitimate action, are posited as a pair of antithetical values." But even so it is the action itself that is the object of such a judgment, not the agent: "The agent is caught in the action. He is not its author. He remains included in it."[13] The agent here is part of a whole for which his 'responsibility' is decidedly limited: had circumstances been different that agent might have been able to do otherwise, and though he may be responsible for his actions within the particular circumstances, he has little or no control either over those circumstances or over the extent of his knowledge of them. In a sense one may say that action is inherent in circumstances rather than in an agent effecting such action. Such a conception is completely coherent with that of the "passive mind" imprinted with "actual knowledge."

More recently, Vernant has refined his commentary by continuing Emile Benveniste's discussion of the two different nominal endings in Greek that can be attached to agent-nouns. In the case of endings

12. Kristeller, *Renaissance Thought*, p. 26.
13. Vernant, "Ebauches de la volonté," pp. 54, 56.

in *-tēr*, he remarks that "the agent is immersed in his action, which is conceived as a function; he blends with an activity to which he is unavoidably given up and in which, by destiny, aptitude or necessity, he is as if shut up." In the case of nominal endings in *-tōr*, "the agent possesses, in the form of a quality belonging to him, the act seen as already accomplished, completely carried out." There are therefore two kinds of act and two sets of relations between such acts and their 'agent.' In the first kind, "the activity viewed in its functional aspect is superior to the agent, primary in relation to him." It is a *techne* inherent in a particular kind of metier and which operates, so to speak, *through* the agent, just as "actual knowledge" is the imprint of preexistent "potential knowledge" on embodied mind.

The act of the second kind is still neither "inherent to the agent nor is the agent present to his act." The act does not concern the "series of productive operations that the artisan develops in the course of his work; it dwells in the made object, the produced piece of work." Whatever may be the status of such a concept of act and action, it evidently ignores, indeed precludes, any treatment of the agent "as source and origin of its acts."[14] This is clearly the case for both modalities of act and agent.

Anthony Kenny goes even further than Vernant in his analysis of these terms as they are found in Aristotle (though he does so only by means of a narrower definition of the term *action*). With the aid of a useful clarifying example, he comments: "'*Hekousion*' for Aristotle is not a predicate reserved for actions; both what happens around us and what we can do can be divided into things which are *hekousia* and *akousia*. If I see a child drowning and don't jump in when I can and should, then, Aristotle would say, the child's drowning, so far as I am concerned, is voluntary, or perhaps rather, is voluntary for me."

He adds that in the *Nichomachean Ethics* something is defined as "voluntary with respect to a particular agent if there is no compulsion, if there is an appropriate degree of knowledge, and if the originating cause of the situation (the *arche*) is in the agent."[15] We may note in passing that the definition of *hamartia* given by Aristotle in the *Poetics* refers precisely to the lack of these elements. It is not therefore a 'fault' or a 'tragic flaw' but rather an 'unwittingness.'

14. Jean-Pierre Vernant, "Catégories de l'agent et de l'action en Grèce ancienne," in his *Religions, histoires, raisons* (Paris, 1979), pp. 88–89, 91–92. Cranz has a useful commentary on *techne* within this configuration in "Technology and Western Reason" (lecture, April 1980).

15. Kenny, *Will, Freedom, and Power*, p. 15.

Kenny makes this explicit by observing that in *Topics* (148a8) as well as in the *Nichomachean Ethics* (1110b29), Aristotle speaks of *hamartia* as one kind of *agnoia*.[16] One recalls blind Oedipus's cry:

> It was Apollo, friends, Apollo,
> that brought this bitter bitterness, my sorrows to completion.
> But the hand that struck me
> was none but my own.

That is just what makes it possible for the protagonist of *Oedipus at Colonus* to assert that all he did was done "unwittingly." One thinks, too, of E. R. Dodd's discussion of how Agamemnon explains his theft of Achilles' mistress in the *Iliad*, overcome, he says, by "wild *ate*."[17]

Like Vernant (and Aristotle himself), Kenny remarks that such an account of *will* can clearly include animals. For him, this is itself a "failure" of conceptualization. Referring to an argument advanced by G. E. M. Anscombe, Kenny thus approves what he takes to be her implication that "the weakness in Aristotle's account is a lack of the concept of intention" (another rendering of *prohairesis*).[18] Such a view is akin to the one he expresses in his later volume on the subject where, speaking of a passage in the *Nichomachean Ethics* that appears to make no distinction between classes of action and individual actions, Kenny continues: "A bizarre metaphysic seems implied, according to which one and the same individual action may have certain properties before being performed and others while being performed, and may have certain properties if it is performed and different properties if it is not performed." At the very least Aristotle's "mode of expression is clumsy."[19] But surely, one may ask, such a metaphysic would have to do with events and actions conceived not as static 'objects,' not as provided with some kind of fixed (and once and for all knowable) ontological status, but rather with *praxis*

---

16. Kenny, *Aristotle's Theory of the Will*, p. 49 n. 1.

17. Sophocles, *Oedipus the King*, tr. David Grene, ll.1329–33, in *The Complete Greek Tragedies*, ed. David Grene and Richmond Lattimore, *Sophocles I* (Chicago and London, 1954), pp. 68–69. E. R. Dodds, *The Greeks and the Irrational* (1951; rpt. Berkeley, Los Angeles, and London, 1961), ch. 1. This entire volume is eloquent on the lack of any clear notion of the self and of person among the Greeks. In this regard, I should also mention Bruno Snell, *The Discovery of the Mind: The Greek Origins of European Thought*, tr. T. G. Rosenmeyer (1953; rpt. New York and Evanston, 1960).

18. Kenny, *Will, Freedom, and Power*, p. 16. The reference is to Anscombe's affirmation that Aristotle fails to see deliberation as "a key concept in the theory of action" (G. E. M. Anscombe, "Thought and Action in Aristotle: What Is Practical Truth?" in *New Essays on Plato and Aristotle*, ed. Renford Bambrough [London, 1965], p. 147).

19. Kenny, *Aristotle's Theory of the Will*, p. 31.

as 'ongoing process,' as a movement that acquires meaning as it goes, so to speak ("je peins le passage," as Montaigne was to write later)?

My own view is that to speak of a "weakness," to dismiss the discussion as "clumsy" or the metaphysic as "bizarre," is to endow something like an analytico-referential concept of *will* with a permanent, true reality and to assert that Aristotle was simply unable to contain that truth in an adequate theory. My argument is rather that such concepts as those of *will* and *intention* (as well as the actions and events that 'follow' from them) are epistemic developments borne in specifiable classes of discourse. The lack of our concepts of *will* and *intention* in Aristotle is not a "weakness" but the mark of a different sort of human functioning, a different social and individual praxis, a different kind of conceptualization and action. Such, too, is Vernant's implication. Kenny asserts another view, arguing further that though we may find Aristotle's account "greatly improved" by Aquinas later on, we will find that St. Thomas's account is also, in other aspects, "wrong": the argument there being that although the extent to which the Angelic Doctor developed a concept of intention is admirable, his notion of "deliberate action" is simply unacceptable, because it fails to account for certain permanent human realities (familiar to us and, presumably, to Aquinas—and Aristotle before him).[20]

I would suggest that if the Greeks lacked our modern concepts of *will* and *intention,* if Aquinas omitted our notion of *deliberate action* and thought that the end of man was in God and the human soul in its essence a mediation of the Divine, then that is not because Aristotle was insufficiently intelligent to see that he "ought" to have elaborated deliberation as "a key concept in the theory of action" or that Aquinas was too obtuse to realize that he ought to have provided an even fuller "account of practical reason." Rather is it because they did not *need* such theories and such "complete" accounts (for Aristotle does provide "fragments" of an account of practical reasoning, and Aquinas does give a partly "adequate" one).[21] Human action and human relations, we may suppose, *were* different. What is this residual claim to cultural hegemony which asserts that humanity "must" always have functioned as we think we do—or else be condemned as less intelligent or insufficiently sophisticated, as "primitive" or "pathological"?

Indeed, Kenny seems to recognize such a fundamental difference

20. Kenny, *Will, Freedom, and Power,* pp. 19–21. In other ways Aquinas's view is similar, says Kenny, to Aristotle's (e.g., pp. 24–25).

21. Ibid., pp. 71–73, 94–95, 97–98.

when he speaks of both Aristotle and Aquinas as basing their concepts of practical reasoning upon a first premise that assumes such reasoning to be transmitting an objective and universal value or plan of life—the good—and when he asserts in consequence that "such a line of thought is very alien." Unfortunately, what it is alien to is not an entire practice of human thought and action but "contemporary philosophical fashion" taken as more "correct" than that of its predecessors, of which it would therefore be desirable "to attempt a serious evaluation."[22] Such a view strikes me as simply insufficient to the evidence Kenny himself provides. Like Vernant, Else, and Cranz, I think we can give Aristotle and Aquinas the benefit of an intellectual doubt—should they perchance require it. It may well be they were speaking of something else. Only a certain cultural complacency permits us to assert that they were simply unsuccessful in an attempt to describe experiences and phenomena familiar both to them and to us because a permanent part of things human. It is perhaps more useful to assume that they were at least as successful as analytical philosophy may be at describing a kind of human praxis that is as different from what is familiar to us as is their description of it. Kenny's 'solution' to his difficulty is to use the *Eudemian Ethics* to show that Aristotle's views actually "bear a remarkable resemblance" to those of such analytical philosophers as Ryle and Wittgenstein. But we may well prefer the view expressed by Rousseau in his *Discourse on the Origin of Inequality*: "Humankind of one age is not the humankind of another, and the reason why Diogenes did not find the [kind of] man [he sought] is that he was looking among his contemporaries for a man of a time that was no more."[23]

Will and intention, following the evidence provided by Vernant, Else, and Kenny, and a reading such as the first two imply, are the product of a particular sociohistorical organization. Rousseau is not simply adopting the tradition of the "ages of man" but is insisting that human sensibility, thought, and practice undergo change of so radical a kind as to make the participants in one age of social order incomprehensible to those of another. Will and intention are by no means a permanent given reality, supposed as proper to the human species and a fundamental part of its very definition. The term translated as "will" appears rather as the sign of a discourse functioning in terms of an assumed immediate perception of supposedly

22. Ibid., pp. 93–94. Such an evaluation has now been undertaken, of course, in Kenny's *Aristotle's Theory of the Will*, where the study of the *Eudemian Ethics* reveals that the "mature Aristotle" achieved a view closer to that of the analytical philosopher.

23. Jean-Jacques Rousseau, *Discours sur l'origine de l'inégalité*, in *Du contrat social ou principes du droit politique* [and other political works] (Paris, 1962), p. 91. The preceding quotation is from Kenny, *Aristotle's Theory of the Will*, pp. vii–viii.

enveloping phenomena: the agent is an actor *within* the action. The interpretation of that (social) world must be attempted in its terms and not in ours: in terms, that is to say, in which the human has no dominant control over that of which it is merely a part. I myself doubt such an interpretation is possible for us, and that we will have to be content with simply noting the difference. A conceptualization of this kind is more akin to Lévi-Strauss's "ordering of the mind by the world" than its contrary, and it is utterly different from what we can see in neoclassical discourse. This last creates its phenomenal events as a function of its own system: at first avowedly, later covertly. The *will* is then the name given to the subject that enunciates the predicative discourse of analysis and reference.[24]

At this point we may begin both to broaden the argument and to extend it up to the Middle Ages. For the concepts of *will* and *intention* are but two (very important) aspects of our concept of 'person.' This is itself a concept the Greeks seem simply not to have had. Colin Morris comments on the great difficulty we have today in understanding the ancient Greeks, Hellenistic philosophy, and the Greek fathers, a difficulty "largely due to the fact that they had no equivalent to our concept 'person,' while their vocabulary was rich in words which express community of being, such as *ousia,* which in our usage can be translated only by the almost meaningless word 'substance.'" We may note that this word is the principal component of the words commonly translated as "willful" and "nonwillful." Morris goes on later to remark that a similar situation is the case with regard to our relation with the Middle Ages.

In the twelfth century, he writes, the "nearest equivalents" to the modern word "individual" were such terms as "*individuum, individualis,* and *singularis,* but these terms belonged to logic rather than to human relations." Indeed, in this matter human relations were subordinate to the logical problem: "a central problem of medieval philosophy was the relation of the individual object (*unum singulare*) with the general or universal class to which it belonged, and humanity was often taken as a test case in this argument."[25] The consequences of such a relation were grave. A belief in the reality of

24. For a slightly different but parallel and more complete discussion of this matter, see Michel Foucault, *The Discourse on Language,* in *The Archaeology of Knowledge,* tr. A. M. Sheridan Smith (New York, 1976), Appendix, pp. 218–19. In his "Two Debates about the Intellect," Cranz has in fact attempted a description of the late classical configuration 'in its own terms,' not to mention that of the Renaissance. See, too, his "The Renaissance Reading of the *De anima,*" in *XVIe Colloque International de Tours: Platon et Aristote à la Renaissance* (Paris, 1976), pp. 359–76.

25. Colin Morris, *The Discovery of the Individual, 1050–1200* (New York, 1972), pp. 2, 64.

universals, for example, such as one finds in Anselm, was likely to imply that individuals were simply a part of them, but not so much a divisible part as an indivisible component, an integral feature. Here the "individual" could not be conceived of as preceding the universal, and if, as Cranz suggests, Anselm marks a moment when *conjunction* is replaced by *disjunction*, then it is safe to say that it is a disjunctive form of thought that spends its time trying to reason its way back to conjunction. Indeed, the celebrated "ontological argument" put forward in the *Proslogium* and the *Reply to Gaunilon* is perhaps comprehensible only in such a light. If one understands universals to be primary, then words are present as concepts in the mind only as they reflect the reality of such universals. Only thus does the association between the mental concept of a Perfect Being (whose perfection must include existence) and the actual existence of the Divinity become not only comprehensible but *essential*. Anselm's ontological argument assumes an Augustinian framework and background and a discourse of conjunction: the reliability of concepts in the mind and of human reason in general depends upon the prior reality of universals, of which the guarantor is the ultimate Universal, the Divinity itself. The difficulty we have today in comprehending such a view may explain (apart from other factors) why we may have more sympathy for a thinker such as Abelard, whose tendency toward nominalism seems to place more emphasis on the individual. But we should not place too much faith in any similarity with our own views, for the underlying concepts are quite different.

It seems clear, for example, that despite many commentators' insistence to the contrary, Augustine's *Confessions* do not at all portray a willful self entirely responsible for its own 'individual life.' They portray rather the discovery of the Divine in and through reflection. They do not affirm an individual, but show the absorption of the human into the Divine. The human is significant (in the full sense of the term) only to the degree that it becomes visible as a part of and a path toward God. The memory of internal ("imprinted") knowledge is the sacred memory of a sacred history: Augustine's confessions of 'his' life necessarily conclude with the spiritual interpretation of the beginning of all life as recounted in Genesis, the scriptural memory of the passage from the Divine to the material. This relation of the human to the Divine also explains why John of Salisbury concludes his *Metalogicon,* a book defending the Trivium, with a lament over the world's decay and a call to prayer (addressed to Thomas Becket), that the reader may be joined with Christ. Just as speech and its necessity proceed from the Divine, so they must lead back into It.

The exemplary text here is of course the *De Trinitate,* which I will discuss later as positive evidence of the presence of a non-analytico-referential discourse.

A conjunctive mode of discourse still seems dominant even in a thinker as 'modern' as Abelard. Though Morris and many others have argued that Abelard is such a modern in some ways, it appears doubtful whether he would have viewed himself in so radical a light. If a disjunctive "center of knowing" (but by no means yet anything like a 'self') has replaced a conjunctive manner of being, that center still conceives of its genuine fulfillment only in some kind of 'union' with the Divine. Robert Elbaz suggests that the letters of Abelard vacillate between a view that emphasizes God's control over all human life and lives and one that accentuates man's responsibility for his own decisions. This is also the opinion of so important an interpreter of Abelard as Jean Jolivet.[26]

Yet it is clear at the end of Abelard's first letter, for example, that his life's process as he has just finished recording it is to be viewed as figured in Christ's and as exemplary of man's suffering on earth within the divine plan. This, it seems to me, is the implication of Abelard's taking for himself St. Jerome's view of *himself* as figured in Christ:

> St. Jerome, whose heir methinks I am in the endurance of foul slander, says in his letter to Nepotanius: "The apostle says: 'If I yet pleased men, I should not be the servant of Christ.' He no longer seeks to please men, and so is made Christ's servant" (Epist. 2). And again, in his letter to Asella regarding those whom he was falsely accused of loving: "I give thanks to my God I am worthy to be one whom the world hates" (Epist. 99).[27]

In the light of such a view, Abelard's "vacillation" becomes itself an image of all the ambiguities inherent in the concept of Christ as the Divine Word made flesh. And if the Eucharist is the means by which man can reverse that process—through flesh to union with God— then Abelard's letters, too, are the image of that means. They are not merely the relating of Abelard's own passage through suffering of the flesh to identification with Christ, but that of the reader (particularly if the principal reader was intended to be Heloise).

26. Robert Elbaz, "From Confessions to Antimemoirs: A Study of Autobiography" (Ph.D. diss., McGill University, Montreal, 1980), p. 115; Jean Jolivet, *Arts du langage et théologie chez Abelard* (Paris, 1969), passim.

27. Peter Abelard, *The Story of My Misfortunes: The Autobiography of Peter Abelard,* tr. Henry Adams Bellows (1922; rpt. New York, 1972), pp. 76–78; this quotation, p. 77.

The "eucharistic" value of Abelard's letter (or its aspect of "*imitatio Christi*") puts us once again face to face with the concept of human thought and practice as *memory*, and indicates the full potential of Augustine's theorizing about speech and teaching in the *De magistro*. That potential is realized in the *De Trinitate*, but for the moment I merely want to suggest the extent to which it carries through to the so-called renaissance of the twelfth century. Eugene Vance can rightly comment on the "special importance" granted by medieval culture "to the faculty of memory." Indeed, the "commemorative model" is absolutely central to that culture.[28] For Augustine, but still for Abelard and Aquinas (and the continuity of the overwhelming ideal of the *imitatio Christi* is further evidence), memory provides access to the presence of the Divine in man. It is in just that sense that medieval discursive structures may still be considered *conjunctive*.

These views of 'person' and 'self,' of 'will' and 'intention,' are utterly different from what will be found by the time of the Renaissance. I suggest that anything like discursive control of the "other," whether as event in the world, as object or person, or as a concept humanly originated, could simply not be enunciated. (Institutions based on such control may exist, but they do not yet provide tools permitting the analysis of diverse human practices.) The lack of these concepts implies that the human creation of order is literally inconceivable. It argues that the view of true knowledge as the application of an abstract *human* schematization to the concrete is in the strict sense unthinkable. I would therefore affirm that the first objective is refuted: there can be no continuity of a hegemonous analytico-referential discourse from the Greeks on because of the lack of an absolutely fundamental element of such discourse. We have, quite clearly, already been brought to the corollary of that first objection: that is, the matter of continuity between the Middle Ages and our modernity. And already the suggestion had been made that the same element may be lacking through most of the Middle Ages.

Nonetheless, it remains a fact that many of those very commentators who readily accept the radical heterogeneity of the Greeks find it perfectly possible to insist that many medieval thinkers are direct ancestors of the moderns. One can argue, for example, that Cartesianism and Scholasticism are chronologically unified as the continuous development of one perennial structure of human thought— as Etienne Gilson has tended to do in his book about the relation

28. Eugene Vance, "Roland and the Poetics of Memory," in *Textual Strategies: Perspectives in Post-Structural Criticism*, ed. J. Harari (Ithaca, 1979), pp. 374–75.

between medieval thought and the system of Cartesian philosophy.[29] The same philosopher-historian is able to write elsewhere that "the Averroistic tradition forms an uninterrupted chain from the Masters of Arts of Paris and Padua, to the 'Libertins' of the seventeenth and eighteenth centuries." A Fontenelle is the direct descendant of John of Jandun and Marsilius of Padua. And while Ockham marks the "final divorce of reason and Revelation" in favor of reason, Erasmus establishes the end of the same line in favor of Revelation. We are thus provided with a kind of genealogy of the Renaissance that runs from Duns Scotus's disagreement with St. Thomas, through Ockham, Gehrard Groote, Thomas à Kempis, and Erasmus himself. In this way, while it may be admitted that Cardinal Cajetan (died 1534) represents the end of the Thomist road ('reason' and 'faith' being part of a single pattern), it also becomes possible for the reason of neoclassicism to be viewed as the immediate and uninterrupted successor of medieval discursive practices.[30]

In a similar way, both Colin Morris and F. Edward Cranz assert continuity between the work of an Abelard on the one hand and the conceptual developments achieved by Descartes on the other, just as Arthur O. Lovejoy could do between that same medieval thinker and Spinoza. Walter Ullmann argues that there is no real break between certain aspects of medieval political thought and that of the era since Machiavelli (though the subtlety of his arguments suggests that the continuity is of a very complex kind).[31] But assertions of some kind of simple continuity are possible, it seems to me, only at the cost of taking isolated elements from different discourses and aligning them on the prior assumption that, for example, Abelard, Descartes, and Spinoza (not to mention Augustine and Ockham) are all representatives of the same unchanging human mind, which itself is in some way unbound by the discursive network of sociohistorical praxis. The critic's 'knowledge' of that supposedly self-identical mind precedes his examination of the thinkers in question. It proceeds, whether one recognizes it or not, from a modern view of which the opening line of Descartes's *Discours de la méthode* is doubtless the most cele-

29. Etienne Gilson, *Etudes sur le rôle de la pensée médiévale dans la formation du système cartésien*, 3d ed. (Paris, 1967).

30. These arguments are made in Etienne Gilson, *Reason and Revelation in the Middle Ages* (New York, 1938), pp. 65, 86–88, 92, 85.

31. Morris, *Discovery of the Individual*, pp. 64–75 and passim; unpublished papers of F. Edward Cranz, esp. "Nicolaus Cusanus as a Paradigm of Renaissance and Reformation" (1979); Arthur O. Lovejoy, *The Great Chain of Being: A Study in the History of an Idea* (1936; rpt. New York, 1960), pp. 71–72; Walter Ullmann, *Medieval Political Thought*, 3d ed. (Harmondsworth, 1975) and his briefer examination of the same thesis in *The Individual and Society in the Middle Ages* (Baltimore, 1966).

brated example—and model: "Good sense is the most evenly divided (widespread) thing in the world." But isolatedly similar strains of thought do not make up the network of relations of an episteme, even though they may form an element within it. Emergent and residual elements are always present within a dominant discourse. What we need to recognize are the elements that are essential to the dominance itself: that is, the elements that are a fundamental part of the episteme.

I have suggested that our concepts of 'will,' 'intention,' 'person' and so on are not even available to the Greeks, and that they are barely so even as late as the European twelfth century. The difficulty commentators have experienced in unearthing such notions as 'individual' in that period is itself a sign of their relative lack of importance. In this manner, speaking of the *Chanson de Roland* (eleventh century), Eugene Vance reminds us that the voice of the "individual" is not that of "an individualizing psychology." The formulae of conquest spoken by Roland himself just before he dies "belong to a repertory of deeds that are not his alone, and his voice becomes more and more that of history itself speaking to us." Once again we are dealing here with a *commemorative* effect grounded in the Divine, for Roland's "silent interlocutor" at this moment is Durendal, his sword, given to Charlemagne by God (through an angel) and therefore brilliant "with the light of good works that originate, ultimately, with the Father in heaven."[32] As Vance has written elsewhere: "Roland's heroism was always to have remembered Charlemagne in his ordeal at Ronceval; then, as he died, to have remembered God." What is clearly expressed here is that conjunctive network indicated by F. Edward Cranz as characteristic of the Greeks. Vance writes: "in the poetics of voice and memory there was to be no separation of word from gesture, of hero from poet, of the knower from what was known."[33] But the same author views the *Roland* as marking a moment of change from such a conjunctive and commemorative episteme to something quite different.

Charlemagne's presence does away with any efficacious commemoration. The end of the *Roland* is thus marked by a kind of dispersion of signification, where language is no longer clear and

---

32. "Roland and the Poetics of Memory," p. 389. Vance has elaborated on this analysis in "Roland, Charlemagne, and the Poetics of Illumination," *Oliphant*, 6 (1979), 213–25. See, too, his earlier introductory book, *Reading the Song of Roland* (Englewood Cliffs, N.J., 1970).

33. Eugene Vance, "Love's Concordance: The Poetics of Desire and the Joy of the Text," *Diacritics*, 5, no. 1 (Spring 1975), 41.

joyous, but opaque, dark and painful, sign of the passing of the old as yet unreplaced by any new form of totalization. Words lose their familiar meaning, and with it their life. Vance recalls here a passage from John of Salisbury's *Metalogicon*, a text more or less contemporary with the *Roland*: "To inquire into the effective force of speech and to investigate the truth and meaning of what is said are precisely or practically the same. A word's force consists in its meaning. Without the latter, it is useless, and (so to speak) dead. Just as the soul [*anima*] animates the body, so, in a way, meaning breathes life into a word."[34] This is a passage we will have good cause to remember later on, for the operation of *anima* will appear to be particularly central to medieval discourse.

If *Roland* does mark a particular discursive development, it is not toward a discourse whose center would be some concept of self-identity. Of Gace Brulé, for example (late twelfth century), Vance warns us against hypostatizing "the authorial figure of Gace into any kind of subjective principle, into any kind of unifying 'original' presence, in terms of which his poems might take on 'meaning': indeed, the flatly conventional surface of these poems discourages any such temptations." In Gace, he notes later, the *je* is almost always negated, a fact that corresponds to a more general discursive habit: "The *je* of medieval lyric is merely the index of a basic principle of activity, and no more."[35] The dispersion of meaning Vance sees in the *Roland,* the presence of *je* as no more than a mark of enunciation in the lyric, is confirmed by his reading of Chaucer's *Troilus,* in which he traces a gradual decay of language, of truth, of meaning. Finally the reader is placed before the only guarantor of "truth," the Divine, in "prayer and illumination."[36]

The movement of the text of the *Troilus* is thus identical to that of the *Metalogicon* as it advances toward its final prayer. The same movement is the subject of the epilogue to this chapter from Aquinas's *Summa contra Gentiles.* It suggests that if there is indeed the growth of a disjunctive mode of discourse from this period through the remainder of the Middle Ages, then such discourse is no less marked by a straining to overcome that disjunction in a new 'wholeness' that will be completely foreign to what will later develop. But

34. "Roland and the Poetics of Memory," pp. 391–99; John of Salisbury, *The Metalogicon: A Twelfth-Century Defense of the Verbal and Logical Arts of the Trivium,* tr. and ed. Daniel McGarry (1955; rpt. Berkeley and Los Angeles, 1962), p. 81 (bk. II, ch. 4).
35. "Love's Concordance," pp. 42, 50.
36. Eugene Vance, "Mervelous Signals: Poetics, Sign Theory, and Politics in Chaucer's *Troilus," New Literary History,* 10 (1979), 335.

negative suggestions of this kind are not sufficient for my purpose (and all the authors mentioned would be willing to recognize the ambiguity of their claims). The only genuine way to refute the notion of short continuity is to show that some other class of discourse is dominant throughout this period. Whether or not one accepts my claim that the discourse of primary importance was that of patterning, I believe it can indeed be shown that another discourse was hegemonous.

It has been argued that the division between patterning and analytico-referentiality (as I am calling it) was already assumed in the Middle Ages to have occurred in time immemorial. Thus Philippe Wolff writes: "There was a general idea that what had been lost among these diverse tongues was the essential and primitive bond which had united a thing and its name ever since the time of the Creation. The languages created at Babel were arbitrary and had no connection with things."[37] The similarity of the concept mentioned in the first sentence here to the views of Paracelsus (for example) is apparent. But we have also seen that the term "arbitrary" is not one to be used loosely. It is not necessarily evidence of a disjunctive discourse such as Wolff clearly has in mind. The question, therefore, is whether a statement such as Wolff's is tenable. I will suggest that it is at best only partly correct: it is clear that the assertion of "no connection" is quite inaccurate.

If such were the case, then etymologizing of the kind practiced by Isidore of Seville in the ninth book, on "languages and kingdoms," of his *Originum sive etymologiarum libri XX* (c. 600 A.D.) would be an utterly senseless operation. If there is "no connection" at all, what is the purpose of looking for it? The diverse references Wolff himself provides at this point demonstrate the opposite of his contention and assert that some such link was believed still to exist: there was some inherent relation between a thing and its name, making of the latter a simple feature of the object it named.[38] The immediate presentation of the object gave the name, if only the nature of the original link could be rediscovered. For it is indeed the case that for Isidore, in these fallen times, the process has to be followed in reverse. But the underlying ideology is the same: the inherency is not doubted. It is simply that it has been hidden from immediate comprehension and must now be sought out by interpretation. Indeed, in the pre-Babel language *interpretation* would have been

37. Philippe Wolff, *Western Languages, A.D. 100–1500*, tr. Frances Partridge (London, 1971), pp. 111–12.
38. Ibid., pp. 110–11.

quite unnecessary, just because the connection *was* immediate between the word and the world: as an inherent feature of the object, the name presented it without ambiguity. On the other hand in analytico-referential discourse interpretation would be incomprehensible.

Only in between, when the link was taken as existing but seen, as it was said, *per speculum in aenigmate,* "through a glass darkly," could interpretation have (and make) sense. This is exactly what Augustine's *On Christian Doctrine* is all about. Whether or not this may then be accepted as the sign of a patterning discourse remains to be seen, but I will take the opportunity of quoting here from Erich Kahler, who asserts unequivocally that "throughout classical antiquity and until the end of the Middle Ages, mythic and hieratic bonds deeply affected everyday life. Men lived in myth, lived its patterns, performed in their lives an *imitatio* of myth."[39] That is a strong statement, and perhaps unjustifiable as it stands: certainly it needs nuancing.

One should not overestimate Isidore's own influence in the late Middle Ages. But that period as a whole would seem to be within an episteme of patterning and of a class one may perhaps call 'mediation' (for I certainly do not seek to deny that several classes of discourse may have been of equal importance during this period, as I remarked at the beginning of Chapter 1). By a discourse of 'mediation' I mean to suggest a discursive relation where the emphasis falls on the actual producing of discourse, where 'concepts' (recognizing this to be a term taken from analytico-referentiality) are inseparable from enunciation. One could oppose something like an operative concept of *process* to a fixed concept of models. For whether it is a matter of "an ordering of the mind by the world" or of "an ordering of the world by the mind," both operate upon a model composed: 'things' fit into a fixed schema (however flexible it may be). The relation of mediation would accentuate rather the very process of modeling.

Isidore of Seville and the "Cratylism" he endorses are doubtless less important than the succession of thinkers working in the Stoic tradition. This is generally taken as resolutely anti-Cratylist. Yet recent research makes it less clear than ever that such was entirely the case throughout a Middle Ages supposed to be following a Cicero-

39. Erich Kahler, *The Inward Turn of Narrative,* tr. Richard and Clara Winston (Princeton, 1973), p. 14. Needless to say, Kahler's view is a radical version of the traditional one: for him, the sixteenth century marks the beginning of an era of essential change in consciousness and reality (pp. 9–66). In this respect his view (and occasionally its expression) is similar to Michel Foucault's.

nian and Augustinian tradition. In the first place, the mere opposition Cratylism/anti-Cratylism is a serious oversimplification of a very complex theoretical discussion. In the second place, the situation of the Stoics themselves is not unambiguous. We may well be dealing in their case with a discourse of mediation. Claude Imbert's recent work on Stoic logic is very suggestive of such a view. She is able to note that for the Stoics, the term *"Logos* has three interconnected meanings: those of divine reason organizing matter, of human reason and of discourse. The qualifier *logike* reminds us that representation obtains its discursive state from the human reason that gives it birth, and that this reason is a fragment of divine reason, and therefore able to penetrate the physical organization of sensible appearances."[40]

An argument of this kind suggests a view of human reason and discourse as ordered by and from the Divine: that is, as a part organized by and within some overarching totality. At the same time it emphasizes the productive role of discourse itself. John of Salisbury had spoken in similar terms of the Stoics. He remarks that for certain purposes we may well imitate their practice in order to reach back to the "truth," a practice of etymologizing: "In imitation of the Stoics, who are much concerned about the etymology or resemblance [literally: the analysis or analogy] of words, we observe that [Latin] *uerum* [true] comes from the Greek *heron,* which means stable or certain and clear." Such a technique, writes John, enables the interpreter to work back to the divine origin, even though, he says, the Stoics here go astray: "the Stoics believe that [both] matter and the 'idea' are coeternal with God." John denies this belief, agreeing with Bernard of Chartres that God precedes and makes both matter and idea. For John, therefore, the analysis of words is indeed a way toward the Divine, but it is very definitely at a considerable remove. He distinguishes his view from that of the Stoics on the grounds that for the Stoics the discovery of matter and idea, through that of the etymon, was also the discovery of the Divine.[41] John's view is supportive of Imbert's analysis. Furthermore, though a certain disjunction has been introduced into the series of signifying relationships, it is clear that John's arguments remain relatively close to and situated in terms of Stoic theory.

The fact that divine reason and human reason are identified with one another in that theory is of prime importance. It enables discourse to be viewed as self-sufficient and, in a way, 'auto-referential,'

40. Claude Imbert, "Théorie de la représentation et doctrine logique dans le stoicisme ancien," in *Les Stoiciens et leur logique* (Paris, 1978), p. 226.
41. John of Salisbury, *Metalogicon,* pp. 255, 259 (bk. IV, chs. 34, 35).

while at the same time permitting the fact of that self-production to be an entirely adequate *presentation* of reality. The utterance itself, *qua* utterance, presents the interconnection:

> It follows that discourse has no claim to express external reality, save only to the extent that it refers to a representation of internal language, to a thought [itself referred to divine reason]. Properly speaking, there is therefore [in Stoic theory] no semantics to bind the parts of speech to some division or other of physical reality; no discursive truth outside the situation in which the protagonists state or interpret it.[42]

As Imbert observes, following Erwin Panofsky, this is not at all Platonic. It does not ascribe the possibility of conception to Idea, but to an incessant and indivisible interplay of divine reason, human reason, and discourse. Though John of Salisbury deliberately opposes Stoic theory to Platonism, preferring the latter, it may be just this 'interplay' that makes certain aspects of Stoic aesthetic theory peculiarly similar to medieval theories of interpretation. One starts with a "presentation" which "can go proxy for a feeble perception and prepares a commentary suitable for God." This presentation does have properties associated with Platonic views. It is (1) a "reflection," presenting "a vision of reality, less rough than that given in sensory contact or simple sense-impression, and containing only the essential differentiating properties (*notae*) of the object." It is (2) like a mirror, in that it composes "fictional presentations," particularly focused or synthesized images of the real. It is (3) like an "eye," in that "it links rays of external light with the inner movements of the soul: cutting through appearances, it identifies its object under the bright light of revelation." It provides "a paradigm of cognitive activity." We may note, too, that this view is very similar to Augustine's concept of the intellectual "eye" that emits a point (*acies*) of vision allowing it to be informed with the remembered intelligibles. In the Stoics, the theoretical movement corresponding to these properties starts with mere wonder, progresses to analysis and to "interpretation by a master, which involves a detour into things divine," and concludes with an initiation into "the truth behind appearances."[43]

How can we not see in this movement an anticipation of the most

---

42. Imbert, "Théorie de la représentation," p. 241.
43. Claude Imbert, "Stoic Logic and Alexandrian Poetics," in *Doubt and Dogmatism: Studies in Hellenistic Epistemology*, ed. Malcolm Schofield, Myles Burnyeat, and Jonathan Barnes (Oxford, 1980), pp. 183, 200–201, 204–5. For the Augustinian *acies*, see F. Edward Cranz's unpublished "The Eyes of the Mind: Antiquity and the Renaissance" (1975) and Eugene Vance's "Roland, Charlemagne, and the Poetics of Illumination," pp. 214–16.

familiar medieval theories of interpretation? There we pass from the
literal (for example, "Jerusalem" as the name of a city geographically
situated in Palestine: Stoic "reflection") to the metaphorical ("Jerusalem" as the Church Triumphant: Stoic analysis), to the allegorical
or moral ("Jerusalem" as the soul of man: Stoic "interpretation"), to
the anagogical ("Jerusalem" as divine union in Paradise: Stoic "initiation"). From the spiritual allegorical reading of Scripture, for which
Augustine's *On Christian Doctrine* was the exemplar, to the interpretations of secular poetry made popular by Boccaccio, the theory was
standard. Let us glance at Dante on the subject:

> In order to make this manner of treatment clear, it can be applied to
> the following verses: "When Israel went out of Egypt, the house of
> Jacob from a barbarous people, Judea was made his sanctuary, Israel
> his dominion." Now if we look at the letter alone, what is signified to us
> is the departure of the sons of Israel from Egypt during the time of
> Moses; if at the allegory, what is signified to us is our redemption
> through Christ; if at the moral sense, what is signified to us is the
> conversion of the soul from the sorrow and misery of sin to the state of
> grace; if at the anagogical, what is signified to us is the departure of the
> sanctified soul from bondage to the corruption of this world into the
> freedom of eternal glory.

Probably one should not insist on too close an identification between
this and Stoic theory, though a brief quotation from Varro suffices
to indicate just how traditional a commonplace this concept was. In
the *De lingua latina*, a text generally considered to be heavily influ-
enced by Stoic linguistic theory, the Roman polymath writes:

> Now I shall set forth the origins of the individual words, of which there
> are four levels of explanation. The lowest is that to which even the
> common folk has come. . . . The second is that to which old-time
> grammar has mounted, which shows how the poet has made each word
> which he has fashioned and derived. . . .
>   The third level is that to which philosophy ascended, and on arrival
> began to reveal the nature of those words which are in common use. . . .
> The fourth is that where the sanctuary is, and the mysteries of the
> high-priest. [Bk. V.7–8][44]

44. Dante Alighieri, "The Letter to Can Grande," in *Literary Criticism of Dante Alighieri*, tr. and ed. Robert S. Haller (Lincoln, Neb., 1973), p. 99. A more celebrated, but
much longer, exposition is to be found in the *Convivio* (ibid., pp. 112–14). The Boccaccio material is most readily available in English in *Boccaccio on Poetry: Being the
Preface and the Fourteenth and Fifteenth Books of Boccaccio's "Genealogia Deorum Gentilium,"*
tr. and ed. Charles G. Osgood (Indianapolis and New York, 1930). The Varro quotation is from Marcus Terrentius Varro, *On the Latin Language*, tr. and ed. Roland G.
Kent, 2 vols. (Cambridge, Mass., and London, 1938), I.9.

That such an order and such a similarity should exist at all suggests on the one hand that Stoicism moves in a discursive class quite different from the analytico-referential, and on the other that elements of such a class are strong in the Middle Ages.

So far as this difference from a later discursive class is concerned, then (since that is what I wish to emphasize above all here), we should note that it is utterly misleading to insist upon the arbitrary nature of the sign (essential in analytico-referentiality) as we may find it from Augustine on, if we attempt to interpret such 'arbitrariness' in the light of a post-Saussurian linguistics. Such terms as *ad placitum* and *voluntas significare*, used in this connection by the Bishop of Hippo, are caught up in a particular epistemology that is not to be confused with what develops during the European Renaissance. Words may be learned from men ("at least the alphabet"); they may be arbitrary in the sense that they are not inherent in the thing they signify, but they are not arbitrary in the sense that their meaning is determined by human control. They are *pointers* toward an inner truth set in man by the Divine: "Although I can lift my finger to point something out," says Augustine, "I cannot supply the vision by means of which either this gesture or what it indicates can be seen."[45] He is speaking here specifically of the use of words to interpret Scripture. Clearly the context of *voluntas* is quite akin to the meaning of the term *hekōn* as explored by Vernant, Else, and Kenny.

In her admittedly disputed book *The Mirror of Language*, Marcia Colish has observed that for Augustine

> words may represent really existing things truly, if partially, and . . . they function either commemoratively or indicatively in the subject's mind, depending on his previous relationship to the object. Although seen as an epistemological necessity, verbal signs are never held to be cognitive in the first instance. They must be energized by the action of God in the mind of the knower in order for them to conduce to the knowledge of their significata.[46]

Verbal signs depend on the object for their meaning, not the reverse: being, that is to say, always precedes knowing. And the object in question is an "inner" object, imprinted upon the mind and retrievable through memory, activated by the commemorative verbal sign. It is in that sense that the sign, as Augustine writes in the *De magistro*, is learned through the 'object' not the object through the

45. St. Augustine, *On Christian Doctrine*, tr. and ed. D. W. Robertson, Jr. (Indianapolis and New York, 1958), p. 4.
46. Marcia Colish, *The Mirror of Language: A Study in the Medieval Theory of Knowledge* (New Haven and London, 1968), p. 84.

sign.[47] This is also the way the child learns from adults as recounted at the beginning of the *Confessions*: but it is worth noting Augustine's emphasis there, to the effect that everything adults can teach a child is owing to the grace of God. If the child learns the names of things because adults constantly relate those names to objects, this is only possible because God has implanted this capacity in the adults to start with: signs are learned from objects, but the necessary connection predates human utilization of that relation.

Words are not to be confused with things, for then they would be immediately cognitive; but clearly some kind of natural relationship enables the combination of verbal signs and divine action to provoke a true knowledge of the object. We find that we are not, after all, so very far from a "conjunctive" tradition: "Augustine also follows the Stoics in arguing that the natural significance of words provides a basis for the science of etymology." The discussion of the term *grammaticus* in Anselm's *De grammatico* six centuries later still has much in common with such a notion of etymologizing and moves in the same tradition.[48] This relationship, and all signification, is seen in terms of a natural connection between individual words and their "objective significata." What is signified may be either a real object or a conceptual one, but either is considered to be an "entity identifiable outside of any relation and susceptible of being designated properly by its name, in such a way that not only is every word a name, but every name is the proper name of something in the mind," as Claude Panaccio writes of Augustine's conception of naming.[49] I have already suggested that Anselm's ontological argument depends on the assumption that such natural connection and such "properness" both suppose and are guaranteed by the priority of universals.

It thus appears clear that the distinction made by Augustine and his successors (one cannot underscore too heavily Augustine's overwhelming influence right through the Middle Ages) between natural and conventional signification is entirely misunderstood if we seek to interpret it in terms of our modernity. In Augustine the distinction depends upon the "intentional or unintentional character" of signs:

47. This passage is usefully discussed by Claude Panaccio, "La métaphysique et les noms," in *Culture et langage*, ed. J. P. Brodeur (Montreal, 1973), p. 269.

48. Desmond Paul Henry, ed. and commentary, *The "De Grammatico" of St. Anselm: The Theory of Paronymy* (Notre Dame, Ind., 1964). The quotation is from Marcia Colish, "The Stoic Theory of Verbal Signification and the Problem of Lies and False Statements from Antiquity to St. Anselm," in *L'archéologie du signe*, ed. Lucie Brind' amour and Eugene Vance (Toronto, 1982).

49. Panaccio, "La métaphysique et les noms," p. 271. The preceding phrase quoted is from Colish, "Stoic Theory."

His natural signs are unintentional. A fire signifies its presence unintentionally through the smoke it produces; a man signifies his feelings unintentionally through his facial expression. These signs do indeed signify physical and psychological realities, but they do so involuntarily. Augustine's conventional signs also correspond truly with the things they signify. But they are signs used deliberately by animate or intelligent beings to express their ideas, intentions, and feelings to other beings.[50]

Without any doubt we are dealing here with a concept of the voluntary and involuntary that is in the tradition noted with reference to the analyses of Vernant, Else, and Kenny.

But, we are told, it was a commonplace in the Middle Ages that the order of discourse was the living expression of the order of society. In that case the relationship of words is a societal creation and therefore arbitrary so far as the signification of words themselves is concerned. Words were in some sense the communicative cement of society. Language and society are born together. Society and language are both human artifacts. Again, we should beware of anachronistic interpretations. Such a view implies a concept of political society perfectly alien, as we will see, to the Middle Ages:

> Now if man were by nature a solitary animal the passions of the soul by which he was conformed to things so as to have knowledge of them would be sufficient for him; but since he is by nature a political and social animal it was necessary that his conceptions be made known to others. This he does through vocal sounds. Therefore there had to be significant vocal sounds in order that men might live together. Whence those who speak different languages find it difficult to live together in social unity.[51]

Here in Aquinas, language and society may refer to one another but they do not seem to be coeval. The latter is made possible by the former: words precede society, which is their setting into discourse, just as objects and their concepts precede words, of which they are the natural significata. The view of the relation between discourse and society suggested here did not spring full-blown from the mind of the Middle Ages: "the notion that the order of language consti-

50. Colish, "Stoic Theory."

51. Aristotle, *On Interpretation: Commentary by St. Thomas and Cajetan (Peri hermeneias)*, tr. Jean T. Oesterle (Milwaukee, 1962), p. 24. This passage is also quoted by Eugene Vance, "Désir, rhétorique et texte—Semences de la différence: Brunet Latin chez Dante," *Poétique*, no. 42 (April 1980), p. 139.

tutes the living order of society was already central to a tradition of classical oratory that any poet such as Chaucer, Dante, or Petrarch knew very well." Vance goes on to assert that after Dante, "beliefs about the homology between the orders of discourse and culture become articulated as a full-blown philosophy of history, and such doctrines were to be amplified during the late Middle Ages and the Renaissance."[52]

We need to remember, however, that human society is God-given, not a free human construction. Whatever may happen to later views, at least in Aquinas, as in John of Salisbury, the relation between the Divinity, discourse, and society seems clear enough. Human society, writes John, is made possible by language. Language itself started from the naming of things, and this activity comes from the Divinity: "In accordance with the divine plan, and in order to provide verbal intercourse in human society, man first of all named those things which lay before him." If the order is not clear at this point, it was certainly so at the outset when John had considered what happens to society when language is withdrawn. Anyone, he asserts, who attacks the proper use of language ("Eloquence"), as does his adversary, "Cornificius," takes on an immense responsibility. For

> he undermines and uproots all liberal studies, assails the whole struc-
> ture of philosophy, tears to shreds humanity's social contracts, and de-
> stroys the means of brotherly charity and reciprocal interchange of
> services. Deprived of their gift of speech, men would degenerate to the
> condition of brute animals, and cities would seem like corrals for live-
> stock, rather than communities composed of human beings united by a
> common bond for the purpose of living in society, serving one another,
> and cooperating as friends.[33]

The misuse of language is a subversion of humanity itself, since for John humanity is defined (as for Aristotle) as a political and social animal. It is also blasphemous, since both discourse and society are marked by the Divine: "when language became detached from a commitment of faith—faith of any kind—it became a tool of subver-sion." So writes Vance of the confrontation between the "feudal" bond represented by Charlemagne, Roland, and the *"pairs"* and the treachery of Ganelon which provokes the utter downfall of that feudal world.[54]

---

52. Vance, "Mervelous Signals," pp. 294, 299.
53. John of Salisbury, *Metalogicon*, pp. 39, 11 (bk. I, chs. 14, 1).
54. Vance, *Reading the Song of Roland*, p. 33; see, too, "Désir, rhétorique et texte."

The arrangement, then, is a kind of 'contractual' one (a word I use here with hesitation, given its later connotations). The correct use of words permits the continuation of society and makes its existence ever more firm. For while particular discourse may be associated with particular sociohistorical circumstances, it is also bound by the proper meaning of words. To misuse words is a derogation of society and indeed of humanity as taken up in it. In that sense words are not at all arbitrary. But what, one will ask, enables one to speak of a "misuse" of words or of discourse? How can such a misuse be judged?

The judgment must rely on two elements: (1) words as naturally given are not the creation of society, but only their ordering, the use to which they are put. Once again we find ourselves in the paradigm of intentionality and unintentionality. (2) We can know correct signification through the "ear of the heart." This is a faculty of the soul and, as such, is confirmed in its functioning by the Divinity, by the *Logos* itself. The relationship is that of soul to body: the sign is bound on the one hand by its material existence as the expression of society, while on the other its correct use is guaranteed by its participation in the *Logos*. It is in just that sense that Augustine can write that the "mouth of the heart" (the "ear's" counterpart) cannot lie in itself, for it "doth reach to the hearing of the Spirit of the Lord, Who hath filled the whole earth." Human passions of one kind or another may make the voice of the heart into a lie when it is embodied in a verbal utterance or when it is transformed into material action, but in itself the heart utters the truth of God.[55] Here is the root of true discourse and genuine society. As the reference to Augustine just indicated, like all things human since the Fall, this situation was held to be corrupt and fallible in virtue of its material existence, but it was 'potentially' perfectible in virtue of Creation and the dispensation of Grace.

The relationship of meaning and knowledge with society is identical to the kind of relationship we find at what we might consider the 'political' level. Walter Ullmann has observed that the combination of Christian doctrine with the Roman social and legal heritage meant for the Middle Ages that "the Christian was a member of the all-embracing, comprehensive corporation, the Church." The act of baptism effected entry as a fully fledged member of that corpora-

---

55. St. Augustine, *On Lying [De mendacio]*, tr. Rev. H. Browne, in *A Select Library of the Nicene and Post-Nicene Fathers of the Christian Church*, ed. Philip Schaff, vol. 3: St. Augustin, *On the Holy Trinity, Doctrinal Treatises, Moral Treatises* (Grand Rapids, Mich., 1956), p. 471.

tion. Nor was it "merely a liturgical or a sacramental act" but a profoundly political one, making of the baptized person a "reborn" member of the society and recognizing him to be "a participant of the divine attributes themselves." Thus he became a "*fidelis*," obedient to a law represented and made concrete by "those who were instituted *over* him by divinity." Such law was often referred to as the *anima* (or 'soul') of society, just as that is also the name given to the presence of the Divinity in man.[56] One is rather forcibly reminded here of Erich Kahler's comment regarding the patterns lived by medieval man.

The relationship here is not one of analogy, but of identity. The discursive functioning of sociopolitical relations is the same as that of logico-epistemological ones (which is why to take humanity as a "test case" for a logical relationship has such profound implications). The corporate social relation between the Divinity and societal participant, mediated by the law (*anima*), and that participant and society as a whole, mediated by baptism, is the same as the relation that holds between the Divinity and the sign, guaranteed by the soul (*anima*), and the sign and society, guaranteed by concrete discursive practice. The sign's ordering and the person's status are both fixed by the discursive organization of society; the sign's meaning and the mere fact of a person's participation are bound by the mediation of *anima* (whose meanings, writes Ullmann, are multiple: immortal law, society itself, King, God, soul, society's laws).

The term *anima* may therefore be seen as a kind of focal point. It is an operator, rather than simply a sign bearing 'meaning.' It permits the transformation of one set of relations into another. It reveals, as it establishes, the identity of apparently heterogeneous sets of relations.[57] Such a view is confirmed by Colin Morris who, while claiming to show the development of a 'modern' concept of the individual during the Middle Ages, actually indicates something quite different. He asserts that the use of such terms as "knowing oneself," "descending into oneself," or "considering oneself" illustrates that a concept of the "self" is developing during the twelfth

56. Ullmann, *Individual and Society*, pp. 7–10; for the last assertion see pp. 46–50. The term "*fideles*" was used in an 828 decree of the Emperor Louis the Pious, for example, of merchants "described as the ruler's 'vassals' (*fideles*)" and considered as belonging to the Prince's household: Georges Duby, *The Early Growth of the European Economy: Warriors and Peasants from the Seventh to the Twelfth Century*, tr. Howard B. Clarke (London, 1974), p. 100.

57. I have in mind here Lévi-Strauss's concept of a totemic or mythic operator, explored in *The Savage Mind* (Chicago, 1966). A useful rapid analysis of the concept is to be found in Roger Poole's excellent introduction to Lévi-Strauss's *Totemism*, tr. Rodney Needham (Harmondsworth, 1969), pp. 50–63.

century (even though a term such as "individual" remains essentially a logical one). He then remarks that "another common term was *anima*, which was used, ambiguously in our eyes, for both the spiritual identity ('soul') of a man and his directing intelligence ('mind')."

We have seen that it was used for much more than that. But such use is "ambiguous" only if one is determined to find a modern *meaning* for the concept of self, taken as unchangingly human. The examples I have given indicate rather that human 'self'-awareness, here, is quite inseparable from a sense of participation ('knowledge') in the Divine: God, says Augustine, who "in the eyes of the twelfth century . . . was the master of the art of self-knowledge," is *within* the soul (*anima*): self-knowledge, for the Bishop of Hippo, is "the path to God."[58] I suggested before how this was indeed the case for both Augustine and Abelard, and we saw a trace of the mediatory *anima* in John of Salisbury's *Metalogicon*. Nonetheless, it is above all Augustine who is most clear on the subject of *anima* as an operator of transformational patterns.

He relates, for example, in the *Confessions* how he gradually discovered the right path to God, noting how he came across certain Platonist writings which, however pagan, were nonetheless able to give him a true idea of the relation between the soul (*anima*) and God: "that the soul of man, though it bears witness to the light, yet itself is not that light; but the Word of God, being God, is that true light that lighteth every man that cometh into the world."[59] The central text in this matter, however, is the *De Trinitate*. There, St. Augustine teaches that memory, understanding, and will are three faculties of the soul (*anima*), which is itself the image of God, as is learned through Revelation. This relationship between the soul and its faculties is in every way analogous to the definition of the Divinity, widespread at the time Augustine was writing and to which he makes constant reference, as "*mia ousia, treis hupostaseis.*" This virtually untranslatable definition (containing the same word, *ousia*, whose 'difficulty' we have already seen), is rendered by Augustine as "a trinity of persons mutually interrelated, and a unity of an equal essence."[60]

The second eight books of the *De Trinitate* set out to show in just what ways the soul of man is a mediation to the Divine. It is in the light of *this* connection that we have to understand the Augustinian 'self,' not in that of some imaginary Cartesianism *avant la lettre*. The

58. Morris, *Discovery of the Individual*, pp. 65–66.
59. St. Augustine, *Confessions*, tr. Edward B. Pusey, intro. Fulton J. Sheen (New York, 1949), p. 130 (bk. VII).
60. *De Trinitate*, in St. Augustine, *On the Holy Trinity*, p. 125 (bk. IX, ch. 1).

work sets out to explain the Trinity, and to do so has to follow the path through will (passions) to reason, to faith, to the hope of eventual redemption. It is in that conjunctive sense that Father E. Hendrikx can view the *De Trinitate* as "the most personal of all Augustine's works," even though the Bishop "introduces us at once to the mystery of God's inner life [*la vie intime*]," for it is at the same time an introduction "more than elsewhere, to the inner life of his own soul": the two are inextricably bound together.[61]

It is useful to linger over the *De Trinitate,* which was perhaps the most read of Augustine's works throughout the Middle Ages. For my present purpose it is exemplary, as I will indicate in a moment. But it is important, too, because of its immense influence. Hendrikx remarks that more than 230 manuscripts of the Latin text are extant to this day, most of them dating from the twelfth to the fourteenth century, while we still possess twenty manuscripts of a Greek translation made at the beginning of the fourteenth century. Quite apart from this evidence of widespread popularity during the birth and heyday of Thomism, Hendrikx can assert that methodologically as well, it was in the *De Trinitate* that "scholasticism was born."[62] By its dialectical interrogation of the texts in its search for a true knowledge of God, by its logical and 'psychological' interpretation of them, and its submission of both activities to the necessity of faith, the *De Trinitate* simultaneously originates a tradition and typifies it to an exemplary degree.

More than any other, it is the Augustinian tradition that holds sway through the thousand years of the Middle Ages. What the *De Trinitate* tells us about the intimate relationship between the human soul and the Divine Trinity explicitly confirms my present argument about the dominant class of discourse throughout this period. In the second half of the text, Augustine provides us (as he had sought to do in earlier texts, from the very earliest to the *City of God*) with a series of triads seeking to show in what way the soul of man is such an image and mediation of God as he suggests. The first of the series is *mens, notitia, amor*: spirit, knowledge, will. This triad is an incomplete analogy with the Trinity, says Augustine, because Father, Son, and Holy Spirit are three equal "substances" (*hupostaseis*) of one "essence" (*ousia*), whereas *mens* is substance, *notitia* and *amor* its acts.

61. *La Trinité*, vols. 15 and 16 of *Oeuvres de Saint-Augustin*, text of the Benedictine edition, tr. and ed. M. Mellet, O.P., and Th. Camelot, O.P. [vol. 16 by P. Agaësse, S.J., with J. Moingt, S.J.], intro. E. Hendrikx, O.E.S.A. (Paris, 1955), vol. 15, pp. 10, 12.
62. Ibid., pp. 14, 16–17.

The second of the series is more satisfactory as an analogy: *memoria (sui), intelligentia, voluntas.* Here, intuitive self-consciousness is at once the foundation of and equal to understanding and will, while the three are united in that together they form the soul (*anima*).

The third and final analogy of the presence of the Divine in the soul comes in the triad *memoria (Dei), intelligentia (Dei), amor (in Deum).* Here, however, we are no longer, properly speaking, in the presence of an analogy, for this is the image of the soul that has come to know God, to know itself as a manifestation of and a participation in the Divine. Self-consciousness, self-knowledge, and self-love have become consciousness of God, knowledge of God, and love of God.[63] As in the *Confessions,* as in the *De magistro,* as in the *City of God,* Augustine practices here what he preaches: the search for truth, the search for a complete knowledge of the 'self,' leads to a final absorption into the Divine. Indeed, the mind given up to itself, given up to its own 'willfulness,' can only fall into error, falsehood, and subversion, as the *De Trinitate* continually insists. The 'individual's' ultimate 'self'-understanding (and the inadequacy of the terms is by now obvious) is in the unveiling of God's image in the soul. "Know thyself" is the urging toward that particular understanding. That is just what the *Confessions,* too, are all about. Yet, in life, there can be no more than a constant passage *toward* such a goal, because the final unveiling can only be achieved with the soul's own end in God. The final prayer of the *De Trinitate* still marks a distance that can only be overcome in death. But it also marks the continuation of a process toward conjunction through mediation:

> And when the last day of life shall have found any one holding fast faith in the Mediator in such progress and growth as this, he will be welcomed by the holy angels, to be led to God, whom he has worshipped, and to be made perfect by Him; and so he will receive in the end of the world an incorruptible body, in order not to punishment, but to glory. For the likeness of God will then be perfected in this image, when the sight of God shall be perfected. And of this the Apostle Paul speaks: "Now we see through a glass, in an enigma, but then face to face."[64]

The *Divina commedia* can easily be read as an "interpretation" (in the medieval sense) of this Augustinian process. We are clearly a very long way indeed from the voluntary 'angelic' reason whose

63. This analysis refers basically to bks. IX, X, and XIV of the *De Trinitate,* but I am also deeply indebted to Hendrikx's analysis in his introduction, vol. 15, pp. 70–74, of which these lines are more or less a résumé.

64. *On the Holy Trinity,* p. 196 (bk. XIV, ch. 17).

concept and practice will be developed throughout the seventeenth century. Morris notes that the Augustinian concept was adopted by such as Bernard of Clairvaux, William of Saint Thierry, Aelred of Rievaulx, and others. He adds to the list, lest we be led into believing that it was an entirely Cistercian strain, such non-Cistercians as Guibert of Nogent.[65] I do not see how a view such as this can be considered in any way 'modern' (as a dominant discursive class, that is to say). Yet it is one which seems to predominate among the principal thinkers of the twelfth century, those very ones whom Morris considers the forerunners of the modern concept of the self. The pattern of relations that organize the meaning of signs in discourse and the place and role of participants in society indicates a quite different class of conceptualization, a different process altogether.

In the light of all this there can be no question but that the *voluntas significare* of Augustine echoes a concept of 'will' that is essentially that of the Greeks (which can scarcely surprise us). It has to do with a concept of conjunction and 'corporate community.' It has no connection at all with the Cartesian concept of will as that element in man by which he is equivalent to God (see the *Passions de l'âme*) and which can thereby become the *individual* origin of discourse, of thought, of knowledge, of society, and so on. Clearly, too, the Augustinian pattern is not dissimilar to the Stoic divinity/human mind/discourse relation as Claude Imbert discusses it. But we have seen that we are actually dealing with an all-embracing discursive network, in which the 'individual' can only be defined as a *path toward* conjunction with an overarching ("divine") totality.

This class remains manifestly dominant certainly throughout the twelfth century. And speaking of a distinction between Augustinianism, "Cratylism," and Stoicism, we may well wonder whether the glossing of accumulated metaphors (for example, to discover the true meaning of the Bible or other authoritative text) or the Stoic analysis and interpretation of a "presentation" are epistemologically very different, as has been claimed, from the etymological researches of an Isidore, undertaken to discover the true denotation of a word and to reveal the object/concept with which that word is taken to be ultimately identical. To be sure, the first place the emphasis on the signified, while the last puts it on the signifier, but one wonders, first, whether such 'modern' distinctions are possible with regard to writers such as Augustine and Isidore (though the distinction was

65. Morris, *Discovery of the Individual*, pp. 66–67.

clearly made by the Stoics: a fact which again suggests a different class of discourse), and second, whether the necessary reliance on a 'right reading' of the Divinity for the confirmation of both true meaning and true identity does not bring both kinds of argument to the same point. For there, the supposition must be that meaning and identity are one in perfection.

In practice both views would have the same consequence: that the confirmation of right discourse depends on the authority of the Divinity (mediated through *anima*), and rather less on any societal anchoring. How otherwise can one explain, for instance, the lack of relation between actual socioeconomic practice and economic theory? Thus, though the outcries against usury, for example, no doubt refer to current practice, they refer above all to Biblical, Patristic, and Aristotelian authority rather than to the needs of a developing mercantilist economy. Again, though the domain and referent (for us) are utterly different, the same kind of gap is apparent in scientific discourse. Even in a field such as that of momentum theory, already very advanced long before the advent of Galileo, the references—with the notable exception of the Oxford 'line' running from Grosseteste through Roger Bacon to Bradwardine and the Mertonians—are back to Aristotle and his commentators: 'truth' was sought through the word, not through the thing. There was experimentation, but it was very rare.[66] Here, too, truth was to be unearthed by following a path inward. Walter Ullmann has shown a similar disjunction between theory and practice in regard to political theory, where a dominant theocratic model largely ignores customary, feudal, and local corporate practices. In all this, the extreme example is usually taken to be that of Ockham, who is thought of as having reduced the entire question to one of definition, and as thereby having cut through the potential contradictions between theory and practice.

The matter is, of course, far more complicated. In his weighty reevaluation of Ockham's role, Gordon Leff writes, "for him the central question was no longer to explain the individual by reference to the universal but rather to account for universals in a world of individuals." The first order of explanation corresponds, of course,

66. The dates of these scientists may be useful: Robert Grosseteste, 1168–1235; Roger Bacon, 1214(?)–1292; Thomas Bradwardine, 1295–1349. This line and Ockhamism led directly to the series of great French scientists that produced Buridan's theory of *impetus* and culminated in Oresme's law for the acceleration of falling bodies: Jean Buridan (c. 1300–c. 1370); Albert of Saxony (c. 1325–1390); Nicole Oresme (c. 1330–1382).

to the concept that universals reside in the mind and can be reached by techniques of memory. That these universals, once attained, will explain any individual instance is precisely why theoretical models seem (to us) divorced from the 'realities' that are their concrete embodiment. In the discursive class we have been looking at, such individual embodiments do not lead us toward universals: on the contrary, they are *second* in relation to those universals. Ockham emphasizes that concepts are first of all present in the mind thinking of them rather than attained by a mind gaining access to the imprint of a universal whose essence is outside the individual mind. Leff continues: "He thereby substituted a logical for a metaphysical order. In doing so he discarded the long-standing assumption of a pre-existing harmony between concepts and reality, transforming what had been taken as a hierarchy of being into a diversity of ways of signifying individual beings."[67]

This is to place a world of meaning over against a world of being. The problem of late Scholasticism was to regain access to a world now ruled by disjunction. The increasing complexity of the theory of signs was evidence of a mighty conceptual struggle to which the theory of signatures sought perhaps to put an end by simply cutting the Gordian knot and placing all things at the same level of apprehension. It was an unsuccessful expedient. Terence Cave has recently argued that not only Rabelais (and others already mentioned here), not only Thomas More (as we will see in some detail in the next chapter), but such writers as Erasmus, Ronsard, and Montaigne all manifest a kind of "discursive outpouring" that could well be taken as yet another manifestation of crisis.[68] But by that time it is shortly to be displaced by the elaboration of a quite new class of discourse.

Ockham's period of greatest activity was in the thirty years between 1319 and 1349. As already indicated, the matter of the replacement of a conjunctive "harmony between concepts and reality" by an essential disjunction has been argued by F. Edward Cranz as having occurred around 1100 in the work of Anselm and Abelard. It would, he argues, have been confirmed by Petrarch (1304–74), by Cusanus (1401–64), and by Luther (1483–1546).[69] These last names

67. Gordon Leff, *William of Ockham: The Metamorphosis of Scholastic Discourse* (Manchester, 1975), p. xxi.

68. Terence Cave, *The Cornucopian Text: Problems of Writing in the French Renaissance* (Oxford, 1979).

69. Cranz explores this view especially in "Nicolaus Cusanus as a Paradigm of Renaissance and Reformation." He argues that Petrarch, Cusanus, and Luther in turn sought to respond to Anselm and Abelard by a return to Antiquity, a return which can only be defined as based upon an essential and inevitable misinterpretation. See also Cranz's "Petrarch's Transformation of St. Augustine" (1971).

and dates suggest that it was rather between Ockham and the mid-sixteenth century than from the time of Anselm and Abelard that something potentially new was emerging. I am suggesting it is as yet no more than potential. It cannot even begin to start consolidating, and does not, until that disjunction becomes absorbed in a whole network of elements to which the hypostasis of the enunciating subject as a possessive internally sufficient *self* is essential—along with other elements whose development and consolidation subsequent chapters will follow. Such a *self* does not yet exist.

To be sure, there is ambiguity. Both the potential for the existence of a new class of discourse and the power of the still dominant model are clearly indicated by the condemnation procured on December 10, 1269, by the Parisian faculty of theology against views of which Siger of Brabant was taken as the exemplary representative. The archbishop of Paris, Etienne Tempier, acted against thirteen articles asserted to be proclaiming, among other things, "the unicity of the human intellect, determinism of the will, the eternity of the world, the mortal nature of the soul, the complete detachment of God from all knowledge of the universe, and the negation of divine providence." The dominant model could clearly not accept such views as those (whether or not they were actually expressed). But nor could such a 'radical' as Ockham have done so either. As Leff remarks: "it cannot be emphasized too strongly that Ockham totally accepted the regularities of nature and the constancy of moral norms. If his was a universe of individuals they were not self-contained or discrete."[70]

The assumption of regularity and constancy is what affords a foundation for a theory of signatures that will last into the seventeenth century. But the increasing difficulty of founding the assumption itself leads to the necessity of a quite different axiomatic grounding. At that point the discreteness of the individual (both logical and ontological) will become fundamental. But at least in Ockham, so far as man himself is concerned, the model remains that of Augustine: "Ockham like virtually every Christian thinker accepts St. Augustine's view of the soul as formed in the image of the uncreated Trinity." The soul's likeness to God is partly in its substance as image, but chiefly "through the soul's conjunction with its acts of knowing and willing." And Leff is then able to discuss the centrality of the Eucharist in Ockham's thought as in a sense its conclusion. For Ockham no less than for Augustine or Abelard, the Divine is the

70. Leff, *William of Ockham*, p. xxiii. The preceding quotation is from David Knowles, *The Evolution of Medieval Thought* (1962; rpt. New York, n.d.), pp. 272–73.

completion of nature, attained by commemorative illumination.[71] Here, too, disjunction strains toward conjunction; commemoration is by no means replaced by reference; the individual is conceivable only as part of a whole whose existence may indeed be becoming increasingly tentative but which remains intact for the moment.

Fundamentally there remains the assumption of an overarching totality within which the word and the world (whether social or physical) are situated at the same level. The dominant model is a collective one in which the sign as a 'unit' of meaning or the human as an 'individual' in society has no significance at all save as it can be referred to the corporate community or social discourse on the one hand and guaranteed by the Divine on the other. Like Erich Kahler, Walter Ullmann also underlines this aspect of the matter at a social level, speaking of "the absorption of the individual by the community or by society," as evidenced, he writes, by such "collective punishments : . . as the interdict of a locality or the amercements of towns, villages, or hundreds, and so on." He continues: "Society was pictured as a large organism in which each member had been allotted a special function which he pursued for the common good." The two "characteristic facts" of such a society were its division into fixed estates (what I earlier referred to as a "person's status") and the obligation of every member to fulfill his "vocation" (what I called the "participant's role"). This order is, of course, a version of "the great chain of being" as explored by Lovejoy. Indeed, it may well be that we can read that *great chain* as an operator having a similar function to that of *anima,* permitting the transformation of different 'conceptual' levels among one another.[72]

Whether or not one accepts that the dominant discourse underlying this unfamiliar kind of conceptual organization is one of patterning, it is clear that such a disposition indicates a very different epistemology of sign process from that of the analytico-referential. To such thinkers as Augustine or Bernard, William of Saint Thierry or

---

71. Leff, *William of Ockham*, pp. 529–30, 596–613.

72, Ullmann, *Individual and Society*, pp. 32, 40, 41–43; Lovejoy, *Great Chain of Being*, pp. 67–98 (for this period). Ullmann, notes, as a further indication of the growth of the individual, the fact that a growing number of writers are naming themselves (pp. 33–35), but Curtius tends to imply the contrary: the very fact that one can count such named authors so easily suggesting that anonymity remains normal (*European Literature and the Latin Middle Ages*, pp. 515–18). Paul Zumthor makes much of such anonymity as a fundamental characteristic of the collective or communal nature of medieval poetic modes (*Essai de poétique médiévale* [Paris, 1972], passim). As Peter Haidu has remarked, what counts above all is that the names of medieval authors are by and large "empty": for we usually know nothing but the name and the text with which it is joined.

Aelred, Aquinas, Anselm, or Abelard, it could not have occurred to *use* the 'arbitrariness' of the sign so as to give a specifiable relatum in the phenomenal world, a relatum whose confirmation depends upon the *will* of an individual who estimates himself (insofar as *will* is concerned) the equal of the Divinity. The key concepts of *use, arbitrariness, will, intention, individual, person,* and *self* are all quite different. They cannot but provide an utterly dissimilar practice of discourse.

It is in the light of such a difference that the realism/nominalism dispute should be considered, rather than by identifying it with a later opposition between rationalism and empiricism, to which it is often mistakenly assimilated. The two disputes do not pose the problem of knowledge in at all the same way. They belong in different epistemes. In this connection Nancy Struever has noticed striking similarities between Sophistic discourse and that of nominalism and fourteenth-century Italian humanism, similarities that immediately recall Claude Imbert's discussion of Stoic logic. Referring particularly to Gorgias and Isocrates, Struever writes of the Sophists:

> Quite simply, the early Sophists decided to deal with the impure: to shun the ideal sphere where pure reason and perfect justice reside for the shifting and uncertain field of action and discourse. In effect, they issue a series of Self-Denying Ordinances in their axiomatic statements. These ordinances assert that only a world of flux and impurity exists, and that a mental operation cannot be divorced from this disorderly matrix. The desire for purity of thought and communication is a delusion, and even the force of logic is a form of violence (*bia*) mediated through the passions. Sophistic thought denies any stability except the stability of the relationships which it creates.[73]

One is vividly reminded here of Frege's remark that "if everything were in continual flux, and nothing maintained itself fixed for all time, there would no longer be any possibility of getting to know anything about the world, and everything would be plunged in confusion." Frege, as I commented earlier concerning the metaphor of the telescope, was himself writing toward the beginning of a period of discursive passage. That passage also marks the closing of the dominance of the analytico-referential with whose rise I am concerned here, and one may well compare Frege's fear to Charles S. Peirce's emphasis on incessant semiosis, and that opposition in turn

---

73. Nancy Struever, *The Language of History in the Renaissance: Rhetoric and Historical Consciousness in Florentine Humanism* (Princeton, 1970), p. 10; see also pp. 46ff.

to the case presently under discussion (though without identifying them in any way together).[74] The realism/nominalism dispute is really over the question of 'exteriority': whether or not there exists any nondiscursive anchor for discourse (thought).

One is tempted to place that dispute in an arena where patterning is opposed to mediation. It is in such an arena that Platonic Ideas (nothing but logic itself, we may recall, in Ramus's transformation of them) answer the Sophists' claims for "pure" discourse. In effect nominalism claims that human thought is nothing but 'anchorless' discursive mediation. Platonic realism asserts the creation of logical patterns whose anchor is the nondiscursive (and hierarchic) world of real Ideas. That is a quite different concept of external anchor from what is claimed in the rationalist/empiricist quarrel. In the latter some form of objectively knowable *material* reality is asserted by *both* parties. *Their* argument (among other things) concerns the question of how one can know such 'objective reality,' the division exterior/interior being a mutually accepted given. Far more was at stake in the realist/nominalist dispute: nothing less, perhaps, than the Renaissance and the subsequent era of technology, which required the development of analytico-referentiality.

It may be that what I have just been calling a discourse of mediation is less a 'class' (like patterning or analysis) than a kind of constant reminder of indecision, an indication of the fallibility of conceptual models. But whatever the case, I have myself argued elsewhere that an episteme may be considered as composed of *two* dominant discourses. The first is the "visible dominant discourse model." This is the discourse that provides 'meaningful concepts,' the discourse that orders all theories of reality and that judges all activities. In the Middle Ages it was the 'theocratic' model; in the period between the sixteenth century and our own time it was one of 'experimentalism' (whose emergence this book will be exploring). The second discourse is the "occulted dominant discourse practice." In the Middle Ages it was a particular 'feudal' disposition of often conflictual relations (which in England were codified as early as Magna Carta, making common law out of a conflict between King John and the barons).[75] When such practice is transformed into a meaningful

74. Gottlob Frege, *The Foundations of Arithmetic: A Logico-Mathematical Enquiry into the Concept of Number*, tr. J. L. Austin, 2d ed. (Oxford, 1953), p. vi. I have discussed the implications of this difference between Peirce and Frege in my article "Peirce and Frege: In the Matter of Truth," *Canadian Journal of Research in Semiotics*, 4, no. 2 (Winter 1976–77), 5–39.

75. This was, of course, a later interpretation, notably the result of various parliamentary statutes passed throughout the fourteenth century, and of the interpretation put on the Charter by Coke at the beginning of the seventeenth century and by later

model (as I suggest eventually happens), then the earlier model is itself discarded. A new episteme develops (and, as part of it, a new occulted practice).[76]

A process of this kind is implied in Walter Ullmann's analyses of medieval society and political order. He suggests the existence of an opposition between a "descending thesis of government" and an "ascending" one. The first is the theocratic model. It situates God at the summit in His plenitude with, immediately beneath Him, His annointed King. The King himself is placed over a society whose members, the *fideles*, are "incorporated" and conjoined within a permanently fixed and hierarchically structured totality. The ascending thesis is a feudal practice that allows considerable freedom to the individual and that also includes the customary practices of everyday life (largely indifferent to the divine theory of order). The latter, Ullmann suggests, is the older of the two. However, he also argues that in some sense they reemerge in the period between the thirteenth and fifteenth centuries, in the form of a "humanistic thesis," giving increasing importance to the concept of man as simply *natural*. The principal representatives of this later development were such figures as John of Paris, Dante, Marsilius of Padua, and Bartolus of Sassoferrato, as well as some others less obviously radical.[77]

English and American radicals, the latter especially calling on the Charter in the period leading up to 1776. But in 1215 and 1225 (the dates of the original version and of that ratified by Henry III), it was a concession of feudal privileges granted by the Crown to the barons. J. C. Holt observes that, as such, it was by no means exceptional in the period: similar grants had been made by Frederick Barbarossa in 1183 to the towns of the Lombard league, by Alphonso VIII of Leon in 1188 to his vassals, by the Emperor Frederick II in 1220 to the ecclesiastical princes of the Empire, by Andrew II of Hungary in 1222 to his vassals, and so forth (J. C. Holt, *Magna Carta* [Cambridge, 1965], pp. 20–21). As in the English case, all these concessions were necessitated by war, and the King's need for the support of the other parties involved. Holt adds that such grants were so far from being unusual that only the Capetian monarchy of France escaped having to make any (a condition that lasted, however, only until the early fourteenth century). Magna Carta was to become exceptional because of its history. To any "dispassionate observer" at the time, Holt comments, "grants of liberties would have seemed to embody the natural reaction of feudal societies to monarchical importunity" (p. 22). In large part, he adds, the Charter was "a statement of principles about the organization of a feudal state" (p. 63). Nonetheless, he concludes, even at the time—and increasingly thereafter—Magna Carta was interpreted as representing the claim "that authority should be subject to law which the community itself defined" (p. 292). Differences of interpretation then depend, of course, on differing interpretations of community and who is taken as representing it.

76. These matters have been advanced in more detail in my "The Environment of Literature and the Imperatives of Criticism," *Europa*, 4 (1981), to appear, and are being explored at length in a book in preparation.

77. These arguments are made principally in Ullmann's *Medieval Political Thought*, pp. 189–219, and in his *Individual and Society*, pp. 130–44.

But by the late fifteenth century we are already leaving the Middle Ages behind in any case.

F. L. Ganshof, agreeing with Ullmann as to the order in which the feudal and the theocratic orders appeared, provides us with some important indications as to how a practice can be absorbed into and occulted by a dominant model: a matter that is naturally significant for the analyses of my next chapters. According to Ganshof, the earliest forms of feudal legal arrangements implied "in the fullest sense a mutual contract." By the Carolingian era, the second half of the eighth century, however, this aspect was becoming increasingly concealed as the feudal rite of vassalage, though still conceived as instituting a mutually binding relationship, came to be the seal of a fundamentally hierarchical one (for the "contract" had never in any case been reckoned as between equals). The act of commendation (by which the vassal placed himself in debt to his lord for service in return for protection and livelihood) was accompanied by an oath of fealty (the vassal's *fides* or *fidelitas*), which at least in appearance is more binding on the vassal than on the lord. At the same time, it emphasizes the hierarchical relation. Ganshof quotes to this effect from "a commentary on the Rule of St. Benedict ascribed to Paul the Deacon," which distinguishes between the slave's service by fear and the vassal's service by faith: "'the vassal serves his lord in virtue of the faith (*propter fidem suam*) by which he has promised to serve him, so that he shall not be taken as a breaker of his word.'" The vassal assumes a position "in relation to his lord," rather than the contrary, and he does it by the symbolic enclosing of his hands between those of his lord (the so-called commendation with *immixtio manuum*), by an oath of fealty and, at least in the case of an important vassal, by touching a *res sacra*.[78]

It is doubtless the case that later texts will continue to point out the lord's obligations, even while emphasizing the vassal's. Ganshof quotes a letter from Bishop Fulbert of Chartres to this effect, dated 1020, and is able to suggest other instances. Nonetheless, one can say that by the late eighth century, and certainly by the ninth, the contractual aspect of the relationship has definitely become subordinated to that of a model of hierarchical domination—placed under a theological sign (the touching of some *res sacra*). By 802, an oath sworn to Charlemagne indicates clearly the obligations of the vassal, but appears not to involve specific stated obligations on the part of Charlemagne, whose legal obligation is presumably simply implicit in

78. F. L. Ganshof, *Feudalism*, tr. Philip Grierson, 3d English ed. (New York, 1964), pp. 8, 27–30.

his enfolding of the vassal's hands, while the latter in addition takes his oath and swears on the sacred relics. Indeed, once the oath was taken, fealty appears to have been terminable only with the lord's agreement, the contrary not being the case (though practice differed as vassals became stronger). Throughout this same century, feudal benefices (later called "fiefs") became increasingly hereditary, and this, too, implies the gradual disappearance of the contractual element (at least visibly) with a corresponding hardening of hierarchical relationships. For such benefices became less and less a matter for the creation of feudal vassalages, less at the lord's disposal, but increasingly a permanent sign of status and place within a fixed hierarchy (for the debt of service and fidelity did not thereby disappear).

The almost entirely oral procedures of Carolingian feudalism had always marked an attempt to increase and maintain the power of the King, though it soon started to have an opposite effect in practice (leading to the downfall of the Carolingians). From the very earliest times there had been a clear tension between the vassal's urge to independence and the lord's attempts to increase his own authority. In ninth-century France it was leading toward the downfall of the Carolingians. Elsewhere it was to lead to such concessions as Magna Carta. But at the same time, as I have been suggesting, a visible model of hierarchy (terminating in the Divinity itself) was gradually becoming dominant, whatever actual practice may have been. This model is gradually coming to cover an originally more clearly contractual arrangement, and the vocabulary of serfdom is increasingly applied to the relationship, not as a form of deprecation but as indicative of a certain order. Ganshof refers to the virtual "sovereignty" exercised by the king over his vassal (even though the latter remained free in law) and to "the religious character of the oath of fealty." In this regard, too, it is important to notice that feudal relations and rights of justice were not the same, though they were linked. The holding of a fief, that is to say, did not give the vassal jurisdiction over that area (though in practice some seized it): a fief implied property rights, not judicial ones. So far as civil law was concerned, such judicial rights remained in the lord's hands, whatever may have been the variety and ambiguity in fact. By the late twelfth century, at least in England and France, the Crown had succeeded in its claim to overall legal jurisdiction.[79]

Such a claim was not simply a legal one. It also emphasized certain elements of the entire hierarchical order by now firmly established—

---

79. Ibid., pp. 83–84, 30–33, 46–49, 56–57, 156–67.

and firmly established in accordance with a theocratic model. To be sure, even in Western Europe there were many varieties of what we tend today to subsume under the single term "feudalism," but by and large this model ruled from the eleventh to the thirteenth century. Certainly the tensions remained. For the time being, however, the occultation of a practice that would fundamentally question the dominant model enabled a great outburst of new activities. In terms of a particular order of conceptualization, Arthur Lovejoy speaks of a similar kind of opposition inherent within the idea of a Great Chain of Being. Throughout this period the image contained a contradiction it was unable to resolve, a contradiction whose eventual resolution would lead, I suggest, to the destruction of the episteme of patterning (together, of course, with such elements as the reappearance, in 'usable' form, of the conflictual and contractual nature of feudal relations). Lovejoy indicates that the concept of the Great Chain contained on the one hand an assumption of necessary and inevitable descent from God himself through the multiplicity of creation to the lowest nonsentient piece of matter, and on the other a supposition of a full Creation achieved by God's will. Such an opposition between necessity and freedom, writes Lovejoy, produced a whole series of contradictions,[80] of which that between a static hierarchical order and a moving conflictual practice is obviously but one example.

It is such practices as these last that compose what I have called the occulted dominant discourse practice. They are not conceived as a means of theorizing reality. Indeed, as Ullmann shows, they are ignored by the dominant model—even though, as my references to Ganshof suggest, they may be instrumental in enabling such dominance.[81] Eventually, however, elements from such practices do give rise to a modeling theory. More precisely they are transformed into such a theory (feudalism was not a theory of the social order but the form taken by specific kinds of social relations and the legal order prescribed for particular kinds of property rights). The consequence of Machiavelli's conflictual analysis was to render obsolete the domi-

---

80. Lovejoy, *Great Chain of Being*, pp. 76–98.

81. Lynn White, Jr., has suggested that a "practice" even less conducive to theorization underlay the development of feudalism itself: the arrival in the West of the iron stirrup in the time of Charles Martel. This immediately provoked a change in the style of warfare by making possible mounted shock combat. The instantly increased effectiveness of such troops necessitated their training and maintenance as well as that of their horses. This meant also that they had to be provided with sufficient land and financial means. At the same time the ruler had to be able to rely on their presence in time of war: thence the whole system of service in return for land benefice, of fealty in return for protection and livelihood, and so on (Lynn T. White, Jr., *Medieval Technology and Social Change* [Oxford, 1962], pp. 1–2, 28–38).

nant theocratic model. It necessitated the development and invention of new analytical elements, some of which were quite new indeed, some of which were already emergent in the earlier dominant model. This transformation of practice into a meaningful analysis eventually produced the experimentalist model, at the same time as it left space for a 'new' occulted practice ('new' in the sense that it becomes epistemically essential—as feudal practices had been before): those relations Karl Marx was to analyze as socioeconomic relations of production. That analysis in turn will give rise to a new dominance and a new occultation (as I suggest in Chapter 12).

In a number of recent writings, Peter Haidu has shown how a kind of unease in the poetic writings of the twelfth century, especially certain of Chrétien de Troyes's writings, is indicative of a latent contradiction such as I have been suggesting—though it falls very far short of what will be seen in a text such as *Utopia*. We have already had occasion to observe some of Eugene Vance's similar observations on texts running from the *Chanson de Roland* to Gace Brulé, from Dante to Chaucer. Both Haidu and Vance interpret such a contradiction, following Georges Duby, as the sign of a new emergent discourse that later interpretation will be able to view as being in opposition to feudalism: that is, as elements of a "capitalist" discourse. In certain areas like Champagne, the argument runs, the growth of the use of money started changing the way people functioned in relation to one another and the way they conceptualized such relations. This increasing process of exchange came into collision with habitual structures of thought and practice: a collision visible, for example, in the previously mentioned poetic productions. It will culminate much later in the sixteenth century. The argument is no doubt based on unimpeachable data, but I think the interpretation is inexact, because it tends to conflate feudal practice and theologico-theocratic theory, dominant model and dominant practice.[82]

82. The Vance paper mentioned here is "Love's Concordance," esp. p. 44. The Haidu text I am above all referring to is his unpublished and important paper "Semiotics and History" (1980). For both his other and Duby's writings, see the Bibliography. Duby's briefest text on contradictory discourses (discussed under the name of "idéologies") is "Histoire sociale et idéologies des sociétés," in *Faire de l'histoire*, ed. Jacques Le Goff and Pierre Nora, 3 vols. (Paris, 1974), I.147–78; but see, too, *Les trois ordres, ou l'imaginaire du féodalisme* (Paris, 1978), esp. pp. 387–402. For Duby, the notion of the "three orders" remains for a long time at once potentially antagonistic to the dominant order and yet preservative of the social equilibrium made precarious by the aforementioned contradictions. In this sense it confirms what I have been saying about feudal practice and theocratic model. Until the thirteenth century, writes Duby, the notion operates at the level of society's "imaginaire." The turning point is marked by Philippe Auguste's victory at the battle of Bouvines on July 27, 1214, where the King was placed symbolically outside the tripartite social order he will now maintain as such (*Les trois ordres*, pp. 414–25).

Feudal practice and new processes of monetary exchange are not at first in conflict with one another. Feudal practice contains many elements of exchange and contract, potentially available to praxes other than feudal ones.

Whether such practice eventually becomes a "capitalist" analytic (as I suggest happens in Machiavelli) or is crushed by it (as Duby, Haidu, Vance, and others suggest) is less important for my purpose than the perception of the presence of such contradictions. Haidu, after Duby once again, has argued rather strongly that elements of a later dominant "textuality" (as he terms it, following others who speak of "social text") are already present in medieval practice.[83] I would suggest that feudal practice provides those elements rather than denying them. The difference is that they are not yet tools for analysis. It is in just this sense that J. G. A. Pocock has been able to show how Continental and English lawyers and antiquarians gradually "discovered" feudalism. Their theory of what feudalism was grew with the new analysis of what society and the state were. Toward the middle of the sixteenth century, Cujas and Hotman in particular came to view what we (but not they) would call the feudal system as a legal, social, and political practice produced out of a tradition quite separate from the Roman. In 1603, the Scottish historian Sir Thomas Craig produced a work in which the feudal law was treated not as a whole complex of practical relations but "as a system of royal and hierarchical authority binding all men to personal dependence on the king." Shortly thereafter, the English antiquarian Sir Henry Spelman produced a series of works tending to imply, though with far more complexity, the same state of affairs. Feudalism, that is to say, is being used to provide historical justification for a theory of the King's absolute authority (that done, all manner of arguments may then be developed as to how subjects are in fact bound to such authority—including the Hobbesian covenant). Pocock can then conclude of James Harrington's *Oceana* (1656) that the concept of

> feudalism, as was happening everywhere in English historical thought, helped him to see how the pattern of custom, law and government had changed in modern history, and helped him to see also that law might be largely a matter of land, and social relationships a matter of tenure.

83. The distinction between the use of the term "text" and my use of *discourse* is essential. For Peter Haidu, Fredric Jameson, Julia Kristeva, Juri Lotman, and others, *text* is something whose existence and production one interprets (even if one plays with words to assert that such interpretation is itself a new production of such text). *Discourse* is something one inhabits and is inhabited by, one uses and is used by. One is *in* discourse, *against* text.

It is the marriage between this and the essentially classical and Italian concepts of the one, the few and the many, of the degenerative cycle, of the legislator, of the citizenry as a voting militia and the militia as an armed citizenry, that produces the thought of the "Preliminaries" [before *Oceana*], which posterity has agreed to consider the important part of Harrington's legacy. Viewed in this light, *Oceana* is a Machiavellian meditation upon feudalism.[84]

All this argues that feudalism as a theoretical analysis of society developed in parallel with and as a consequence of the "Machiavellian" analysis. It was at once an effort at differentiation and at historical justification. In any case, what is above all important here is to be able to avoid confusing emergence with dominance. I wish to show in the following chapters how emergent elements, facing insuperable contradiction, develop into a dominant process (remembering always, of course, that to speak of "emergence" can only be retrospective: neither the twelfth nor the sixteenth century, nor any other, could see the elements of its discourse in such terms). The crisis of discourse I have suggested as gradually growing is not simply manifested in language and thought, in logic, epistemology, and metaphysics. It is revealed in every kind of human practice, as it is in events which it does not seem possible to ascribe directly to human causation.

On March 7, 1277, the thirteen articles condemned eight years earlier were increased somewhat in number. Etienne Tempier condemned 219 propositions. It was during Ockham's early teaching years, in the period between 1315 and 1319, that "the greatest famine of the Middle Ages struck." In the Low Countries at least 10 per cent of the population died. Between 1347 and 1350 the outbreak of bubonic plague, the Black Death, decreased the population of Europe by an estimated 33 to 40 per cent. Not for 250 years—not until 1600—would this population be made up once again. That this partly corresponded to a change in climate seems unquestioned, the period between the mid-fourteenth and the mid-seventeenth centuries in Europe being very cold and damp (the same climactic conditions were accompanied by an earlier outbreak of bubonic plague between the sixth and eighth centuries of our era). At the same time, falling agricultural productivity as a result of the over-use of land

84. J. G. A. Pocock, *The Ancient Constitution and the Feudal Law: A Study of English Historical Thought in the Seventeenth Century* (1957; rpt. New York, 1967), pp. 146–47. The earlier quotation is from p. 87. Similar implications as to the relation between a new historiography, a growing science, and political liberalism, with particular reference to Ralegh, Bacon, and Coke, have been explored by Christopher Hill, *Intellectual Origins of the English Revolution* (Oxford, 1965), esp. pp. 173–203, 250–61.

was becoming a serious problem by the third decade of the four-teenth century: cultivation could no longer provide for a population whose increase over the previous two centuries had been dramatic. Four centuries later agricultural technology and population growth in Europe would be able to keep pace with one another, but this was not the case in the fourteenth century. Where agricultural technology was lacking military technology provided a less pleasant "solution." To famine and plague was added war. The same third decade of the fourteenth century saw cannons in general use, and this led directly to the early English victories of the Hundred Years' War.[85]

Between 1337 and 1453, the fortunes of that war ebbed and flowed across the battlefields of France. It was fought partly because the Plantagenet English rulers of the vast French fief of Aquitaine anomalously refused vassalage services to the French kings, partly because English and French merchants were battling over the wool trade in Flanders, and partly because a new national consciousness was beginning to develop in France as it already had in England. Feudal concerns, mercantile dominance, national awareness were therefore all mixed up together in this symptomatic war. Ockham's defense of the Holy Roman Emperor's power in his writings after 1328, matched more radically by the *Defensor pacis* of Marsilius of Padua and John of Jandun (1324), fits in theoretically with the grow-ing 'individuation' of 'national' consciousness. The Hundred Years' War is the practical manifestation of a growing crisis: philosophical, economic, political, and social.

By the mid-fifteenth century matters have quieted to a degree where certain nation states can begin to consolidate themselves. But this is only partially the case, for they still have to confront a feudal order which, having at first made use of the rising mercantilism, now finds itself threatened by its political consequences. The ele-ments of contract and conflict inherent in the feudal relationship could easily pass into the emerging structures of economic exchange. Like Ganshof, Marc Bloch also commented on the essential bilater-ality of the feudal contract, and remarked that it would eventually have a profound influence on social and economic relations in the West—noting at the same time the importance of the "warrior ethic."[86]

85. Ozment, *Age of Reform*, p. 8; Jean Gimpel, *The Medieval Machine: The Industrial Revolution of the Middle Ages* (1976; rpt. Harmondsworth, 1980), pp. 182–83, 205–13. For the relation between climate and disease, Gimpel, pp. 56, 205–6; for falling productivity, p. 213; for use of cannons, pp. 233–35. Many of these matters are also discussed in Robert S. Lopez, *The Commercial Revolution of the Middle Ages, 950–1350* (1971; rpt. Cambridge, 1976).

86. Marc Bloch, *La société féodale* (1939; rpt. Paris, 1970), p. 617.

But other elements, most notably that of a fixed and static hierarchy, could not fit into a new class of discourse. Indeed, they were insuperably threatened by an order founded upon a whole set of dynamisms. The death throes of feudalism and the birth pangs of a new nationalism were nowhere more savagely experienced than in Italy, ravaged all these years by the internecine squabbles of diverse city-states and the errant brutality of the *condottiere* armies.

In the second two decades of the sixteenth century Machiavelli, in the context of these developments, provides the possibility of a new theoretical departure. At the same time he poses a problem for political theory (and practice) that will not be resolved until Hobbes: how could one live in a nation-state whose very being depended on a constant play of personal power? And how could nation-states live together in peace if the definition of their "health" is constant expansion at the expense of one another? Simultaneously, Luther takes up where Marsilius and Ockham had left off, putting into question not only the temporal power of the "universal church" but also the universality of its theological dominion. The same struggles for power were everywhere visible. If the Concordat of Bologna (1515) gave François I some power over the church in France (to match imperfectly the power Henry VIII had simply seized in England), the Affair of the Placards (1534) indicated only too clearly that an alternative theology threatened not only the Catholic Church but also the unity of the nation-state. As such it led straight into the overwhelming bitterness of the religious wars.

The theologico-political Concordat of 1515 was closely followed in 1517 by the Treaty of Cambrai. This put an end to the wars between Italy and France which had so complicated the struggles of the Italian city-states. But that treaty was immediately followed by the beginning of the struggles between the Hapsburgs and the Valois (and later the Bourbons) over the control of Spain, when François failed to obtain nomination as Holy Roman Emperor in 1519. This war of succession was destined to continue in a desultory and intermittent fashion for almost two hundred years, until the beginning of the eighteenth century. By that time, of course, our new discourse will also have been consolidated. Relative peace will reign in Europe, for disputes between European states will tend to be fought out over the oceans of the world and over others' lands (not without such major exceptions as the Seven Years', the Napoleonic, and the Franco-Prussian wars).

The Hundred Years' War may have ended, then, in 1453, but it very soon gave way to the religious wars of a century later, and to a diversity of ongoing broils between Italy, Savoy and France, Spain and France, and so forth. The mid-sixteenth century was racked by spiraling inflation, while a little later the massive influx of South American gold began to make its impact felt. All these events, characterizing the two centuries between Ockham and Machiavelli, are at once the symptoms and effects, the causes and reflections of a total theoretical and practical dilemma, whose solution was to be found finally by the end of the seventeenth century, with the complete consolidation of a class of discourse that still remains by and large our own.

My argument is that no new discourse of this kind consolidates between the thirteenth and sixteenth centuries, that the dominant discourse (certainly through Ockham, and I would suggest until the beginning of the sixteenth century) remains the totalizing one of patterning, and that the crisis grows as contradictions become ever more visible. It seems to be in something of this sense that Steven Ozment speaks when he comments on that age's "continuity and discontinuity with the Middle Ages." As a corrective movement, he argues with many others, the Reformation was a "failure." It did not succeed in installing any kind of new discourse. But it was a failure only to the extent that it strove in vain both to maintain and to surpass a dominant discourse whose internal contradictions and problems were becoming thus increasingly visible. The attempt "to ennoble people beyond their capacities," as Ozment puts it, may well be interpreted, for example, as a (somewhat) secularized version of the soul's passage to God.[87]

The sixteenth century is a time of "plural narratives," to use Terence Cave's phrase once again. The seventeenth century will displace and recast a set of problems that this plurality was incapable of resolving. The new discursive dominance, then, is made both possible and necessary, first by the internal contradictions of the previously dominant discourse (in this case, the totalizing theologico-theocratic one of the Middle Ages: a patterning discourse) and second by the gradual cohesion of emergent elements that together will become more powerful conceptual tools than the discourse within which they were produced (more powerful in their correspondence with the needs of a particular conjuncture, not in any absolute sense). Of the first condition, I am taking More's *Utopia* as an exemplary demonstration. The remainder of the book will dem-

---

87. Ozment, *Age of Reform*, pp. 435, 438. The relations of thought and society are dealt with magisterially by Ozment, pp. 182–222, 245–89.

onstrate the emergence to dominance of the new (analytico-referential) discourse, starting with the case of Kepler's *Somnium.*[88]

88. An omission needs perhaps a brief comment here. Aquinas of course discussed at length and in depth such matters as will, intention, free choice, voluntary versus involuntary, and so on. Space and competence both forbid treatment in detail here. I have, however, been concerned only to provide indications of a dominant discursive class distinct from the analytico-referential, not with any attempt to exhaust the question for the Middle Ages, though St. Thomas has not been set altogether aside. For his discussion, see esp. *Summa theologica,* pt. I, Qq. 82–83; pt. II, Qq. 6ff. It should also be mentioned here, perhaps, that the argument about "will" in ancient Greece presented between pp. 60 and 69 above, and the view of Stoic thought suggested between pp. 77 and 81, have been explicitly denied by André-Jean Voelke, *L'idée de la volonté dans le stoïcisme* (Paris, 1973). He asserts that the Stoics had in fact elaborated such concepts as will, individual, deliberation, self, and so on, in a manner prefiguring what was to be elaborated fifteen centuries later. To do so, however, he is forced to treat the Old, Middle, and New Stoas as though they were simultaneous. Even if Cicero's views may be used to determine those of Panaetius, one may be skeptical as to the value of arguing back from Marcus Aurelius or Epictetus to discover those of Chrysippus, and even more from Sextus Empiricus, Clement of Alexandria, Diogenes Laertius, and Simplicius, to illuminate those of Cleanthes (though Voelke claims that this can be done "without deforming" their thought, p. 7). Such an ahistorical approach seems at best methodologically dubious. Voelke himself is obliged to conclude that the concept of will undergoes a pronounced change during the first century B.C. Vernant's remark about Diodorus Siculus then comes into its own again (as do various critics' remarks about Seneca and the "Roman spirit" or concerning the possible Christian influence on Epictetus). Where the texts are unavailable for study, it seems best to renounce all hope of "understanding" rather than invent a conceptual history in the image of our own desire.

3 · *From the Middle Ages to the (W)Hole of* Utopia

But who could have handed down to us
The story of those times of innocence?
Did they inscribe their happiness
In the temple of memory?
The vanity of the art of writing
Would soon have made it fade away;
So without a thought of describing it,
They were satisfied with its mere enjoyment.
                        —Jean-Jacques Rousseau, *Le siècle pastoral*

A moment must come when the contradiction between the visible and the occulted becomes insuperable. A seemingly insoluble conflict arises. A hole gapes open where neither meaning nor practice seems any longer possible. Perhaps we occupy such a moment in our own time, and therefore the exploration of how it arises and how it has in the past been overcome is by no means a matter of indifference.

The present chapter will try to show how More's *Utopia* writes itself into an insoluble conflict of this kind. It is a response to a crisis in the episteme that seals off for us a whole area of discourse: what I have been calling patterning. More's text itself is neither medieval nor modern. It is the mark of a moment when the very possibility of discourse finds itself, so to speak, teetering before an abyss of non-meaning (as Dr. Johnson was to put it with regard to an author who should be placed rather at the moment when a new discursive practice is finally consolidating its dominance: John Dryden).

Subsequent chapters will show how a new dominant discourse model gradually emerged. They will show how such a model had first of all to uncover and differentiate the specific form of the earlier dominant model (that of patterning). They will show how it produced from within that very form the elements of its own dominance, and how, in doing so, it overcame the 'hole' created by a work like *Utopia*, set aside forever that kind of textuality.

This chapter will therefore also suggest that *Utopia* was not only the first of its kind, but that it was *unique* of its kind: a joke, a carnival repudiation of discursive authority doomed to disappear with the discourse it placed in question.[1] For if we may say with Robert Elliott, following Dostoevsky, Berdyaev, and Zamiatin, that utopia is a product of the Euclidean mind, we must take it as a most ambiguous and subversive one.[2] And that is certainly the case of the nominal ancestor of the genre, *Utopia* itself. I would say that this text makes the invention of the 'Euclidean' mind necessary, but that it is not itself a product of it. It may be, here, that the Euclideanism of the interpretive critic betrays its textual victim.

Utopia partakes simultaneously of the satiric rejection and of the affirmative vision of a humanly created and, at least to some degree, obtainable Golden Age.[3] It is, however, doubly paradoxical. For there is a necessary 'failure' involved in any 'hope' inspired by the nostalgia for a Golden Age, whose 'proper' place is the no-time and eternity of a discourse of patterning. The linear achievement (involved in the term "Euclidean") of such a Golden Age would in that sense be a contradiction in terms. And indeed, it is that contradiction which leads to the inescapable paradox to be discussed in the rest of this chapter. For the logic of linearity demands not only a first term and its product (which *are*), but also the process making such a product possible and filling the gap between the first and 'last' terms (except that such a 'last' term is supposed to be at infinity). It needs the process of *becoming*. Yet we know that there can be no such process leading from the finite to the infinite, from the temporality of *now* to the atemporality of *then* (and of the 'yet to come'), from the present geographic situation of, say, sixteenth-century London to the absent unsituated and atemporal Amaurotum.[4]

1. On this see Timothy J. Reiss, "Le non-lieu de la fête et le projet d'ordre," in *La fête en question,* ed. Karin R. Gürttler and Monique Serfati-Arnaud (Montreal, 1979), pp. 92–108.

2. Robert Elliott, *The Shape of Utopia: Studies in a Literary Genre* (Chicago and London, 1970), pp. 9off.; Fyodor Dostoevsky, *The Brothers Karamazov* (the Grand Inquisitor episode), etc.; Nicholas Berdyaev, *Dostoevsky,* tr. Donald Attwater (1934; rpt. New York, 1969), pp. 84–88, 188–204; Eugene Zamiatin, *We,* tr. Gregory Zilboorg (1924; rpt. New York, 1952).

3. Elliott, *Shape of Utopia,* pp. 3–24 ("Saturnalia, Satire, and Utopia"), and pp. 3off. ("The Shape of *Utopia*").

4. The concept of Euclideanism is explored more fully at the beginning of Chapter 11. Delaying such discussion seems appropriate because the concept itself is part of the discursive development this volume is examining.

Furthermore, once it has been written into existence, utopia presents a signifier that may be—and generally is—inserted in at least two different types of discourse: that of literature, as a self-referential kind of text, and that of politics or of polity. In turn, both of these "insertions" participate at once in the satirical and in the 'utopian' modes (the term 'utopia' indicating both a genre and a more general, almost ethical, characteristic). At least in the so-called traditional utopia, both these types of discourse are frozen.[5] Given their accession to textuality, this is necessarily so.

The discourse of polity, to the extent that it is satirical, is a circular discussion around an already existing sociopolitical situation (or one that is at least assumed to exist). We may take this existing situation as the 'mathematical' base. In so far as such a discourse is visionary, it is a static (and ideal) end product. The discourse of literature, inasmuch as it is satirical, has a structure composed of similar sets of syntactic arrangements that repeat themselves, not in an open-ended series, but rather in a kind of parallel process.[6] They *re*produce themselves, so to speak. The utopian mode of the literary discourse repeats this structure: the difference being that it is not based on an externally observed (referential) situation (implicit with regard to the text itself), but on an internally posited hypothesis, the 'vision' itself (explicit with regard to the text).[7]

5. In view of what I have been arguing, I would clearly deny that one can find any such thing as "traditional utopia" prior to More's. The Atlantis of the *Timaeus* and *Critias* is not even ambiguous in this respect, though the unexplored 'archaic' Atlantis may have been 'utopian.' It is the conqueror, ancient Athens, that is presented as the epitome of the ideal republic in what small reference there is to it (*Timaeus*, 23d–24d; *Critias*, 111e–112e), though its destruction, together with that of Atlantis itself (*Timaeus*, 25d), suggests the impossibility of ever attaining it. Even in that the ambiguity is maintained: "Well, then, said I, do you admit that our notion of the state and its polity is not altogether a daydream, but that though it is difficult, it is in a way possible and in no other way than described" (*Republic*, vii, 540d—Paul Shorey's translation). There is still further ambiguity in Plato's city: it is at once a myth of origins (the city is supposed once to have existed, inhabited by "the fairest and noblest race of men which ever lived" [*Timaeus*, 23b–c—Jowett translation]), associated with a nostalgic Golden Age (*Laws*, 713b–714b), and at the same time a myth of a future utopia (*Republic*). Projected into the past, it has much in common with the Christian paradise; into the future, it participates in the structure that produces the City of God, unattainable on earth (cf. Northrop Frye, "Varieties of Literary Utopias," in *Utopias and Utopian Thought*, ed. Frank E. Manuel [Boston, 1966], p. 39). The satirical mode, not emphasized by Plato, comes between these, as a commentary on and corrective for an extratextual condition in the present. Still, we cannot speak of a utopian text in Plato's case, because, excluding the *Republic* (which may be of utopian intention but is not a utopia), there are only scattered remarks in texts whose design lies elsewhere.

6. I.e., *not* as A/B/C/ . . . , but as A/B, A/B . . . In this sense, it clearly takes the form of a patterning order of discourse, as opposed, for example, to the analytico-referential (which would correspond more to the first situation).

7. If we were to consider the text in terms of polity and of its political 'meaning' (signified), we would have to reverse the places of the explicit and the implicit.

In the case of both types of discourse, it can readily be seen that there is no possibility of process, of continuity as we will see it, for example, in Bacon's *New Atlantis,* in Cyrano's *Voyages,* or in Defoe's *Robinson Crusoe.* Here, the discourse of polity is broken between the base and its product, the textuality is ruptured in that its two identical structures are set on two different bases. More's utopian discourse would thus seem to be characterized first and foremost by an *absence,* by the default of process embodied in its very text, by a lack of becoming. It has a hole at the core. As a product of the Euclidean mind, it would be inescapably scarred by its inability to grasp what will be the most original aspect of that mind: the capacity to 'know' logical progression, to make will into action, to mathematize the process of becoming. Both probability theory and the infinitesimal calculus will be the marks of that achievement. More's *Utopia* textualizes a discursive paradox that will remain an insuperable contradiction until its two sides are separated: we will see this in Kepler as an opposition between 'process' and 'entropy.' *Utopia* condemns medieval discursive practices, and its successors will escape the dilemma of its paradox by passing into another class of discourse. *Utopia* is less the product of the Euclidean mind than it is its producer.

It is in this light that the kind of opposition invoked by Alexandre Cioranescu between Machiavelli's *Prince* and More's *Utopia* needs important revision: "On the one side there stands the champion of political realism, on the other the out-and-out idealist. On the one side, the State conceived as will expressing itself in action; on the other, the republic viewed as a devout beehive. There, government as personal power and as a way to climb up the ladder; here, the State as communal duty and as sanctity in civil life."[8] It is certainly true that *Utopia* can be read in many ways as a late medieval treatise on civil life. But it also shows the impossibility of the very society it is taken as idealizing. One could almost say that it renders Machiavelli inevitable.

For the Florentine is among the first moderns to make his matter conform to a certain kind of textual exigency, in which the subject has complete control over his progressive system: hence his concern with personal possession of the other, with mastery, with conquering by force, with overcoming bodily (concepts expressly belittled and dismissed by such as More and Erasmus, Elyot and Budé, for exam-

---

8. Cioranescu, *L'avenir du passé: Utopie et littérature* (Paris, 1972), pp. 87–88. While Cioranescu does try to palliate this opposition, he does so by reference to More the statesman (despite his constant insistence that he is concerned only with textual structures) and not to the text of *Utopia* itself, whose discussion he in any case bases on an inexact and tendentious description.

ple).[9] That is why Machiavelli places his text under his own aegis, under the weight of his own "knowledge of the actions of men" and his own "long experience of contemporary affairs." But Machiavelli's text is not only homologous with the possessive society whose practice it analyzes and makes significant, and whose will to action it seeks to express. It also has a 'monetary' role to play within the exchange systems of that society: "Will Your Magnificence [Lorenzo de' Medici], then, deign to accept this little gift in the same spirit that I send it?" Machiavelli wants some return. That dedications are a commonplace may well be, but what is important here is that the text is not so much a mediation (though it is also that) as a value in its own right: the system seeks now to replace what it ostensibly merely relates.[10] With Machiavelli we are already passing into a new class of textuality. It is with reason that Bacon's discourse of knowledge is often identified with the Florentine's discourse of politics.

More's text is constantly torn. On the one hand it fits into that textual production demanded (and determined) by the society of humanists (a production with which Hythlodaeus risks 'contaminating' the Utopians).[11] On the other, it strives at all times (unlike *The Prince*) to maintain a strict use value, and a function of pure mediation that seeks to deny its own literariness and to express a condition (here, of the Utopians) of the pretextual. That opposition perhaps explains why the narrator of *Utopia* divides the text physically and structurally at precisely the point of process:

> So we went in and dined. We then returned to the same place, sat down on the same bench, and gave orders to the servants that we should not be interrupted. Peter Giles and I urged Raphael to fulfill his promise. As for him, when he saw us intent and eager to listen, after sitting in silent thought for a time, he began his tale as follows.
>
> THE END OF BOOK ONE
> BOOK TWO FOLLOWS   [P. 57]

9. Niccolò Machiavelli, *The Prince*, tr. and ed. Robert M. Adams (New York, 1977), p. 72 (ch. xxv).

10. Ibid., p. 3. These questions are a principal topic of the book mentioned in note 76 to Chapter 2.

11. St. Thomas More, *Utopia*, ed. Edward Surtz, S.J. (New Haven and London, 1964), pp. 106–7. I quote throughout from this edition, which is that of the Yale St. Thomas More Project's *Selected Works of St. Thomas More*. Page references will henceforward be placed in the text. Wherever my discussion has necessitated a verification of verbal accuracy with the Latin original, I have used the edition of Edward Surtz and J. H. Hexter, which is vol. 4 of the *Complete Works of St. Thomas More* (New Haven and London, 1965). It should also be made quite clear at this point that except when the contrary is specifically noted, references to More in the present chapter are *not* to the historical personage but to his textual namesake.

The first book was presented very much in terms of policy (More the statesman being sent to Flanders as Royal Commissioner), in terms of travel, and, above all, in terms of "dispute," "discussion," and public "eloquence" (pp. 9–10). Indeed, the first book is a dialogue throughout. The second book becomes an individual narration ("he began his tale"). Instead of movement (around the Continent, after the negotiations with Charles collapse), there is syntopy (we remain seated in a garden—on whose 'sameness' More insists). Instead of dialogue, there is to be uninterrupted narration. Instead of extroversion and a looking outward, there is introspection and introversion ("after sitting in silent thought for a time"). Furthermore, it is a narration twice sealed and blocked by its own structure: it is a narrated 'history,' presupposing foreknowledge; it is told in accordance with a "promise." I have suggested elsewhere that the promise (or the vow) represents an absolute term to the process of discourse, that it seals it off utterly from any progression.[12]

Here, then, what follows is preset. It is already known: "There is nothing," says Hythlodaeus, "I shall be more pleased to do, for I have the facts ready to hand" (p. 57). There can be no development. The tale is twice-told. Raphael indeed, quite unlike the narrator of *New Atlantis*, for example, makes no voyage, discursive or otherwise (in the text): it has already been done. We are placed directly on the "island of the Utopians" (p. 59), even more abruptly than we will see Campanella's reader obliged to engage the City of the Sun.[13] The absence I have remarked upon cannot be filled. The text itself insists that there *is* no becoming, no process to get us from here to there, from now to then. *Utopia* implies, too, that the apparent movement of social and physical reality as perceived cannot be grasped in the text.

No doubt it may be affirmed that this is a necessary condition of all textuality (though a discourse of mediation would certainly deny it). Even if this were the case, it is clear that post-Renaissance discourse has succeeded in occulting that condition. That is clear in *The Prince*, in *New Atlantis*, in a text such as *Robinson Crusoe*. The novel in general, until quite recently, always purported to possess some external referent and justification, which it 'followed' as it represented

12. Timothy J. Reiss, *Tragedy and Truth: Studies in the Development of a Renaissance and Neoclassical Discourse* (New Haven and London, 1980), esp. pp. 59–71; also Reiss, "Vers un système de la tragédie renaissante: Buchanan, Montaigne, et la difficulté de s'exprimer," *Canadian Review of Comparative Literature*, 4 (1977), 166–68, 170 ff.

13. The title of the second book of *Utopia* should be noted here: "THE BEST STATE OF A COMMONWEALTH, THE DISCOURSE OF RAPHAEL HYTHLODAEUS AS REPORTED BY THOMAS MORE, CITIZEN AND SHERIFF OF LONDON" (p. 59).

it. Writing was claimed as *report*. And it was not simply a mediation, for it asserted that it 'made sense of' what it described, that it systematized the otherwise 'incoherent' mass of sensible and intellectual data. It had its own particular value in the lines of production and the systems of exchange. It could become a surrogate for any and all experience. Romantics and symbolists, realists and naturalists, classicists and revolutionaries, all may have claimed a special and separate, an isolated and privileged, status within society for themselves (setting themselves in a way *outside* society), but they did not assert such absolute separateness for their production (if only because they needed a public). The text had a role to play in the social process: its system repeated that of society, of history, of science (assuming these to be other than identical).

Utopia shows the impossibility of such a claim at the time when it was written (1516). But it also shows the ambiguous tension of a growing desire to be able to act out such a claim—as we will see. *Utopia* emphasizes the distance between a patterning discourse and some other that it is yet unable to produce, because the attempt to produce it loses itself in unredeemable contradictions. Patterning discourse is in movement to the extent that it can continue to incorporate new elements, but such elements merely confirm a fixed overarching structure: dialogue repeats itself. The other progresses formally, again in the repetition of certain linear elements, but it is utterly static epistemologically—we can learn nothing new from it at all; it is a series of tautologies. Furthermore, it is undermined from within by its attempt to grasp elements that appear to belong in a different logical or discursive space. Both systems come out as equally hollow.

The stasis of the promise seeks to enforce an affirmation. It seeks to oblige the reader or listener to accept a particular sort of verity (a fact that explains why the Utopians make no use of treaties, pp. 116–18). This is made clear from the outset. In the prefatory letter to Peter Giles, More (and I mean 'More' as textual presence) is almost exclusively concerned with the truthfulness of the narration concerning the "state of Utopia," and with the unreadiness of readers and listeners to accept *any* discourse that does not coincide with their own. As Bacon will do a century later, More remarks that such unfamiliar discourse will appear to the Other as quite incoherent: "Very many men are ignorant of learning: many despise it. The barbarian rejects as harsh whatever is not positively barbarian. The smatterers despise as trite whatever is not packed with obsolete expressions" (p. 7). Therefore, he writes, the present narration must at least be internally coherent: "Just as I shall take pains to have nothing incorrect in the book, so, if there is doubt in anything, I shall rather tell an objective falsehood than an intentional lie—for I would rather be honest than wise."[14] The term "incorrect" here refers to some 'objective' referent, but the phrase "objective falsehood" indicates that such an idea may be unattainable and that even if it were not, there would be no way of knowing. From the start, then, the status of any new discourse is thrown into question, at the very moment its necessity is recognized.

The prefatory letter serves only to lead the reader into the circular dialogue of the first book through its own circular structure, and through its own contradictions as to the nature of this writing. On the one hand, the writer remarks: "Certainly you know that I was relieved of all the labor of gathering materials for the work and that I had to give no thought at all as to their arrangement." Or again: "there was no reason for me to take trouble about the style of the narrative" (p. 3). Yet on the other, he comments: "since I have gone through the labor of writing . . ." (p. 8). Indeed, the very effort to maintain narration as affirmation is itself tautological (as I implied above), because, in itself as predication and in its very sequentiality, the narrative discourse is *necessarily* affirmative. It creates what it seeks to affirm by its own internal process; but *Utopia* also tries to deny this, as a signifier with no signified other than itself:

> We forgot to ask, and he forgot to say, in what part of the new world Utopia lies. I am sorry that point was omitted, and I would be willing to pay a considerable sum to purchase that information, partly because I am rather ashamed to be ignorant in what sea lies the island of which I am saying so much, partly because there are several among us, and one in particular, a devout man and a theologian by profession, burning with an extraordinary desire to visit Utopia. [P. 6]

In another way, too, this preface emphasizes the text's 'circular' limits. Its speaker ('More') proceeds from simplicity and eloquence (Hythlodaeus's), to proper public intercourse (the speaker's own official life), to happy home life (pp. 3–5), all of these placed under More's control. But the preface concludes with a loss of control, with

14. "Potius mendacium dicam, quam mentiar." Surtz explains that the "objective falsehood" is self-deceiving, while the "lie" deceives others (*Selected Works* ed., p. 5 n. 5). It is self-deceiving *because* it is absolutely coherent within its own discourse. (It is perhaps worth repeating that I consider this prefatory letter to be a part of the whole discourse of *Utopia*: 'More' here is the textual personage, the inscribed writer of Hythlodaeus's discourse.)

unhappiness, ingratitude, discourtesy, and the confusion of the critics (pp. 7–8). This pattern forms a chiasmus with the order of the two books of the text 'proper,' which proceed from the satirical dialogue concerning political, social, and conceptual confusion of the first book, to the visionary and well-ordered narrative of the second.

From the very outset, then, the text denies, as it were in spite of itself, both process and reference. Like Montaigne's later *Essays*, the discourse of *Utopia* paints its own passage as it goes, for according to its own premise the most solid base (the situation of the island itself) is *absent*: not only is it out of memory, but it is forgotten by discourse itself ("we forgot to ask, and he forgot to say"). Utopia cannot be placed within the very text whose discourse it names, other than as a mere act of naming. And that naming is, as we have just seen, a denial, a negation. Utopia 'exists' only to the extent that it is promised in the narration that seeks to predicate it, by the simple act of naming. The process of the narrative, affirmative as it may be in itself, fails to make possible an imposition that would be external to itself. That is why this particular narrative, far from progressing, even within its own textual limits, constantly circles back upon itself. The beginning and end of discourse is identical: from the naming of "the island of Utopia" at the beginning (p. 59), to the naming of "the Utopian commonwealth" at the end (p. 152). The name, the promise, corresponds precisely to the discourse that it makes possible and by which it is made possible. Can we not see in this a fundamental questioning of the name/object-concept relation we saw as dominant during the Middle Ages? It is not, here, a formal questioning, but one of practice. (One may perhaps add that in other popular writers of this period, such as Pierre Fabri, Geofroy Tory, and John Palsgrave, attempts to delineate the relation between the sign and a 'referent' led to the invention of ever more intermediary levels of signification and to a potentially insoluble infinity: a certain indication that the nature of discourse is becoming increasingly problematic.)

In *Utopia* the city-states, "identical in language, traditions, customs, and laws," are also as similar in material layout as the land permits (p. 61). The same applies to the physical cities themselves, "exactly alike insofar as the terrain permits" (p. 63). The textual repetitions I mentioned as characterizing the first book are resumed in book two, where it may be observed in every aspect of the description: clothes are of "one and the same pattern" (p. 69), families are identical, skills are the same, streets, houses, gardens, and the rest are all of a piece.

The introduction, inasmuch as it speaks of the text that is to follow, speaks only of the narrative (affirmation of Utopia) and of making that narrative internally coherent. Yet, as I suggested, the dialogue is formulated in the letter by means of More's personal and public life:

> I am constantly engaged in legal business, either pleading or hearing, either giving an award as arbiter or deciding a case as judge. I pay a visit of courtesy to one man and go on business to another. I devote almost the whole day in public to other men's affairs and the remainder to my own. I leave to myself, that is to learning, nothing at all.
>
> When I have returned home, I must talk with my wife, chat with my children, and confer with my servants. [P. 4]

The circularity of this constant exchange ("the day, the month, the year slip away" without any change), its repetitive nature ("pleading or hearing," "giving or deciding," "pay a visit," "go on business," "talk," "chat," "confer"), characterizes the first part of this text in both its aspects: the circularity of the sociopolitical discourse in its satirical mode; the repetitiveness of the literary discourse in the same mode.

It is time, I think, to show rather more precisely how all this applies to the dialogue book of the text. I have suggested that the satirical political aspect of the text is circular and referential to the extent that it sends the reader to the present state of English polity. This state is characterized as aristocratic, composed of essentially separate small (still 'feudal') societies each out for its own advantage: the rich, the idle, the luxurious; societies in which a philosopher/councilor could find no place, argues the writer (thus denying the text any effective purpose, as we have seen him do for any external referent or process).

The microcosm of this situation is Raphael's account of his time spent in the circle of Cardinal Morton, a circle presented by the narrator as the best and most outstanding—at least with respect to its leader's own qualities (p. 19). Those who surround the Cardinal are classified as flatterers, jealous, self-serving (p. 18). The talk quickly centers on the condition of thieves in England, before it passes on to other circles in which the philosopher/councilor might hope and be supposed to find a useful place. The structure of the entire subsequent discussion may be indicated as follows (the finer details being omitted):

First discussion
  I. Base: Morton's society (paradigm of all, despite its central figure)
 II. Proposition: Raphael unacceptable as councilor in such a society
III. Discussion: 1. Condition of thieves
            Cause A: Idle, possessive rich
            Result: Servants, idlers turned out = beggars = robbers
               (pp. 21–23)
            Cause B: Greedy rich
            Result: Farmers turned off grazing land = beggars =
               robbers (pp. 24–26)
            Cause C: Luxury
            Result: Desire for ostentation = robbers (p. 27)
        2. Hytholodaeus's proposed cure (pp. 29–34)
             Example of Polylerites (pp. 31–34)
             i. refused by lawyer (p. 34)
     [2a. Cardinal's agreement with Hythlodaeus (pp. 34–35),
            and addition of vagrants
             ii. Accepted by all flatterers (p. 35)
       2b. Jester's agreement with H. and Morton, and addition of
            friars, etc. (pp. 35–36)]
             iii. General dispute, violent argument, break-up of
             discussion
 IV. QED II, given I.

Second discussion
  I. Base: French king's council (pp. 40 ff.)
 II. Proposition: same as II above
III. Discussion: 1. Cause B above: ways for king to possess more lands
              (pp. 40–42)
        2. Hythlodaeus's proposed cure (pp. 42–43)
             Example of Achorians, near Utopia (pp. 42–43)
             i. Refused by council (p. 43)
 IV. QED II, given I.

Third discussion
  I. Base: Any king's council (pp. 43 ff.)
 II. Proposition: same as II above
III. Discussion: 1. Cause A above: ways for king to possess more money
              (pp. 43–45)
             (Structure of discussion identical to above)
        2. Hythlodaeus's proposed cure (pp. 45–47)
             Example of Macarians, by Utopia (pp. 47–48)
             i. Refused by council (p. 48)
 IV. QED II, given I.

It is hardly necessary to belabor the matter by observing how this structure always returns to what I have termed the base (which rules the proposition), how it always, and necessarily, returns to its own point of departure. The form is that of the syllogism. Changes are out of the question.

It is worth observing, however, that Hythlodaeus's examples gradually bring us toward Utopia itself, that this tends to make of the discussion in the garden and of the narrative of Utopia yet a fourth general discussion on the acceptibility of Hythlodaeus as a philosopher/councilor, and finally that the recorder of this narrative (More) concludes with a rejection analogous to those that followed the other discussions: "though in other respects he [Raphael] is a man of the most undoubted learning as well as of the greatest knowledge of human affairs, I cannot agree with all that he said" (p. 152). Repetition is compounded: the second book becomes an expanded version of a segment of the first, the longest proof that even in the very best humanist society Raphael's healing would be unacceptable.

In terms of the text's 'literary' organization, one can easily see how each small system repeats the one before it, sometimes down to the very words: those who become thieves as a result of idleness (p. 22) and those who do so through greed (p. 25) are described in an almost identical way. And the above model is scarcely more schematic than is the text itself. This is simply underscored when the lawyer who first proposes to answer Hythlodaeus says that he will do so by repeating what has just been outlined: "First, I shall repeat, in order, what you have just said . . ." (p. 28). The model also indicates clearly how the second two discussions, while repeating in themselves the overall structure of the more extended first one, duplicate at the same time the two major causes (A and B) put forward in the first example.

At this point, More signals in effect all the difference between this organization and Hythlodaeus's efforts to break it by means of his proposed exemplary cures. This difference is precisely why Raphael's advice cannot be heeded, unless he tries half-measures—which can naturally only lead straight back into the aforementioned discursive contradictions:

> So it is in the commonwealth. So it is in the deliberations of monarchs. If you cannot pluck up wrongheaded opinions by the root, if you cannot cure according to your heart's desire vices of long standing, yet you must not on that account desert the commonwealth. You must not abandon the ship in a storm because you cannot control the winds.

On the other hand, you must not force upon people new and strange ideas which you realize will carry no weight with persons of opposite conviction. On the contrary, by the indirect approach you must seek and strive to the best of your power to handle matters tactfully. What you cannot turn to good you must make as little bad as you can. For it is impossible that all should be well unless all men were good, a situation which I do not expect for a great many years to come! [Pp. 49–50]

That impossibility is confirmed by More's own refusal at the end to "agree with all that he said."

Throughout the first book, Raphael's very proofs demonstrate that the discursive circularity can never be other than self-sustaining, *unless* it permits the necessary rupture. But such a rupture would destroy the discourse itself and replace it with a new structure. Raphael's tactful strategy is therefore to approach Utopia slowly and without making the fact evident: through the Polylerites in Persia, to the Achorians ("without place, region, district," p. 42, n. 95), and to the Marcarians ("The Happy, Blessed Ones," p. 47, n. 106), "a people not very far distant from Utopia" (p. 47). Tact makes the narration of the second book a repeated element of the first. Narration itself makes it 'incommensurable' with the entirely dialogized first book. It is as though we were confronted with a new kind of discursive practice, but without its being presented as such; as though the new were entirely contained in the first, even if, both by what it seeks to say and by how it says it, that new discourse fundamentally undermines the old.

For the world is mad, says Raphael. It speaks only to its own habitual systems: "I should accomplish nothing else than to share their madness as I tried to cure their lunacy" (p. 50). Raphael, emphasizing the example of Court, underlines the impossibility of breaking the circle from the inside (p. 52). All these small societies are closed structures: but so, too, is Utopia itself. Its very difference, signified as equality, abundance for all, pleasure, and so on (p. 53), is possible only so long as it retains the very organization that is being put in question. The will to action and possession that is placing these mini-societies in jeopardy is answered in Utopia only by a 'return' to an older nostalgia, and by an affirmation of the very discursive structure whose efficacy is now in doubt.

It is perfectly accurate to remark that Utopia *appears* to open up that structure: hence, for example, the tale of the shipwrecked Romans and Egyptians, "twelve hundred years ago," whose knowledge is absorbed. In Europe, it is said, the contrary would be the case: just as Raphael's advice is refused, so such knowledge would be quickly and completely forgotten (p. 56). We should, however, be wary of this. In Utopia, too, what can be absorbed is only what already coincides in some way with the system, just as More's critics can accept only what they have already heard, only what is habitual with them (pp. 7–8). The Utopians are as frozen in the text as all writing (*écriture*) seems to require:

> You know, Phaedrus, that's the strange thing about writing, which makes it truly analogous to painting. The painter's products stand before us as though they were alive, but if you question them, they maintain a most majestic silence. It is the same with written words; they seem to talk to you as though they were intelligent, but if you ask them anything about what they say, from a desire to be instructed, they go on telling you just the same thing forever.[15]

There is no discussing with written narrative, and what it affirms there is therefore no "hope of seeing realized" (p. 152). The dialogue of the first book admits discussion, but its only outcome is refusal of the very difference advanced in the narration. The issue remains ever the same.

The entire theme of *Utopia*, indeed, is the uselessness of the writing of it. At every moment, Hythlodaeus remarks that the new cure he brings will necessarily be refused by the (European) reader. The new word, separated from its true 'father' (Utopia itself, where Raphael's dead text would have been replaced by the living organism), cannot but remain without offspring. Caught, like Plato's *Phaedrus*, as both remedy and poison,[16] it is bound to remain outside the two organisms it describes, outside both Europe and Utopia: hence the absence at the center.

The entire text—or, more precisely, the bringer of the tale as inserted into the dialogic social situation the text presents—attempts to endow itself with a higher self-sufficiency than that of mere textual circularity. It strives to attain a particular kind of nonreferentiality: "One day I had been at divine service in Notre Dame. . . . Mass being over, I was about to return to my lodgings when I happened to see him [Giles] in conversation with a stranger" (p. 11). The text endeavors to place itself, as it were, under the sign of the Divine Word. That would permit the begging of the whole question of *absence,* in so far as for the Divinity the problem of reference or of

15. Plato, *Phaedrus,* 275d—Hackforth translation.
16. Cf. Jacques Derrida, "La pharmacie de Platon," in *La dissémination* (Paris, 1972), pp. 92–93. My debt to this work in the following dozen paragraphs is sufficiently obvious and extensive as to allow me to dispense with further acknowledgments.

signified is without meaning: for the Divinity the sign would be 'whole' and 'entire' (that is, it would not be a *sign* at all). The desire to report that Divinity in the text is why *Utopia* is 'impossible.' For it will be apparent that such divinity is the would-be role of Utopia itself. (I will note in passing here that the effort to incorporate some unmediated 'divinity' in the text is utterly different from what we will see as Kepler's project of organizing the diverse and multiple manifestations of some unmediatable "world soul" that characterizes the *Somnium*. It is just precisely that difference that makes Kepler a fruitful point of departure. for a new discourse of the future, while *Utopia* remains the mark of an inescapable discursive contradiction.)

If *Utopia* were able to achieve such incorporation, then the question of any logical *becoming*, of *process* founded upon an idea of difference, would be avoided. Though the problem of process may be present surreptitiously (and potentially subversively) in the text, the writer/narrator/reader here bypasses it by not naming it: it occurs between dialogue and narrative. The Utopians' own efforts to escape such process are indicated by their refusal of mediation, by the exclusion of money and usurers, of lawyers, by the search for the perfect *given* of "Greek" literature and for a language that seeks not to mediate but to *be* what it says. All these elements express a striving to incorporate the Word in the text—and with respect to *Utopia* the religious overtones are unavoidable. All these diverse efforts remain only approaches to such a goal. Their eventual failure is inescapable.

In Derrida's terms, *Utopia* is a genuinely "patricidal" text. The island itself cannot be precisely located (or even located at all). As I suggested earlier, it is in a sense absent from the very text that tries to narrate it. It has to be. The attempt to make present in the text the very denial of mediation is clearly doomed to failure. Utopia's presence would be the death of More's text, which exists nonetheless to relate the constant attempt to make Utopia present. But a text that genuinely denied the mediation which is all communication could be neither written nor read. Still, Utopia is not the only absent 'father' of the text: Hythlodaeus himself is gone from his own narrative. It is More who must relate him to us, in the third person. The text of *Utopia* seems remarkably torn between what it endeavors to do and what it is obliged to be. Part of what I will attempt to show in this volume is how the Renaissance and neoclassicism found a discursive solution to the 'impossibilities' of *Utopia*.

Utopia strives, then, to incorporate the 'Divine Word.' But mass is over, it *has been* said, and the word is passed not in church but in a garden. The Word cannot be attached directly to the text. No longer can any text have the virtually eucharistic posture of Abelard's correspondence. Only the separation can be written. More can only recapture *a* logos. He works, to adopt Derrida's terminology, on the interest, on the product of a capital that can no longer be touched. The description of Utopia will conclude with the divine service whose primary characteristic, we will see, is the attempt to dispense with discourse as mediation (p. 145). Unfortunately, the text that relates such an effort cannot do so.

Raphael, "healing of God," "most learned in Greek" (p. 12), is the doctor who would heal his listeners/readers by overcoming the absence subversively underscored in the text. Hythlodaeus, whose "sailing has not been like that of Palinurus but that of Ulysses or, rather, of Plato" (p. 12), is the would-be purger of humanity. He would rid humankind of its separation from the Divine. He would overcome the dichotomies of system. Indeed, the very combination of his name, Raphael ("healing of God") and Hythlodaeus ("learned in trifles"), eludes the utopian dichotomy of satire and vision that has been mentioned.

Raphael, however, is twice absent. He has related the tale to More who, in turn, writes him for us, the reader. Once the mediator and his mediation are introduced, there is an immediate proliferation— and I will recall here my earlier note about such writers as Fabri, Tory, and Palsgrave, with their production of an increasing number of "intermediary levels of signification." Raphael, like Theuth and Hermes, belongs in the no-place of Origin, denying mediation. Originally "Portuguese," now (perhaps) in the Low Countries, Hythlodaeus is a constant traveler (or he is *said* to be), who strives to reside in the infinite: "These two sayings are constantly on his lips: 'He who has no grave is covered by the sky,' and 'From all places it is the same distance to heaven'" (p. 13). His two sayings retreat beyond the two Delphic commands reported by Plato in the *Charmides* (164d–165b), whose "Know thyself" and "Nothing in excess" mark the accession to a certain kind of selfhood. Indeed, Colin Morris has referred to the Delphic "Know thyself" and to its duplicate in the Song of Songs ("If you do not know yourself, go forth") as "the two foundation-texts of the movement for self-exploration" in the twelfth century.[17] I argued that this self-knowing was not in any way a discovery of the self in a modern sense, but that it was entirely a mediatory passage to God. In retreating beyond these sayings, it is as though Raphael seeks to rediscover a 'wholeness' that would dispense with such mediation.

For the angelic Raphael is not the visitor of oracles, like More and

17. Colin Morris, *The Discovery of the Individual, 1050–1200* (New York, 1972), p. 78.

his reader. He *is* the oracle, right hand and messenger of God, mediator between God and man (*Tobit*, 12), bringer of the Word and, therefore, original introducer of mediation. Like Hermes, like Theuth to the Egyptians, like Prometheus to the Greeks, like his namesake to the Jews, Raphael has born the Word to the Utopians as he would now wish to do to the Europeans. Plato writes of Theuth: "He it was that invented number and calculation, geometry and astronomy, not to speak of draughts and dice, and above all writing" (*Phaedrus*, 274d). Like him, Raphael has sought to make the Divine Word available to the Utopians as human discourse. He has brought them Greek literature (whose language, it is asserted, is derived in the first place from that perfect source—along with Persian). In that, Raphael is not simply the bearer of origins; he is the healer who will return the Utopians to their own original condition.

The role is an ambiguous one, because like Hermes he risks destroying that condition in the very quest to restore it. It is also the role More would have him fill toward the Europeans, with the same risks. Not only does Raphael bring the Utopians 'their' literature, he brings them printing, the record of writing and yet another twice-removed mediation (pp. 106–7), similar to More's recounting of Hythlodaeus's tale of Utopia. Though the Utopians already have two games "not unlike chess," Raphael brings them knowledge (like Theuth) of dice, a kind of game they were "not acquainted with" prior to his arrival (p. 71). Since the aim of dicing is to make money it, too, is a double form of mediation (money itself being a mediation). When Raphael leaves Utopia, it is no longer clear that its inhabitants did not know the game before he came, since it is a "madness they know not by experience but by hearsay only." They now know it well enough to pass a condemning judgment upon it: "What pleasure is there, they ask, in shooting dice upon a table?" (p. 97). Yet inasmuch as both are forms of double mediation, we may well find ourselves inclined to ask why their knowledge of dicing should turn out to be any more innocent than that of printing, which they have put into operation without the slightest delay or hesitation.

Hythlodaeus has brought technology to the previously unmediated order of the Utopians with whom he was left by Vespucci (unmediated both internally, in respect to the discursive class, as we will see, and externally, because they were, until now, quite unknown). Without Raphael's continued presence, without the constant influence of the 'father,' it is carefully noted that these people may only too easily end up on the shoals of a misused technology: "there is a risk that what was likely to be a great benefit to them may, through their imprudence, cause them great mischief" (p. 15). The medicine is also a poison. This ambiguous contradiction runs right through the lesson in systematic combinations that is Raphael's discourse (now becoming text): "To be sure, just as he called attention to many ill-advised customs among these new nations, so he rehearsed not a few points from which our own cities, nations, races, and kingdoms may take example for the correction of their errors" (p. 15). These "corrections," we have just seen, may, however, cause "great mischief."

Raphael is the angelic man, bearer of a lost knowledge. In that sense he is not unlike his ubiquitous successors of following centuries; Cartesian man bearing knowledge to humanity. But his knowledge is not the self-created willful science of analytico-referential discourse. That is no doubt why, like the monstrous strangers in Racine's later tragedies who must be cast out before a new political society can be safety constituted, Hythlodaeus remains a "stranger" (p. 11), absent from what would have been his own text.[18] He possesses no *I* expressed in that text. Once his "promise" is made, the text has been sealed and no further process is possible. Raphael himself *is* the nonmediatory discourse whose expression is by definition impossible: hence both his absence and his apparent superiority to those with whom he comes in contact. He enjoys more "wit" and knowledge than those about him, needs no more of anything: "desirous neither of riches nor of power" (p. 17), he represents a perfect equilibrium. Carrier of the Divine Word, he has need of nothing and of no one, he is freed of all ostensibly social demands. Thus he *must* be absent, too, from his own text.

The pattern for the 'perfect state' is similar. The first thing the Utopians have done is cut off their land from any intercourse with the Other (by removing the neck of land that connected them to the mainland, p. 60). No state with any real material existence, it is implied, would (or could) do this, and that is why the second-best social system is both half-present in the text (it can be found "in Persia") and half-absent from it ("among the people commonly called the Polylerites"). The Polylerites compose

a nation that is large and well-governed and, except that it pays an annual tribute to the Persian padishah, otherwise free and autonomous in its laws. They are far from the sea, almost ringed round by mountains, and altogether satisfied with the products of their own land. In consequence they rarely pay visits to other countries or receive them. In

18. Reiss, *Tragedy and Truth*, esp. pp. 77, 243, 249–51, 255, 266–71, 280–81.

accordance with their long-standing national policy, they do not try to enlarge their territory and easily protect what they have from all aggression by their mountains and by the tribute payed to their overlord. Being completely free from militarism, they live a life more comfortable than splendid and more happy than renowned or famous, for even their name, I think, is hardly known except to their immediate neighbors. [P. 31]

The ambiguous intermediary position of this Persian state of the "people of much nonsense" is indicated by the constant hedging: "except that . . . , otherwise," "almost ringed round," "rarely." And what are we to make of a people whose name is "hardly known" being yet "*commonly called* the Polylerites"? They seem in fact to bear much the same relation to Utopia as does *archaic* Atlantis (before its imperialist impulses) to Plato's Ideal State or, again (and perhaps more to be emphasized here), as More to Hythlodaeus. These are the secondary mediators—or tertiary, if we start with the 'Divine Word.'

Hythlodaeus is presented to the reader as one who has the cure to the present ills of European politics and society. The entire discussion of the first book concerns the efficacy of this healer. Raphael asserts that Europe is already so far from common sense and the original justice of the rediscovered "new" world that no such cure would be accepted (the now-familiar opposition nature/culture, primitive/civilized is apparent here [p. 56], and "new" has not only the sense of unfamiliar, because previously unknown, but also that of being closer to its origins). The "stranger" speaks of Europe as of "sick bodies which are past cure [and which] can be kept up by repeated medical treatments" (p. 54). We have already mentioned More's reaction to such a view: "If you cannot pluck up wrong-headed opinions by the root, if you cannot cure according to your heart's desire vices of long standing, yet you must not on that account desert the commonwealth" (p. 49). But his own disagreement with Raphael at the end of the second book confirms that Hythlodaeus is right to reply as he does at this point.

His response seems in all ways inevitable. If he turns his back on the cure he has, on his immediate bearing of the Word, he will simply be including himself in the contradictory but fixed discourse that characterizes European practices of all kinds, practices which, by their very nature, betray the reality to which they supposedly refer and which they claim to present unproblematically. These practices have forgotten they play an entirely mediatory role:

"By this approach," he commented, "I should accomplish nothing else than to share the madness of others as I tried to cure their lunacy. If I would stick to the truth, I must needs speak in the manner I have described. To speak falsehoods, for all I know, may be the part of a philosopher, but it is certainly not for me. Although that speech of mine might perhaps be unwelcome and disagreeable to those councilors, yet I cannot see why it should seem odd even to the point of folly. What if I told them the kind of things Plato creates in his republic or which the Utopians actually put in practice in theirs? Though such institutions were superior (as, to be sure, they are), yet they might appear odd because here individuals have the right to private property, there all things are common." [P. 50]

Raphael wants to resolve a discursive contradiction by excluding an element that is becoming increasingly important as the only begetter of meaningful relations. He wishes to remove the *I* as enunciator and possessor of its own discourse, as creator and supporter of conflictual relations with other such enunciators. The future Euclidean mind is his enemy, and that is the real reason why Raphael must remain an exile from the courts of kings. Nations that seek to impose themselves (as certain kinds of text do as well), "where whatever a man has acquired he calls his own private property" (p. 53), must be hostile. As referential text would seek to trap the Word in the particular tale of its own telling, so the possessive *I* grasps the other. (It is perhaps worth recalling here that theocratic medieval discourse held that all property was ultimately the King's, and therefore in effect common to society as a whole inasmuch as the King was both society's microcosm and the direct mediator of God: society's laws, society itself, the King, God, and eternal Law could all be called by the same term, *anima*.)

Raphael's 'communistic' state is the necessary analogue of what we may call his 'antitext.' The very fact of its being written down is a denial of its own postulate. That is why the absence of all process is emphasized by the rupture at the center (between the first and second books). Plato snared Socrates in his text, the first in truth absorbing the second: why, in modern editions, does the death of Socrates invariably precede his subsequent dialogue? More has denied Raphael in his. For the written text, it is suggested, must deny 'real' communication ("telling you just the same thing forever"), just as the individualist state must deny 'real' society:

Where every man aims at absolute ownership of all the property he can get, be there never so great abundance of goods, it is all shared by a handful who leave the rest in poverty. It generally happens that the one class pre-eminently deserves the lot of the other, for the rich are greedy, unscrupulous, and useless, while the poor are well-behaved, simple, and by their daily industry more beneficial to the commonwealth than to themselves. I am fully persuaded that no just and even distribution of goods can be made and that no happiness can be found in human affairs unless private property is utterly abolished. While it lasts, there will always remain a heavy and inescapable burden of poverty and misfortune for by far the greatest and by far the best part of mankind. [Pp. 53–54]

More must perforce write this into his text and deny both it and its proponent as he does so: just because this "principal foundation of their whole structure" (p. 151) negates the very contradiction upon which his own discourse depends even as it strives to get around it. To cast aside conflictual possessive practices and return to an unmediated totality: there is the ideal. But the necessity of human mediation to achieve it demands that the discourse bearing that ideal be discarded in favor of some other, more efficacious. For, remarks Hythlodaeus, there cannot be "a cure and a return to the healthy condition as long as each individual is master of his own property." The one contradicts the other: "Nay, while you are intent upon the cure of one part, you make worse the malady of the other parts" (p. 54). Such will be the case, Raphael insists, until there can be a reciprocal healing, an overcoming of the contradiction, a return to the unity of organism: that is, by the existence of a situation that would deny any posture of mediation, and therefore the very existence of a text such as this. More, as writer, is constantly questioning the goals of his own text, closed upon itself in a permanent self-contradiction.

It is revealing that the question concerning the reliability of his text as a true affirmation of things, as an overcoming of the distance between words and things, should be put in terms of a dispute concerning the length of a *bridge* (p. 5). What is still more significant, however, is the decision simply to efface all doubts about it and allow the discourse itself to affirm the length, a discourse that will likewise choose to change it should it deem that useful: "If you agree with him, I shall adopt the same view and think myself mistaken. If you do not remember, I shall put down, as I have actually done, what I myself seem to remember" (p. 5). The bridge as an object is, of course, indifferent. It is the bridge as a sign of potential textual mediation of the exterior that is of interest, as a sign of the relation between system and things systematized. The uncertainty over the bridge's length corresponds, if you will, to the proliferation of mediatory signifying levels to which I have already referred. The contradictions become insoluble, and discourse passes out of its depth. The bridge, the distance, the relation, fluctuates according as the text requires. The very imperiousness of this requirement is what Hythlodaeus rejects. It is why he, in turn, is rejected. The inescapability of that fluctuation is also why Utopia itself must cast out and annul all the would-be arbitrators of difference, all the potential mediators of such distance. The exemplary forms of such arbitration here are money, language, society itself, and literature. We must take a look here at how these concepts and the practices accompanying them are dealt with by the Utopians.

The passage of money from measure of value to store of value (from token to capital), marked by the mercantilist ethic spreading throughout Europe since before the sixteenth century and clearly signaled, for example, by Copernicus only ten years after the publication of *Utopia*, is evidenced in More's text.[19] For Raphael (or rather, Utopia), money as capital and interest, as possessing any other than simple use value, is the cause not only of all economic ills but of every vice current in a capitalist society: "it appears to me that wherever you have private property and all men measure things by cash values, then it is scarcely possible for a commonwealth to have justice and prosperity" (p. 52). That, too, is why, among the Polylerites, the further corrupting gift of money to a prisoner (already guilty of having attempted to corrupt society in some way) is considered a capital offense (pp. 32–33), and it is why

> in Utopia all greed for money was entirely removed with the use of money. What a mass of troubles was then cut away! What a crop of crimes was then pulled up by the roots! Who does not know that fraud, theft, rapine, quarrels, disorders, brawls, seditions, murders, treasons, poisonings, which are avenged rather than restrained by daily executions, die out with the destruction of money? Who does not know that fear, anxiety, worries, toils, and sleepless nights will also perish at the same time as money? What is more, poverty, which alone money seemed to make poor, forthwith would itself dwindle and disappear if money were entirely done away with everywhere. [P. 149]

For the Utopians, treasure in gold and silver has only such value as the use to which it can be put: as chamber pots, as chains for

19. On Copernicus's theories and for a translation of his principal text on the matter see Timothy J. Reiss and Roger H. Hinderliter, "Money and Value in the Sixteenth Century: The *Monete cudende ratio* of Nicholas Copernicus," *Journal of the History of Ideas*, 40 (1979), 293–313.

prisoners, and as symbols on the convict's person of his misdemeanors. Money is given no chance to proliferate usuriously or create activities whose sole purpose is in such proliferation: "For, in a society where we make money the standard of everything, it is necessary to practice many crafts which are quite vain and superfluous, ministering only to luxury and licentiousness" (p. 72). The absence of money from the Utopian system comes up many times in the course of the narrative (pp. 63, 77, 85, for example). It is indeed a major factor in the "principal foundation" of their society: "their common life and subsistence—without any exchange of money" (p. 151).

The Utopians keep a store of treasure only because it can be used to buy mercenaries on behalf of nations who work by money. It is kept uncoined until it is so needed: that is to say, though the Utopians accept gold and silver in foreign trade, it is kept quite out of circulation within their community and has no opportunity to pass from use to capital. But this storage of precious metals is not a means to prevent its leaving the country; it is not the measure of the island's wealth, as a later mercantilist ethic might maintain. It is merely that the Utopians have no internal use for it. Internally, indeed, money can never even become mediation (pp. 84–89): the inhabitants are too well aware of its "true nature." For the same reason, treasure must never be *merely* hoarded (simply for its own sake, that is; p. 97).

The Utopians are possessed by the wise fear lest money become the only meaning of production (what a later analysis will refer to as its "fetishization"). They are apprehensive lest the text replace what it can at very best only hope to mediate: "They wonder, too, that gold, which by its very nature is so useless, is now everywhere in the world valued so highly that man himself, through whose agency and for whose use it got this value, is priced much cheaper than gold itself . . . as if he were a mere appendage of and addition to the coins!" (p. 89). In every other society, Raphael asserts, money has indeed replaced human necessities or human pleasure as the sole meaning of production and of the circulation of goods. The system of mediation has replaced what it mediated. It is just because money is 'patricidal' in this way that it must be banished from Utopia.

The same holds true of language. Inasmuch as systematic communication is necessary, language is necessary. Nonetheless, that of the Utopians strives to come as close to something like direct apprehension as it may. Their entire effort is concentrated on reducing language to a minimal mediation, which is why "Greek" comes so easily to them.

Throughout the sixteenth century, Greek (along with Hebrew, no doubt) was considered by the humanist grammarians, poeticians, and philologists to be the nearest thing to a natural 'unmediated' language known to men. It was supposed to allow so precise an expression of, to be in so perfect a correlation with, concepts and things immediately apprehended as to come very close to not being a symbolic system at all. For Greek, argues Ramus (or, as he would have it in this case, "old Gaulish," which he claims to be early Greek), dates from the time when "languages were still whole," when *raison* and *oraison,* parts of speech and 'parts of reason,' were coincident, not conventionally or arbitrarily, but essentially.[20]

The terms used by Raphael to describe the Utopians' language are almost identical to those used later by so many writers to describe Greek: "their native tongue . . . is copious in vocabulary and pleasant to the ear and a very faithful exponent of thought. It is almost the same as that current in a great part of that side of the world, only that everywhere else its form is more corrupt, to different degrees in different regions" (p. 90). Words, however, remain nothing but insufficient surrogates (despite their approach to perfect presentation), and as far as possible should give way to the thing itself: "If a person does not regard nature, do you suppose he will care anything about words?" asks Raphael, as he discusses the Utopians' refusal to make use of written treaties (which are therefore already a dead letter, p. 116). The same attitude is held toward laws (p. 114)—a point that will later be stressed by Montaigne among many others (in "De l'expérience," for example): laws should be few, simple, and pleaded by those most immediately concerned so that the situation is more in evidence than the law whose interpretation may concern it.

No innate mediatory power is granted to language. It has no value of its own, any more than has money. It has what is strictly a use value, and any meaning apart from that use is eschewed. Yet here, too, the contradictions are apparent, for the effort to avoid mediation leads straight back into it. Thus even (or especially) the word

20. Pierre de la Ramée, *Traitté des meurs et façons des anciens Gavloys, traduit du latin* [de 1559] *par* Michel de Castelnau (Paris, 1581), p. 53ʳ. See also, e.g., Henri Estienne, *Conformité du langage français avec le grec* [1562], ed. Léon Feugère (Paris, 1853), pp. 18–19, and his *La précellence du langage françois* [1579], ed. Edmond Huguet (Paris, 1896), pp. 10 ff. The same arguments are to be found in the Italian and English writers on the subject, particularly those around Roger Ascham (see, e.g., diverse remarks scattered throughout *The Scholemaster* [1570]). The terms *raison/oraison* (*ratio/oratio*) are used by (among many others) John Palsgrave, *L'eclaircissement de la langue française* [1530], ed. F. Genin (Paris, 1852), pp. xxivff. See also Geofroy Tory, *Champ fleury ou l'art et science de la proportion des lettres* [1529], ed. Gustave Cohen (Paris, 1931), passim.

denoting the Divinity is held to be arbitrary and conventional, not able to become capital in itself, or interest either: "They invoke God by no name except that of Mithras. By this word *they agree to represent* the one nature of the divine majesty *whatever it be*" (p. 143, my italics). The whole difficulty of textualizing the Word may be seen in this confrontation between the avowedly conventional and arbitrary name Mithras and the supposed unnameable totality which is God. As soon as mediation is admitted, essence ("whatever it be") disappears and becomes utterly unattainable.

The effort to overcome that flaw remains, however. It is because language is viewed in this way that the Utopians are so far "from ability to speculate on second intentions" (p. 90) that only the direct apprehension of the nature of things in "first intentions" is meaningful to them (though the term "meaningful" is perhaps misleading here: for the Utopians, things *are* before they acquire meaning—as we saw in the case of Augustine).[21] Since their language is viewed by them as at best an inefficient mediation, the second intention, which may be held as residing only in discursive systematization, has no role in their conceptual process. It might well be asserted, indeed, that pure sound would be the only means by which second intentions could be avoided: for words inevitably produce the intellect's reflection upon itself, upon its manner of comprehending, and upon the manner of the existence of a thing in the intellect. And the Utopians' 'universal' language does tend toward such a pure ideal. Only thus could there be an expression and communication of immediate (unmediated) sensible apprehension:

> All their music, whether played on instruments or sung by the human voice, so renders and expresses the natural feelings, so suits the sound to the matter (whether the words be supplicatory, or joyful, or propitiatory, or troubled, or mournful, or angry), and so represents the meaning by the form of the melody that it wonderfully affects, penetrates, and inflames the souls of the hearers. [P. 145]

In so ideal a situation, words serve no purpose at all.

Unfortunately, the ideal situation is somewhat elusive. Utopia has found itself obliged to cross the threshold of a 'Euclidean' textuality even before Raphael and More combine to kill the ideal for good.

21. Surtz, p. 90 n. 9: "Whereas the first intention is the direct apprehension of a thing according to its nature, the second is the form resulting from the intellect's triple reflection: upon itself, upon its way of apprehension, and upon the manner in which the nature of a thing exists in the intellect."

Despite all its efforts to remain in the realm of the *pharmakon,* Utopia in the text is among the most repetitively systematized of all ideal states. Nor is it the least militaristic, the least aggressively willful—even if only in its external relations. Nonetheless, within the limits of its own 'geographical' (and discursive) boundaries, it does strive toward the complete reduction of mediation. There, its system seeks (in vain, once textualized) to cancel the bonds of mediated System.

For the very structured social organization of Utopia also corresponds to such a search to reject mediation. The patriarchal society is founded on a kind of pyramidal familial organization (always ruled by the father), according to which the family 'proper' is the basic form of increasingly large units: family, agricultural groupings, sets of thirty families, of three hundred, city, state, each under its own patriarch (pp. 61, 67). The goal of the state is the equal satisfaction of the material and intellectual needs of all its citizens, and the highest aim is a "pleasure" that signifies a complete harmony with "nature": "The Utopians define virtue as living according to nature since to this end we were created by God" (pp. 92–93). Ideally this pleasure would cancel all dichotomies, and humankind, considered both as 'individual' and as society as a whole, would be absorbed into the patterns of an enfolding totality, the Divine itself.[22]

It is not without reason that Guillaume Budé, in his letter-preface to the 1517 Paris edition, remarks that primitively organized society, Utopia, "is itself divided into many cities, but they all unite and harmonize in one state, named Hagnopolis" ('pure' or 'sacred' city).[23] Yet it is in fact striving for a *lost* unity. Utopia *was once* named Abraxa, while the *unknown* Deity is named Mithras, two words once supposed to be in some unmediated contact with the Divine: Abraxas, whose component letters in the Greek numerical system make 365, was the name given by Basilides the Gnostic to the highest of his 365 heavens; while Mithras, a name with the numerical value of 360, denotes "roughly the number of days it takes the sun to complete its cycle."[24] The words are both sacred and contain in their very composition an immediate relation (supposed) with the yearly and seasonal cycles.

The society strives to avoid becoming a system of mediated process. It functions as a single, totalizing organism that seeks as few

22. For the discussion of pleasure, see esp. pp. 92–103. The matter is taken up at length by Surtz in *The Praise of Pleasure: Philosophy, Education, and Communism in More's "Utopia"* (Cambridge, Mass., 1957).
23. Letter to Thomas Lupset, in Surtz and Hexter, *Complete Works* ed., p. 13.
24. Surtz, *Selected Works* ed., p. 60 n. 5, p. 130 n. 5.

bonds as possible with an exterior. That is why its entire 'exchange' system is internal (if, indeed, it may be called 'exchange' at all). From other lands it needs scarcely anything but iron (p. 84), while its own list of exports is relatively large: "a great quantity of grain, honey, wool, linen, timber, scarlet and purple dyestuffs, hides, wax, tallow, leather, as well as livestock" (p. 83). Apart from iron, the only appreciable imported commodity is "a great quantity of silver and gold" (p. 84). As we know, this is quite useless to them as a merchandise for the internal market and, because it is obtained simply to be in accord with their neighbors' systems of exchange, cannot really be classified as an 'import' at all (that they receive it as bullion though the process would rather require they obtain it in the form of coin is another sign of contradiction).

This bullion can be used, again, only in an outgoing direction, and even then in a peculiarly pure and direct form of 'exchange' that in effect maintains the Utopians' own absence from it. They use this bullion only to pay off foreign mercenaries in wars fought on behalf of those other peoples from whom they acquired the gold and silver in the first place (pp. 84, 122–23). So little need have they of exchange with the exterior that the greatest percentage of the trade balance takes the form of "credit," for most of which "the Utopians never claim payment" (p. 84). As a social and economic organization, Utopia strives toward the 'original' state of nonmediation, just as it does with respect to those other forms of mediation of which it is perforce obliged to make use.

As such a social organism, Utopia remains decidedly ambiguous. Though it may be removed (both formally and topically) from the emerging 'Euclideanism' of European societies, it remains very far distant from the perfected, nonmediated totalizing organism of theocratic theory. Utopia does need its healer, if less than most. The medical works brought by Hythlodaeus and his companion (the gods of mediation are also those of medicine), while of considerable interest to the Utopians as "a branch of philosophy," are of no physical use to them: "there is scarcely a nation in the whole world that needs medicine less" (pp. 105–6). Real medicine in the eyes of the Utopians is a kind of 'pure' mediation between the world and humankind—'pure' because it operates with things instead of with the names of things. That does not make it an unmediated form, and while the island inhabitants may need medicine "less," they still need it.

The Utopian social organization pursues an urge toward 'primitivity.' But it is a highly sophisticated organization and can therefore only strive in vain. That is why it does have some need of a healer.

Inscribed within More's text (and Raphael's before him), it is already seized in writing. It has no option. Yet it strives at all points to deny that it is so seized.

Emile Durkheim, among others, has studied at some length the ritual exile of the new initiate into primitive societies. The initiate must expiate the diverse interdictions that help compose society's structure. Marcel Mauss, in his turn, showed how in ancient Rome, for example, the very nonstatus of the slave represented a permanent exile from the structure of the civil organization *in equilibrium*.[25] Exile, in some more or less ritualized form, seems to be the manner in which 'organic' societies maintain a 'perfect' equilibrium: as though it were expelling the destabilizing or sick element (let us recall once again Raphael as a "stranger" and Racine's asocial monsters). So, at least, is the manner in which they *signify* the maintenance of such equilibrium. Again, the ideology of such societies would affirm that the doing and the signifying are identical. It is no doubt the case that *any* system will have to find some way of excluding whatever threatens its order. In an analytico-referentially organized society, the solution tends to be enclosure. It is a perfectly logical solution. For such a society claims to be open-ended and always in expansion. The only way, therefore, to be certain of protecting itself from elements of menace is by sealing them up within the system: if it merely excluded them, it would always run the risk of catching up with the threat once again. A society that conceives itself as a self-sufficient total organism can use exclusion: either exile or slavery. Moreover, as in Utopia, such exile is redeemable, for the reabsorption of once undesirable elements then occurs when society wishes and not simply as part of an irrepressible process (p. 112).

In Utopia slavery is so much the standard punishment for what society takes to be crimes against itself that it may almost be said to be the only one (p. 112). It is genuinely a civil exile, slaves being the only ones who are totally excluded from the entire set of civil relationships. In them the social organization is turned on its head: they work constantly and as a punishment, instead of intermittently and as a pleasurable service to the commonwealth (p. 108); they wear chains of gold as a sign of disgrace, while citizens wear nothing to restrict their freedom and no signs of rank whatsoever (p. 86). Slaves are truly a mirror image of society. Death, the only other punish-

---

25. Emile Durkheim, *Les formes élémentaires de la vie religieuse: Le système totémique en Australie* (Paris, 1912), pp. 441 ff.; Marcel Mauss, "Une catégorie de l'esprit humain: La notion de personne, celle de 'Moi,'" in *Sociologie et anthropologie* (Paris, 1950), pp. 331–62.

ment used as a rule by Utopian society as a public discipline, is only inflicted for repeating a fault already punished by slavery (p. 112).

One exception is recorded, and it is extremely revealing. It concerns the single case of an attempt to persuade the Utopians to institutionalize *difference* within their social organization, to create and accept a definitive dichotomy in the civil organism. The case is that of a zealous new Christian who tries to convince them that his belief is the only one corresponding to reality. His argument, then, does not only demand that social divisions be installed; it also insists upon the referential truth of sign systems as it can be instituted by human decision (what Hobbes will later refer to in his introduction to *Leviathan* as the human "*Fiat*").

The guilty verdict is automatically followed by the offender's exile. Indeed, adds Raphael, there was no choice in the matter for his judges: exile or slavery being the obligatory punishment for such an offense (p. 133). All the punishments mentioned are, clearly, forms of exclusion, whether slavery, exile, or death. They represent the social means of maintaining that wholeness of the organism of which the refusal of money and the search for a language that denies its mediatory role are also characteristic. We may perhaps, though hesitatingly, add literature to the types of discourse just mentioned, though there are few references to what we may call 'literature.' Raphael's remarks about reading and writing seem to be concerned with 'moral' and 'philosophical' letters. Prior to his having brought them printing and the *given* of Greek, public literature seems to have consisted only in reading aloud to accompany meals. This oral/written opposition in the present context tends to confirm what we have seen elsewhere: a striving to escape mediation confronted with its inevitability (on "literature," see pp. 81, 89–90, 106). The three (or four) types of discourse, then—money, language, society, and literature—all attempt to remain as near as possible to a state of 'undifferentiation,' to a condition where there would be no division between self and other, between individual and society, between object and value, between the Word and the world, between the human and the Divine. The Utopians strive toward the wholeness of an organism that they seem nonetheless to recognize obscurely as belonging to an irrecoverable past. Raphael must mediate to them, just as through More he mediates to us.

More's writing is the most tense, indeed the most embarrassed, of utopias. Striving to return to a nostalgic no-time (*illud tempus*), to the theocratic wholeness of a 'medieval' organic society, or to an ever postponed process of Derridian *différance* (perhaps), Utopia is already trapped in the text necessary to mediate it: hence the circularity of that text, with its lack of process signaled by the hole at the center—circular dialogue, repetitive narrative, the latter sealed in the former by the barrier of Raphael's promise and its repetition of the structure that already controls the dialogue.

The text that seeks to *embody* some nontextual Reality concludes by being able to *signify* only itself. In effect More concludes: "I cannot agree with what I have just finished writing." And that disagreement focuses on the very "feature which is the principal foundation of their whole structure. I mean their common life and subsistence—without any exchange of money" (p. 151). No doubt More, the real person, is now commenting satirically upon his own text; but that simply reinforces our point: he is echoing a general view that such a society as sought by the Utopians belongs, if anywhere, in a past that is no more than a memory. Indeed, the satire that the text is comments not only on the society of More's time but also on that of the Utopians. Utopian organicism is no more possible than the 'new' European societies are desirable. The satirical aspect of the text, therefore, by the "shifting of the traditional values of words," succeeds in subverting the text from within:

> he says that Utopian communism would deprive a commonwealth of "nobility, magnificence, splendor, and majesty, which are, in the estimation of the common people, the true glories and ornaments of the commonwealth" [p. 151]. The reference to the "estimation of the common people" only reinforces the satirical thrust of this list of "true glories." For earlier in the book More has already switched the signs on three out of four of these traditionally honorific terms—nobility, splendor, majesty. Of commonwealths they are not the true but the false glories.[26]

This ambiguity, this subversion from within endemic to More's text, will later be seized upon by Swift, who turns it inside out and makes the medicine overtly a poison (but he is unable, as we shall see, to switch the signs at all). Even in that case the ambiguity is not entirely evacuated, as the endlessly contradictory critical lucubrations over and 'clarifications' of *Gulliver's Travels* testify only too well. *Gulliver* after, like *Utopia* before, brings the profoundest of critiques to bear on such texts as *New Atlantis* and *Robinson Crusoe*. But *Gulliver* criticizes a class of discourse without being able to break out of its

---

26. J. H. Hexter, "The Composition of *Utopia*," in Surtz and Hexter, *Complete Works* ed., p. liii; see also p. lii.

limits. *Utopia* necessitates the development of it. In More's text the tension is essential and inescapable: it is the contradictory attempt to mediate what cannot be mediated. The writing appears to want to show that Utopia itself *is* the inexpressible. It cannot be mediated. Nor can it mediate, and that is no doubt the reason for More's ultimate 'disclaimer.'

Utopia is a far cry from the 'paternalistic' texts of a later era. More seeks to deny the linear textuality of his writing: they will its imposition. Utopia would have been the unmediated, pretextual Word, the rediscovered organic, patterned, and conjunctive society. To attempt its embodiment in the texture of *Utopia* is necessarily a contradiction. No more than any other text of the period can More's writing rediscover the soul's transcendent passage to God or society's to wholeness. The real absence at the center of this text is the no-place of Utopia itself, the antitext that denies More its inscription. And before the event, it denies the possibility of the narration of knowledge in the neoclassical sense of some permanent truth concerning a reality not itself discursive.

The "antitext" asserts that society cannot be simply the result of a contractual agreement between equally possessive individuals, an arrangement to put a halt to the constant struggle for "power after power" characteristic of Hobbesian natural man and of the Machiavellian state. It gives the lie to the later practice of literature as the self-assured moral and didactic discourse of an educated elite. It repudiates the use of money as capital 'replacing' the commodities whose exchange it facilitates—and if the travels of a Sir Walter Ralegh become the future metaphor of a new concept of knowledge and action, so too his exemplary mercantilist opinions about money run quite counter to the Utopians': "Where there is store of gold, it is in effect nedeles to remember other commodities for trade."[27] Such a view would clearly be anathema to Raphael, and utterly foreign to the Utopians.

Utopia suggests that any discourse that occults its own discursivity (as analytico-referential discourse will eventually do) is merely blind to what is most essential to it. Terence Cave has recently proposed that in certain kinds of Renaissance writing this blindness is de-occulted. At first this leads to a kind of outpouring of discursivity itself, a flood of writing whose lost totalizing meaning is not yet

27. Sir Walter Ralegh, *The Discoverie of the Large, Rich, and Bewtiful Empyre of Guiana, With a Relation of the Great and Golden Citie of Manoa* . . . (London, 1596), p. 95. The exemplary representatives of views such as these are, of course, writers and traders like Gerard Malynes and Thomas Mun.

replaced by any specifiable direction of signification, taking its origin for example in the intentionality of a subject. He thus writes of Montaigne: "All that the *Essais* can do, with their ineradicable self-consciousness, is to posit paradigms of wholeness as features of a discourse which, as it pours itself out, celebrates its own inanity."[28] On at least one occasion, this leads Montaigne to imagine the existence of a mediation-free society not entirely dissimilar to what we have seen in *Utopia*:

> It is a nation, would I answer *Plato*, that hath no kind of traffike, no knowledge of Letters, no intelligence of numbers, no name of magistrate, nor of politike superioritie; no use of service, of riches or of povertie; no contracts, no successions, no partitions, no occupation but idle; no respect of kinred, but common, no apparell but naturall, no manuring of lands, no use of wine, corne, or mettle.[29]

The emergence of analysis out of patterning as we will see it in Kepler, its elaboration in Bacon and his successors, its consolidation as the dominant discourse at the end of the seventeenth century: all this development is a response to the contradictions of an earlier discourse that is no longer able to function satisfactorily as a whole conceptual system. *Utopia* was an exemplary case.

28. Terence Cave, *The Cornucopian Text: Problems of Writing in the French Renaissance* (Oxford, 1979), p. 321.

29. Michel de Montaigne, "On Cannibals," in *Montaigne's Essays,* tr. John Florio, intro. L. C. Harmer, 3 vols. (1910; rpt. London and New York, 1965), I.220 (I.xxx—the essay is I.xxxi in French editions).

4 · *Kepler, His* Dream, *and the Analysis and Pattern of Thought*

What, I may be asked, is the use of knowing nature, and what use is the whole of astronomy on an empty stomach? . . . Painters and musicians are tolerated because they delight our senses, though they are of no use to us. The pleasure their work gives us is considered decent and even honorable in man. What abject ignorance and stupidity to withhold from the mind what is willingly granted to the eyes and ears! Whoever is against such delight is against nature itself.

—Johannes Kepler, *Dedicatio* to *Mysterium cosmographicum*

Galileo's telescope marks a total distancing of the mind from the world and the imposition upon that world of a system which belongs to the realm of discourse. It is as though the system expressed the essential structure of the world by becoming that world (so Descartes, in *Le monde,* invents a fiction of the world which by the end of the text is understood to express the essential nature of *our* world). The system is not restrained or bound by the fundamentally perspectival nature of the human mind. It is taken as a form of mediation dependent upon the actuality of the world in such a way that eventually all "qualitative phenomena" of whatever kind will be seen as "causally dependent upon spatio-temporal occurrences in some simple unilateral way."[1] The relationship between the distancing in question and this subsequent imposition of the system is emphasized suggestively by the fact that Ramus, who has already been mentioned in this connection, is one of the first to endorse wholeheartedly the Copernican system.[2]

1. Aron Gurwitsch, "Galileo's Physics in the Light of Husserl's Phenomenology," in Ernan McMullin, ed., *Galileo, Man of Science* (New York, 1967), p. 399.

2. See the *Scholae physicae,* and especially his celebrated letter to Rheticus: Marie Delcourt [ed. and tr.], "Une lettre de Ramus à Joachim Rheticus (1563)," *Bulletin de l'Association Guillaume Budé,* no. 44 (July 1934), pp. 3–15.

Scientific discourse sought first of all to grasp an exterior, coming to view itself as a simple translation of the world of objects into a conceptual order. It claimed there was an adequately explicable correspondence between a referent supposed to be in nature and a sign which was assumed to mediate the other entirely passively. The order itself was to become ever more 'simplified' (and thus more generalized) as it was refined to the point of representation in mathematical, algebraic, or logical notations. The order of representation became a shorthand, and the shorthand became the world. A simple purpose was served. It was a matter, declared Descartes, of finding a "practical philosophy" which would allow men to "become as masters and possessors of nature." "Legitimate" knowledge, Bacon had already affirmed some thirty years earlier (c. 1607), involved the "invention of further means to endow the condition and life of man with new powers or works."[3]

The quotation from Kepler's *Dedicatio* to the *Mysterium cosmographicum* (1596) which heads this chapter places that scientist squarely among those whom Bacon criticizes as seeking knowledge merely "for delight and satisfaction."[4] Though the future Chancellor does not name Kepler (even assuming him to have been in a position to have done so), it would be little wonder if he had. For Kepler, in this first work of his on astronomy, uses a possible quantitative mathematical discourse as a part of a discourse of patterning. Even when he applies this discourse to the planetary movements, beginning in 1599 (but the *Astronomia nova* will appear only in 1609), the same practice is revealed, as Gérard Simon has shown. The analytical ordering does not replace the older discourse which performs a semi-concealed connection between concrete events outside the mind and some sort of logical order. It is simply a part of the performance of that connection, a composition of the mind as in some way bound to those concrete events: the world is not outside the mind, it is its container bound to it.

By means of this patterning, the mind 'subordinates' itself to an order of concrete events exterior to it, though that is an analytical way of putting it. Emphasizing a lack of accountability in terms of some *real* or of some *truth,* the discourse of patterning, at least as it

3. René Descartes, *Discours de la méthode*, in *Oeuvres philosophiques*, ed. Ferdinand Alquié, 3 vols. (Paris, 1963–73), I.634; Francis Bacon, *Filum labyrinthi, sive formula inquisitionis*, in *The Works of Francis Bacon*, ed. James Spedding, R. L. Ellis, and D. D. Heath (1857–59; rpt. Boston, 1863), VI.420. This kind of remark is of course constant in Bacon.
4. Bacon, *Filum labyrinthi*, p. 419.

appears in Kepler's work, is able even to indicate the ludic nature of all 'choices' concerning the form of what contains it. For the semes attached to the elements composing the pattern are not at all limited. In a letter to his friend Joachim Tanck at the time of the *Astronomia nova*, Kepler is able to write:

> I play, indeed, with symbols, and I have started a book called *The Geometric Cabbala*, which is concerned with reaching the forms of natural objects by means of geometry. But when I play, I never forget that I *am* playing. For nothing is proved in symbols alone; nothing hidden is arrived at in natural philosophy by geometrical symbols . . . unless it is shown by conclusive reasons to be not only symbolic but to be an account of the connections between things and their causes.[5]

All phenomena are thus subject to an unlimited series of interpretations, and any 'explanation' to a limitless series of variations. This is why Kepler is not "prevented" (as Arthur Koestler puts it) from discovering his three laws of planetary movement, "despite" his organization of the universal order as a superimposition upon one another of the five Pythagorean solids, whose proportions would correspond to the progression of the distances of the five known planets from the sun. And for Kepler it is indeed a question of an order in the divine intellect, corresponding to some manifestation of the "world soul." The possibility of varying the details of the elaborated pattern allowed him, thanks to the precision of Tycho's figures, to find the first 'real' laws of nature.[6] So Koestler. But that is to "ruin" Kepler's edifice to some extent. For Kepler did not betray his fidelity to that pattern, as may be seen from the *Harmonice mundi* of 1618. The German scientist viewed this work as the very capstone of his labors.

He indicates that the analytical discourse (of causality, for example) is only a form of shorthand for a part of the older discourse. It is a special case of interpretation. That is why Kepler himself attached but small importance in the *Harmonice* to his three laws, organized as one more element in a discourse of patterning. For him, the notion of harmony was the principal one. It is true, as Wolf-

5. Johannes Kepler, *Opera omnia*, ed. Christian Frisch, 8 vols. (Frankfurt, 1858–71), I.378, quoted by Ernst Cassirer, "Mathematical Mysticism and Mathematical Science," tr. E. W. Strong, in McMullin, *Galileo*, p. 349. Cassirer calls this "the key to his [Kepler's] entire life's work."
6. Article "Kepler," in *Encyclopedia of Philosophy*, ed. Paul Edwards (New York, 1967), IV.329–33; see also Arthur Koestler, *The Sleepwalkers: A History of Man's Changing Vision of the Universe* (New York, 1963), pp. 247 ff.

gang Pauli has noted, that in Kepler's argument a symbolic structure (an order of discourse, as I would call it) precedes and leads to the discovery of natural laws and the production of events in the world —though Kepler does not so produce them. That is an order of operation corresponding to one of Lévi-Strauss's definitions of the functioning of a scientific logic.[7] However, those events are then treated, as Simon demonstrates, as "remains and debris" inserted into the "overall" structure which they help to compose, to elaborate, and to "understand." In 1618 they are a part of the greater harmony (into which the third law will also be injected), but far from organizing that harmony, they are seen merely as a part of its pattern. So much is that the case that later commentators have often accused Kepler of having "buried" his laws. They do not control events, they are one element in a vaster pattern in which both man and the world are orchestrated, and whose benefit is not that it can be *used* for the material betterment of mankind but simply that it gives joy and delight: the words which are constantly at the tip of Kepler's pen to characterize his enterprise are *gaudium, laetitia,* and *voluptas.*

The considerable increase in the production of utopias and analogous formulations from this period on appears not so much an attempt to reaffirm a disappearing class of discourse (that of patterning) as the mark of its production of analytico-referential discourse and its gradual occultation by it. Kepler's *Somnium* was published in 1634, but it had been written over a period of many years: its initial conception coinciding with the period of the *Mysterium cosmographicum* (or even slightly earlier, when he was still a student at Tübingen), the writing of the text of the dream occurring around 1609, that of the notes between 1621 and 1630. Simon has remarked that if one were to measure the respective importance of Kepler's astronomical works in time then it is the *Rodolphine Tables* which occupy the greatest place in his researches (from 1601 to 1624).[8] In

7. Wolfgang Pauli, "The Influence of Archetypal Ideas on the Scientific Theories of Kepler," in Carl Gustav Jung and W. Pauli, *The Interpretation of Nature and the Psyche* (New York, 1955), pp. 151–240; Claude Lévi-Strauss, *The Savage Mind* (Chicago, 1966), pp. 19–21.

8. Gérard Simon, *Kepler, astronome astrologue* (Paris, 1979), p. 421. The original edition of the *Somnium* has recently been published in facsimile: *Ioh. Keppleri Mathematici olim Imperatori Somnium, seu Opus Posthumum de Astronomia Lunari.* Divulgatum à M. Ludovice Kepplero Filio, Frankfurt, 1634, ed. Martha List and Walter Gerlach (Osnabrück, 1969). The work is in vol. 8 of the *Opera omnia.* There are two American translations: John Lear, *Kepler's Dream, with the full text and notes of* Somnium, sive astronomia lunaris, Joannis Kepleri, tr. Patricia F. Kirkwood (Berkeley and Los Angeles, 1965); and *Kepler's Somnium: The Dream, or Posthumous Work on Lunar Astronomy,* tr. with a commentary by Edward Rosen (Madison, Milwaukee, and London, 1967).

fact that place would rather appear to be occupied by the lunar speculations of the *Somnium,* since the conception dates from his university days while the text as we have it appeared only posthumously. He returned to it intermittently throughout his life, notably with the addition of the majority of the notes after 1620, having concluded the *Harmony* and the summing-up of the *Epitome of Copernican Astronomy* (1618–21). It is almost as though the *Dream* text posed a constant problem that Kepler eventually sought to elucidate in his notes by the use of an analytical tool developed elsewhere. In doing so he accumulates a series of possible readings of the text.

The *Somnium* is presented deliberately as corresponding at once to literary and scientific preoccupations. The latter occupy the central portion of the text of the *Dream* and most of the notes, the former appear most particularly in the prologue and the conclusion. I will suggest that the text fairly clearly divides, therefore, a discourse of patterning from one of analysis and reference. I will propose that the notes represent the appearance from within a discourse of patterning of the order of what will shortly become the dominant discourse.

The notes are a series of propositions *intended* to explain what "occurs" in the *Dream* itself. They place various types of order in a text which does not otherwise distinguish such types. Together they compose a series of different analyses in which the two most notable elements, apart from the analysis itself, are the constant claim to objective referentiality (corresponding to the implication that a variety of realities are being analyzed) and the equally constant imposition of the knowing *I,* of the enunciating self of the *cogito.* The series of analyses thus performed by Kepler, each of which seeks to provide a specific *meaning* for the text, are discussions of allegory, autobiography (both fictive and real), science, scientific methodology, literary fiction itself, and, to the extent that it enters into certain of the others, history.[9] The several analytical systems all correspond to

---

In the text page references will be given to the Rosen translation, preceded by an E, the corresponding page of the Latin original being indicated by an L. Details of the dates of writing of the *Somnium* can be found conveniently in Rosen's edition, pp. xvii–xxi, and in Max Caspar, *Kepler,* tr. and ed. C. Doris Hellman (London and New York, 1959), p. 351. Caspar writes that the work was partially conceived during Kepler's student days in Tübingen, the text itself being mostly written in 1609, and the notes being added mostly after 1620 when he realized that his "little writing [contained] problems to be solved in an astronomical, physical or historical way."

9. I will not attempt to make a complete catalogue here because the quantity of notes involved would make it unnecessarily long. The following figures will give some suggestion (parentheses indicate notes whose status is ambiguous). Allegory: 3, 10, 34, 35, 36, 37, 38, 51, 55, 56, 64, 72, 82, etc.; Autobiography: 6, (7), 8, (16, 19, 20, 21,

the order of what is called "ordinary" language, in that they follow a linear unidimensional system apparently predicating individual denotated meanings. They could, if one wished, be reduced to a single logical formulation by the necessary removal of their semantic variables. They all adopt a rigorous expository order of cause and effect. That is to say that they do for the *Dream* just what Livy and Florus, in Dumézil's exposition of the matter, did for the Horatii paradigm. They offer us the "set of parallel readings" of which I spoke previously.

The dream voyage that is narrated functions quite differently. On the one hand it does follow an order of linear seriality, since it is inscribed in diachrony by virtue of its being the *relation* of a *journey* (or journeys) in space, and because in however disorganized a way, it does follow the order of a 'scientific' descriptive discourse: indeed it must, since it is written on a page. At the same time it opposes this linearity, for it occurs synchronically within the pattern of what may be termed for the moment a 'lunar myth,' as well as syntopically (if I may again be allowed the word) insofar as neither the supposed writer nor, more to the point, the narrator moves from his 'position' to make the journey.

In the *Somnium* the patterning of concrete events still organizes discourse in such a way that the presumably unlimited syntagms which can be produced by the rational code of an analytical discourse enter only as a "debris", as products of operators which within 'their own' discourse produce a quite different order. The notes form a posterior analysis in 'new' terms. This is in strict agreement with Lévi-Strauss's conception of "mythical thinking," though not with the form taken by his statement of it: "natural phenomena . . . are . . . the *medium through which* myths try to explain facts which are themselves not of a natural but a logical order."[10] The use of the word "explain" here is as problematic as is Simon's use of "objectivity" in his discussion of the different "conceptuality" he finds in Kepler.

It strikes me as of dubious utility to apply such analytical concepts to a form of discourse functioning so differently from our own, and to assume they provide us with some *truth* about its *purpose*. The

---

22), 24, 25, 26, 27, 33, 58, 60, etc.; Science: (12), 13, (15, 17, 18, 23, 28, 29), 30, 39, 40, 43, 53, 54, 55, 57, 62, 63, 66, 67, 68, 69, 70, 73, 74, 76, 77, 78, 80, 81, etc.; Scientific methodology: 14, 44, 46, 47, 48, 49, etc.; Fiction: 1, 2, 4, 11, 65, etc. The proportions here correspond roughly to those of the complete notes, but this is no more than indicative because the notes vary considerably in length.

10. Lévi-Strauss, *The Savage Mind*, p. 95.

"phenomena" are taken as "natural" to the extent that they are *observed,* not *observing,* and to the extent that these operations are not taken as intricate with one another but as opposite poles within the organization of knowledge. The danger in this notion of "explanation" and of "objectivity" is that it adopts the metaphor of the telescope as expressive of the necessary form all knowledge must take, and tends therefore to make the a priori assumption that we *can* look for meaning in a class of discourse different from our own in the same way as we do in our own. It leads to the supposition that other classes of discourse, at least to an appreciable degree, follow the same forms of intentionality as our own, despite the recognition that its organization is quite different.

Simon observes in this regard that the objects of Kepler's knowledge are in no way susceptible of being superimposed on ours, just because the classificatory grid he uses is quite different.[11] It might therefore appear that my object of showing in what way our analytico-referential model is already present in the *Somnium* is a self-contradiction: it would seem to be an attempt to divide Kepler's work into what can and what cannot be so superimposed. But this would be a double misunderstanding. In the first place, it will be clear that I view the presence of an analytical discursive order in the *Somnium* as simply one piece of a whole by which and in which it is subsumed. A later analysis can well extract it, just as it also extracted the three laws of planetary movement, provided that the analyst remains aware that such an undertaking is the ruin of Kepler's edifice. In the second place, the present aim is less to show how Kepler's work itself functions (though I certainly hope there is some indication of that) than to distinguish it from the practical functioning and consequences of what grew out of it into opposition. So far as the *Somnium* is concerned, I do not so much superimpose as decompose. The purpose here will be to indicate, by means of an opposition present for us in the text of the *Dream,* the operation of a discourse of patterning which has already given birth to and is confronted by another class of discourse.

Kepler's commentary in the notes represents an attempt to systematize the text which is inspired (apparently, when looked at retrospectively) by the distancing mechanism characteristic of analytico-referential discourse. Kepler is aware that he is attempting such a systematization ("that is to say . . . ," "I meant by this . . ."), before such a process is even potentially a dominant order of dis-

11. Simon, *Kepler,* p. 12.

course. "No important later [imaginary] voyage," Marjorie Nicolson has written, "will employ so fully the supernatural, yet none will be more truly 'scientific' than that *Dream,* which was the *fons et origo* of the new genre, a chief source of cosmic voyages for three centuries."[12]

The first paragraph of Kepler's text draws the modern reader progressively into a fictional, literary scheme. It places what is given as history into some other 'place' and 'time'; it relates the 'reality' of history to the mystery of the supernatural and the legendary:

> In the year 1608 there was a heated argument between the Emperor Rudolph and his brother, the Archduke Matthias. Their actions universally recalled precedents found in Bohemian history. Stimulated by the widespread public interest, I turned my attention to reading about Bohemia, and came upon the story of the heroine Libussa [*historiam Libussae Viraginis*], renowned for her skill in magic. It happened one night that after watching the stars and the moon, I went to bed and fell into a very deep sleep. In my sleep I seemed to be reading a book bought from the fair. Its contents were as follows.
>
> My name is Duracotus. My country is Iceland, which the ancients call Thule. [E 11; L 1]

The narrator/dreamer 'travels' not only in space, from Kepler's Bohemia to the semi-'mythical' Thule, but also in time: from the precise historical date of 1608 to some vague period characterized only by its relationship with antiquity, or, better, with storytelling. The figure which is the operator of both these transformations (literally becoming a 'crossroads') is the "virago" Libussa, the legendary founder of Prague, "primal mother-figure of the Bohemian people," whose "gift of prophecy was such as to bring her the nickname, Sibylla Bohemica."[13] From what is presented as historical fact, we are transferred into some unsituated (and perhaps unsituatable) time, and immediately into the dream. That dream will be governed by the image of the "stars and moon" by which it is directly preceded. The sun and the moon, indeed, will provide two pieces of "material debris" organizing discourse, concrete sensible images acting as discursive operators.

The dream is presented here in the guise of a book to be read and annotated. The narrator even underlines the *literary* context by references to the Frankfurt book fair both at the beginning and at the end of the dream, as though the book itself were to make possible

12. Marjorie Nicolson, *Voyages to the Moon* (New York, 1948), p. 41. See also Caspar, *Kepler,* p. 352.
13. Lear, *Kepler's Dream,* pp. 74–75.

some kind of equilibrium between history and the science of Kepler's own present study on the one hand and atemporality and magic on the other.[14] In this first paragraph it is as though the narrator were producing the tale of a discourse which he presents as difficult, if not impossible, of comprehension to anyone imbued with the habit of a scientific discourse—supposing such a person yet to exist. The dream is a discourse whose "overload of information" must be reduced to the manageable proportions of a meaning or meanings which can be shown to be analyzable in terms of truth or falsehood. It is to be subjected to a series of different analyses, and those analyses can be viewed not simply as interchangeable interpretations but as parallel readings.

For Kepler insists that his analytical notes are not only scientific (chiefly physical and mathematical) confirmations and explanations, but that they represent at the same time an effort to organize a fictional structure whose meaning would otherwise remain unclear, if not unknown. In this connection Kepler finds it occasionally useful to remark, in his notes, upon his own mystification as to a number of similarities between his *Dream* and certain earlier fictions which he is unable (he says) to explain. A not inconsiderable portion of the notes was added in order to offer an alternative to the biographical interpretation which almost took his mother to the stake as a witch. This alternative thesis is the analysis of an allegory concerning the relationship of Science, Ignorance, and Reason, an allegory which is presented as a passage into the scientific material which is subsequently to be presented. Such analytical interpretations accompanying the text appear to perform the same serialization as that noted by Dumézil in his discussion of the Horatii paradigm.[15]

I suggest that Kepler's *Somnium* manifests a moment when two different classes of discourse function with equivalent power—a moment of transition which must obviously be brief, for the one is

14. The Latin word at the beginning of the text is *nundinae*, which strictly means a market occurring every nine days: here it simply means "fair." As Lear notes, to speak of a book market in Kepler's day first of all meant that of Frankfurt. At the end of the *Somnium* the dreamer's brusque awakening not only disturbs his sleep but has the unfortunate effect, he writes, of "wiping out the end of the book acquired at Frankfurt" (Rosen, p. 28; L 28). The printing of the *Somnium* was itself completed at Frankfurt.

15. For extensions of the autobiographical order, see Caspar, p. 245; Lear, pp. 22–27; Nicolson, pp. 43–45, and her "Kepler, the *Somnium*, and John Donne," in *Science and Imagination* (Ithaca, 1956), pp. 58–79. The allegorical has been noted and examined (other than by Kepler himself) by Ludwig Günter, in his edition of *Keplers Traum vom Mond* (Leipzig, 1898), pp. 37 ff.; Lear, pp. 39–50. The scientific has received attention from Günter, pp. 45 ff.; Nicolson, *Voyages*, pp. 45–47; Koestler, *Sleepwalkers*, pp. 416–19; Lear, pp. 52–72. See note 9 above.

being produced from the other. And it may be possible to generalize here and suggest that a whole type of literary discourse is being undermined as well. The allegorical dream was a literary genre much cultivated in the Middle Ages (one might mention the *Roman de la rose, Piers Plowman,* the names of Chaucer and Alain Chartier, among others), and while its ambiguity might be resolvable to a degree by the four stages of medieval interpretation, it could certainly not be reduced as it is by Kepler to the production of a discourse by and about a self (I am thinking of the autobiographical notes and the *I* of the notes) whose intention is given as providing truths about the world (the scientific and methodological notes). The allegorical interpretation is explained in the *Somnium* as a merely convenient way to pass from the expression of self to the presentation of the scientific material.

There is here no mystery to which allegory can offer an initial approach: on the contrary, allegory is no more than a discursive device connecting the thought of the self (and its expression) to the grasping of referential truth. It is almost as though the allegorical interpretation fulfilled the activity of the *ergo* between the *cogito* as the thought of self and the *sum* as the concept of other. But that is the explanation provided in the notes. In the text of the *Dream* itself the operation is not analytical. The spatial and temporal passage that precedes the dream proper, which may also be taken as a 'cognitive' passage proceeding from the known (history) to the unknown, from reality to fiction, from fact to dream, from, indeed, self (Kepler) to other (Duracotus)—that passage occurs through the presence of the figure of Libussa. The analyses of the notes propose to permit what is *contained* in the dream to become a part of an analytical knowledge. In doing so they would change the very structure of discourse. Even so, the fact that allegory permits the commentator to pass from autobiography to objectivity in the notes themselves makes of those allegorical notes a form of the operator, Libussa: such a passage is no longer needed, for example, by the Descartes of the *Discours de la méthode* who *reasons* from autobiography and an autoreflexive thought to the generalized objectivity of method.

During the transformation made possible by the "buying of the book," the very person of the narrator changes. From Kepler, Imperial Mathematician, he becomes Duracotus, a character whose name attaches him to mysterious and legendary elements.[16] He under-

16. In his first note, Kepler adds: "The very sound of the word was suggested to me by my recollection of proper names of similar sound in the history of Scotland, a country which looks out upon the Icelandic Sea" (E 30; L 29).

goes a final metamorphosis when he becomes the Daemon, presented as of superior wisdom and science—indeed, as mind itself and
knowledge, as we will see. This last change is a surreptitious one, for
it occurs not narratively, not through what the narrator *says* (as does
the change from Kepler to Duracotus), but syntactically, by what he
does: the use of the third person of the verb to refer to the Daemon
gives way definitively to that of the first person. It is as though in the
text a further and different means from that of the notes had been
found to pass from the self (under the names "Kepler" and now
"Duracotus") to the incorporation in that self of a knowledge exte-
iror to it (the Daemon and his science). Organized very differently
from the analytical systematization of the notes, though not from the
use of the allegorical notes, this discursive passage moves within a
different order.

The change of character performs a transformation parallel to the
spatiotemporal one which occurs in the opening paragraph. Indeed
the relationship between Duracotus and his mother, Fiolxhilde,
matches that of the 'original' narrator with Libussa. Fiolxhilde provides a 'crossroads' just as Libussa does: like the latter figure, like
the allegorical notes in their functioning, "Fiolxhilde" is an operator of transformations. I will come back to that aspect later. What
is important here is that knowledge ("Daemon," asserts Kepler in his
note 51, comes from the Greek *daíein*, "to know") is associated with
the accumulation of patterns which are anything but analytical: it
forms the end of this patterning before it becomes the aim of analysis (though there is, of course, nothing to prevent the process of
patterning from being endless). It is as though analysis were *contained* in the patterning as the central portion of the text of the
Somnium is contained in the dream. Nor is it perhaps indifferent to
this matter that Aristotle (with whom Kepler was as familiar as any
of his educated contemporaries) refers to dreams as "daemonic," as
following, that is to say, "the laws of the human spirit."[17] Through
the Daemon the patterning of the *Dream* and understanding can be
identified with one another.

In this connection my analysis will take up certain material offered
by Bachelard and Jung which, it deserves repeating, is useful here
only to the extent that it indicates discursive difference, not that it
offers either a latent or a manifest content of the text. No attempt

17. Sigmund Freud, *The Interpretation of Dreams*, in *The Standard Edition of the Complete Psychological Works of Sigmund Freud*, ed. James Strachey (1953; rpt. London,
1975), IV.2. The reference is to Aristotle, *De divinatione per somnium*, II, and *De
somniis*, III.

will be made to use these writers in such a way, for example, that "when the work of interpretation has been completed, we perceive that a dream is the fulfilment of a wish."[18] I do not wish to repeat in a different key the kind of analysis suggested by the diverse series of notes added by Kepler: and to make either a Jungian or a Freudian psychoanalytical reading would simply be to add further parallel readings. The use of material drawn from such research is not arbitrary, however, inasmuch as it corresponds to certain of Kepler's (and the narrator's) own preoccupations. The use of such material must, nonetheless, be treated merely as indicative because it is impossible to describe 'correctly' (that is, in its own terms) a class of discourse functioning differently from our own.

Bachelard, then, suggests that in certain kinds of "poetic" texts there is a relationship between the image of water and that of the moon. Certainly in Duracotus the two images come together. On the one hand he is constantly surrounded by or crossing over water, while eventually he is metamorphosed into the lunar Daemon. The figure accords with Bachelard's description even more closely: "The being destined to water is an ever-changing being. At each moment he is dying, some part of his substance is endlessly crumbling away."[19] The changes of the narrator do rather resemble the successive lifting of a series of skins. If Duracotus combines the two images, the figure of his mother, the sorceress Fiolxhilde, itself has a connection with that of the goddess Luna, the great and power Hecate; capable of granting or denying to man victory, wealth, and wisdom; goddess of the crossroads.[20] It is Fiolxhilde who, by withdrawing into the darkness at a crossroads, permits the transformation of the narrator into the lunar Daemon. Libussa can then be understood as another form of the same figure. (It is, of course, this connection that led to the accusations of witchcraft which were brought against Kepler's mother.)

The appearance of such figures in a text which is to treat of the moon and of the difficulties and possibility of a lunar journey with

18. Freud, *Interpretation of Dreams*, IV.121; and see esp. pp. 122–33.

19. Gaston Bachelard, *L'eau et les rêves: Essai sur l'imagination de la matière* (Paris, 1942), p. 9. The same connection is made by comparative mythologists: see Mircea Eliade, *Images et symboles: Essais sur le symbolisme magico-religieux* (Paris, 1952), pp. 165–68.

20. See *Encyclopedia Americana*, art. "Hecate." *La grande encyclopédie* (art. "Hécate") adds that she was originally a lunar goddess (associated with Selene), that she later acquired traits from Athene, Demeter, and Artemis. At first she was an agent for both good and evil, but during the Middle Ages she was gradually stripped of her overt ambiguity and the accent was eventually placed entirely on her malevolent aspects: Kepler seems to be using the figure's more 'ambiguous' aspects.

all its scientific and technical ramifications may well be a cause for some surprise in the modern mind: no doubt it is why the text has not been taken 'seriously' until very recently. For us that appearance accentuates the nonanalytical bases of the experience (and of experimentalism itself), thrusts it into the "material imagination," into a discourse different from ours.

In his notes Kepler indicates from the outset the use being made of such material:

> In our German language this means "Ice Land." But in this remote island I perceived a place where I might fall asleep and dream, in imitation of the philosophers in this branch of literature. For Cicero crossed over into Africa when he was getting ready to dream. Moreover, in the same Western ocean Plato fashioned Atlantis, whence he summoned imaginary aids to military valor. Finally, Plutarch, too, in his little book on *The Face in the Moon*, after prolonged discussion ventures out into the American ocean and describes to us such an arrangement of islands as a modern geographer would probably apply to the Azores, Greenland, and the territory of Labrador, regions situated around Iceland. Every time I reread this book by Plutarch, I am exceedingly amazed and keep wondering by what chance it happened that our dreams or fables coincided so closely. [E 30–32; L 29][21]

In this same note, he remarks on the place of Hekla in mythology as the entrance to purgatory, and on that of the moon as "the purgatory of souls," according to "the belief of pagan theology" (E 34, L 29). Such notes, while suggesting an 'explanation,' simply act as markers: for the distance demanded by the attempt to systematize in an analytical way and the consequent inability to grasp what is essential to the discourse of patterning is not only our difficulty. It is also Kepler's as he "plays with" the shorthand which is to become analytico-referential discourse.

The first journey Duracotus undertakes is narrated as the consequence of an accident: one might almost say that he 'undergoes' it. It results from his mother's anger that he opened out of curiosity a charm-bag of herbs gathered on Hekla which she was in the process of selling to a sea captain. The herbs are scattered, and to repair the captain's loss Fiolxhilde gives him her son:

> On the next day he unexpectedly sailed out of the harbor, and with a favorable wind steered approximately toward Bergen in Norway. After

---

21. *Somnium*, note 2. The last sentence of this passage is an example of Kepler's 'mystification.' Does he imply that there lies underneath a 'truth' indicated by the discourse of patterning but closed to analysis?

a few days a north wind sprang up and drove the ship between Norway and England. He headed for Denmark and passed through the strait, since he had to deliver a letter from a Bishop in Iceland to the Dane, Tycho Brahe, who lived on the island of Hven. The tossing of the boat and the unaccustomed warmth of the air made me violently sick. [E 12; L 2]

It will be worth lingering a moment over these herbs culled from the slopes of volcanic Hekla. As material of the patterning relation they are the plants which mediate between the regions of fire and those of earth.[22] Connected with Fiolxhilde, the herbs themselves become discursive operators: they mark a passage from earth and water to fire and air. It is strictly in accordance with the order of 'resemblance' that these aromatic herbs should be directly responsible both for Duracotus's (horizontal) voyage between his original law of earth and water (Iceland) and the later knowledge of air and fire to be acquired at Hven (already indicated by the phrase "the unaccustomed warmth of the air"), and for his (vertical) journey, as the Daemon, from the earth to the moon.

The prefiguration of the lunar journey which will be 'made' later is contained, so to speak, in the herbs and is emphasized here in the narrator's description of the rough journey to Hven, with its winds and heat (whatever the meterological explanations of the wind and the rest provided in the technical notes). Concerning the trip to the moon, too, particular attention will be paid to the harshness of the elements, to the risks of illness and death, and so on.

As potential material of discourse the image of a difficult sea voyage toward what is often some lonely island lost in the midst of a vast ocean (for example, the utopias of Plato, More, Campanella, Bacon), sometimes *interpreted* as the search for knowledge or as the descent into the unconscious (and more), is often associated with the loss and rediscovery of discourse, with 'a return to the primitive' in the sense of a kind of purging of certain habitual ties to the external world. We find this here, too, and it is 'translated' into the terms of a pattern which makes use of a set of oppositions whose principal operator is the image of the moon itself (though that image takes various forms).

Duracotus is abandoned by his captain on the island of Hven, and is obliged to learn a new language in order to exchange with Tycho and his students his knowledge of his own country for theirs of various "marvels" concerned with the heavens (E 12–13; L 2). The

22. Jean-Pierre Vernant, introduction to Marcel Detienne, *Les jardins d'Adonis: La mythologie des aromates en Grèce* (Paris, 1973), pp. xxx–xxxi.

narrator himself emphasizes the relationship of this exchange with the one he will later have with the Daemon concerning the moon, associating once again the patterned and analytical aspects of the fiction: "I was delighted beyond measure by the astronomical activities, for Brahe and his students watched the moon and the stars all night with marvelous instruments. This practice reminded me of my mother, because she, too, used to commune with the moon constantly" (E 13; L 3). This connection is asserted once again when he writes that after his return to Iceland his mother was "deliriously happy that I had become acquainted with that science [of the heavens]. Comparing what she had learned with my remarks, she exclaimed that now she was ready" to introduce her son to other mysteries (E 13; L 3).

It is then that the fiction itself arrives at its crossroads: from dream relation it will become a kind of scientific treatise. Duracotus, through the power invested in the figure of Fiolxhilde and the syntactic order of discourse, is to be transformed into the Daemon:

> Without any delay I agreed that she should summon her teacher. I sat down, ready to hear the entire plan for the trip and description of the region. It was already spring. The moon, becoming a crescent, began to shine as soon as the sun set below the horizon, and was in conjunction with the planet Saturn in the sign of the Bull. My mother went away from me to the nearest crossroads. Raising a shout, she pronounced just a few words in which she couched her request. Having completed her ceremonies, she returned. With the outstretched palm of her right hand she commanded silence, and sat down beside me. Hardly had we covered our heads with our clothing (in accordance with our covenant) when the rasping of an indistinct and unclear voice became audible. It began at once as follows, albeit in the Icelandic tongue. [E 14–15; L 4]

At this crucial point in the text, then, the proposed lunar journey is associated with elements drawn from the "system of transformations" (as Simon calls it) that is astrology. The very many notes to this passage in Kepler's text (notes 43–50), seeking to explain why this particular conjunction is necessary (the time of year, the need for darkness, for a crescent moon, and so on), become little more than aspects of the astrological element in question, as though the analyses were a necessary part of the transformation which is occurring: human (Duracotus) to inhuman (Daemon), terrestrial (Iceland) to celestial (moon). The analyses themselves can thus become simply a transformation of the patterning, as though the very production of analysis from within the discourse itself amounted to an affirmation of the power of patterning to be all-embracing. For us it suggests a discursive union which could not be long-lasting. In a sense, by the union of certain images, the coexistence of discourses is itself indicated in the text.

In the *Mysterium coniunctionis,* Jung quotes Pico's *Heptaplus* and John Dee's *Monas hieroglyphica* respectively as follows:

> [Luna] has an affinity with Venus, as is particularly to be seen from the fact that she is sublimated in Taurus, the House of Venus, so much that she nowhere else appears more auspicious and more beneficent.

> And when the semi-circle of the moon was brought to be the compliment of the sun, there was evening and there was morning, one day. Be that (day) therefore the first, on which was made the light of the Philosophers.

Jung remarks that "the union of ☉ and ☽ gives the sign for Taurus, ♉ ruler of the house of Venus. The marriage of day (sun) and night (moon) is the reason for the rather rare designation of the lapis [philosopher's stone] as the 'filius unius diei' (son of one day)."[23] This astrological union is, therefore, the crossroads which is associated in the text with the goddess Hecate through the figure of Fiolxhilde, with Libussa, with the herbs from the slopes of Hekla, with the role played by the allegorical notes, perhaps with that of the "book buying" itself.

The scientist gives explanations in his footnotes for much of this passage, even remarking in passing on its being a "magica ceremonia." He notes how many of these activities were for scientific purposes, how covering the head with a cloak made it possible to observe heavenly bodies more easily, how his house had itself become a crossroads for learned men, and so on. All this does not change in the least the patterned order of this passage. All that seems to be achieved by Kepler's continuing attempt to supply a series of systematic explanations of an order which escapes such explanations is to underline their common use of the material of language. He merely underlines Lévi-Strauss's claim that "symbols are more real than what they symbolize, the signifier precedes and determines the signified."[24] The text of the *Dream,* confronted with the footnotes it

23. Carl Gustav Jung, *Mysterium coniunctionis: An Enquiry into the Separation and Synthesis of Opposites in Alchemy,* tr. R. F. C. Hull, in *Collected Works* (London, 1963), XIV.144 and n. 260.

24. Claude Lévi-Strauss, "Introduction à l'oeuvre de Marcel Mauss," in Marcel Mauss, *Sociologie et anthropologie* (Paris, 1950), p. xxxii.

produces, emphasizes precisely that the semes associated with its diverse images can be extended without limit. The order of a discourse of patterning will be relatively strict and limited, as the conclusion of the present chapter will try to indicate, but its 'meanings' are not so restricted.

The marriage of the Sun and the Moon, then, 'is' that of Logos and Eros, of "discrimination, judgement, insight" with "the capacity to relate," as Jung interprets it.[25] It is perhaps the coincidence of an analytical discourse and one of patterning: Dionysus as Apollo, to recall Nietzsche's metaphor. That precarious coincidence is perhaps the design of the text of the *Somnium,* which does not fail to recognize the difficulty: "Should it [the moon] regain its full light while we are still in transit, our departure becomes futile" (E 15; L 6). The figure of Duracotus, as Daemon, will be the operator of this transformation.

Duracotus, enamored of the moon, has insisted that his youth was passed under the sign of the sun: "In the earliest days of my boyhood my mother, leading me by the hand and sometimes hoisting me up on her shoulders, often used to take me to the lower slopes of Mt. Hekla. These excursions were made especially around St. John's Day [*festum divi Joannis*], when the sun is visible all twenty-four hours, and there is no night [*nocti nullum relinquit locum*]" (E 12; L 2). Needless to say, the notes again add 'scientific' reasons for the time chosen. We may add, however, that a certain ambiguity in the matter makes possible a further transformation between sun and moon. While the summer solstice, occurring shortly before the Feast in question, places it under a twenty-four hour sun in Iceland, its date also narrowly precedes the earth's aphelion: what better time, one might ask, for communing with the lunar elements than when Apollo is at his furthest? One other element may be noted (of which Cyrano will make particular use, we will see). The popular Feast of St. John was (and in some places still is) accompanied by a kind of fire ritual which strikingly resembles what ethnologists and historians of religion have been able to tell us about the techniques of the shaman as he prepares his entry into the regions beyond. The Feast was furthermore understood as the celebration of a resurrection and spiritual rebirth.[26]

25. Jung, *Mysterium,* pp. 179–80.
26. The summer solstice occurs on June 21 or 22, aphelion around July 2; the Feast of St. John takes place on June 24. *La grande encyclopédie* (art. "Le feu de la Saint-Jean") says: "A popular custom still continued in many villages and hamlets . . . fires are lit, around which people dance, and over which they leap." (In its transformation as the National Day of Quebec, the celebration occurs to this day in North America.) *The Catholic Encyclopedia* (New York, 1910), VIII.490d, adds that apart from its being

Kepler, of course, was well aware of all this (though not, doubtless, of the import of the shamanic ritual as such). Certainly he was familiar with the details of the fire rituals surrounding the Feast of St. John; his intimacy with astrology and its significance in his researches is now well documented by Simon's work. More than that, however, the order of this discourse with its attached notes corresponds entirely with the concept of science which was indicated at the beginning of this chapter: analytical ordering not as a dominant form of rationality, but as a part of an all-embracing discourse. It is here that one may look for what might be called the 'motivating force' behind the narrator's transformations.

The obvious analytical associations with a "rising from the underworld" (Hekla, writes Kepler), with a resurrection; the ambiguity of an ascent from one purgatory to what might well prove another (the moon), and that by a figure which is itself ambiguous (for the Daemon, like Hecate and her avatars, is not only a 'good' spirit of knowledge but also a potentially 'evil' spirit which can bring death)—these elements, like others already mentioned, suggest some statement of union, however precarious and momentary. It is a 'marriage,' an equilibrium whose symbols the narrator constantly elaborates.

His return to Iceland thus occurs when "autumn was approaching, to be followed by those long nights of ours, since during the month in which Christ was born the sun barely rises at noon and sets again at once" (E 13; L 3). Duracotus insists upon the parallel between his voyage to the island of Hven and the journey to the moon. The Daemon, having appeared once mother and sun have cut themselves off from the exterior, presents the moon: "Fifty thousand German miles up in the ether lies the island of Levania" (E 15; L 5). The notion of *distance* is indeed emphasized, for he declares that it lies *in aethero profundo*—even as Kepler once more adds a technical explanation of this distance (note 53). Yet even in the footnotes the similarity of the two is emphasized: "It does not lie; rather, it floats, if we consider its resemblance to an island" (note 54).[27]

---

the oldest feast of the Greek and Roman liturgies, this feast is peculiar in that it celebrates a saint's *birthday*. See also Sir James George Frazer, *Balder the Beautiful: The Fire Festivals of Europe and the Doctrine of the External Soul*, vols. 10 and 11 of *The Golden Bough: A Study in Magic and Religion*, 3d ed. (London, 1911–18), esp. X.160–219. For the techniques of shamanism see various writings of Eliade, but particularly, *Le chamanisme et les techniques archaïques de l'extase*, 2d ed. (Paris, 1968); *Mythes, rêves et mystères* (Paris, 1953), pp. 83, 85–86, 127–37; *Forgerons et alchimistes* (Paris, 1965), pp. 81–88. In Chapter 8 we will see Cyrano using this material in a quite different way from Kepler.

27. Given the implications of this passage, I add the original: "Non sita est, sed natat potiùs, si ad Insulae similtudinem respicimus. Sed hic jam ad imaginationem

The Daemon makes of the passage to the moon something like an opposition of life and death. He is himself the operator of this balancing act, just as was Duracotus between sun and moon, and the herbs between fire and earth.[28] The Daemon remarks: "The road to it from here or from it to this earth is seldom open. When it is open, it is easy for our kind, but for transporting men it is assuredly most difficult and fraught with the greatest danger to life" (E 15; L 5). That Duracotus does not actually make the journey, according to the narrative, but remains with his head covered in Iceland, is of particular interest. To describe the voyage as though he were in the process of undertaking it would be to take a certain distance from it. Instead the journey occurs by means of a syntactic change to which I have already referred: the change in the person of the verb. All of a sudden the "they" being used by the Daemon to refer to men becomes "we":

> The fixed stars look the same to all Levania as to us. But its view of the movements and sizes of the planets is very different from what we observe here, so that its entire system of astronomy is quite diverse. . . . One of these [Subvolva; i.e., the side of the moon facing earth] always enjoys its Volva [i.e., the Earth], which among them takes the place of our moon. [E 17; L 8]

The Daemon, no longer talking as a spirit of the moon, has 'become' the narrator with his terrestrial viewpoint. A transformation, terrestrial/celestial, has occurred. It is, indeed, a point worth remarking that to my knowledge *all* commentators of Kepler's *Somnium* have discussed the text as though the narrator, Duracotus, does make the journey to the moon in the narration: as though they had readjusted the operation of the text to the needs of analysis. But the analytical need for a descriptive explanation of the passage to the moon is not a problem which patterning has to confront. We soon find ourselves 'on the surface of' the moon, and there follows a description apparently according to the possibilities allowed by physical laws.

I would say that we are thus 'transported' to the surface of the moon precisely because there is no description of any actual journey: for the narrator that is technologically impossible, and to recount it

---

visus loquendum fuit. Nam qui in Luna esset, omninò is Lunam stare loco fixam estimaret."

28. Bachelard notes at some length the association between the moon and death. See, e.g., *L'eau et les rêves*, pp. 62, 119–21.

would be foolish in the very terms of the technical analyses with which Kepler associates his text. Some other operator functions therefore, and the passage to the moon consequently takes on a multiplicity of meanings in which the common denominator is the balancing of opposites. That is perhaps the reason why, in the central part of the *Somnium*, the narrator chiefly emphasizes the abrupt oppositions of light and shade, hot and cold, wet and dry, insisting upon them as the main characteristics of the moon. It is presented as a place where contraries meet but never coincide, where all is larger than familiar life. And the life of the moon, we gather, is such that "in general, the serpentine nature [*natura viperina*] predominates" (E 28; L 27).

Jung adds that "the union of consciousness (Sol) with its feminine counterpart the unconscious (Luna) has undesirable effects to begin with: it produces poisonous animals such as the dragon, the serpent, scorpion, basilisk, and toad."[29] Indeed, this fiction echoes in microcosm the entire work of Kepler, conceived as a series of possible interpretations of a system present in the divine intellect. Science was a kind of interrogation of the manifestations of the "world soul" whose essence must forever remain indistinct for humans, by virtue of their own participation in it, but whose limitless appearances were available for ordering into a pattern which would reflect in some way such an essence.

The presence of the image of the moon in the discourse of patterning—as death, as the unconscious, as "the capacity to relate," or however it may be interpreted by analysis—marks that that discourse has attained a balance which is excluded from analytico-referential discourse. As a product of patterning, analysis reveals thereby, in its very project, a central contradiction: the aim of the linear discourse of analysis is to be a continuing process providing its user with an eventually '*complete*' knowledge. Descartes, indeed, was able to claim that that end would be achieved in not more than a few centuries.[30] But such knowledge would be the negation of its own ordering, for it would put an end to the continuing process. Analytico-referential discourse is thus a process which inscribes stasis as its goal: it is aimed, so to speak, at entropy. Perhaps, again, that is why it is in the nineteenth-century creation of thermodynamic theory that this discourse itself is brought into crisis. In a sense the discourse of patterning can 'cope with' its *own* death in a way which is unavailable for

29. Jung, *Mysterium*, p. 144.
30. See the letter-preface to the French translation of the *Principes de la philosophie*, in *Oeuvres philosophiques*, III.783–84.

analytico-referential discourse. The former has a way of coping with 'things' that are inexpressible for the latter, and because analysis nonetheless lays claim to completeness, such 'things' can only signal its failure and death, not because it has finally said everything but because it is unable to do so.

Kepler's notes are symptomatic of the development of analytical knowing: and so, too, is their accumulation. The development is marked by their continual suggestions (both implicit and explicit) that such a systematization is possible. It is even more clearly marked by the fact that they even try to reduce the telling itself to *mythology* through an ongoing attempt to explain the *denotation* of certain elements of the text: Fiolxhilde, Duracotus, the beasts of the moon, the magic, the movements of the moon, the positions of the stars and sun are all elements to be explained in terms of some real event. By such means the 'mysterious' elements would be made the syntagmatic equal of the other accumulating readings.

The pattern produced by the sun and the moon, Iceland and Hven, Libussa and Fiolxhilde, Duracotus and the Daemon, by the herbs, the allegorical notes, and the change from third to first person of the verb (a collection of which one could make the same remark as we earlier saw Hacking make with regard to Paracelsus's lists of signs): that pattern is precisely what cannot be *explained*— except reductively, by seeking for singular meanings. That pattern can only be viewed as a system of transformations. The elements of the text perform the union which the notes are unable to grasp. That is what I mean by the moon as 'death' of discourse: as the movement of analysis itself contradicts (and is contradicted by) the stasis of its goal, so patterning denies the very premise of analysis. Patterning *shows*, it does not *say*.

Analysis, however, cannot permit this potential death to remain without explanation. To do so would be to inscribe (as opposed to occulting) the denial of its goal at the very outset. It must find a way to represent it, even as an exclusion—madness, for example, or myth: but not myth as a discursive relation; myth as an object of analytical study, as that "primitive thought" or "savage mind" which Ernst Cassirer, with seeming innocence, is able to equate with madness: "It may be pointed out in passing that the belief in the 'substantiality' of the word, which dominates all mythical thinking, may be observed in almost unchanged form in certain pathological phenomena."[31]

31. Ernst Cassirer, *The Philosophy of Symbolic Forms*, tr. Ralph Manheim, 3 vols. (1953–57; rpt. New Haven and London, 1968), II.41–42 n. 13.

The accumulation of the notes of the *Somnium* appears for us as an effort to achieve that representation. Precisely because the two discourses are incompatible that accumulation could have been endless. Patterning can do no more *for* analysis than supply information out of which the latter will have to multiply meanings. That is why the notes of the *Somnium* are three times as long as the text they seek to explicate, and that is perhaps why the period of its writing covers Kepler's entire lifetime: "To write so as not to die, as Blanchot said, or perhaps speaking so as not to die is a task no doubt as old as speech. The most mortal of decisions inevitably remains suspended for yet the time of a tale."[32]

In this way analytico-referential discourse is a kind of everlasting retarding of its own death. Confronted with the very discourse which produced it, it reveals that its claim to the production of true knowledge about the real is a means of occulting this necessity of speech as the mark of immortality (rather than as the mere mediator and container of knowledge). Speech was taken as the guarantor and index of humanity from the time of the oldest theories of language down to the most modern (at least before Derrida). Plato's fear of writing, like Saussure's, was just the fear of a kind of death in stillness, of a passage out of life into memory: but neither then nor perhaps now was that aspect concealed as it was when the analytico-referential took over. Speech, then, was no longer simply the mark of humanity, of a human activity *in* the world; it became the guarantor of man's rationality and the sign of a human use *of* the world.

Kepler's *Somnium* reveals the production of analytico-referential discourse from within the very discourse which puts it in doubt (as other than a 'shorthand'). Patterning appears to succeed in balancing discourse and death. The *Dream* may fail to produce an *explanation* of the union I have been indicating in its various analytical sequences and be 'obliged' to break off abruptly.[33] It nonetheless composes that union from various elements. We have seen in the text a set of sequences whose syntagmatic orders seem similar: Kepler thinking about Bohemia and its history; the dreamer opening his book and coming upon Iceland; Duracotus upsetting the herbs and journeying to Hven; Duracotus 'becoming' the Daemon and finding himself before a view of the moon through the change from the first to the third person of the verb. Each of these sequences is made possible

32. Michel Foucault, "Le langage à l'infini," *Tel Quel,* 15 (1963), 44.
33. But Kepler appears to have thought it finished. Just before his death he wrote to Philip Müller that six sheets of text and notes were in proof: see Carola Baumgardt, *Johannes Kepler: Life and Letters* (New York, 1951), p. 187.

through an operator to which I have frequently referred as a 'cross-roads.' Indicators drawn from a variety of sources suggest that underlying these transformations is the 'need' for some kind of 'union,' of equilibrium: Libussa makes possible an 'exchange' between history and magic, between the natural and the supernatural; Duracotus between the moon and the sun, death and life, and so on; the herbs between earth and water, fire and air; Fiolxhilde between the terrestrial and the celestial. This balance is achieved in the text not by what it says but by how it says it, or, better yet, by the mere fact of inscribing these diverse elements. I suggested that this overflowed into the notes due to the role played there by the allegorical interpretations, making possible a passage from the autobiographical to the objective.

It seems to me that the four-column model proposed by Lévi-Strauss can help us divine something of the difference all this implies between two classes of discourse:

Kepler	Libussa	History	Bohemia
Dreamer	(Interpreter/Reader?)	Book	Iceland
Duracotus	Captain (and/or) herbs	Sea voyage	Hven
Duracotus	Fiolxhilde	Daemon	Moon
SELF	OTHER	PROCESS	STASIS

This is similar to what Simon suggests. Speaking of Kepler's use of the zodiac in astrology he notes that the semes attached to the zodiacal sign are capable of infinite extension and can be multiplied without limit. This is because their function is to serve as "mediators between absolutely heterogeneous fields, such as heaven and earth, the world and man, nature and society." It seems quite apparent that the patterning of the *Somnium* works in just the same way. We are justified in calling the elements of the diagram and those of the other transformations mentioned in the course of this chapter "intellectual operators," as Simon does the signs of the zodiac and Lévi-Strauss the animals which appear in "mythical thought" or in the totem.[34]

One could, of course, propose other models, but since a model is at best only indicative there would be small point in doing so. Similarly, it is clear that the nomenclature of the columns is open to dispute, but the names given are merely those proposed by analysis, and several different 'possibilities' have already been suggested. What does not seem to me doubtful is the existence of the relation

34. Simon, *Kepler*, pp. 109–10.

between the elements in something like this form. Here discourse simply acts as mediation between 'self' and 'other,' it does not set up a paradox between process (life) and stasis (death)—or between any of the other "absolutely hetergeneous fields." It does not seek any single *explanation*. The system of transformations simply places the diverse elements in 'equilibrium' and leaves it at that. The possibility of explanation is displaced into another discourse.

Such a model nonetheless provokes a number of questions, only one of which strikes me as of immediate and real importance: Could one not compose just such a plan for *any* text ('literary' or other)?

The fundamental question here is not whether one *can* construct such a plan (to which the answer is necessarily affirmative) but whether, once constructed, it suggests a *different order* from that of our linear expectations: as an equilibrium of 'opposites' (for us), for example, rather than a linear progression (cause → effect; origin → descent; class → species) or exclusive contrast (true/false). In the Kepler text we can see something of both. Inevitably, since the text is written, it is composed in diachrony, but the sequences and the various elements we have been observing do not become coherent until the diachrony is broken down and recomposed in some such model as that suggested. Then it presents just such a pattern of figures and images as I have been discussing. And they are 'images.' For, really, the symbolic interpretations sought by a Jung, a Bachelard, or an Eliade owe their meaning to the existence of the pattern and not vice versa: the images are *there* in the text, to be provided only subsequently with their 'meanings,' their one-to-one correspondences with the concepts of the psychoanalyst, the poetician, or the historian of religions.

As Lévi-Strauss and others have observed, what is important is not the singular meanings but that they are derived from the relations between the images. That is also what we can perceive in the notes of the *Somnium*, in those analytical projections which are at odds with a kind of harmony in the text, which echoes the implications of the letter to Joachim Tanck and of such works as the *Mysterium cosmographicum* and the *Harmonice mundi*. Those texts appear to seek a science which would not be the useful imposition of the discursive *I* but which would be a manifestation of *laetitia*, of *voluptas*, of participation in the "world soul" and of a spoken 'presence' in a world whose elements order discourse rather than the contrary: a discourse in which the order of speech constructs the world.

The point is just that *the overall pattern reveals something different from the isolated syntagms*. The laws of nature applying to the planetary movements are not to be seen as points of departure for the construction of theories and the ordering of referential knowledge. They are simply bits and pieces of an overall harmony. That is why the equilibrium manifest in my (minimal) model of the text of the *Somnium* provides an index of a project different from the 'voyage to understanding,' or into the unconscious or whatever, of which the individual syntagms (the various separate sequences) might provide the symbol. Thus the patterned order is not at all to be confused with what might be called theme, motif, or topos. These are the functional elements of an analytical order. Patterning functions at odds with analysis: if the two discourses function simultaneously (as they seem to here), they subvert each other. The simultaneity does not add a supplementary layer of meaning (for example) but disperses meaning into a quite different optic. An element of patterning may well become a theme in a different discourse (say, the telling of a 'myth'), but then its purpose is one of analysis. Indeed, we will see Cyrano do this with some of the very elements found in Kepler's text. Cyrano takes them up and uses them for purposes of an analytical discourse. I return therefore to my question.

Can one do the same thing for later texts as one can for Kepler's? That is, can one as a general rule (for I am speaking of dominance) show a plan whose order seems to be different from the ostensible direction of the narrative? One might attempt to suggest that it can be done for much later texts, as some from the nineteenth and twentieth centuries. But it would not seem to be possible in the same way, and one would suspect indeed that the kind of coherence that patterning provides is no longer available to us—it would, on the whole, be dismissed with scorn as "mysticism," as Bertrand Russell does the conclusions of Wittgenstein's *Tractatus* in the introduction to that work. In modern texts, the presence of the "material image" could only be disruptive, not constructive: at least, if it could be constructive, it would construct a different discourse altogether.[35]

35. Concerning an apparent example of such disruption see Reiss, "Cosmic Discourse, or, The Solution of Signing," *Canadian Journal of Research in Semiotics*, 8, no. 1–2 (Winter 1980), 123–45. With reference to certain holistic views of society, and subsequent to a willful misreading of Marxism, Karl Popper produces a fine example of the kind of rejection I have in mind: "The doctrine that we may obtain a kind of concrete knowledge of 'reality itself' is a well-known part of what can be technically described as *mysticism*: and so is the clamour for 'wholes'" (Karl R. Popper, *The Poverty of Historicism* [1957; rpt. New York and Evanston, 1964], p. 78 n. 3). It may with some justice be doubted that the discourse Popper has in mind corresponds very precisely (to put it mildly) with what I am calling 'patterning' when he equates dialectical materialism with "utopianism" (thus reversing the evaluation of Marx and Engels themselves), but he does appear to have in mind something like a 'patterned whole.' That such an equation would annul history is precisely what the dispute between Popper and the Marxians was all about. See also note 4 to Chapter 5, below.

In later chapters I will use certain texts of the later seventeenth century primarily to indicate the occultation of a discourse and the rise to domination of another. A quick forward glance at the *Voyages* of Cyrano de Bergerac can give us an initial response to the question. For there, despite numerous other ambiguities, this is not one of them: if I try to apply the same model the peculiar thing is that the order disengaged by the columns is quite precisely that of the individual syntagms themselves. The order produced is a linear one of cause → effect: observation; first discussion of that observation and the statement of a hypothesis; experimental test; confirmation (full or partial) and new observation. But this order is *already* evidenced in each syntagm taken separately. Moreover, each sequence is given as *open,* in the sense that it is given as the beginning of the next sequence and as leading *causally* into it.

This kind of finding seems predominant in such later texts, and the lack of difference suggests that the analytico-referential order (in Cyrano's case following closely a Galilean experimentalist model) has by then become the dominant discourse. The two-dimensional model thus serves to show a difference between two forms of discourse: in the case of the analytico-referential the two dimensions coincide; in that of patterning they do not. In the latter case, therefore, we can simply note a mode of functioning; there is no question of ascribing 'meaning' to it. The lion has spoken, and we cannot understand it. For my present purpose that is all that is necessary, because what I am seeking to indicate is discursive functioning and its changes, not whatever might lie 'behind' or 'before' such functioning.

It is clear that the problem raised most urgently for the seventeenth century in the margins of Kepler's text is an epistemological one (and as an adjunct to that for us as critics, the question of the nature and functioning of discourse). A choice is now offered between the production of patterns and the construction of an analyzable meaning about the world, between a discourse of "joy and satisfaction," as Bacon scoffed, and one of utility and power. The ever more precise correspondence being achieved at the end of the Renaissance between an analytico-referential discourse and the world of phenomena made of the European seventeenth century perhaps the first after the fifth century of ancient Greece to feel the problem of knowledge as one having urgent need of a *solution.* This was so not only for the scientist and thinker but also for the technician and artisan who was to apply the abstracted system of the world to its controlling and possession: medicine and agriculture, geology and demography, education and economics, commerce and industry were just as much a part of this transformation as the "hard" sciences. The fate and significance of a discourse of patterning were tersely expressed at the time by another great scientist: "I am the more astonished at Kepler, than at any other," avers Salviati in Galileo's *Dialogue.* "Despite his open and acute mind, and though he has at his fingertips the motions attributed to the earth, he has nevertheless lent his ear and his assent to the moon's dominion over the water, to occult properties, and to such puerilities."[36]

Galileo was, of course, aiming his criticism more generally, but the fact that in this instance he was wrong, that the "moon's dominion over the water" should correspond both to scientific fact and to "popular superstition," might give us pause. The perhaps not altogether untimely lesson of the *Somnium* is that although we may refer to "fact" and "superstition" as to two mutually exclusive classes of discourse, they are not so much "opposites" as complementary, different from one another in their constructs of the same.

Indeed, the most appropriate answer to Galileo is perhaps to be found in the work of an equally celebrated scientist of our own time: "Science and the majority of educated people smile if they are set the task of interpreting a dream. Only the common people, who cling to superstitions and who on this point are carrying on the convictions of antiquity, continue to insist that dreams can be interpreted." Freud goes on in the same text to assert that such interpretation can and should only be the disclosing of relations, of a pattern: "Nevertheless all such systems of nomenclature and classification of the different kinds of delusion [he is referring specifically to paranoia and fetishism] according to their subject matter have something precarious and barren about them."[37]

Freud is not, of course, repeating Kepler's attempt to associate two different classes of discourse (or what will *become* two); at least not in the same way. For if one cannot classify by subject matter, one *can* classify in accordance with the "laws" that control the processes in question. Freud's purpose (unlike Jung's or Eliade's) is eventually to

36. Galileo Galilei, *Dialogue Concerning the Two Chief World Systems—Ptolemaic and Copernican,* tr. Stillman Drake, 2d ed. (Berkeley and Los Angeles, 1970), p. 462 (Fourth Day). Shakespeare, as in so many other cases, offers a pleasant example of such popular views, when Falstaff remarks to Prince Hal: "and let men say we be men of good government, being governed, as the sea is, by our noble and chaste mistress the moon, under whose countenance we steal." To which Hal replies: "Thou sayest well, and it holds well too; for the fortune of us that are the moon's men doth ebb and flow like the sea, being governed as the sea is by the moon" (*1 Henry IV,* I.ii.27–34). The play was probably written in 1597.

37. Sigmund Freud, *Delusions and Dreams in Jensen's 'Gradiva'* (1907), *Standard Edition,* IX.7, 45.

unveil "the structure of the apparatus of the mind and . . . the play of forces operating in it." This, he asserts, cannot be achieved by the investigation of any "mental function taken in isolation" but only by "a comparative study of a whole series of such functions," and by examining these processes, structures, and contexts from a diversity of viewpoints.[38] Freud's aim is not to provide singular meanings (though they may exist) but to 'discover' the processes that make the provision of such meanings possible (in mental functioning in general, in the case here of a given dream in particular, and also in consequence of the very process of analysis itself). Unlike Kepler, Freud views the relations (structures and processes) in question as both human and knowable. Unlike Galileo, he emphasizes structure and function over whatever precise 'content' they may be held to possess.

I will return to this matter later. For the present I will simply assert that like Frege, Peirce, and so many others, Freud shows the limits of the discursive class whose inception I am seeking to demonstrate here. It is therefore of considerable interest that in the first major psychological text of his career, *The Interpretation of Dreams* (1899–1900), Freud should have used the metaphor of the telescope to express the functioning of human mental processes. Indeed, the commentary concerning structure, function, and process to which I have just referred simply leads up to this introduction of the telescope.

I do not wish to interrupt the examination of the instauration of analytico-referentiality at this point, though it is useful—indeed essential—to keep the signs of its end in mind. I will therefore return in some detail to the question only in the concluding chapter. There I will suggest that Freudianism is a kind of 'mythical' repetition of a specific discursive history, the hypostatization of that history in the form of the human psyche and its permanent functioning. The matter is important because it tells us something about how a waning discourse can seek to maintain its dominance. It informs us of the possible consequences of ignoring the details of a discursive history. In the particular case of psychoanalysis, it also tells us something significant about our modernity and its ordering of certain forms of knowledge as power. But we need more information before we can draw conclusions in that direction, and so I will return to earlier developments.

38. Sigmund Freud, *The Interpretation of Dreams, Standard Editions,* V.511.

5 · *Campanella and Bacon: Concerning Structures of Mind*

Knowledge is the action of the soul, and is perfect without the senses, as having the seeds of all science and virtue in itself; but not without the service of the senses; by these organs the soul works: she is a perpetual agent, prompt and subtle; but often flexible and erring, entangling herself like a silkworm: but her reason is a weapon with two edges, and cuts through.

—Ben Jonson, *Discoveries*

The compass opened, if I may so express myself, the universe.

—Montesquieu, *De l'esprit des lois*

"The first century of modern science," to use Whitehead's phrase once again, opened in Italy with two martyrdoms, not one. On February 7, 1600, ten days before Bruno was burned at the stake in Venice, the civil authorities in Naples began their interrogation of Tommaso Campanella. In June, still holding out against the savage torture he was being made to undergo, the utopist started to feign madness. By such means he could (and did) avoid the almost certain death penalty that would be the reward for his leadership of the Calabrian conspiracy against Spanish rule. An insane person could not be shriven, and could not therefore be executed. Campanella was to spend the next twenty-eight years in a confinement that fluctuated between the almost unbelievably harsh and the relatively gentle.

These two martyrs were both equally at odds with the old and the new. Both teetered in the gap betwen an old discourse of analogies and a new one of analysis. But no longer were these presented as contradictory elements within a single class of discourse, or even as a class and a 'subclass' of emergent elements. More's paradoxes and the emergent solution of them in Kepler had now led almost to a situation where a *choice* was possible. Both Bruno and Campanella

168

claimed to see direct observation as the means to a complete knowledge of things. Thus we might imagine they held views and wrote in a manner akin to what we find in a Galileo or a Bacon. We would be mistaken: their choice was not the same.

In both Bruno and Campanella the term 'direct' tends to imply some form of nonmediated knowledge. At the same time, the term 'complete' refers us rather to a knowledge having to do with the Divine: indeed, to a kind of 'immediate awareness' of the Divine in all things akin to that 'organic participation' we have already seen. Their goal is not a gradual analysis of things with a view to their potential use, but rather a kind of accumulation of all possible elements of knowledge leading to some 'union,' to some conjunction within an all-embracing totality: "For in this condition of ours we cannot desire or attain greater perfection than that which is ours when our intellect through the medium of some noble intelligible species is united either to the separate substances, as some say, or to the divine mind, if we employ the idiom of the Platonists."[1]

It is significant, moreover, that Bruno's *De gli eroici furori*, from which I have just quoted, is couched in the terms of a variant of the schoolmen's fourfold interpretive reading of a group of poems and emblems. Such an unfolding of meanings forms part and parcel of the 'directness' and 'completeness' in question. "They say," adds Campanella concerning his Solarians, "that it is first necessary to look at the life of the whole and then at that of the parts."[2] We might find ourselves inclined to affirm that the entire *Città del sole* is an illustration of Bruno's assertion.

Here, reason guided by the will is not going to lead us to the use of things and to power over them, nor is it going to conduct us to

1. Giordano Bruno, *The Heroic Frenzies* [*De gli eroici furori*, 1585], ed. and tr. Paul Eugene Memmo (Chapel Hill, N.C., 1964), p. 117 (pt. I, 3d dialogue).

2. Tommaso Campanella, *La città del sole*, in *Opere di Giordano Bruno e di Tommaso Campanella*, ed. Augusto Guzzo and Romano Amerio (Milan and Naples, 1956), p. 1098. References to the Italian will be to this edition, indicated in the text by an I, followed by the page number. The Italian text was begun in 1602, and was translated, somewhat adapted, into Latin for its appearance as the *Appendix politicae civitas solis idea reipublicae philosophiae*, following Campanella's *Realis philosophiae epilogisticae partes quatuor* . . . (Frankfurt, 1623), pp. 417–64. The only English translation is by T. W. Halliday, which can be found in at least three anthologies. I have used Henry Morley, *Ideal Commonwealths* (London and New York, 1901): references to this will be indicated by an E, followed by the page number. The translation is not good: it is abridged and often rearranged in places where the translator has censored 'indecent,' theological, astronomical, and astrological discussions. In my text, therefore, the English reference will sometimes be lacking, and in such cases the translation is my own. I have also made use of the excellent modern French translation, *La cité du soleil*, ed. Luigi Firpo, tr. Arnaud Tripet (Geneva, 1972).

the greater material comfort of a section of humankind. This kind of reason is to bring the human soul to unity with the divine whole. Such is the revelation of *The Heroic Frenzies,* and such is what is illustrated in the very construction of *The City of the Sun.*

According to Marx, the utopian thinker writes as a bourgeois, who in the silence of his study gives free play at once to his reason and his imagination.[3] One might suppose that this assumed (psychological) duality of cause is reflected in the result. For the utopian ideal (at least after More) is at once a meditation upon history or a historical situation, which could be thought of in that respect as scientific, and the proposal of an 'ideal' solution that would close and eradicate history.

Of course, on the one hand one can hardly refer to Campanella as writing "in the silence of his study," while on the other no utopia can be scientific in the Marxian sense. For they are comparable only to thought experiments, which have been isolated from the particular sociohistorical situation that alone could make them scientific. I am not, however, as Marx and Engels were, concerned with the applicability of the *content* of such documents: in that regard Engels is perhaps justified in dismissing them as "phantasies" which may be left to "the literary small fry to solemnly quibble over."[4] The concern here is with the discursive functioning that produces such 'content,' that directs and controls it. I am assuming that it is a functioning that organizes at the same time the dominant forms taken by most other types of discourse produced in the same time and place: sociopolitical, economic, philosophical, scientific, critical, and the rest.

Utopian texts conceived as containing some kind of discussion *about* a historical situation may well be reckoned to be unusable

3. Paraphrased by Georges Duveau, *Sociologie de l'utopie et autres "essais"* (Paris, 1961), p. 7.

4. Friedrich Engels, *Socialism: Utopian and Scientific,* in Karl Marx and Friedrich Engels, *Selected Works* (New York, 1968), p. 403. See also *The Communist Manifesto,* ibid., p. 61. Such a view of the 'scientific' is combatted, at the same level of content, by Karl R. Popper in *The Poverty of Historicism* (New York and Evanston, 1964). Popper argues that all science works on more or less isolated experimental systems, and implicitly, therefore, would consider utopias to be valid as social (thought) experiments. They would indeed, he asserts, be more 'scientific' than the holistic approach of dialectical materialism, which constructs its theory of the development of the state, according to Popper's reading, from an a priori set of hypotheses concerning a particular and unique human history on the pretense that they are universal laws. This strikes me as a willful misreading of Marx, who seeks to show that human history is a developing set of coherent and traceable relations: they are not conceptual a prioris but observable realities. This gets us into problems with which we are not immediately concerned here, but the dispute in itself is worth noting as a significant example of the point of view from which written utopias have always been considered (by 'literary' as well as social or political critics).

fictions. But that cannot change the fact that as discursive practice they are necessarily one of the elements of the semiotic field that is the episteme in which they function. Their ordering will reproduce that of a specific ideology: "The domain of ideology coincides with the domain of signs. They equate with one another. Wherever a sign is present, ideology is present, too. *Everything ideological possesses semiotic value.*" In that sense it is impossible to separate any discourse from the social situation (for example) which makes it possible and for which it is in turn partly responsible: "*the sign and its social situation are inextricably fused together.* The sign cannot be separated from the social situation without relinquishing its nature as sign."[5]

To the extent that the utopia formulates an ideal 'out of history' at the same time as it presents a reasoned attempt to permit the insertion of that 'non-time' into the stream of a recognizable and localized history, it partakes of that discursive division characteristic of the European sixteenth and seventeenth centuries. In this it is comparable to science fiction—though I know of no utopia that seems to 'overcome' the split in the way Kepler's *Dream* does. Utopias seem rather to fall neatly onto one side or the other of the epistemic gap—though the complexity of their nominal origin, *Utopia* itself, makes of it the special case already examined. None other, of course, falls at a moment of such a crisis in discourse. Subsequent utopias always appear to make the choice which I have mentioned.

In so far as a utopia is 'dynamic,' as is the case of Bacon's *New Atlantis* (1627), it offers a kind of *construction* and *continuation* of history: an open-ended series which may be said to be adapted to the process of analytical thinking. When a utopia is 'static'—a term appropriate to *The City of the Sun* (1623) or to Andreae's *Christianopolis* (1619), for example—it suggests that halt to history to which I have just referred. Such a 'halt' is always found in the shape of a 'myth,' characterized by what one can only call a completeness of knowing and the known, a kind of fullness of being. In a way, just as the Marxians can argue that no utopia can be scientific, so it can also be asserted that utopias are always static—as Alexandre Cioranescu has done.[6] For such texts always suggest to some extent the sublimation

---

5. Valentin Nikolaevič Vološinov, *Marxism and the Philosophy of Language*, tr. Ladislav Matejka and I. R. Titunik (New York, 1973), pp. 10, 37 (original Russian edition, 1929).

6. Alexandre Cioranescu, *L'avenir du passé: Utopie et littérature* (Paris, 1972), p. 23: "The very structure of the genre forces it to remain within horizontal structures, in which epic details provide only an artificial relief: the great enterprise of vertical or diachronic cross-sectioning is not open to it." It is not therefore to be wondered at that he finds himself obliged to add later: "One may say that Bacon's utopia is not utopian" (p. 149).

of an existing social order in which they are nonetheless said to find their origin, or at least of some model abstracted from that order.

That a distinction can be made, however, between the static and the dynamic utopia, and that for the period with which I am concerned here such a distinction corresponds to that between patterning and analysis, is one of the things I hope to be able to show. For the two best-known utopias of the early seventeenth century represent an almost exemplary demonstration of two different classes of discourse in collision. Campanella's *City of the Sun* stands virtually as the paradigm of knowledge by analogies, resemblance, or the formation of patterns. Bacon's *New Atlantis* is the epitome of the new experimentalism, of the search for knowledge by a process of induction, by analysis and reference.

To be sure, Campanella was anything but ignorant of the expanding knowledge and technical know-how characteristic of his age. He is aware in some detail of the voyages of discovery: his dialogue between the steersman and a "Grandmaster of the Knights Hospitallers" is reminiscent of Pigafetta's relation of Magellan's voyage to the Grandmaster of the Knights of Rhodes.[7] His seamen served with Columbus, his Solarians have discovered flight, various forms of sea and land travel, and diverse other mechanical devices.[8] He hesitates between the systems of Ptolemy and Copernicus (I 1108; E 177), avoids pronouncing on the delicate question of the infinity of worlds, one of the charges brought against Bruno (I 1110–11; E 179), and refuses authority in learning, declaring a preference for the direct experience of things (I 1081; E 151–52).[9] All this may be gathered from even the most superficial reading of the utopia itself. Campanella was also, of course, so ardent a supporter of Galileo as to offer himself in 1632 as the scientist's defender before the papal commission, and he had previously risked his life and successfully put a stop to the process leading to his own freedom by his *Apologia pro Galileo* (1622, begun in 1616, the year of the first ecclesiastical injunction against Galileo). In that text he had, as De Santillana puts it, "called Aristotle and the Scholastics all sorts of names, had come out boldly for the Copernican system, and had propounded new and arbitrary interpretations of scripture."

7. See Charles E. Nowell, ed., *Magellan's Voyage around the World: Three Contemporary Accounts* (Evanston, 1962), pp. 85–260.

8. These last two details are omitted by Halliday.

9. This summary obviously does gross injustice to Campanella's thought as a whole, but I am concerned here in the main with what can be gleaned from *The City of the Sun*. For the rest see, for example, Léon Blanchet, *Campanella* (1920; rpt. New York, n.d.).

Nonetheless, as De Santillana elsewhere observes, these particular "perilous fantasies" serve Campanella rather to affirm than deny that science is the handmaiden of a humanism based in theological speculation.[10] Scientific discoveries are more or less satisfactory explanations, in the form of geometrical constructions, of the myriad workings of divine providence. Such discoveries are, that is to say, parts of the divine whole, union with which is the goal of life. Campanella's Solarians seek, as Luigi Firpo puts it, "the constitution of an organic and universal knowledge."[11] The entire city is shaped in terms of such an 'encyclopedia,' whose center and soul is the sign of God Himself, the Sun.

The Copernican system struck Campanella as a particularly happy model. In that he differs scarcely at all from Osiander's position in the preface to the *De revolutionibus*. He accepts the new cosmology as a suitable mathematical model for purposes of human knowledge but denies that it is reality.[12] This position, Renaissance humanist rather than anything else, is the very echo of the mode of thinking of the pre-Galilean philosopher. Speaking of Urban VIII, De Santillana makes the following remark:

> This is where his thinking was backed by the great schemes of the Renaissance and its hope in unknown harmonies. "There is nothing that is incredible," Marcilio Ficino had said. "For to God all things are possible, and nothing is impossible. There are numberless possibilities that we deny because we do not happen to know them." This was also what Pico della Mirandola had maintained, hinting at reaches of "natural magic" beyond our dreams; and Campanella, too, was supporting Galileo in the hope of results such as no scientist could ever produce. It was "Platonic theology" itself, urging man to extend his imagination beyond what he could see and test; it was Leonardo's belief in the creative power of artistic "fantasy."[13]

When Bruno writes that "the most brilliant and the most obscure, the beginning and the end, the greatest light and the most profound

10. Giorgio de Santillana, *The Crime of Galileo* (Chicago, 1959), p. 199 n. 7; pp. 19, 168.

11. Luigi Firpo, *La cité du soleil*, p. xxiii.

12. See Blanchet, *Campanella*, pp. 244 ff. Campanella writes: "Before presenting in Chapters IV and V the arguments from ancient and modern theologians which support and oppose Galileo, I shall construct from Holy Doctrine, the law of nature, and the agreement of mankind, *the most probable and substantial hypotheses or foundations* essential to their foundation" (*The Defense of Galileo*, tr. and ed. Grant McColley [Northampton, Mass., 1937], p. 14; my italics).

13. De Santillana, *Crime of Galileo*, pp. 167–68.

darkness, infinite potency and infinite act coincide,"[14] he is expressing a viewpoint essentially similar to what lies behind Campanella's criticism of scholastic learning, when the Solarians argue that the bookman "has contemplated nothing but the words of books and has given his mind with useless result to the consideration of the dead signs of things" (I 1082; E 151).[15] This is little different from their (and Campanella's?) acquiescence in the Copernican system:

> They praise Ptolemy and admire Copernicus, but put Aristarchus and Philolaus ahead of him. But they say that the one does the reckoning with stones, the other with beans, but none with the things themselves that are counted [*le stesse cose contate*], and that they pay for the world with calculating chips [*li scudi di conte*], not with gold. But they research this business [*questo negozio*] with much subtlety, because it is important to know the construction of the world. [I 1108]

The signs of things serve only to conceal them. Between the bookmen's activity of playing with the signs for themselves (say the Solarians) and that of the future technocrat who will take the signs for their referent, the choice is that of one side or the other of the same coin. The choice is visible (as it was not before), but it lies between two evils. The phrase "*stesse cose contate*" is a revealing one. It presents the goal to which the Solarian will bend his energies: a knowledge of things in themselves, without the mediation of signs, whether these be monetary, linguistic, or any other.

The Solarians have incorporated the elements of this knowledge within the very code through which their city is built. The gradual deciphering of these material elements will conduct the Solarian to the temple at the center of the city, where Sol is to be found, symbol of unity with the Divine. The world cannot therefore be ordered by humankind for its own use, because humanity is simply one further bit (debris, perhaps) among all the many to be pieced together. Like Kepler, the Solarian plays with shapes and figures that compose a plan of whose overall structure he is ignorant. Nonetheless, and again like Kepler, he fits some of them together into a discourse for whose order he *is* responsible, hoping thereby to fulfill a goal similar to what Andreae's Director of Learning proposes: "for he insisted that a close examination of the earth would bring about a proper appreciation of the heavens, and when the value of the heavens had

14. Bruno, *Heroic Frenzies*, p. 77.
15. The Italian is briefer: "perché non contempla le cose ma li libri, e s'avvilisce l'anima in quelle cose morte."

been found, there would be a contempt of earth."[16] *The City of the Sun* is an attempt to place heaven on earth, to inscribe all possible 'pieces of the world' into the order of its own construction. From this point of view it makes not the slightest difference whether the city's plan is to be found in the pages of a book or executed in stone in the hills of Calabria (as Campanella had indeed tried to do, before writing the text).

The city thus looks back to the Great Chain of Being for the ordering of the knowledge it contains, and to the *Critias* and the earlier Renaissance utopias of Doni and Stiblin for the outward shape of its succession of circular walls. The structure of the *Città del sole* directs the traveler inward, and ultimately through the microcosm that it is, to the infinity of the Divine that it seeks to produce.[17] It is not therefore surprising that its theme appears directed to a future and to a knowledge of the natural sciences: "It represents an unlimited will to know [*Wissen-Wollen*], which is directed at all natural objects."[18] "Appears" is the operative word, however. Such knowledge of nature is not simply a "will to know." It is the will to know God—in the very strongest theological sense of knowing. To this end the Solarians direct all their science. It cannot, therefore, be directed toward a future in any historical sense, for the Deity is not accessible to such a concept of 'natural' (or humanly ordered) history.

The Solarians are striving to put together the pieces of an ever-existent total order which subsumes them within its fabric. Perhaps such a totality is what is contained in the book written "in letters of gold of most important things, kept in the center of the temple" (I 1075; E 144). Of this book nothing more will, or can, be said. No doubt it is akin to the "cyclical" book of Borges's "Library of Babel," containing all possible knowledge, all possible forms of sense and of nonsense—in short, all discourse. And which is God.[19] Thomas More

16. Johann Valentin Andreae, *Christianopolis* [*Reipublicae Christianopolitanae descriptio*, 1619], tr. and ed. Felix Emil Held (Urbana, Ill., 1914), p. 187.

17. See, e.g., Charles Rihs, *Les philosophes utopistes: Le mythe de la cité communautaire en France au xviie siècle* (Paris, 1970): "*The City of the Sun*, a political work, is a description of the ideal State, an image of the divine order" (p. 293). Or again: "The Solarian approaches knowledge more as a Platonic philosopher than as an expert technician" (p. 299 n. 8).

18. Martin Schwonke, *Vom Staatsroman zur Science Fiction: Eine Untersuchung über Geschichte und Funktion der naturwissenschaftlich-technischen Utopie* (Stuttgart, 1957), p. 10.

19. Jorge Luis Borges, "The Library of Babel," in *Labyrinths: Selected Stories and Other Writings*, tr. and ed. Donald A. Yates and James E. Irby (Harmondsworth, 1970), p. 79. Michel Foucault has written some parallel remarks on this matter in "Le langage à l'infini," *Tel Quel*, 15 (1963), 52–53.

had sought to elaborate such 'wholeness' in his text, and found himself confronted with insoluble contradictions. Campanella is content to intimate something of the kind and then forget it.

The city "is divided into seven rings or huge circles named from the seven planets, and the way from one to the other of these is by four streets and through four gates, that look toward the four points of the compass" (I 1074; E 141). After the visitor has entered through the outer walls, of which the traveler remarks that "so thick are the earthworks and so well fortified . . . with breastworks, towers, guns, and ditches" (I 1074; E 142) that they would be impossible to storm, he passes through the subsequent rings and arrives at the foot of an ascent. "On the top of the hill is a rather spacious plain, and in the midst of this there rises a temple built with wondrous art" (I 1075; E 143). Like the Athenian Acropolis or the theocratic medieval discursive model, this summit embodies the mind of the civil society whose high point and center it is. The temple is not divided from the city but like the intellect or, perhaps, the soul (*anima*) it incarnates, it is opened up to it. A constant intercommunication can take place: "it is not girt with walls, but stands upon thick pillars, beautifully wrought," while at its center is to be found the dome with the altar beneath (I 1075; E 143). The occupants of the temple are the forty "priests and religious officers" (I 1075; E 144: the number is forty-nine in the Latin) of whom the principal is Sol.[20]

Sol is a godlike figure, all-knowing, analogous to the Borgesian book, the ideal of both Bruno and Campanella: he "is, as it were, *the architect of all science, having rule over all. . . . Sol is ashamed to be ignorant of any possible thing*" (I 1102; E 171: my italics). A far cry, this, from the ideal of a later scientist, who might well be ashamed of not *trying* to get to know everything, but certainly not of not actually doing so. Indeed, the priests, who are named after various human virtues, moral, intellectual, and physical, are described in a rather revealing manner. They are essentially the mediators between ordinary citizens and the government of Sol: "The priests, moreover, determine the hours for breeding and the days for sowing, reaping, and gathering the vintage, and they are, as it were, the ambassadors and intercessors between God and man" (I 1106; E 175).[21]

---

20. It may be noted that all the Italian MSS have the astrological sign ☉ for the name of the Metaphysician: the first Latin edition transcribes this as *Sol*, the second as an *o* preceded and followed by an *h*. The English translation has used *Hoh* throughout. I have replaced this in every case by *Sol*.

21. The Italian reads, "e serveno come mezzani tra Dio e gli uomini."

The ordering of the city is such that the traveler passes through the material walls to the pure intellect and soul at the center, and it is this structure that informs life within the city in all its forms and at all levels. The learning process itself is impressed upon the citizens by its means. The rejection of mere signs is a further indication of such a process, though their necessity for purposes of communication is recognized. The purely human symbolic languages of alphabet and mathematics are relegated to the fortified outer wall that would be the first to fall (though mathematics are given pride of place on its inner surface): for while the way to knowledge must initially lie through the outer skin, the learner must, so to speak, come through to the inside. As in Andreae's city, the observation of earthly signs is simply a moment in the passage to the unity of all things in the Divine (that being, in this sense, simply a way of patterning—necessarily, for in this conception *any* discourse can only be a *piece* of such overall plan). The alphabets are accompanied by the image of the whole earth on that same outer wall. Things are finally learned, not by talking about them, but by a direct observation of their images: that is to say, "by walking around them" and through them (I 1080; E 149).

Such symbols are replaced, as the visitor approaches the inner temple, by the depiction of natural objects (successively minerals, rivers and streams, vegetables, birds, and animals), until he comes to "the mechanical arts" and "the inventors in science, in warfare, in law" (I 1077; E 146), the prophets of natural religion, and arrives at last at a final resolution of the microcosm/macrocosm tension with the world on the altar, where is also to be found the soul/mediator, the ruler of the City of the Sun. The sun (who is also Sol, of course) is worshiped as the image of God, placed as it is in the heavens as His most visible sign (I 1109; E 178). It is at the same time the center of the city and the soul which receives illumination from the Divine. *Anima* as patterning operator seems clearly visible in this organization.

We are also very close, once again, to Bruno, who likewise uses the sun as a metaphor (and more) for the soul. The eye of the mind receives the light of God and translates it into love: "All love proceeds from the sight, intellectual love from the eye of the mind; sensible love from the view of the senses. [Sight] is not desired for itself, but surely because of some object, inasmuch as the apprehension of an object cannot take place without it."[22] Heart and eyes,

22. Bruno, *Heroic Frenzies,* pp. 131–32. For the sun as soul, see p. 137. The entire fourth dialogue of the first part is devoted to this discussion.

intellect and soul produce a kind of 'dialectic' of knowledge tending toward that unity of which I have already spoken. Through the eyes (whether physiological or spiritual) the object kindles desire, and that desire creates a dialectic whose object is to efface itself in a complete and perfect knowledge. And Bruno concludes his *Heroic Frenzies* with an allegory concerning the nine ways in which their humanity makes men blind to the light proceeding from "the divine object."[23]

Campanella's city is a kind of practical version of the "Song of the Illuminated" with which Bruno concludes the dialogues called *De gli eroici furori*.[24] It is a world in harmony, whose outer wall reveals "an immense drawing of the whole earth" (I 1076; E 145) and whose inner space is occupied by the image of the Divine and the seat of unity, at once political and spiritual, intellectual and material. Between them lie all the bits and pieces that make possible such a pattern. That it must always remain to some extent imperfect, that it must admit the possibility of finding a more appropriate contender for the position of Sol than the person presently occupying it, is the mark of an ordering that considers itself to be receiving its light from beyond. It views itself as striving to compose a whole from an accumulation of parts, under the inevitable constraint of being itself just one more such part. The Solarians sum up this situation in one of their pieces of wisdom: "The world is a great animal, and we live within it as worms live within us" (I 1110; E 178). One is tempted to recall Kepler's similar affirmation.

This plan and the harmony are fixed. They compose a variant of the older order of the Scholastics. It is by a logic in perfect accord with such an order that the city is communistic, and not at all as a prophecy of things to come. Here the dynamism of the individual, the impulse behind possession, the imposition of will have no role. It is not an accident that Campanella's system was originally planned and started as a dwelling place for and with the participation of many people (the Calabrian revolt), before it became a writing for the contemplation of the individual reader (and written in the solitude of prison).

What is depicted on the walls are the pieces of a static natural grandeur that is neither controlled by man nor controls him. It informs all activities and the entire system of the city. To be sure, there is a social hierarchy within the city (albeit very underplayed), but within each step there is equality of possession (though the

23. Ibid., esp. pp. 228–40 (pt. II, 3d dialogue), and p. 249 (pt. II, 4th dialogue).
24. Ibid., pp. 265–66 (pt. II, 5th dialogue).

Solarians are uninterested in material possession in any case) if not
of talent: and each talent, too, has its proper and permanent place in
that organized hierarchy. This is precisely the theocratic model of
certain medieval discursive theory. Given the static form of things,
all work in harmony (and the pieces can be ordered indeed only
because they do not change according to a willful human ordering). It
is to be expected that things are done by the inhabitants only "when
it is a pleasure to them" (I 1097 [*con gusto*]; E 167), and because it is
natural to do so (I 1089; E 158): "each one according to his natural
propensity [does] his duty well and pleasantly, because naturally" (I
1094; E 158). The harmony of the natural extends to include mankind.

Campanella's city is a kind of static refuge (not, I would insist, a
retreat) from the problem posed by an episteme on the verge of
confirming the adaptability of a discourse of analysis and reference,
of imposing a 'light' entirely human rather than accepting illumination from the outside, of affirming the difference between thinking
man and material substance taken as 'outside' his intellect. It is,
remarks one commentator, "an enchanted island, miraculously pre-
served at the Ocean's end, a perfect ark rediscovered at the end of a
dream."[25] Still, the Solarians are well aware of new developments.
They seem bent on seeking knowledge: "And when I asked with
astonishment whence they had obtained our history, they told me
that among them there was a knowledge of all languages, and that
by perseverance they continually sent explorers and ambassadors
over the whole earth, who learn thoroughly the customs, forces,
rules and histories of the nations, bad and good alike" (I 1077; E
147).

Yet this 'dynamism' is absorbed into the monolithic structure of
the city, just as the planetary laws were absorbed into Kepler's universal harmony. They are absorbed as a potential force for change
into a form that can accept no change. Where the harmony is perfect, the only hope for 'survival' is, quite precisely, no change. The
knowledge brought back from these searches becomes just so many
more bits and pieces to be inscribed upon the walls. The circles that
are at once the order of knowing *and* the order of the world that
is known, cannot but predicate their essential identity and constancy. That is why the movement to knowledge, the visitor's passage
through the walls, is inward. It is directed toward the divine intellect,
toward the soul, into the static knowledge and unity at the center of

25. Jean Servier, *Histoire de l'utopie* (Paris, 1967), p. 26.

being. There, all the bits and pieces of the world, through whose ordered inscription on the walls the traveler has passed, lose their multiplicity and partiality. A performance such as this in the early seventeenth century was, I submit, already almost archaic, distinctly conservative, the mark of a residual discourse.

Speaking of the necessary structure of all utopian fiction, Cioranescu has noted that its articulation is most similar to that of a lawyer's brief: "The hypothesis is its basic fact: the deduction is its logical scaffolding."[26] This forms the whole fiction: the static construction presented in the form of a closed and finished city. Now while this may not be a wholly inapt characterization of *La città del sole*, of *Christianopolis*, or even of *Utopia* itself (though it tends then to become a meaningless generalization), what are we to do with it when the fiction makes deduction (or induction) not merely the means of its scaffolding but its very subject? A recent utopia such as B. F. Skinner's *Walden Two* (1948), for instance, sets the idea of logical (experimental) progress at the very foundation of its functioning. And what is most frightening *for us* about *Brave New World* or *1984* is just exactly their static, sealed nature, and the quashing of the hope of experimentalism by extending it to its logical limits. There seems no a priori reason why the discourse of utopia should present a lack of movement, even though it shares the general aim of all analytico-referential discourse and therefore embodies the process/entropy contradiction.

Sir Francis Bacon lies at the other end of Huxley's and Orwell's dreary ladder, and in *New Atlantis* it is perhaps not surprising that a serial process should become its own subject. James Spedding, in his introduction to *New Atlantis*, remarks that while Bacon had only to write down "as known all that he himself most longed to know" in order to show the ideal result of the experimental labors of his state, yet "he could not describe the *process* of a perfect philosophical investigation" because he had not yet expounded such method in the *Novum organum*.[27] I would suggest that such a view reverses the *necessary* priorities, and that a discursive practice in fact precedes the formalization of such a method as content.

New Atlantis actually does the opposite of what Spedding claims.

---

26. Cioranescu, *Avenir du passé*, p. 25. This position is taken by most commentators of utopian fiction.

27. *The Works of Francis Bacon*, ed. James Spedding, Robert Leslie Ellis, and Douglas Denon Heath, 15 vols. (Boston, 1861–64), V.350. The text of *New Atlantis* occupies pp. 359–413 of this edition. Future references in this chapter will be indicated in the text by page number only.

That aspect is what contrasts most clearly with *La città del sole*. While the prospective *content* of knowledge is by no means a given (as it would also be according to Cioranescu's characterization), the discursive *process* by which it may be achieved is *shown* quite clearly, even if it is not spelled out (or *said*) in all its formalized details—which it could not be. The process is akin to that of a 'journey' and is constantly emphasized as such throughout Bacon's text. Its details will later be shown by Cyrano de Bergerac (see Chapter 7), for whom the journey, already in Bacon something more than simply a metaphor for the discursive process, will be hypostatized into the potential reality of a new technological capacity.

The fundamental structure controlling Bacon's utopia is based on a movement not toward the interior but toward the exterior, toward what is different, whether the structure itself be indicated as a voyage or as an observing gaze. In that connection the voyages of Columbus, Magellan, and others were as much a symbol of a new kind of discursive habit as they were real events—in much the same way as the telescope became a generalized metaphor for a certain class of discourse. If the City of the Sun can be compared to a prey contracted and trapped in a corner, situated near the Taprobana of an already outdated geography, then New Atlantis is an octopus, situated in a New World and sending its tentacles toward both the Old World and the quite unknown.

Campanella's interlocutor dismissed the voyage itself in a word (as he did those undertaken by the Solarians). The subjective narrator of *New Atlantis* insists upon it. In his discourse, movement and its accompanying troubles take on what initially appears an almost inordinate emphasis:

> We sailed from Peru (where we had continued by the space of one whole year), for China and Japan by the South Sea; taking with us victuals for twelve months; and had good winds from the east, though soft and weak, for five months' space and more. But then the wind came about, and settled in the west for many days, so as we could make little or no way, and were sometimes in purpose to turn back. But then again there arose strong and great winds from the south, with a point east; which carried us up (for all that we could do) towards the north: by which time our victuals failed us, though we had made good spare of them. So that finding ourselves in the midst of the greatest wilderness of waters in the world, without victual, we gave ourselves for lost men, and prepared for death. [P. 359][28]

28. It may be objected that I am making too much of the originality of this emphasis. Andreae also begins *Christianopolis* with the recounting of a voyage, storm, and

Once again the influence of the voyages of discovery is manifest. But in *La città del sole* dialogue placed the emphasis on intercommunication in a state of closure. Whether or not Pigafetta's tale of Magellan was the model, the situation of Campanella's interlocutor is, like that of Pigafetta, a subsidiary one: he, like every Solarian, is a small though necessary part of a greater encompassing whole. Bacon's narrator relates and emphasizes his voyage of discovery more from the viewpoint of a Walter Ralegh directing his own ships at the Americas. He can take responsibility for what can become his own "history of the world."

Ralegh's *Discoverie of Guiana,* for example, is not related as one single voyage. The principal journey represented by the passage of his ship is accompanied by his own short trips along the coasts of the islands he comes across, during which he "landed in every cove." The single long voyage is narrated as though it were the sum total of many short ones, culminating in his four-hundred-mile, month-long journey up the Orinoco. That trip itself is recounted as having been preceded by those of many other explorers. A similar technique is evident in Drake's *World Encompassed,* whose story was published the year after *New Atlantis.* Single voyages without sight of land for long periods were very definitely an uneasy experience, and fifty-two days in a tempest at sea, "with great trouble, long time, many dangers, hard escapes, and finall separating of our fleet," is more awful and brings greater fear than coasting up the shores of an enemy continent, raiding the Spaniards with one small ship and vastly inferior numbers of men, and constantly facing the unknown risks of the native Indians.[29] It is indeed a fact that such voyages were composed of miriad small trips: landings were constantly necessary to revictual and repair ships at sea for long periods, to explore and if possible take possession of the land, to obtain some idea of the inhabitants, and, in Drake's case especially, to raid the Spaniards. What I am suggesting here is the metaphorical value of such activities for a newly developing class of discourse.

---

shipwreck. There, however, it is completely allegorized: a voyage in the ship "Phantasy," across the "Academic Sea," toward true religion that has fled with "the companions whom she regarded the most faithful" (p. 144). Moreover, the island containing Christianopolis is a haven of rest, and once arrived there the sole survivor of the wreck will find himself in a city akin to Campanella's. Bacon's island is a place of constant journeying.

29. Sir Walter Ralegh, *The Discoverie of the Large, Rich, and Bewtiful Empyre of Guiana* . . . (London, 1596), pp. 2, 12–24; Sir Francis Drake, *The World Encompassed, Being His Next Voyage to That to* Nombre de Dios, *Formerly Imprinted* . . . (London, 1628), pp. 39–40 and passim (Drake's voyage around the world took place from 1577 to 1580).

The steady accumulation of such small bits and pieces is what will lead to honor and wealth. Such is ultimately Drake's goal. Ralegh makes no bones about it: "the shining glorie of this conquest will eclipse all those so far extended beames of the Spanish nation," his specific examples being Cortez "in *Mexico,* or *Pazzaro* in *Peru.*" Discovery is worthy of kingship, and the voyager may be considered a king, concludes Ralegh, as he asserts that if Elizabeth will not send a fleet to Guiana: "I will judge those men worthy to be kings thereof, that by her grace and leave will undertake it of themselves."[30] The men of Bensalem view matters and go about acquisition in much the same way: knowledge, power and gain, spiritual profit, and material utility go together.

So autonomous and self-dependent an activity carries with it its own risks. In Ralegh's case they were economic and, finally, political. Like Bacon himself, though with consequences even more disastrous, Ralegh expiated politically his collision with the entrenched order. Only a dozen years later the same opposition was to bring Galileo's case to a head: at his trial the confrontation of two different classes of conceptualization, 'science' and 'theology,' echoes the conflict elsewhere taking a political and economic form. In full awareness of such a contextual network, Descartes finds it useful, in the second part of his short treatise on what is presented as a *scientific* (or, at most, philosophical) method, to comment on his present inability to change the *political* order. The tone of the opening passage of *New Atlantis* may well remind us of Pascal's anguished cry before the fearful silence of unlimited space that will be heard only a short time later. Provoked by the same emerging elements, that cry is a reaction to the risks undertaken, too, by such as Ralegh, Bacon, Galileo, Descartes, or the earlier Drake.

Despite his own very real physical and spiritual risks and sufferings, that awe does not touch Campanella in at all the same way, and the interlocutor of *La città del sole* remains safe within the "animal of the world." The tenants of Bacon's text are very different indeed. Not only his travelers but his islanders as well experience the awe of being cast adrift upon the "vasty deep." Like Francis Fletcher, recorder of Drake's voyage, Bacon's islanders are concerned to avoid the dangers of an unknown that fascinates them.

For the moment, in *New Atlantis,* the voyage comes to a halt in a land in a quite unknown area of an unexplored ocean (p. 360): "in the secret conclave of . . . a vast sea" (p. 374), where they enter a

---

30. Ralegh, *Discoverie of Guiana,* pp. 94, 101. The present volume has room for only skeletal references to Ralegh. In some exemplary pages, Christopher Hill provides the meat: *Intellectual Origins of the English Revolution* (Oxford, 1965), pp. 131–224.

welcome harbor fronting a beautiful city. Pascal's dread leads him toward his two infinities and to the disavowal of analytical science as being the choice of constraining humanity within the limits of a flawed finitude.[31] That of Bacon's voyagers will produce the means to a scientific knowledge that lays claim to a potential completeness. Such knowledge will be achieved by means of such ever-renewed journeys as those composing *New Atlantis*. It is a 'completeness' not in the sense of an embracing totality but as an accumulation of discrete units—a totality, therefore, that is the sum of its parts and no more, following the manner of Drake's or Ralegh's quest.

In the text of *New Atlantis*, just when one might expect the journey to be at an end, a whole series of journeys gets under way. The initial voyage from the shelter of the old, safe world to this unknown island of Bensalem is to be repeated in several forms (though, in fact, this one is itself not the first voyage: for the reader enters in the very midst of the process, the travelers already having made the journey to Peru). It becomes the central figure of *New Atlantis*. Anchored in port, the sailors are not allowed to disembark, or even approach the town. It is only after several trips to and fro, after much discussion and ceremony, that the islanders permit them to land, and then only after waiting a night. From the prison their boat has become, they make the short trip that brings them to the "Strangers' House" (p. 364), where they will once again find themselves sequestered, this time for three days (p. 366). This one is a short journey in distance, but it is enormous spiritually.

Before being allowed ashore, the travelers find themselves in a no man's land, "between life and death . . . beyond both the old world and the new" (p. 367). Their habitual gestures are of no use, and they have yet to acquire new ones. They are to experience a kind of new beginning, stripped of the accoutrements of the old usages: "let us behave ourselves as we may be at peace with God," the narrator urges his companions, "and may find grace in the eyes of this people" (p. 367). They will become as children before the governor and priest of the House of Strangers, whom they regard as "gracious and parent-like" and whom they ask to accept them as "true servants" (p. 369).[32] In a sense, the travelers have not yet landed: away from the

31. On this matter see Louis Marin, *Critique du discours: Sur la 'Logique de Port-Royal' et les 'Pensées' de Pascal* (Paris, 1975), esp. pp. 18–19, 103–11; and my own comments in "Sailing to Byzantium: Classical Discourse and Its Self-Absorption," *Diacritics*, 8, no. 2 (Summer 1978), 34–46.

32. At this period the word "parent" meant not only father and mother—or simply "progenitor" at no matter what remove—but also anyone of close kinship. It seems legitimate to interpret the word here in the former sense, for he comes as governor

ship they are nevertheless not allowed into the city itself. When they do come forth (and even before doing so) it will be to learn an entirely new way of social and intellectual ordering, and what they will eventually be given "leave to publish . . . for the good of other nations" (p. 413) is far more than the surprising information about the established order of a City of the Sun: it is a whole new way of observing and controlling the world. To be sure, they will not be permitted to reveal the whereabouts of Bensalem, even if they knew it, and the knowledge gained by the "Fathers" of Salomon's House remains their secret, but the narrator can and does bring back the elements and system making possible that knowledge.

Some of the principal marks of the system are indicated from the outset. If the travelers are to begin afresh from a sort of 'zero point' in the acquisition of knowledge ('zero' both as to the how and to the what), if they undergo a 'spiritual rebirth,' the inhabitants for their part find themselves experiencing the fear of the unknown, facing the danger that is posed by the difference of what comes from the outside. Only later is it explained to the sailors why they are initially warned off by "divers of the people, with bastons in their hands, as it were forbidding us to land" (p. 260). They will be informed of "the laws of secrecy which [the islanders] have for [their] travellers" and of their "rare admission of strangers" (p. 370), the idea being to protect the integrity and knowledge of the island and inhabitants of Bensalem. The "interdicts and prohibitions" concerning strangers had been laid down by that enlightened lawgiver, Solamona, because he saw that the land could "be a thousand ways altered to the worse, but scarce any way to the better" (p. 381). "Perceiving the good which cometh from communicating with strangers, and avoiding the hurt" (p. 382), he had sought means to get to know foreigners without putting his own subjects to the risk of being known by them.

The discursive practice they maintain is thus marked at what is given as its points of origin—the island of Bensalem itself topographically and the King, Solamona, chronologically—by secrecy and an elitism of no uncertain kind: the island of Bensalem in respect of the rest of the world, the Fathers of Salomon's House as regards the rest of the island, the father in relation to the family. It becomes increasingly clear that the discourse of knowledge as a jour-

---

and priest, and he has just, at the moment the term is used, given the travelers the command not to go beyond a mile and a half from the House. It is true that after they ask him to accept them as his servants, he refers to their "brotherly love" for one another (p. 369). It is nonetheless clear that they regard him as their superior and guide.

ney always recommencing at the end of a previous one (which we will find 'translated' by Cyrano de Bergerac into the exact form of experimentalism) depends on the secrecy of the knowledge gained and then put into play again for the next 'journey,' and upon the superiority of the enunciator of that discourse.[33] In *New Atlantis* these elements are laid unbashedly bare, and I will return to them shortly.

After three days in the House of Strangers, the travelers still do not leave. Instead the islanders renew those trips to and fro that characterized their wait in port, and the governor of the House comes for a series of discussions. These are no less centered on sea voyages than the account itself up to the present. On the fifth day (the fourth having been given over to their instructions), the governor relates how a mysterious "ark or chest of cedar" (p. 372) brought them by sea the word of an apostle of Christ, to which event they owe their faith: if their Christian beliefs are the foundation of their society, as they are said to be, then they in their turn are founded in a sea voyage, whose telling is a part of the travel discussions held by the governor of the House of Strangers, themselves enveloped in the journeys that compose *New Atlantis*. Only much later do we learn that secrecy and superiority are an integral part of this faith as well: for "Moses by a secret cabala ordained the laws of Bensalem which they now use" (p. 391). They are set apart even from other Christians—which no doubt explains why the Jews who live on the island do so in such harmony (pp. 390–91), being also a chosen race!

The following day, the governor describes to them the state of navigation in the past, the flood of the Americas, and how his country was alone in maintaining a knowledge of foreign lands and the means to go there (p. 380). He goes on to tell that one of the principal activities of Bensalem is the dispatching every twelve years of two ships to go out into the world,

> appointed to several voyages; That in either of these ships there should be a mission of three of the Fellows or Brethren of Salomon's House, whose errand was only to give us knowledge of the affairs and state of those countries to which they were designed, and especially of the sci-

---

33. This accords precisely with analytical science as it is elaborated by Galileo, for example: see Reiss, "Espaces de la pensée discursive: Le cas Galilée et la science classique," *Revue de synthèse*, no. 85–86 (Jan.–July 1977), pp. 5–47. It also agrees with neoclassical juridical practice as explored by Michel Foucault, *Surveiller et punir* (Paris, 1975), pp. 39 ff. I do not seek to give a precise reason for their similarity here, but such elements are essential to the functioning of this class of discourse. As far as the succession of journeys is concerned, the very title page of Drake's *World Encompassed* is an example worthy of notice: " . . . being his next voyage . . . " (see note 29 above).

ences, arts, manufactures, and inventions of all the world; and withal to bring unto us books, instruments, and patterns in every kind. [P. 384]

After the revelation of this recurring and continuous voyage of research, the visitors, the strangers, begin to leave their "refuge" and see the country.

Ultimately, one of the "Fathers" from the House of Salomon returns, and they watch his ceremonial passage from the harbor, through the town, to some solitary retreat: "his coming is in state; but the cause of his coming is secret" (p. 395). After three more days, the narrator is admitted to his presence and permitted to join him in discussion. It takes the form of an instruction concerning the reason and justification for the House of Salomon, its activities, its journeys: "The End of our Foundation is the knowledge of *Causes*, and *secret motions* of things: and the enlarging of the bounds of *Human Empire, to the effecting of all things possible*" (p. 398: my italics).

The well-known passage that follows describes a veritable experimental institution with its means and experiments (pp. 398–409). Yet what is given are almost entirely descriptions of the material from which experiments *could* be made (which is why I have twice suggested that the *content* of knowledge is not given, but simply the means to achieve it). It is, affirms Cioranescu, "a veritable programme, to the extent that all programmes remain open and leave the door open behind them. It was thus that it was understood immediately: and as early as 1645 a philosophical College was founded in London, in imitation of Salomon's House, and which was the ancestor of the illustrious Royal Society." It is almost certainly too much to put the founding of the Royal Society down to the fiction of Salomon's House, but the latter's methodical repetitiveness, its continuity, and its open-endedness indeed lent themselves to such a descendant.[34]

---

34. Cioranescu, *Avenir du passé*, p. 149. In his introduction to *Christianopolis*, Held claims that Bacon had taken the idea of his center of learning from Andreae (pp. 41–74). This is nonsense. Andreae's center owes more to the kind of humanistic science of Paracelsus than to anything that comes later: it seeks out "the forces of agreement and opposition . . . poisons and antidotes . . . things beneficial and injurious to the several organs of man's body" (p. 200). It investigates "according to their characteristic marks and signs thousands of herbs, classifying them with respect to diseases" (p. 201). Others have offered different models: see, e.g., Rosalie L. Colie, "Cornelis Drebbel and Salomon de Caus: Two Jacobean Models for Salomon's House," *Huntington Library Quarterly*, 18 (1955), 245–60. Arthur Johnston observes that the "germ of this institute" is to be found in Bacon's own work: the *Gesta Grayorum* of Christmas 1594 and the *Commentarius solutus* of 1608 (Francis Bacon, *The Advancement of Learning and New Atlantis*, ed. Arthur Johnston [Oxford, 1974], p. x n. 16). Charles Webster, *The Great Instauration: Science, Medicine, and Reform, 1626–1660* (London, 1975), passim, seems to have given the definitive word on the matter, showing how

After the description, and after the Father has left the narrator with a reward of two thousand ducats, the tale comes to its abrupt close. To be more exact, it does not end, but leaves off the telling with the words, "the rest was not perfected" (p. 413). Spedding comments that Bacon had intended to show "a model political constitution, as well as a model college of natural philosophy" (p. 350), but asserts at the same time that "though not finished [the work seems] to have been intended for publication as it stands" (p. 349). This is not, I think, as contradictory as it looks on the surface: for the non-end does serve as an explanation of sorts of the series of voyages within voyages and suggests the direction indicated by the inductive discursive movement. It is a journey outward whose conclusion can always be only temporary—a time for the contemplation of the new knowledge gained before beginning once again (and always) a subsequent journey.

The narrator himself has followed just this pattern: a journey untold, followed by a year in Peru; a journey followed by the confinement in port on shipboard, "between life and death"; a journey to the House of Strangers, followed by "servitude" during three days; a journey to the solitary abode of the "Father" from Salomon's House, and the instruction of a new means and system of knowledge; a further untold journey home, and the writing of *New Atlantis*. The story, in a way, could not be otherwise. The experimental (analytico-referential) discourse must be open-ended and repetitive. The continual voyages, their halts for 'meditation,' the arrival at an empirical knowledge that leads the narrator into another journey, and so on ad infinitum, are the very image of the experimental discourse being elaborated throughout the period. At the same time, these elements echo the contemporary voyages of discovery and, at a different level, such general situations as the enormously increasing social mobility of the individual—a mobility at once vertical and horizontal, one of class status and geographical location. Later texts will show more clearly yet how such movement forms the very basis of their organization.

This dynamism is reinforced by what appears to become an essential element in the discourse of analysis and reference, in addition to

---

the Royal Society was a gradual consolidation of a whole network of intellectual activists chiefly in Oxford and London. I am not concerned with protecting Bacon's originality but with observing the fundamental distinction to be made between different discourses and their goals. Like the Solarians, the inhabitants of Christianopolis are undertaking to decipher the *world*. What we have there is not Galileo (or Bacon) but Fiolxhilde, Paracelsus, or Agricola.

secrecy and the superiority of the enunciator of discourse: the use throughout the fiction of the first person, both singular and plural. Such use may be contrasted with the almost exclusive use in *La città del sole* of the third person—despite its superficial use of dialogue (such dialogue being, in a manner of speaking, 'collective' rather than 'personal'). The usage corresponds exactly to what we find in Galileo, in Descartes, and in other writings of Bacon: the new scientist *imposes* the discursive *I* upon the world outside him. He is a conqueror enforcing his will, a man ravishing a woman: whether it be Galileo tearing the veils concealing the moon's nakedness in the *Sidereus nuncius*, diverse later grammarians disrobing a language they speak of as a woman, or Sir Walter Ralegh bluntly asserting the future rape of a yet relatively untouched part of South America:

> To conclude, Guiana is a countrey that hath yet her Maydenhead, never sackt, turned, nor wrought, the face of the earth hath not beene torne, nor the vertue and salt of the soyle spent by manurance, the graves have not beene opened for gold, the mines not broken with sledges, nor their Images puld down out of their temples. It hath never been entred by an armie of strength, and never conquered or possesed by any Christian Prince.[35]

That was just the attitude that had been savagely attacked by Montaigne in his essay "Of Coaches" only a few years before (1588), and utterly condemned by Las Casas in his *Brief Relation* of 1552, written against Spanish behavior in the "Indies."

In the *Passions de l'âme*, Descartes will hypostatize that *I* of discourse into the psychological self of possessive individualism, as Hobbes will into the political self in the almost simultaneous *De cive*. In literary discourse such a development will be paralleled by a new writing of introspection, revealed in "a minute examination of psychological detail [that] can make a gradual impression only on the consciousness of a persistent and solitary reader."[36] When that occurs, the secrecy, the superiority, and the power of the enunciating *I* have all been occulted: a new class of discourse has become dominant, thanks to the concealing of certain elements essential to the discur-

35. Ralegh, *Discoverie of Guiana*, p. 96. On Galileo, see my "Espaces de la pensée discursive," pp. 15–17, and on the grammarians, my "Du système de la critique classique," *XVIIe Siècle*, 116 (1977), 3–16.

36. Paul Delany, "*King Lear* and the Decline of Feudalism," *PMLA*, 92 (1977), 438; also his *British Autobiography in the Seventeenth Century* (London, 1969), passim, and pp. 19–23 for the relation between individualism, autobiography, and social mobility. See also Hill, *Intellectual Origins*, pp. 220, 295–96 (discussing especially Ralegh's poetry).

sive inception, but whose visibility would put in doubt the possibility of such discourse (if only for ethical or epistemological reasons).

Bacon's seeker is an individual *I* in search of knowledge that will allow him to enlarge "the bounds of human empire." It is a way to personal possession, with all the difficulties, hesitations, and fears that may be involved. The Fellows of the House of Salomon are searching for *personal* honors and riches as much—or more—as they are enrichers of the general store of knowledge: "For upon every invention of value we erect a statua to the inventor, and give him a liberal and honourable reward" (p. 412). It is significant that the narrator's own 'discoveries' (what he can reveal on returning home) should be rewarded in advance by a sum of money (p. 413).

It is certainly the case that Campanella's Solarians also received rewards: but in the first place *all* could win honors, and in the second such honors were entirely symbolic. In Bensalem such rewards take the form of material possessions, the very image of what is made possible by the invention itself. One may well be reminded of the aims of sailors from Columbus to Magellan, from Vespucci to Drake and Ralegh. Some three hundred years later, in 1896 (and almost simultaneously with Frege's 're-telling' of the telescope metaphor), Charles Sanders Peirce was to write: "But it is easy to see that the only kind of science the principle [of individual greed] would favour would be such as is immediately remunerative with a great preference for such as can be kept secret, like the modern sciences of dyeing and perfumery." And he continues by noting the difference between a science of the kind sought by Kepler and that of his successors:

> Kepler's discovery rendered Newton possible, and Newton rendered modern physics possible. . . . But Kepler's discovery would not have been possible without the doctrine of conics. Now contemporaries of Kepler—such penetrating minds as Descartes and Pascal—were abandoning the study of geometry (in which they included what we now call the differential calculus, so far as that had at that time any existence) because they said it was so UTTERLY USELESS.[37]

As a commentary upon the mode of activity of the Fathers of the House of Salomon, this is clear enough. Kepler's science had so little of the gainful or secret about it that he was on the one hand always

37. Charles S. Peirce, *Philosophical Writings*, ed. Justus Buchler (1940; rpt. New York, 1955), p. 48.

out of money, and on the other had no hesitation, in the *Astronomia nova* of 1609, in leading his reader through his incorrect calculations concerning the movement of Mars before arriving at the correct ones. That is unimaginable in a Galileo, for example, who uses his discoveries for purposes of profit and who never communicates (except unawares) any but his correct, final conclusions. To do otherwise would be to reveal the fallibility of the enunciator of the discourse—a revelation that Peirce will consider essential to the activity of science. Like Galileo, the Fathers of Salomon's House reveal only such finished artifacts as they choose, "such profitable inventions as [they] think good" (p. 412, the term "profitable" being used in the sense of 'useful' rather than 'financially rewarding,' though it is also that for its inventor).

It goes without saying that such remarks as these are intended not to make a pejorative moral judgment but to stand as statements of fact concerning the establishment of the hegemony of a particular class of discourse. Opponents of the new philosophy raised many questions of this kind. Montaigne had objected half a century before (in the 1588 edition of the *Essays*), in a voice echoing that of Las Casas and to be left behind like the Spanish Dominican's, that the new knowledge might have been used for a kind of new beginning, to benefit from a contact with "minds yet so pure and new," to elevate both itself and its potential pupils among the newly discovered natural souls of the Americas, conspicuous for their "yeelding naturall beginnings." Instead of which, the emphasis was being placed entirely upon increasing wealth and property: the Cortezes and the Pizzaros, the Cartiers, Drakes, and Raleghs shared an attitude utterly typical. Though less strong than the bitter fury that informed Las Casas's life work, the outrage expressed by Montaigne is far greater than later objections could be, once the new discourse had become firmly established:

> contrarywise, we have made use of their ignorance and inexperience, to drawe them more easily unto treason, fraude, luxurie, avarice and all manner of inhumanity and cruelty, by the example of our life and patterne of our customes. Who ever raised the service of marchandize and benefit of traffick to so high a rate? So many goodly cities ransacked and razed; so many nations destroyed and made desolate; so infinite millions of harmelesse people of all sexes, states and ages, massacred, ravaged and put to the sword; and the richest, the fairest and the best part of the world topsiturvied, ruined and defaced for the

traffick of Pearles and Pepper: Oh mechanicall victories, oh base conquest. Never did greedy revenge, publik wrongs or generall enmities, so moodily enrage, and so passionately incense men against men, unto so horrible hostilities, bloody dissipation, and miserable calamities.[38]

Like so many others of the sixteenth century, Montaigne's was a voice of passage, no doubt admired, but now long overcome by the dominant discourse of analysis and reference. Nonetheless, voices were raised even from within that dominance. Cromwell himself, in the manifesto of 1655 (perhaps written by Milton), justified his war against Spain with the claim to be avenging Spanish cruelty against the American Indians, on the grounds that such cruelty constituted an attack on all mankind. The Protector's assertion, of course, implied a convenient forgetfulness with regard to the excessive cruelty visited by his own troops upon the Irish. The emphasis on utility and profitability, if less that on secrecy, is just what Meric Casaubon, Prebendary of Canterbury, was to criticize in the new experimentalism. Writing to Pierre Du Moulin, a *Letter Concerning Natural experimental Philosophie, and some books lately set out about it,* published at Cambridge in 1669, Casaubon strongly attacks the two chief champions of the Royal Society, Thomas Sprat and Joseph Glanvill, for measuring utility by a strictly "materialistic standard." If, he argues, utility was "found only in what affords the necessities and conveniences of life, brewers and bakers, smiths and veterinarians would have to be considered equal or superior to those who have been regarded as the great lights of learning."[39]

Casaubon's essential criticism is aimed at the division of the material and the spiritual, the separation of the physical from the moral and aesthetic. His view is typical of the humanism preceding what Haydn called the "counter-Renaissance," and still alive in such writers as Tesauro and the late Paracelsans. Indeed, the Prebendary's opposition to simply utilitarian specialization (the form eventually to be taken by that initial emphasis on "secrecy") and to the consequent fragmentation of knowledge was not without its antecedent justifica-

38. Michel de Montaigne, *Essays,* tr. John Florio, intro. L. C. Harmer, 3 vols. (1910; rpt. London and New York, 1965), III.144 ("Of Coaches," III.vi). Florio's translation is not a model of accuracy, but is not unfaithful to Montaigne's tone, if anything rather exaggerating the outrage.

39. The quotation is from Richard Foster Jones, *Ancients and Moderns: A Study of the Rise of the Scientific Movement in Seventeenth-Century England,* 2d ed. (St. Louis, 1961). Jones paraphrases and comments on Casaubon's *Letter* at some length, pp. 241–44. For the Cromwell reference, see Christopher Hill, *Some Intellectual Consequences of the English Revolution* (Madison, 1980), p. 86.

tion in the writings of Bacon himself. The Chancellor always insisted that no object of knowledge could be studied in isolation. He went so far as to assert, indeed, that to try to do so would be fatal to the advancement of learning. In 1642 Comenius was making identical assertions. Nonetheless, the conservative nature of Casaubon's intervention is suggested by the fact that his "correspondent" had been one of the royalist theorists in the vituperative dispute with Milton, whose *Pro populo anglicano defensio secunda* of May 1654 had been directed specifically against anti-regicide arguments published by Du Moulin in 1652.

These fundamental aspects of utility, profit, and secrecy run over into other areas of human activity. It is a natural corollary to such a view of the scientific activity that the wise men of *New Atlantis* do not consider the state as a harmonious organism, on the model, for example, of the City of the Sun and the Solarians' view, or, looking a bit further back, on the model of the conjunctive polity of the Middle Ages. By the scientists of Salomon's House, the state is seen almost as a foreign body of which they are scarcely a part: they "take all an oath of secrecy, for the concealing of those [inventions] which [they] think fit to keep secret: though some of those [they] do reveal sometimes to the state, and some not" (p. 411).

Indeed, the state *is* composed, like any form of discursive knowledge of this kind, of discrete, separate units. Of these the family is the principal, being related to the whole much as is the House of Salomon: whenever a father lives to see "thirty persons descended of his body alive together, and all above three years old" (p. 386), then that family unit is celebrated. The father becomes judge, priest, prince, and chief celebrant of the feast, receiving from the King, just as do the inventors in an analogous situation, "many privileges, exemptions, and points of honour" (p. 388). Monogamous individual marriage (as opposed, for example, to the Solarians' collective breeding system) is praised as the essential maintainer of such a unit (pp. 392–94). One is irresistibly reminded, again, of Ralegh's conquering kings sailing to take Guiana, or of Machiavelli's process of princely power through a gradual accumulation of possessions.

We can see that the "political constitution" that was never written down as such is in fact already inscribed in the particular discursive order of which secrecy, willful hierarchy, and the power of the enunciating *I* are such essential elements. There is little doubt that Uscatescu is right in observing: "Machiavelli's conception of politics was in agreement with the fundamentals of the Baconian experimental philosophy. In addition, the idea Bacon has of politics is substantially utilitarian and activist."[40] There is nothing new in a statement of identity between the politics of possessive individualism and the scientific stance of experimentalism: "we do publish such profitable inventions as *we* think good" (p. 412: my italics). It is, remarks Charles Webster, "only a slight exaggeration to regard Baconianism as the official philosophy of the [Puritan] Revolution." And the same author notes the natural alliance between the new economic theorists, of whom William Petty would be typical, and the Baconian natural philosophers.[41] All these discourses are types of the developing analytico-referential dominance. That the structure of Bacon's sea voyage should illustrate such an institution is scarcely cause for surprise. It does need emphasizing, though, that this is revealed not only at the level of 'content' (as Spedding and others have it): the entire form of the fiction is built up from the impulse to control the other, to impose the self—in secret.

The fictions of Campanella and Bacon reveal a fundamental difference of impulse. The access to both is by a long sea voyage, certainly; but how quickly does Campanella jump the southern ocean to go to earth in his island, bound tight in its circular foundations, closed off as far as possible from the exterior expanse of the ocean. That voyage is essential to the entire ordering of *New Atlantis*, and mark of a new discourse of knowledge and power. The City of the Sun seeks to create (indeed, *has* created) a fixed world where the elements of knowledge, with their analogies and union with the divine, have been acquired and sealed on its walls.

Campanella's structure resembles the Platonic, then, in a way more essential than the mere similarity of its outward shape. And that is in the very impulse of its functioning. In the *Republic* knowledge is equated with being itself: "And knowledge is relative to being and knows being."[42] Such 'absolute' knowledge—knowledge of Unity, of Idea—is by definition accession to a 'total being' in something like the sense we tried to grasp when speaking of medieval discursive practices. Translated into Campanella's terms, the perfect knowledge sought by the city will be quite precisely coincident with that identity of the self with God attained at the altar of Sol.

Just as Plato's State is ideal *because* it is at once the homologue *and*

40. George Uscatescu, *Utopía y plenitud histórica* (Madrid, 1963), p. 89. Johnston, with others, tries to distinguish between the scientific and political orders sought by Bacon (ed. cit., p. viii). It is clear that such an argument strikes me as untenable.
41. Webster, *The Great Instauration*, pp. 25, 447–48.
42. Plato, *Republic*, 477—Jowett translation.

the analogue of the ultimate guardian, the perfect philosopher and earthly embodiment of the Divine (and one can, then, speak of an *identity*), *because* its perfect harmony is that of the just soul (in the absolute sense given to the term and concept 'Justice' by Plato), so also with Campanella's city. Moreover, though it is directed at such a unity with the Divine, it can do so only in response to an aura that proceeds from the Divine. Its light, as we saw earlier, does not proceed from within. It is entirely receptive, and its light is received from without and beyond: "Then the sun is not sight, but the author of sight who is recognized by sight."[43]

Bacon has taken each of these terms and inverted them. For him, in accordance with a remark in *The Advancement of Learning*, "the truth of being and the truth of knowing are one, differing no more than the direct beam and the beam reflected." This may well be, but however close they are kept, he has nonetheless separated them: knowledge and being are split into two separate fields, and for Bacon their generalization into concepts will be the responsibility of two different types of discourse. For Campanella and Bruno, as for Plato, being *is* knowing; for Bacon knowing leads toward being: as for Descartes, *cogito ergo sum*. Knowing is action first of all, and it can only lead to being insofar as such being is concerned with the interaction of individuals responsible for their own choices. It is precisely thus that Hobbes will be able to found the new society of *Leviathan*, advancing the claim that his science of human society starts with the same punctual units and the same facts of their motion as any other science of mechanics: the equation of self–knowing–being is that of discrete unit–action–society.

Furthermore, the sun of *New Atlantis* is provided by the human mind, a mind that is no longer the mere recipient of light, but rather its imposer. Descartes will remark that in the power of his will man is the equal of God; Bacon writes that "the spirit of man is as the lamp of God, wherewith he searcheth every secret."[44] The biblical encouragement is put into practice in Bensalem. Salomon's House, the "noblest foundation (as we think) that ever was upon the earth; and the lanthorn" of the island (p. 382) is rather a caster of light than a receiver of it. Its pride is a natural history, written by Solomon and lost to the rest of humanity, that contains the "history" of "all the plants from the *cedar of Libanus* to the *moss that groweth out of the wall, and of all things that have life and motion*" (p. 383). Such knowledge of

43. Ibid., 508b.
44. *Filum labyrinthi*, in *The Works*, VI.422.

external nature is "Light," but it is a light that must be sought by an active process: the purpose of the Fathers from Salomon's House is to find "God's first creature, which was *Light*: to have light (I say) of the growth of all parts of the world" (p. 384).

Thus it is that the twelve seekers who go out from Salomon's House are known as "Merchants of Light" (p. 410), while the three members of the House who are responsible for the fomulation of "new experiments of a higher light" are known as "Lamps" (p. 411). The both seek and produce light, so that even the Atlantans' knowledge of the Divine is brought to them by their scientists: "It so fell out that there was in one of the boats one of the wise men of the Society of Salomon's House, which house or college (my good brethren) is the very eye of this kingdom" (p. 371). Faith, then, is received through science, not the other way about. The eye marks the distance of the discourse of analysis and referentiality from the object it wishes to grasp and know: we are back to the import of the telescope. This is a very far cry from the college as soul that we find in *Christianopolis*, or from the temple of *The City of the Sun*. Salomon's House is "the very eye of this kingdom." It is a very self-contained eye, quite unlike the reactive soul of Plato's State or Campanella's City. It is the very eye that sends forth its beams of light up the telescope to illuminate the object of its gaze that is so dramatic an ingredient of the *Sidereus nuncius*.[45]

Bacon's Bensalem is an island trying to have the best of both worlds: it too has its well-placed and long-lasting foundations, protected from the threats menacing it from the ocean. But Bensalem is constantly caught up in its journeying abroad, and its traveling sages receive the most honor and the greatest rewards. It is a city on the edge of Pascal's empty space, constantly angled toward flux, danger, and the transitory: "The being destined to water is an ever-changing being [*un être en vertige*]. At each moment he is dying, some part of his substance is endlessly crumbling away."[46]

In that, the inhabitant of Bensalem is similar to Duracotus; but now, instead of acting against the analytico-referential discourse, he has become its image. What may perhaps be represented by these islands, lying in the midst of uncharted seas, is the attempt to seize the discursive process of intellection, a certain form of consciousness. Each narrator, it may be, sails through "an oneiric experience"

45. See Reiss, "Espaces de la pensée discursive," pp. 13–15.
46. Gaston Bachelard, *L'eau et les rêves: Essai sur l'imagination de la matière* (Paris, 1942), p. 9.

toward "the revelation of his reality and of his identity."[47] But this should not confuse us into thinking that therefore these consciousnesses are the same: consciousness is the product and embodiment of discourse, itself the ongoing development of sign processes. As Vološinov has written: "*consciousness itself can arise and become a viable fact only in the material embodiment of signs.* The understanding of a sign is, after all, an act of reference between the sign apprehended and other, already known signs; in other words, understanding is a response to a sign with signs."[48]

The utopian structure may best be understood, it would here appear, as the objectivization of a class of discourse into a particular type of content. Between *La città del sole* and *New Atlantis* the difference is clear: the first may be compared most nearly to the text of Kepler's *Dream*, the second to the mode of its notes. They are different responses to a moment of crisis we saw already couched in the terms of More's *Utopia*, a text potentially containing them both but unable to make any decision—or even to conceive of such a decision, locked as it was in the contradictions of an altogether different discursive space. *Utopia* performed the moment of crisis, the *Somnium* revealed the emergence of a solution, Campanella's and Bacon's texts illustrate a further development: the separation and delimiting of the old contradictions. *La città del sole* is linked to a discursive past. *New Atlantis* opens up toward a new discursive future.

47. Ibid., p. 134.
48. Vološinov, *Marxism and the Philosophy of Language*, p. 16.

6 · *The Masculine Birth of Time*

> It appeared to us a land without memories, regrets, and hopes; a
> land where each sunrise, like a dazzling act of special creation, was
> disconnected from the eve and the morrow.
> —Joseph Conrad, *Karain: A Memory*

The paradoxes of *Utopia*, the hesitations of the *Somnium*, the
decision being forged between texts such as *La città del sole* and *New
Atlantis* are leading toward a new kind of dominant certainty. The
difficulty faced by a More is seized upon with scant ceremony by
Francis Bacon, his later successor as Chancellor of England, and all
the non-sense shaken out of it. *Utopia* had treated the act of writing
as essentially problematic. For his part, Kepler had sensed the presence of two different classes of writing, but strove to maintain their
mutual coherence by making the one the servant of the other. The
emerging analytical product will rapidly take over. *The New Organon*
will view a particular class of writing and the specific organization
of discourse it necessitates as the fundamental requirement of all
'right' knowing.

When we talk nowadays of Sir Francis Bacon, we tend to view him
as preoccupied with the foundation of an empirical science of nature. From one point of view this nineteenth-century legacy is well
founded. It is a fact that he often writes of a "legitimate science" and
of the series of "natural histories" that such a science establishes. We
should nonetheless remember at least three things: first of all, that
the restricted sense of the word 'science' is itself in part the result of
a particular later interpretation of Bacon's own work. For him and
his contemporaries the word's meaning was much broader: "It may
also be asked (in the way of doubt rather than objection) whether I
speak of natural philosophy only, or whether I mean that the other
sciences, logic, ethics, and politics, should be carried on by this

method. Now I certainly mean what I have said to be understood of them all" (VIII.159; *NO*, I.cxxvii).[1]

Second (and I will come back at some length to this matter), we may be tempted to find rather strange the application of the word 'empirical' to a science that begins with axioms and descends to "particulars" (as he calls them). Third, we should never forget that Bacon was first and foremost a lawyer and statesman—politician, rather, in modern parlance. He was a Member of Parliament from the Elizabethan era, and, after 1607, successively Solicitor General, Attorney General, Lord Keeper, and finally, in 1618, Lord Chancellor of England.

Bacon himself and his contemporaries viewed his work as at least the prolegomenon to a complete philosophical system. The system was inseparably linked with its author's legal and political activities— as the previous chapter has suggested. When he insists that the single aim of this system—and of all philosophy in general—is the betterment of human life and society, he has the right to expect us to understand such a statement as it comes from a man profoundly immersed in the life of his times, political and social. No doubt that is why the intellectual weight carried by Bacon for his immediate successors was not at all reduced by his political fall in 1621. Charles Webster has shown convincingly that if there is one single voice that resounds through the intellectual, social, and political revolutions of seventeenth-century England, it is indeed Bacon's.[2] In this respect critics often mention the Royal Society—as did the previous chapter. Webster emphasizes, rather, the many reforms in medicine, education, and social and political institutions. He notes that Bacon was perhaps more immediately important in these areas than he was ever to be in the natural sciences.

It is certainly the nineteenth century that insisted on the 'scientific' character of the Chancellor's work, the century during which the dominance of the model drawn from 'experimental science' reached

1. I have used throughout the following edition: *The Works of Francis Bacon*, ed. James Spedding, Robert Leslie Ellis, and Douglas Denon Heath, 15 vols. (Boston, 1861–64). In the references, the first two figures refer to the volume and page, the letters to the precise work (here, *NO*, *New Organon*), the subsequent figures to book, section, and/or paragraph, according to the organization of the work in question. The first reference in the text will give the complete title of a work, followed by the initials(s) I will subsequently use. Quotations from the *Redargutio philosophiarum*, the *Cogitata et visa*, and the *Temporis partus masculus*, are taken from the translations by Benjamin Farrington in his *The Philosophy of Francis Bacon* (1964; rpt. Chicago, 1966). References, however, are to *The Works* as for all other writings.

2. Charles Webster, *The Great Instauration: Science, Medicine, and Reform, 1626–1660* (London, 1975).

its apogee in the claims of scientists like Laplace, and faced its first serious misgivings in the work of such diverse thinkers as Marx and Maxwell, Helmholtz and Peirce. Before the time of this new crisis, no one had committed the same error concerning Bacon's work. Sir William Petty's judgment is typical and, coming from a man who played so very important a role in the intellectual network of seventeenth-century England, of special significance. Petty, it is worth recalling, was a doctor, one of the founders of the Royal Society, and a great friend of both Hobbes and Dryden, as well as one of the founders of demography as a science and of the strain of economic thought whose first great monument will be Adam Smith's *Wealth of Nations*. He chooses to underline above all the political aspect of Bacon's work:

> The *Advancement of Learning*, hath made a judicious *Parallel* in many particulars, between the *Body Natural*, and *Body Politick*, and between the Arts of preserving both in *Health* and *Strength*: And it is as reasonable that as Anatomy is the best foundation of one, so also of the other; and that to practice upon the Politick, without knowing the *Symmetry, Fabrick*, and *Proportion* of it, is as *casual* as the practice of Old-women and Empiricks.[3]

Such an assertion tells us several things. First, it is clear that the human body/political body comparison refers beyond Bacon to Machiavelli, and beyond the Florentine to Greek Antiquity. Petty, who is fully aware of the tradition, chooses to accentuate Bacon's importance. In part that is no doubt for polemical effect, Bacon's name being endowed with the weight already indicated. At the same time he can thereby underline its connection (and his own) with the work of that thinker who was now considered to have elaborated the first *scientific* work of political theory: Thomas Hobbes. For when Petty stresses the words "*Symmetry, Fabrick, and Proportion*" he reminds us of the goal that Hobbes himself had asserted of founding a theory of the state in "geometrical reasoning." At the same time, he implies that the idea is Baconian, and founded in a new discourse that the Chancellor would have elaborated (indeed, there had been a real intellectual and personal relationship between Bacon and Hobbes for the few years preceding the former's death).[4]

If Petty confirms in this manner my points about the breadth of

3. Sir William Petty, *The Politital Economy of Ireland* (London, 1691), preface.
4. Leo Strauss, *The Political Philosophy of Hobbes: Its Basis and Its Genesis*, tr. Elsa M. Sinclair (1936; rpt. Chicago and London, 1963), passim.

the term 'science' and the place of his political activity in the new discourse, he also substantiates my remark about an "empirical science." He says that immediate experience, whether in medicine or in politics, is quite useless. It can lead only to a "casual practice," as by those who practice medicine with no knowledge of first principles. He offers the new ('Baconian') discourse as a radical alternative.

So, too, does Giambattista Vico, whom we may take as a last witness in addition to Petty and Hobbes. In 1725, Vico begins the *Scienza nuova* by insisting that he will build a new science on Baconian principles. This science will exclude any consideration whatsoever of "natural" phenomena, because these were created by God and their innermost causes must therefore remain hidden from humans. It will instead concentrate on human society, for this is the invention of humans and therefore available to their understanding. Views such as these, of course, suggest a comprehension of the term 'empirical' that needs exploring—the more particularly here as it is so central a concept within analytico-referential discourse.

Confronting what he understood as a profound crisis of all human practices, Bacon (like many of his contemporaries) viewed his age as the time of a new "birth" of human thought, of human activities, and of the society that could come from them and be their embodiment. This birth would be enabled by a "legitimate" knowledge, which would produce "works" for "the betterment of men's lives." It is a constant principle of Bacon's discussion that such a birth depends on new discoveries, that such discoveries depend on experience ordered according to some methodical rule, and that such a method depends on *writing*: what Bacon calls *experientia literata* or "literate experience."

The old learning, he asserts (meaning not only that of the Scholastics but also that of his immediate predecessors—one can imagine what scorn he would have poured on the *Harmonice mundi*), does not depend on such literate experience. On the contrary, it gathers up bits and pieces of diverse notions, it tinkers with the results of a disordered 'immediate' experience of the world, which leads only to playing with words: one is reminded of Kepler and Campanella—not to mention Lévi-Strauss. Bacon, therefore, completely rejects the syllogism and scholastic logic, because, he says,

> the subtility of nature and operations will not be enchained in those bonds. For arguments consist of propositions, and propositions of words, and words are but the current tokens or marks of popular notions of things; which notions, if they be grossly and variously collected

out of particulars, it is not the laborious examination either of consequences or arguments, or of the truth of propositions, that can ever
correct that error, being (as the physicians speak) in the first diges-
tion. [VI.266: *Advancement of Learning (AL)*, II.xiii.4]

This kind of reasoning from images of nature taken as immediate
and drawn from 'raw experience' leads directly to "anticipations."
These "anticipations are far more powerful than interpretations"
because the "familiarity" of their expression straightway touches "the
understanding" and fills "the imagination." As soon as one is dealing
with literate or methodic experiences, the matter is no longer comprehensible by this kind of thinking (VIII.73–74: *NO*, I.xxviii). This
failure of language and experience is in need of correction:

> For experience, when it wanders in its own track, is, as I have already
> remarked, mere groping in the dark, and confounds men rather than
> instructs them. But when it shall proceed in accordance with a fixed
> law, in regular order, and without interruption, then may better things
> be hoped of knowledge. [VIII.135–36: *NO*, I.c]

And for this reason, he affirms:

> hitherto more has been done in matter of invention by thinking than by
> writing; and experience has not yet learned her letters. Now no course
> of invention can be satisfactory unless it be carried on in writing. But
> when this is brought into use, and experience has been taught to read
> and write, better things may be hoped. [VIII.136: *NO*, I.ci]

Such a concept of *experiment* is derived, not from some concept of
human relations with nature, but from the domain of political affairs, and Bacon seeks to explain his epistemological abstraction by
referring to the activities of government: "just as if some kingdom or
state were to direct its counsels and affairs not by letters and reports
from ambassadors and trustworthy messengers, but by the gossip of
the streets; such exactly is the system of management introduced
into philosophy with relation to experience" (VIII.133–34:
NO, I.xcviii).

In this matter certain texts of Galileo assert nothing else than what
we can see here. The Italian scientist constantly insists that what he
calls "raw experience" is absolutely useless. "Experience" is only usable when it has been ordered *beforehand* by a mental calculus. And
only a small number of lettered scholars are capable of inventing

such a calculus.[5] Once again we meet with the need for secrecy we saw among the Fathers of Bensalem. Bacon insists on this aspect of a prince's power when he not only urges that all "counsel" should appear to emanate from the prince directly and alone, but argues that the ruler should "extract and select" those "secrets" he wishes to communicate even to his own councilors (XII.146 ff.: *Essays,* XX).

He will go so far as to assert that "he is the greater and deeper politique, that can make other men the instruments of his will and ends, and yet never acquaint them with his purpose, so as they shall do it and yet not know what they do"; so great a politician, he adds, is entirely comparable to God (VI.225: *AL,* II.vii.7). We are once again reminded of Descartes's *Passions de l'âme,* where man is equal to God in respect of his will; and of the scientists of *New Atlantis,* where the secret functioning of power is a part of knowledge. These elements are, as we see, fundamentally tied in with the concept of *experientia literata*; they are the property of a small number of lettered scientists, owners of "legitimate" knowledge.

The reference to Galileo was not meaningless, therefore. It recalled once again the tetrad of Bacon, Galileo, Descartes, and Hobbes, which the quotation from Petty also emphasized. It is precisely within this relationship of will, secret, power, individual enunciator of discourse, literate experience, and human divinity that the new analytico-referential discourse will institute its dominance. Indeed, according to Bacon, the "order and method" of this practical and well-organized human experience correspond exactly to the "order and method that the divine word operated on the created mass" (VIII.115: *NO,* I.lxxxii). Such a phrase clearly contains the embryo of Hobbes's entirely human "*Fiat*" that logically founds the modern contractual state, our civil association called "Leviathan."

Such a relation enables us to glimpse the possible significance of Bacon's all-important "literate experience." Indeed, the *experientia literata* indicates in Bacon a kind of 'dialectic,' a constant play between the elaboration of "axioms," the "descent to particulars," and the return to the former. As he puts it in *The Advancement of Learning*: "all true and fruitful natural philosophy hath a double scale or ladder, ascendent and descendent, ascending from experiments to the invention of causes, and descending from causes to the invention of new experiments" (VI.215: *AL,* II.vii.1). A process such as this

5. See Timothy J. Reiss, "Espaces de la pensée discursive: Le cas Galilée et la science classique," *Revue de synthèse,* no. 85–86 (Jan.–July 1977), pp. 12–13, 18–30.

can clearly have neither a beginning nor an end. Indeed, the study of many examples of this kind of phrase (and they are myriad) shows that Bacon is indifferent as to his placing of axioms and experiments: sometimes the one, sometimes the other is placed first. That is tantamount to observing that there is no way of cornering Bacon in some narrow empiricism (or rationalism either).

Nevertheless, Bacon's literate experience, which seems initially to be a part of a kind of 'dialectic,' will easily take the linear form of a particular discursive elaboration, whose origin is an enunciating subject (rapidly hypostatized into a *self*) under the (communicative) necessity of *hiding* all marks of its own 'presence.' For diverse reasons, epistemological as well as political, logical as well as moral, the discourse must not be seen to take its origin in its own subject. The hypostatization of the 'dialectic' of knowing into the founding collective *Fiat* is one evidence of this. Bacon's *experientia literata* is thus mightily ambiguous. On the one hand, it indicates only the 'self-conscious' discursive organization of human thought and its 'objects,' without which organization there can objectively be no thought whatsoever. On the other, it is already leading toward its own hypostatization into the origin of all thought, of all power, of all authority and will, of all knowledge.

Critics have often claimed that such literate experience is at once a simple recording of experience, previously acquired in the form of disordered and unusable raw images, and the theoretical organizing of such 'experience' as 'experiment.' That is Spedding's view, for example. Benjamin Farrington notes similarly: "It includes i) the recording of experience and, arising out of that, ii) the employment of a certain direction and order in experiment."[6] We are dealing, that is to say, with memory and law. Bacon is thus assimilated, quite simply, to a Western tradition that dates from Plato and maintains (more or less) that writing is merely an efficient means of recording and representing speech: a matter questioned, but differently, in *Utopia* as well.

No doubt there is something of that in Bacon: one does not simply sidestep tradition. But there is much more. It is perhaps not irrele-

6. Farrington, *Philosophy of Francis Bacon*, p. 119 n. 2. The passages particularly noted by Spedding (in the edition of *The Works*) are *NO* (Latin original), I.ci; *NO*, I.ciii; and *De dignitate et augmentis scientiarum*, V.2. Essentially the same view is held by James Stephens, *Francis Bacon and the Style of Science* (Chicago and London, 1971), pp. 87–97; and by Lisa Jardine, *Francis Bacon: Discovery and the Art of Discourse* (Cambridge, 1974), pp. 143–49. Jardine views the concept of *experientia literata* strictly as a practical technique for composing and comparing experiments, even though she does grant it a certain privilege at that level.

vant to recall here the frequency with which the Chancellor refers, beyond both Aristotle and Plato, to the Presocratics. For him, writing is not a mere record. It is the very foundation of knowledge, whose recording it will *then* make possible as well: writing precedes *and* follows knowledge. Such a situation is explicit in Bacon. What remain implicit are the consequences (the Hobbesian *Fiat* being one). Indeed, not only do they remain implicit, not infrequently they are 'deliberately' occulted. A further example is worth noting immediately.

Empiricism itself, as an objective knowledge of reality, is the consequence of such an occultation. And that occultation will permit the installation not only of a certain kind of science but also of the liberal state as corresponding to the permanent reality of human relations and of humanity in general (Vico's argument also, at one level). I quote the following passage as an example of the occultation and because it puts the concept of literate experience in relation with a particular kind of political and historical knowing, and because it does so with respect to a figure Bacon considers one of his most important predecessors:

> And therefore the form of writing, which of all others is fittest for such variable arguments as those of negotiation and scattered occasions, is that which Machiavelli most wisely and aptly chose for government; namely, Observations or Discourses upon Histories and Examples. For knowledge drawn freshly and in our view out of particulars knows best the way back to particulars again; and it contributes much more to practice, when the discourse or discussion attends on the example, than when the example attends upon the discourse. [IX.266: *Of the Dignity and Advancement of Learning*, VIII.ii][7]

What are we to make of such a passage? It seems clear enough that the "Histories and Examples" in question are already literate experience, and not simply raw experience as Bacon appears to suggest. Even if such raw experience were not a priori impossible, Bacon knew as well as any that Machiavelli selected and altered the details of his examples to suit his needs. That is as much as to say that the 'dialectic of knowing' originally implied in the concept of

7. See VI.359: *AL* II.xxiii.8: "But for fables, they were viceregents and supplies when examples failed: now that the times abound with history, the aim is better when the mark is alive. And therefore the form of writing which of all others is fittest for the variable argument of negotiation and occasions is that which Machiavelli chose wisely and aptly for government; namely, discourse upon history or examples." See also VI.360–61, 376: *AL*, II.xxiii.9, 13, 38.

experientia literata is replaced by the notion that experience ordered in accordance with "order and method" corresponds in fact to raw experience, and the implication that such experience is common to all sensible and reasonable beings. Just as Descartes will, Bacon implies that method, once discovered, will allow all the same access to a common and identical store of good sense. In its turn, such good sense is taken as reacting to experiences that are everywhere and always the same.

The concept of a common, general experience—universal and reasonable, as the grammarians will have it—is one that permits the elaboration and practice of the liberal state, founded upon a contract between equal individuals, each possessed of a similar will. Like Descartes, Bacon will have a powerful share in the creation of the 'discursive space' making possible such an idea of knowledge and social practice. What has been occulted in a passage like the one just quoted is the awareness (that is, as a mark in discourse) of experience as itself the result of a certain kind of discursive elaboration: the term "*experientia literata*" is merely one of the indices of such an elaboration. The reference to Machiavelli has its importance as well. For the Florentine, as I observed in Chapter 3, is the writer who 'began' the development of a new class of political discourse, at precisely the moment when the older discourse was showing itself untenable.

By Bacon's time, two particular relationships had provoked a series of questions that needed urgent answers but to which no solutions were as yet forthcoming: the relation between man and nature, and the relations between humans. I am not neglecting the relation between man and God, but it is a fact that theology, despite its continuing force was more and more losing its *dominance* in political and social theory, Vico's "*scienza nuova*." Felix Raab, Christopher Hill, and others have shown that though a certain tension between the secular and the religious continues to mid-century, such is no longer the case by the end of the century—at least in England.[8] Galileo may have been impeached in 1633 in Rome, Descartes may have (so it has been said) withheld publication of the *Traité du monde* as a result, Campanella may have been forced to flee to Paris (there to live an honored guest), but their kind of thinking was common currency not more than twenty years later. It was in the first two areas that the questions seemed in most immediate need of solution.

8. See the various books by Christopher Hill concerning the social and political situation in seventeenth-century England, and Felix Raab, *The English Face of Machiavelli: A Changing Interpretation, 1500–1700* (London and Toronto, 1964).

When no solution is available to such peremptory questions, there is only one way to go: it becomes necessary to change the contextual field which gives rise to the problem—as Machiavelli had already started to do in the case of political theory.

From the beginning, as I have been suggesting, Bacon is working toward what he conceives of as a new discursive or logical space. It is a space essentially of *practice*: "But men must know, that in this theatre of man's life it is reserved only for God and angels to be lookers on," and man's work must aspire to *public* profit (VI.314, 316: *AL*, II.xx.8, 10). He will write in the preface and text of the "Plan of the Great Instauration" that "the true ends of knowledge" are directed only "for the benefit and use of life," that knowledge will exist only "to lay the foundation . . . of human utility and power": "the matter in hand is no mere felicity of speculation, but the real business and fortunes of the human race, and all power of operation" (VIII.36, 53: *NO*).

It is with such a goal in mind that Bacon seeks to lay the foundations of a new discourse, or a new logic (if we recall what we have seen him assert, for example, concerning scholastic logic). He wants neither more nor less than to change the direction of the human race. That is why he constantly affirms the difficulty of understanding and communication posed by these new principles of "writing," of "literate experience," and so on. But these principles, he says, are not refutable for all that, because they are to be found in a completely new space: "for confutations cannot be employed when the difference is upon first principles and very notions, and even upon forms of demonstration" (VIII.75: *NO*, I.xxxv). The terms here are, of course, all logical ones. He says again: "To attempt refutations in this case would be merely inconsistent with what I have already said, for since we agree neither upon principles nor upon demonstrations there is no place for argument" (VIII.89: *NO*, I.lxi). He faces head on, then, this previously dominant discourse, which works by "anticipations of nature," by a kind of 'bricolage' of immediate images of nature, by syllogism and circular argument: "I cannot be called on to abide by the sentence of a tribunal which is itself on trial" (VIII.75: *NO*, I.xxxiii). The problem of communication and closure is acute, and I will return to it in a moment, because as a consequence of it we discover one of the major occultations of this discourse: that of the enunciating subject (later, indeed, to be hypostatized as individual will).

The *New Organon* conceives of writing and the discursive ordering it installs as the fundamental necessity of all "*right*" knowing. Long before, Bacon had written in the *Redargutio philosophiarum* (*RP*, c. 1608): "Our way might properly be described as literate experience [*literata experientia*], the art or plan for an honest interpretation of nature, a true path from sense to intellect" (VII.78: *RP*).

Writing may be an early step toward the restoration of true knowledge, but it is perhaps not the first. Learning the proper way to write experiments (or to accompany them, so to speak, with writing) must precede, it is said, or at least keep step with the invention of suitable experiments themselves; but before correct writing can occur, a language must be discovered capable of mediating thought and things, concepts and causes. For language, writes Bacon, is not initially transparent. On the contrary, it is opaque and a distorting influence on thought, which it controls by organizing it in terms of the "wretched hotch-potch of traditional error" absorbed by children from the very moment when "they learn to speak": "The nature of words," he goes on, "being vague and ill-defined, is another source of illusion, nay, almost of violence to the human understanding. Words are a kind of currency, which reflect vulgar opinions and preferences, for they combine or distinguish things according to popular notions and acceptations, which are for the most part mistaken or confused" (VII.112: *Cogitata et visa* [*CV*]).

Language, thought, and reality are now three separate domains, and the first can be made a 'neutral' mediator between the second and third only with laborious effort. These "Idols," as Bacon will come to call them, must be cured by a retreat from the "Market Place" to a kind of Salomon's House of the mind. For if the effort is not made, there can be no advance whatsoever in "natural philosophy." This is necessarily the case, because "those faulty meanings of words cast their rays, or stamp their impressions, on the mind itself. They do not only make discourse tedious, but they impair judgement and understanding" (VII.113: *CV*).

The distinction between reason and language, between reason and things, between language and things, poses an enormous difficulty, particularly because the distinction cannot in any event be absolute: "for men believe that their reason governs words; but it is also true that words react on the understanding" (VIII.86: *NO*, I.lix). On the one hand, as I have noted earlier, neither words nor thought has any longer a direct relation with things; on the other, reason and language tend to become confused with one another. How then, we must ask, is it possible to distinguish the occasions when reason is governing words from those when words are governing reason? And how can we make *any* judgment whatsoever concerning the expression of things—whether in words or in concepts? These are the obstacles that Bacon, like Descartes, like Galileo and so many others, must overcome if he is to be able to proffer the hope of a (necessarily) written science of nature and of the human.

Bacon deals first with the matter of trying to make words equal to the expression of things. He responds to the question by a kind of ruse. He invents a kind of logical atomism *avant la lettre*. Mere definition of terms, he argues, is insufficient. For if there is no evidence underlying such definition of any right relation between discourse and the world (evidence that would itself depend on the definition in question), then any such attempt leads merely to an infinite regression: "since the definitions themselves consist of words, and those words beget others."[9] Thus, he continues, "it is necessary to recur to individual instances, and those in due series and order" (VIII.87: *NO*, I.lix). It is by no means clear how this can help to overcome the distance between words and things, because we are still at a loss for any guarantee of the adequacy or suitability of our expression of such "individual instances."

In his *Natural and Experimental History for the Foundation of Philosophy* of 1622, Bacon remarks that true knowledge can only be sought in "the volume of creation," because that is where the elements of a true language are to be found: "For this is that sound and language which went forth into all lands, and did not incur the confusion of Babel; this should men study to be perfect in, and becoming again as little children condescend to take the alphabet of it into their hands, and spare no pains to search and unravel the interpretation thereof" (IX.371). This, then, is the ruse—well known and widespread at the time. It is a question of metaphorizing states of affairs in the world as an alphabet.[10] In such a way, Bacon writes, the object of a legitimate science must be "to inquire the forms of sense, of voluntary motion, of vegetation, of colours, of gravity and levity, of density, of tenuity, of heat, of cold, and all other natures and qualities, which, like an alphabet, are not many, and of which the essences (upheld by matter) of all creatures do consist" (VI.220–21: AL, II.vii.5).

These alphabetical elements, solidly set in matter at the same time

9. In this evaluation I disagree with Ian Hacking, who suggests, on the basis of a passage in *The Advancement of Learning*, that for Bacon the difficulty is sufficiently overcome once clear and suitable definitions have been provided: *Why Does Language Matter to Philosophy?* (Cambridge, 1975), p. 5 and passim. If one can assert, as we will shortly see Bacon doing, that our world depends to however limited a degree upon the discourse in which we elaborate it, then it is clear that definitions of meaning are useful only after the precise nature of the discursive relation with the world has been clarified. It is *that* clarification that is most difficult for Bacon, as it is for Descartes—as it is also for us.

10. The most celebrated example is no doubt the "language of mathematics" passage to be found in Galileo's *Saggiatore* of 1623.

as they give form to it, will thereby permit the 'filling out' of a kind of natural grammar. This grammar will correspond in part to what we call natural laws, in part to the letters and syntax of the scientific language that is *experientia literata.* We are thus provided with the beginnings of a lesson whose term will be a right reading and a true writing of the (alphabetical) order of the world. In the "Plan of the Great Instauration," Bacon writes therefore that he had discovered many things of no particular use in themselves and therefore not "sought for on their own account, but having just the same relation to things and works which the letters of the alphabet have to speech and words—which, though in themselves useless, are the elements of which all discourse is made up" (VIII.49: *NO*).

The elements of the material world are thus an alphabet organized in just the same way as the letters that compose a discursive phrase; their order depends on the same kind of organization. A right reading and writing of the world is thus one in which the *projection* of the elements of written language and of those of the world in some way coincide (the Wittgenstein of the *Tractatus* is thus in many ways an exemplary descendant): "So also the letters of the alphabet in themselves and apart have no use or meaning [*nihil significant nec alicujus usus sunt*], yet they are the subject matter [*materiae primae*] for the composition and apparatus of all discourse. So again the seeds of things are of much latent virtue [*potestate valida*], and yet of no use except in their development" (VIII.152: *NO*, I.cxxi).

Eventually he will be able to assert that science—knowledge of things in general—comes at once from the nature of the human mind (which reveals itself in and through language, the witness to reason, words being "competent to express cogitations," VI.283: *AL*, II.xvi.2), and from the nature of things, composed of alphabetical "seeds." The two meet in *writing.* It only remains then to align concepts, whose reference is to reality, with expression (discourse), whose correct *order* corresponds with the *order* of the natural world: as far as their setting in order, their projection, is concerned, the seeds of right discourse coincide with those of matter. Bacon can thus speak of "the power and nature of words, as they are the footsteps and prints of reason" (VI.285: *AL*, II.xvi.4), having already asserted that "the common principles and axioms which are promiscuous and indifferent to several sciences" (=reason) (VI.217: *AL*, II.vii.3) are also "but the same footsteps of nature, treading or printing upon several subjects or matters" (VI.211: *AL*, II.v.3). The first principles of the sciences, which are reason organized according to the legitimate "order and method," *are* the "same footsteps of nature" and isomorphic with words, which *are* "the footsteps and prints" of that same reason.

Well-ordered writing thus provides us with an automatic analysis of the world, a logical analysis: its minimal parts coincide with the minimal parts of the material world. The final aphorism of *The New Organon* asserts that his new 'logic' sets out "to teach and instruct the understanding . . . , that it may in very truth dissect nature, and discover the virtues and actions of bodies, with their laws as determined in matter; so that this science flows not merely from the nature of the mind, but also from the nature of things" (VIII.347–48: *NO*, II.lii). So it is, too, that the monetary metaphor we saw earlier used as an indication of "mistaken or confused" popular thinking about the nature of things will now be employed as 'evidence' of a kind of division of labor and of a greater clarity in knowledge: "this part [in respect of language] concerneth as it were the mint of knowledge (for words are the tokens current and accepted for conceits, as moneys are for values)" (VI.285: *AL*, II.xvi.3).

So written syntax becomes a logical analysis of the world, merely by virtue of its very ordering process. But what evidence is there that such an analysis is *truly referential*, that it can *really* denote objects in the world? that it describes the world as it is 'in reality'? that the concepts ascribed in discourse are not simply more scholastic "spiders' webs" (VII.118: *RP*)? The answer Bacon gives to these questions is essentially that the proof of the pudding is in the eating: "in nature practical results are . . . the guarantee of truth" (VII.131: *CV*). If our discursive logic in fact produces the works it claims to be able to produce, this is the proof that its order and the order of that piece of the world it expresses *do* conform with one another, and that our knowledge is therefore a *true* knowledge: "Truth, therefore, and utility are here the very same things; and works are of greater value as pledges of truth than as contributing to the comforts of life" (VIII.157: *NO*, I.cxxiv). We should not, here, allow ourselves to believe that Bacon is changing his emphasis, or downgrading "the improvement of men's lot." He is at this moment concerned with referential truth, and consequently stresses that aspect of the matter. Finally he will have to give equal weight to both, so that "the improvement of man's mind and the improvement of his lot are one and the same thing" (VII.131: *CV*). Truth, utility, knowledge, and visible material production are identical: "what in operation is most useful, that in knowledge is most true" (VIII.171: *NO*, II.iv).

There remains a considerable ambiguity nonetheless, for it is by no means clear to what extent such truth is or is not limited. At times Bacon appears to suggest that truth of this sort can never be in any sense an 'absolute,' though he also asserts, apparently to the contrary, that "the investigation of nature and of all sciences will be the work of a few years" (VIII.355: *Parasceve*). Like Descartes, he seems to suggest here that his method will lead to the acquisition of all possible truth about nature. This is the line of assertions that will culminate in Laplace's conception of the universe as a mechanism entirely determined and mathematically predictable. But Bacon also argues that human knowledge is absolutely limited: "For the testimony and information of the senses has reference always to man, not to the universe" (VIII.44: *NO*, "Plan of the Great Instauration").[11] He goes so far as to hint that such new human ordering is a new universe of discourse, that the world thus invented consists of a new logical space, so that "by the help and ministry of man a new face of bodies, another universe or theatre of things, comes into view" (VIII.357: *Parasceve*).

We have seen the arguments about analysis and referentiality that permit the instauration of such a space. But if the epistemological difficulty has been 'solved' to some extent, there yet remain two considerable problems as far as communication is concerned (and which considerably affect the epistemological 'solution'). (1) How is one to communicate the new space of such a logic? (2) How is one to resolve the visible ambiguity of a humanly ordered discourse that is nonetheless able to conclude in the affirmation of some completed truths about nonhuman matters? (Vico's answer to the second one was, of course, that no such resolution is possible, and therefore no such affirmation either.)

11. See also VIII.77: *NO*, I.xli ("Idols of the Tribe"). Not surprisingly, John Wilkins makes a similar claim in relation to the kind of discursive habit that he suggests preceded that now being proposed: "There being not any Absurdity so gross and incredible, for which these Abusers of the Text, will not find out an Argument. Whereas 'tis the more Natural way, and should be Observed in all Controversies, to apply unto everything the proper proofs of it; and when we deal with Philosophical Truths, to keep ourselves within the bounds of Humane Reason and Authority" (*A Discovery of a New World, or, A Discourse Tending to prove, that 'tis Probable there may be another Habitable World in the Moon* . . . [1638], 4th ed. [London, 1684], pp. 94–95). Others went even further, making the claim that man can only know his own discourses, and that that is *all* he knows. No doubt, such is the traditional skeptical position: "In truth, if we look closely at the matter, and if we are willing to face facts honestly, man is not capable of knowing the cause [*la raison*] of anything other than what he carries out on his own model [*à sa mode*], or of understanding sciences other than those whose principles he himself composes. This can easily be proven if we consider closely the case of mathematics" (François de La Mothe Le Vayer, *Soliloques sceptiques* [1670; rpt. Paris, 1875], pp. 6–7; my translation). This is what underlies the viewpoint expressed by Vico in the *Scienza nuova* of 1725, as I have suggested.

The two questions point on the one hand toward authority, on the other toward falsifiability. And Bacon introduces the authority of an enunciating subject as the basis of acceptable communication, and a logic of the excluded middle as the foundation of belief. The first must necessarily remain hidden in discourse, because its visibility would deny the 'objectivity' and the 'transparency' of analytico-referential discourse. The 'sight' of this authority would place an irresistible obstacle in the way of any objective discursive truth. Such authority is necessary, however, as well for the needs of communicating a new discursive class (first question) as for those exigencies which concern the clear communication of a new kind of conceptualization (second question).

For this logic depends not only on the 'atomism' already discussed but also on the affirmation that understanding can be placed in adequate contact with material facts. Logically such an affirmation precedes the atomism, which is merely its proof. But the affirmation itself depends upon the exclusion of what Bacon calls all contrary or contradictory instances: "conclusions drawn from a limited number of facts would be valid only on proof that no contradictory instance could be found" (VII.139–40: *CV*), something that is in practice impossible. Yet though the human mind is akin neither to God nor even "to the angels," it is nonetheless "a kind of divine fire" (VIII. 204: *NO*, II.xvi) and its knowledge is to a degree perfectible. It may be possible "only to proceed at first by negatives," but it is also possible "at last to end in affirmatives after exclusion has been exhausted" (VIII.204: *NO*, II.xv).

By such means, explains Bacon, even though we are always dealing with "a limited number of facts," we will end up with certain truths:

> The first work, therefore, of true induction (as far as regards the discovery of Forms) is the rejection or exclusion of the several natures which are not found in some instance where the given nature is present, or are found in some instance where the given nature is absent, or are found to increase in some instance when the given nature decreases, or to decrease when the given nature increases. Then indeed after the rejection and exclusion has been duly made, there will remain at the bottom, all light opinions vanishing into smoke, a Form affirmative, solid, and true and well defined. [VIII.205: *NO*, II.xvi]

But it is impossible so to exhaust all possible instances. The exclusion itself can only come from the authority of enunciation, from a kind of discursive fiat, from the *I* of the new Alexander frequently mentioned by the Chancellor. For such a knowledge to be possible, there must be a new leader for the new discourse. The *I* will install a societal history composed of the truths/works of legitimate, written science, and these truths will be the elements of that history in just the same way as the letters of the alphabet are the elements of written phrases, and as the material seeds are the elements of the world.

Before this can be achieved further difficulties must be overcome. First, as I said, that authority must be invisible. Second, Bacon must succeed in making generally usable a discourse whose logical syntax is quite different from that of the discourse with which his listeners may be expected to be familiar. Like ourselves confronted with the discourse of patterning, Bacon has to deal with Wittgenstein's lion. The difference, as he sees it, is that he is himself the lion. His is the unfamiliar discourse. The new discourse of analysis and reference is an utterly new space making use of an inhabitual set of axioms. To some extent his solution here will enable him to overcome the epistemologically insuperable difficulty: the affirmation of adequacy between words/concepts and things was preceded by the affirmation concerning the excluded middle, that last depending finally on a completeness of knowledge that could only be unattainable. Bacon's solution to the lion problem will bear on this other as well: it will be a matter of situating the difficulty in the area of communication and access to knowledge, rather than in that of knowledge itself. As his surrogate says to the members of the Parisian academy in the *Redargutio*:

> But suppose you were minded to give up all you have been taught and have believed; suppose, in return for the assurance of the truth of my view, you were prepared to abandon your favorite views and arguments; I should still be at a loss, for I do not know how to convince you of a thing so novel and unexpected. The difficulty is that the usual rules of argument do not apply since we are not agreed on first principles. Even the hope of a basis of discussion is precluded, since I cast doubt on the forms of proof now in use and mean to attack them. In the present mental climate I cannot safely entrust the truth to you. Your understandings must be prepared before they can be instructed; your minds need healing before they can be exercised; the site must be cleared before it can be built upon. [VII.63–64: *RP*]

The sentiments expressed are not entirely dissimilar, on the surface, to the protestations of More's Hythlodaeus. The difference is that Bacon's philosopher is demanding a "clearing of the site," a return to some zero-point of the mind preparatory to the erection of an entirely new edifice. Descartes asks nothing else. But Raphael had sought rather to rejuvenate a decaying organism: the goal and the 'construction' are quite different. Indeed, Bacon also ties the matter, through Machiavelli once again, to the creation of the state, or at least to a new political situation:

> It was said by Borgia of the expedition of the French into Italy, that they came with chalk in their hands to mark out their lodgings, not with arms to force their way in. I in like manner would have my doctrine enter quietly into the minds that are fit and capable of receiving it; for confutations cannot be employed when the difference is upon first principles, and even upon forms of demonstration. [VIII.75: *NO*, I.xxxv]

These kinds of assertion imply, naturally, that the speaker himself has already achieved the passage into a new discourse. He is now in a position to lead others out of the wilderness. This is certainly Bacon's own view; and it is important in the present context that he should constantly indicate that what is at stake is two ways of *speaking*. It is in this regard that his dismissal of the old way of speaking is so revealing:

> A syllogism consists of propositions, a proposition of words, and words are the counters or symbols of notions or mental concepts. If then the notions themselves, which are the life of the words, are vague, ignorant, ill-defined (and this is true of the vast majority of notions concerning nature) down the whole edifice tumbles. [VII.125: *CV*]

We have seen other examples of this same critique, which is indeed repeated many times throughout Bacon's writings almost verbatim.[12] The old knowledge is entirely verbal. What is needed, writes Bacon, is true notions, appropriate and well-defined forms of language to render them, and a legitimate explanation of an adequate relation between concepts and things. We have seen that such true notions depend, on the one hand, on the idea that "the understanding [can] be brought into contact with facts in a straightforward unprejudiced way" (VII.138: *CV*) and, on the other, on the concept that the elements of discourse, of *written* discourse (the organization of the "letters of the alphabet"), correspond in their potential ordering to the elements of things. The first is referentiality, the second analysis.

---

12. For example: "The syllogism consists of propositions, propositions consist of words, words are symbols of notions. Therefore if the notions themselves (which is the root of the matter) are confused and overhastily abstracted from the facts, there can be no firmness in the superstructure" (VIII.70: *NO*, I.xiv).

The analysis and the reference are possible because the order of language and of reason is one and situated in a single model: "they are copied," he says in the Epistle Dedicatory to *The New Organon*, "from a very ancient model, even the world itself and the nature of things and of the mind." Yet it remains quite unclear how such a correspondence operates in practice: that is no doubt why there remains the ambiguity of a human discourse about an objective world (whether material, social, or whatever) whose truth is at once limited yet potentially perfectible. Still, to put it in such terms is to make an epistemological and potentially resolvable problem of the radical impossibility of discourse visible in More, and to a degree in Kepler —expressed by the process/entropy contradiction: the ongoing discovery of truth and the completion of knowledge.

Nonetheless the remaining ambiguities require a solution. Some kind of appeal to authority will provide it. Again, the difficulty is to conceal such an appeal. How to show simply that the logic of the excluded middle is founded in the true relation of concept and object, itself confirmed by the proofs of utility and practice, and that it is not simply the subject's fiat? The authority must be that of things themselves and of their seeds. The problem therefore is to displace the authority, to guide it toward its own disappearance (which was indeed one of the aims sought through the contractual installation of the liberal state). It is a matter, if you will, of concealing the limits *a quo* of the new discourse.

So, says Bacon, the true scientist, like Christ, comes "*in the name of* the Father," not *as* the father; unlike an Aristotle, for example, who "is his own authority throughout" (VII.69–70: *RP*, my italics). Such a 'distant' father, whose name one depends upon but whose authority one does not replace, is to have the effect of furnishing the discourse with its own authority, not that of its immediate enunciator. Authority there must be, because if it is to be supposed possible to arrive at final truths by means of a demonstrably complete exclusion of all negative instances, there must be some ground: for who can possibly claim to have exhausted all such contradictory instances? Quite obviously only the master of discourse. Bacon tries to displace that mastership. There is no doubt whence comes this authority in Bacon's eyes—it is the work of the Presocratics:

> I am studious to keep the ancient terms. For hoping well to deliver myself from mistaking, by the order and perspicuous expressing of that I do propound; I am otherwise zealous and affectionate to recede as little as possible from antiquity, either in terms or opinions, as may

stand with truth and the proficience of knowledge. And herein I cannot a little marvel at the philosopher Aristotle, that did proceed in such a spirit of difference and contradiction towards all antiquity: undertaking not only to frame new words of science at pleasure, but to confound and extinguish all ancient wisdom: inasmuch as he never nameth or mentioneth an ancient author or opinion, but to confute and reprove. [VI.215–16: *AL*, II.vii.2]

It is the Presocratics whom Bacon wishes to present as the authors of a complete way to knowledge (and not Plato, whom he accuses of "turning his opinion upon theology" and thus "infecting" his natural philosophy—VI.220: *AL*, II.vii.5). It is well known that Bacon had investigated the work of these his philosophical predecessors and "forbears" (as he calls them) at length and in depth, seeking to discover not so much *what* they may or may not have said as the *form* the saying took: "holding to [his] rule not to enter into controversy on points of doctrine, but to judge by 'signs'" (VII.68: *RP*). These signs consist of context, reception, future development, and the like, as well as the discursive organization itself; for, as he asks of Aristotle, for example: "what solidity of structure can be expected from a man who constructs a world from categories?" (idem). The signs in question are basically those familiar to Renaissance medical textbooks, "as anything by which we may make a prognosis."[13] In this case the prognosis concerns the knowledge that may be derived from a given discursive organization.

Such a demand undermines entirely the Presocratics' authority. For there exists no complete writing, only "fragments and references," as he says. But according to Bacon, "the force of a theory rests on an apt harmony of mutually sustaining parts and on a rounded and complete demonstration, and is weakened when handed down piecemeal" (VII.73: *RP*). Under such circumstances there can clearly be no authority in fragmented writings. What then is the basis for the Presocratics' authority? Well, in a nutshell, it is Bacon's own claim: "I am convinced . . ." (VII.74: *RP*). Authority remains his own: that of a new Alexander (VIII.132: *NO*, I.xcvii).

It is no doubt correct that elsewhere the Chancellor denies the necessity of any systematic demonstration, asserting that aphorisms "leave the wit of man more free to turn and toss, and to make use of that which is so delivered to more several purposes and applications. For we see all the ancient wisdom was wont to be delivered in that

13. Ian Hacking, *The Emergence of Probability: A Philosophical Study of Early Ideas about Probability, Induction, and Statistical Inference* (Cambridge, 1975), p. 28.

form" (XIV.182: *Maxims of the Law*; cf. VI.291–92: *AL*, II.xvii.6–7). But of course as far as the development of a new discourse is concerned he does not wish to leave room for "several purposes and applications": he is concerned with the logic itself, not with its content. He is creating the true logical method permitting the elaboration of the true, legitimate knowledge, with a certain aggressiveness of tone: "I hold that true logic ought to enter the several provinces of science armed with a higher authority than belongs to the principles of those sciences themselves" (VIII.43: *NO*, "Plan of the Great Instauration").

The authority for the new truth is the enunciator of the new discourse in which that truth is revealed. Again, one is reminded of the aggressive vocabulary of Ralegh or Galileo. Although Bacon asserts that the search for "truth" and the search for "magistrality" are not the same thing (VI.234: *AL*, II.viii.5), one of the major premises underlying his discourse is that "human knowledge and human power meet in one" (VIII.67: *NO*, I.iii). Thus he says, for example, that a government that has failed in wisdom justly loses its power (VIII.130: *NO*, I.xciv). Because he believes he has made the fundamental discovery, the basic and essential method which "contains within itself the potentiality of all particular inventions," and since such a discovery must be accounted "the noblest, the truly masculine birth of time" (VII.128: *CV*), it is clear that the only conceivable authority is his own discourse, which *is* and which develops from as it produces that discovery. Like Descartes, he is convinced he has discovered the sole method able to undertake "the management of the childhood, as it were, of philosophy in its course of natural history" (VIII.50: *NO*), the direction of all right science. The governor of the House of Strangers is abroad and all possible objects of discourse are aimed at by the teacher.

Possibly as early as 1603, in perhaps the earliest attempt to set out systematically what will find form in *The Advancement of Learning* and later in *The New Organon* (the opposition to an old discourse, the creation of the structure and goals of a new one), Bacon responds in an indicative manner to the apparent self-contradictoriness and circularity of 'More's' archaic quest, to the contradictions of Kepler's, and to an anachronistic choice such as Campanella will shortly make. The text in which he does so is the *Temporis partus masculus* (*TPM*), and this phrase, "the masculine birth of time," will recur constantly throughout the later works. There, the implications of birth and childhood, of paternal authority and legitimation that it reflects, will be thoroughly explored.

The *Temporis partus masculus* is presented as a patriarch's monologue to his son, and it predicates nothing less than the imposition of an entirely human history upon the world, by means of a precise knowledge of "motions," of the nature of things. This new knowledge will enable humankind to acquire riches and possessions, and to found a science that "is active and productive of works" (VII.114: *CV*). Human history will be the ordering of the world through a new discourse of science, aiming "to restore and exalt the power and dominion of man himself, of the human race, over the universe." It is a dominion that "rests only on knowledge" and will be "accompanied by rewards and blessings" (VII.129: *CV*). As the Chancellor will write much later: "the true and lawful [*vera et legitima*] goal of the sciences is none other than this: that human life be endowed with new discoveries and powers" (VIII.113: *NO*, I.lxxxi).

The new Adam will apply his names to things and create a new world through his control (instrumental knowledge) of them. He will "stretch the deplorably narrow limits of man's dominion over the universe to their promised bounds" and compose a new future fit to be passed on to his son (VII.17: *TPM*). No doubt is entertained that the new world thus made available is the real world. Later on once again, the now-disgraced Chancellor of England will take up this conception in the affirmation that the human understanding is "to be expanded and opened till it can take in the image of the world as it is in fact" (VIII.361: *Parasceve*). Ten years later Descartes will be saying just the same thing in the two treatises on the world and on man (though they will not be published until 1664 and 1662, respectively), in which the mechanistic fiction *becomes* the fact of the world.

Bacon's *mundus alter*—the 'real' world but also the life of the mind made manifest as an 'otherness,' as the place of "things themselves" (VII.31: *TPM*)—will make possible, once it has been made to function for the benefit of humanity, the creation of a new history, accompanied by a new and better society. That the real world and the world of the mind should be conceivable as one is because, as we have seen in respect of later texts, the model of discourse is the same in both. That discovery makes possible the "masculine birth of time" here being proclaimed by the master of discourse, father of the new science. What exactly is this birth? "All concur," he writes, "that truth is the daughter of time" (VII.131: *CV*). Or again: "rightly is truth called the daughter of time" (VIII.117: *NO*, I.lxxxiv).

For time to conceive and give birth to truth requires, one need hardly repeat, a particular progenitor. The father of discourse leads his son into the new order of the future by conducting him into a "marriage" with Nature: "I am come in very truth leading you to Nature with all her children to bind her to your service and make her your slave" (VII.17: *TPM*). Nature already has children, and it can only be the father who has brought them into existence for the understanding. The new scientific discourse (the "son") and its master and progenitor (the "father") are one and the same thing. The text of the *Temporis partus masculus* (as we have it) is enclosed between two such unions, the second and last being more specific yet than the first:

> My dear, dear boy, what I propose is to unite you with things them-
> selves in a chaste, holy, and legal wedlock; and from this association
> you will secure an increase beyond all the hopes and prayers of ordi-
> nary marriages, to wit, a blessed race of Heroes or Supermen who will
> overcome the immeasurable helplessness and poverty of the human
> race, which cause it more destruction than all giants, monsters, or
> tyrants, and will make you peaceful, happy, prosperous and secure.
> [VII.31: *TPM*]

The prime example of the discourse that will make this possible will be *The New Organon*, itself, like truth, "a birth of Time" (VIII.109: *NO*, I.lxxviii).[14]

The above quotation makes it clear that two ideas are constantly linked from the *Temporis partus masculus* on: truth, and the legitimacy of the discourse to be constituted by the father. 'Legitimacy' has to do both with truth as an adequation of words, concepts, and things (that is, with correspondence—or reference), and with the logical system capable of rendering such adequation (that is with coherence—or analysis). The word *legitimus* constantly recurs. Not to follow this legitimate method will be to act "dishonorably" and "undutifully" (VII.16: *TPM*). Illegitimate knowledge, the father asserts, is one that lacks order, that piles fantasy on fact without distinction, that fails to differentiate between types of discourse in respect of their "lawful" objects. Until such lack of differentiation has been replaced by a suitable analytical method (by a discourse that can "dissect" nature and reveal the lawful order of the composition of

---

14. "I am wont for my own part to regard this work as a child of time rather than of wit" (*NO*, "Epistle Dedicatory"). Such a sentence implies the same denial of authority to the enunciator of discourse that we have already seen. But it tends rather to make its authority unassailable, asserting that the truth of this discourse does not proceed from an individual, but from the very nature of things: it would therefore be absolutely 'objective.'

things), mankind, says the master of discourse, will continue to rave on "in this universal madness" (VII.17: *TPM*).

The legitimate science (of the *laws* of nature) must be able to withstand "the ravages of time," he insists. Indeed, it will constitute its own time as real, because its "legitimately" ordered development of "invention" (to use Bacon's terms) *is* the standard of the future. The linear order of analysis is the structure creative of the very idea of a human-historical 'future'; because it is given as a discursive space coherent in terms of its own "first principles" and not in those of some other class of discourse (such as the 'Divine'), it can only constitute *itself* as the shape of history to come. Time and historical society will be composed from the gradual unfurling of those individual and discrete truths that are the components of an eventually complete human knowledge (hence the phrase "Great Instauration"). Such knowledge is composed of particular truths in just the same way as discourse is composed from its separate alphabetical elements, and as the totality of the real world is composed from the "seeds of things" (*semina rerum*).

Once again the necessity for this discourse to assume that the orders of reason, of discourse, and of the material world all follow a singular model is clear. Truth here is a matter of both correspondence and coherence (as it was always to be in neoclassical discourse). By such means, the reins of knowledge and the power that accompanies it are firmly held in the hands of the master of discourse. We are a very long way indeed from Campanella and Kepler, from Bruno and Rabelais, from Agricola and Paracelsus. No matter that "theological beliefs" were so important for later scientific research that "no dimension of human speculation was untouched by their influence."[15] Being "touched" and being organized by are two different things. The progenitor's call "*ad tempus futurum*" that it confirm the success of his new methodical discourse (VII.18: *TPM*), with which the first chapter of the *Temporis partus masculus* concludes, involves a solipsism: if the method is installed it will constitute the only shape this future can take, and it is bound therefore to 'confirm' its own success. Whoever accepts it, as Bacon's surrogate had to say to his Parisian academic listeners, will have passed into a new universe of discourse.

That is why the new men, recipients of this discourse, must become as children. Truth itself and the method that produces it are

15. Webster, *The Great Instauration*, p. 494.

children in the very process of birth. Man too must be born anew if he would enter the new world: "the entrance into the kingdom of man, founded on the sciences, being not much other than the entrance into the kingdom of heaven, whereinto none may enter except as a little child" (VIII.99: *NO*, I.lxviii).[16]

The newborn truth and method answer the need to "set up in the midst one bright and radiant light of truth, shedding its beams in all directions and dispelling all errors in a moment" (VII.29: *TPM*). This is the light of *New Atlantis*, where the paradigm of childhood will be (as we saw) repeated, along with the emphasis placed on the sea voyage of discovery as productive of order and possession, that will be so constant a theme in *The Advancement of Learning* and *The New Organon*. This light is provided by a "machine," a machine whose reliability is assured as the masculine birth of time. It is the method of the new discourse itself, as finally set forth in *The New Organon*, arm in arm with truth, the daughter of time, and both generated by the enunciator and master of discourse: "There remains but one course for the recovery of a sound and healthy condition—namely, that the entire work of the understanding be commenced afresh, and the mind itself be from the very outset not left to take its own course, but guided at every step; and the business be done as if by machinery" (VIII.60–61: *NO*, "Author's Preface").

This is the machine of which he speaks also at the end of the "Epistle Dedicatory" to the same work. Descartes makes precisely similar demands at the beginning of the *Discours de la méthode*. For Bacon, the machinery in question is a set of "progressive stages of certainty" (VIII.60: *NO*), a method that "derives axioms from the senses and particulars, rising by a gradual and unbroken ascent, so that it arrives at the most general axioms last of all" (VIII.71: *NO*, I.xix).

The machinery will function on its own, as though it no longer needed the support of a now-hidden authority. It is clearly visible, for example, in the "great engine" of the state, of which Bacon often speaks and which leads straight to Leviathan. That, too, is an engine functioning on its own once the moment of the founding "*Fiat*" has gone by, and from whence is evacuated any visible presence of willful power, of originating authority (though the prince, first 'subject' of discourse, remains there).

Thus is elaborated the growing dominance of a particular class of discourse: a logic based on referential truth and internal (analytical)

16. "One might say that the kingdom of nature is like the kingdom of heaven, to be approached only by becoming like a little child" (VII.138–39: *CV*).

coherence, asserted by the discursive enunciating subject, and founded on the axiom of the excluded middle. The assertion in question is followed by the occultation of the subject, withdrawn from its own discourse. The discursive imposition of knowledge is concealed (it deals in "secrets"), and the authority and power openly assumed at the outset are gradually eclipsed: an equilibrium between equal speakers and owners of a public discourse is 'invented'—a situation founded on the balance of a contract between equals, and on the *voluntary* cession of individual powers taken to have evacuated the problem of authority and power (we will see this more particularly with respect to a work like *Robinson Crusoe*).

These occultations lead to a 'capitalization' of discourse itself, via a process that takes us through at least three stages. The first involves the acknolwedged imposition of the *I* of an enunciation avowedly producing knowledge and power (Galileo, Bacon). The second sees the surreptitious replacement of that "*I*" by a "*we*" whose claim is to collectivity (Descartes, Hobbes). The process concludes in a discursive practice asserting discourse to be at once a mechanism transparent to the truths it transports and an ordering system whose coherence alone is responsible for the 'value' of those truths.[17] In this mechanism, the social, political, epistemological, and physical realms coincide, thanks to a form of 'logical atomism' and the axiom of the excluded middle, which will permit reason to be hypostatized in the shape of that "good sense" that, according to Descartes, "is the best-shared thing in the world" (*Discourse de la méthode,* part 1); and thanks to the displacement of authority permitting the occultation of the enunciating *I*. This is the mechanism Bacon calls "literate experience," *writing*.

It is this system that becomes the fundamental structure underlying the very composition of a novel like Cyrano de Bergerac's *Histoire comique des état et empire de la lune et du soleil,* whose first part was published in 1657 but had been circulating in manuscript some years before. There the experimental method of Bacon and Galileo (for their underlying theories are very similar) becomes the basic process of discourse:

> But the true method of experience, on the contrary, first lights the
> candle, and then by means of the candle shows the way; commencing as

17. On the matter of the replacement in Descartes of the *I* by *we*, see Reiss, "Cartesian Discourse and Classical Ideology," *Diacritics*, 6, no. 4 (Winter 1976), 21–23, 25–26, and Sylvie Romanowski, *L'illusion chez Descartes: La structure du discours cartésien* (Paris, 1974), pp. 127–30 and passim. On discourse as an objective and public mechanism, see, e.g., Reiss, "Espaces de la pensée discursive," pp. 30–41.

it does with experience duly ordered and digested, not bungling or erratic, and from it educing axioms, and from established axioms again new experiments; even as it was not without order and method that the divine word operated on the created mass. [VIII.115: *NO*, I.lxxxii][18]

Here, too, we have more than a hint of one special element in the masculine birth that we have already seen, and that will be of increasing importance in the development of the analytico-referential. It is what I have referred to as 'a dialectic of knowledge' (a 'dialectic' quite different from what I spoke of regarding Campanella), a constant process of exchange between the method of the new science, experiments, "inventions," and the world of particulars: "from the new light of axioms, which[,] having been educed from . . . particulars by a certain method and rule, shall in their turn point out the way again to new particulars, greater things may be looked for. For our road does not lie on the level, but ascends and descends; first ascending to axioms, then descending to works" (VIII.137: *NO*, I.ciii). It might be said that with his diverse aerial voyages, the narrator of Cyrano's novels takes this aphorism literally!

The significance of this dialectical element will gradually increase, culminating most evidently in Hegel, and then in Marx. But for the present it is less evident than those other aspects I have been discussing. And it seems fitting to conclude this chapter with an exemplary word from a younger contemporary of Bacon, himself destined to celebrity:

> Gentlemen, when universal learning shall once complete its cycle, the spirit of man, no longer imprisoned in its gloomy reformatory, will stretch far and wide until its godlike greatness fills the whole world and the void beyond. Then suddenly the circumstances and consequences of events will come to light for the man who holds the stronghold of wisdom. Nothing in his life will happen unexpectedly or by chance. He will certainly be one whose power and authority the stars, the earth, and the sea will obey. The winds and tempests will serve him; Mother Nature herself will surrender like a goddess relinquishing the empire of the world. She will entrust the world's rights, its laws, and its administration to him as governor.[19]

18. See also *NO*, II.xxi.
19. John Milton, "The Seventh Prolusion: A Speech in Defense of Learning Delivered in the College Chapel," ed. and tr. Thomas R. Hartmann, in *The Prose of John Milton*, gen. ed. J. Max Patrick (Garden City, N.Y., 1967), p. 20.

Thus rejoices the young John Milton in "The Seventh Prolusion," delivered probably in the first half of 1632 to his fellow students and his teachers, when the future poet of *Paradise Lost* was twenty-three years old. At the outset, it reminds us of Hamlet's "paragon of animals," of his "king of infinite space" though "bounded in a nutshell." The enlightened predictability of the world conducts us in an uninterrupted line from Descartes to Laplace, passing through Newton and Kant. Mother Nature's surrender recalls both a Galileo and a Ralegh. The administration of the world's "rights and laws," the "power and authority" over the universe, and all created things summarize a development of which I have been taking Bacon as an exemplary representative.

This is the exultation and glorying of the willful discourse of power and knowledge, of knowledge as "power and authority." A later Milton may view the process less joyfully. In a somewhat contentious reading of *Paradise Lost,* Donald F. Bouchard explores the epic as relating the freeing of humanity from external direction, whether divine or satanic. In that sense, he suggests, there is no difference between the two "idols." Galileo, Bacon, and Descartes all asserted that the human will's own 'eye/I' was identical to the Divine. Bouchard writes of *Paradise Lost* that "only through a radical Christian position verging on heresy, if not atheism, can one begin to value the real import of the epic: God is dead that man may live."[20] *Paradise Lost* can thus itself be read as showing a passage from one discursive class to another. I will argue elsewhere that certain of Milton's political tracts perform an identical role of passage with regard to theoretical political discourse. Such texts perform, in different domains, a role analogous to that I have suggested of Kepler and Bacon. They thus confirm the passage as they make it more complex.

We must now see how the new willful discourse develops after its "birth." In the terms used earlier, we may say that the emergent elements from one discourse have now consolidated themselves into an entirely new class of discourse. What remains to be seen is its growth to dominance, from its first hesitations in a Cyrano, for example, to its final hegemony in a Defoe or a Swift.

20. Donald F. Bouchard, *Milton: A Structural Reading* (London and Montreal, 1974), p. 64.

7 · Cyrano and the
Experimental Discourse

> As Leonard Bloomfield has shown, scientific research begins with a
> set of sentences which point the way to certain observations and
> experiments, the results of which do not become fully scientific
> until they have been turned back into language, yielding again a set
> of sentences which then become the basis of further explorations
> into the unknown.
>> —Benjamin Lee Whorf, *Language, Thought, and Reality*

Francis Bacon asserts that a true science elaborates its axioms from facts ("particulars") by means of a "certain method and
rule." This method is nothing less than a new class of discourse. We
may justly say, with Whorf and others, that "science" in this view is
neither more nor less than the elaboration of a system of sentences.
To say that scientific research begins in a series of sentences which
indicate "the way to certain observations and experiments" is merely
to repeat Bacon's idea of "literate experience." It is Bacon, too, who
is at the root of the idea that such experiments are only "scientific"
when their results have once again been placed in the discourse
which originated those experiments (and observations), in such a
way that the process will be repeated indefinitely: "first ascending to
axioms, then descending to works."[1]
Bacon's is not, then, an idea of science limited to a relatively brief
moment at the beginning of the seventeenth century. It remains our

---

1. The phrase "experimental method" can obviously be invested with a diversity of
meanings (cf. Ian Hacking, *The Emergence of Probability: A Philosophical Study of Early
Ideas about Probability, Induction, and Statistical Inference* [Cambridge, 1975], pp. 35–37).
My use of the phrase "experimental discourse" or "discourse of experimentalism," as
in the previous two chapters and henceforward, is almost as a synonoym for the
phrase "analytico-referential discourse." It is rather more restrictive in that it seeks to
specify the model of that discourse, with specific reference to the development of the
'natural sciences' from the early seventeenth century on. Its precise meaning and
implication here is, of course, part of the point of my entire discussion.

own. It remains indeed by and large the underlying premise behind all our discourses of truth and, therefore, behind all the forms of what we term 'knowledge.' For Baconian experimentalism is not *simply*, as is often claimed, the active manipulation and 'forcing' of natural phenomena. Such manipulation is dependent, as it is for Galileo, on prior theory. Indeed, in his autobiography, John Wallis deliberately associated Galileo and Bacon as the model of "the New Philosophy or Experimental Philosophy" to be pursued by the group which was to form the nucleus of the Royal Society.[2] When Norwood Hanson argues, in a widely held contemporary view, that all observational terms are "theory-laden," he repeats Bacon's or Galileo's position: for in their 'dialectic of knowing' there can logically be no point of beginning either.[3] Thus a relatively recent schematization of our scientific methods depicts an order that could have been derived directly from the new discourse invented (found?) by Bacon, Galileo, and their contemporaries:

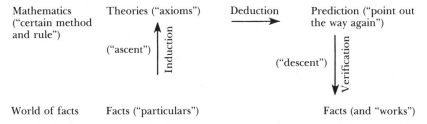

This diagram, without the Baconian analogues, is offered by John Kemeny as the fundamental system of scientific research in a text widely used in North American universities.[4] The analytical order which Kepler places, so to speak, in the margin of his text or seeks to incorporate as merely another piece in an overall organization (in the *Harmonice*); the method which Bacon and Galileo work out as a new space of discourse for which they must initially take responsibility as master—this order becomes with Cyrano the fundamental structure of a literary text. We may add that its doing so in the discursive type called 'literature' is sign that it has done so elsewhere. It is becoming generalized as the only form that can be taken by true knowledge, and the *responsibility of enunciation*, as I termed it earlier,

2. Quoted by Charles Webster, *The Great Instauration: Science, Medicine, and Reform, 1626–1660* (London, 1975), p. 56.
3. Norwood Hanson, *Patterns of Discovery* (Cambridge, 1965). The idea of all description and observation as "theory-laden" is the basic matter of this book.
4. John J. Kemeny, *A Philosopher Looks at Science* (New York, 1959), p. 86.

has been replaced by a notion of discursive *objectivity* (a replacement we see occurring from the very outset in the early works of Bacon, in Galileo, in Descartes . . .).

Following the Galilean model, the order of Cyrano's *Voyage dans la lune*, not to say its sequel the *Voyage au soleil*, is that of an uninterrupted series of experimental sequences, each of which is composed of four (or possibly five) elements:[5] (1) The first element repeats Galileo's epochal gesture of turning his telescope toward the moon. It is the phase of *observation*. Here the medium is always the naked eye. Its object, of course, is not always the moon or other celestial body, although it is in the first sequence—as is no more than appropriate. (2) The second element is an attempt to control what is perceived as exterior by 'internalizing' it, as though to possess it, and to express the resulting 'conceptualization' in (as) language, a sentence. It is an attempt to give *meaning* to the initial observation *within an already known discourse,* an attempt to *explain*. This element in the sequence continues on to a kind of 'double take,' resulting in a reappraisal of the initial attempts to conceptualize. We have a critical examination of the proposed theses, terminating in a *hypothesis* susceptible of verification by the undertaking of specifiable "works." (3) The third element is the carrying out of the *experiment* whose intention is to test the abstraction or the hypothesis put forward in the second element of the sequence. This is the descent to works that follows the ascent to axioms of the first two elements. It represents an attempt to close the distance between mind and events in the

5. The textual history of *L'autre monde* is complicated: even its title is variable. The *Histoire comique des estats et empires de la lune* was published in 1657, after Cyrano's death, by his friend Henri Le Bret, in an avowedly expurgated version. Copies of the manuscript are known to have circulated as early as 1649–50. Two of these are still extant, one in Munich, one in Paris. The basic critical edition of the two novels remains that of Frédéric Lachèvre in the first volume of *Les oeuvres libertines de Cyrano de Bergerac*, 2 vols. (Paris, 1921). For the text of the *Lune* alone the definitive edition is now *L'autre monde ou les estats et empires de la lune*, ed. Madeleine Alcover (Paris, 1977). Cyrano is increasingly published. I have however continued to use a readily available contemporary edition of both: Cyrano de Bergerac, *Histoire comique des état et empire de la lune et du soleil*, ed. Claude Mettra and Jean Suyeux (Paris, 1962); page citations will appear in the text, preceded by an F. The English edition cited is Cyrano de Bergerac, *Other Worlds: The Comical History of the States and Empires of the Moon and Sun*, tr. Geoffrey Strachan (London, 1965), and page citations appear in the text preceded by an E. These texts both give the 1657 edition with the variants from the Paris MS added or substituted, as the case requires. The English includes one or two variants from the Munich MS. Because I am referring essentially to the French, I have omitted these last. For the same reason, I have on occasion silently brought the English closer to the French original whenever my point requires it. In four cases it seemed useful to provide the full text of the French in a note. I will refer to the novels as the *Voyages*, in accordance with what is now customary.

world, and to compose a discourse adequate to things. (4) Finally comes the *confirmation* (full or partial) of the adequate relationship between hypothesis and particulars. It leads always to a new observation and a new experimental sequence.

The first of these sequences starts without delay from the first word of the novel:

> The moon was full, the sky was cloudless, and it had already struck nine. We were returning from Clamard, near Paris, where the younger Monsieur de Cuigy, who is the squire, had been entertaining myself and several of my friends. Along the road we amused ourselves with the various speculations inspired by this ball of saffron. All our eyes were fixed on the great star. One of our number took it for a garret window in heaven, through which the glory of the blessed could be glimpsed. Another assured us that it was the round, copper ironing-board on which Diana presses Apollo's collars. Another that it might be the sun itself, having cast off its rays in the evening, watching through a peep-hole to see what happened on earth in its absence. "And as for me," I told them, "I will gladly add my own contribution to your transports. I am in no way diverted by the ingenious fancies with which you flatter time, to make it pass more quickly, and I believe that the moon is a world like ours, which our world serves as a moon." Some of the company treated me to a great outburst of laughter. "And that, perhaps," I said to them, "is just how someone else is being ridiculed at this very moment in the moon for maintaining that this globe here is a world." But although I informed them that Pythagoras, Epicurus, Democritus and, in our own age, Copernicus and Kepler had been of the same opinion, I merely made them laugh more heartily.
>
> Nevertheless this notion, the boldness of which matched the humour I was in, was only fortified by contradiction and lodged so deeply in my mind that for all the rest of the way I remained pregnant with a thousand definitions of the moon of which I could not be delivered. As a result of upholding this burlesque belief with half-serious arguments, I had almost reached the stage of yielding to it already, when miracle or chance, Providence, Fortune, or perhaps what will be called a vision, fiction, chimera, or madness if you will, afforded me the opportunity that has engaged me upon this discourse.   [F 11–12; E 3–4][6]

6. "La lune était en son plein, le ciel était découvert, et neuf heures du soir étaient sonnées, lorsque, revenant de Clamart près Paris, où Monsieur de Cuigy le fils, qui en est seigneur, nous avait régalés plusieurs de mes amis et moi, les diverses pensées que nous donna cette boule de safran nous défrayèrent sur le chemin, de sorte que les yeux noyés dans ce grand astre, tantôt l'un le prenait pour une lucarne du ciel par où l'on entrevoyait la gloire des bienheureux, tantôt un autre assurait que c'était la platine où Diane dresse les rabats d'Apollon; un autre, que ce pouvait bien être le soleil lui-même, qui s'étant au soir dépouillé de ses rayons, regardait par un trou ce qu'on faisait au monde quand il n'y était pas. 'Et moi, leur dis-je, qui souhaite mêler

So begins the narration of the first *Voyage*. The experimental elements are here articulated in near exemplary fashion. The first observation of the moon leads directly into an attempt at 'explanation' that initially takes the form of a series of 'myths,' or 'pieces' of mythology. These attempts are closed and in the form of a subject-predicate definition: the moon is a "garret window," an "ironing-board," a "peep-hole," each suggested predicate being an element from a different mythology. These suggestions try to seize the moon and place it as a piece of the world into some previously elaborated discourse. The material image of the moon would serve only to fix more clearly the parameters of that discourse, for it is evident that none of these *tell* us anything whatever about the moon itself. Of course, all we see here are these particular pieces of a potential discourse of patterning. For reasons which will become clear in Chapter 8, they go no further than this. The fundamental reason is that the elements of myth are now themselves being aligned with the discourse of analysis and referentiality. They will be taken up later in the characters of Elijah, Socrates, and possibly Campanella, each in turn rejected, displaced, or simply put in doubt. But I will come back to this.

For the present, then, we are given pieces of a Christian myth concerning a Heaven of the *bienheureux,* a pagan myth concerning Diana and Apollo (there is a second one of this type suggested in the Munich manuscript conerning Bacchus), and an animistic myth in which the sun watches the activities of human beings. In a way the last of them *does* perhaps lead toward the new cosmological system which places the sun at the center of a mass of bodies whose motion it controls, and it does therefore lead the reader toward the narrator's own suggestion.

In this first series of suggestions, then, we can see a fairly exact

---

mes enthousiasmes au vôtres, je crois sans m'amuser aux imaginations pointues dont vous chatouillez le temps pour le faire marcher plus vite, que la lune est un monde comme celui-ci, à qui le nôtre sert de lune.' Quelques-uns de la compagnie me régalèrent d'un grand éclat de rire. 'Ainsi peut-être, leur dis-je, se moque-t-on maintenant dans la lune de quelque autre qui soutient que ce globe-ci est un monde.' Mais j'eus beau leur alléguer que Pythagore, Epicure, Démocrite et, de notre âge, Copernic et Képler, avaient été de cette opinion, je ne les obligeai qu'à rire de plus belle.
"Cette pensée cependant, dont la hardiesse biaisait à mon humeur, affermie par la contradiction, se plongea si profondément chez moi, que, pendant tout le reste du chemin, je demeurai gros de mille définitions de lune, dont je ne pouvais accoucher: de sorte qu'à force d'appuyer cette croyance burlesque par des raisonnements presque sérieux, il s'en fallait peu que je n'y déférasse déjà, quand le miracle ou l'accident, la Providence, la Fortune, ou peut-être ce qu'on nommera vision, fiction, chimère, ou folie si on veut, me fournit l'occasion qui m'engagea à ce discours."

illustration of Bachelard's critique of naïve observation, of "illiterate" experience: "The first experience or, to speak more precisely, the first observation is always a first obstacle to scientific culture. Indeed, this first observation is accompanied by a wealth of images; it is picturesque, concrete, natural, facile. All that has to be done is describe it and marvel at it. It is then believed to be understood." Nonetheless, Bachelard's claim that "there is rupture and not continuity between observation and experimentation"[7] is not borne out altogether by the development I see in the series of suggestions put forward by the narrator's companions. For the last of these does appear to lead toward the implications of the narrator's own belief.

To be sure, the narrator's hypothesis is not founded in a fixed system which would 'absorb' the material image of the moon as Campanella's City absorbs its pieces of new knowledge into *its* closed structure. On the contrary, it suggests the possibility of a system of knowing whose models change and 'expand' with each new piece. It supposes a continual exchange between the seer and the seen, for the hypothesis is proposed with the implicit premise that it can be tested: it is not just a way of passing time. The way this hypothesis is presented differs from the form taken by the other suggestions. The moon is thought to be *like* the earth, the earth *like* the moon ("la lune est un monde comme celui-ci, à qui le nôtre sert de lune").

It has been claimed that this clause, and the reversibility it proposes between the earth and the moon, their '*like-ness*,' introduces a "logic of relativity."[8] This phrase, in the present context, does not imply that the status of a phenomenon depends on the position of the observer, but simply that the position of the observer limits his knowledge of the thing. This provides both more and less freedom of hypothesis: less, because it can no longer be assumed that a hypothesis is verified once and for all when it has been incorporated into some 'knowledge system,' since that system is limited; more, because within those limits *any* hypothesis susceptible of verification may reasonably be put forward. In the present instance, for example, there is no possible reason to suppose that there is some absolute order in which the earth would be of a physical composition different from that of the rest of the universe, or that there are not other habitable planets. It is assumed, a priori, that if the observer can change his position he will gain new knowledge.

The hypothesis is assumed to be open to proof by some kind of

7. Gaston Bachelard, *La formation de l'esprit scientifique: Contribution à une psychanalyse de la connaissance objective*, 7th ed. (Paris, 1970), p. 19.
8. Maurice Laugaa, "Lune, et l'Autre," *Poétique*, no. 3 (1970), p. 285.

activity which, in this case, depends on a technical achievement whose very elaboration would be part of the proof. This, indeed, is what is demonstrated at the conclusion of the first experimental sequence in Cyrano's *Voyage dans la lune*: the landing in New France (the third element being the narrator's first flight). The relativity in question, then, simply indicates that our *knowledge* of a thing is 'relative' to our ability to extend the means of our knowledge and to our understanding that this knowledge depends on where we are and what we do with regard to the thing. 'Relativity' is doubtless a misleading word for what is essentially the Baconian exchange between particulars and axioms.

This does not seem to necessitate any kind of 'rupture' between the propositions of the companions and that of the narrator himself. Certainly there is development. By definition, the only way one could prove (or disprove) the first would be by dying and going to Heaven, while the second would require an acquaintance with the pagan gods in question. In both cases, the discourse to which they belong places a taboo on the passage and the acquaintance in question. This does not apply, however, in the case of the third proposal, which could be proven or disproven by the same means as the narrator's own, even though there is no suggestion that it should be: it does not altogether imply a closed system (though it may depend on one in practice). Perhaps this is why the first two propositions correspond respectively to the characters of Elijah and the demon of Socrates, while the third corresponds to that of Campanella.

A certain ambiguity remains, for the "great outburst of laughter" would seem to emphasize clearly the distance between the first three proposals, caught up to a greater or lesser degree in closed discourse, and that of the narrator, insisting on a process of verification guided by discourse but whose means (observation and experiment) are outside it. Indeed, the narrator appears to insist upon that distance: "Nevertheless this notion, the boldness of which matched the humour I was in, was only fortified by *contradiction* and lodged . . . deeply in my mind."

It seems to me that this ambiguity corresponds to a similar uncertainty we have already seen in Bacon: on the one hand the discourse is completely objective and therefore needs no 'personal' authority, while on the other it is totally unfamiliar and it remains necessary to *convince* prospective users of its objectivity. Since such users are confronted with a quite new and different discursive space, they cannot hope to understand unless they are first reduced to a 'clean slate,' and in that case conviction can occur only after the discourse has been inscribed on that slate by its master. Is the discourse 'objective,' or does it create its own objects? Does its acceptance depend on an authoritarian imposition (however enlightened), or is it so related to the order of the world as to be the 'natural' discourse of truth?

The first three proposals in this second element of the first experimental sequence of the novel do not succeed in providing an acceptable (and demonstrable) *meaning* in terms of any familiar discourse—they remain "imaginations pointues"—and the narrator has recourse to an unfamiliar one. When he states it, the others ridicule him. The narrator might well have observed that the previous suggestion already inclines toward a new cosmology and certainly does not preclude the need for, and the possibility of, experiment. But the point perhaps is that the discovery of a "new face of bodies" does require a new class of discourse, however unwilling to admit it may be those who urge such a new class upon their contemporaries. The lack of clear distinction between the proposals in Cyrano's novel, and yet the apparent *claim* of rupture (the emphasis on the growing laughter and on *contradiction*), match Bacon's bewilderment as to how to communicate his new discourse: "I do not know how to convince you."

The ambiguities I have mentioned as regards the relation of the experimental discourse with its predecessor(s) correspond to one within the discourse itself. If this new discourse is to function it requires its method and its axioms; to produce method and axioms it needs the observation of "particulars." The dilemma is that of the chicken and the egg. Bacon 'solves' it by the necessary but implicit assumption that the "ascending" and "descending" process is always underway. In this first sequence of Cyrano's novel it is solved by running through a variety of discursive possibilities until one is found which does not seal the answer in a ready-made discourse, in a past superstition or authority, but which "points out the way again to new particulars." This pointing out demands a recourse to "works."

That this interaction with the world is possible indicates the incorporation of an essential axiom of the Baconian discourse which the Englishman expressed most clearly perhaps in the negative: the rejection of that "exalted but deceitful view" which is "the doctrine that truth is the native inhabitant of the human mind, not something that comes into it from outside, and that the sciences do not inform the understanding but merely awaken it." Bacon refers to the view thus rejected as "this error or (to give it its true name) this alienation of the mind" (VII.115: *CV*). Truth, in the opposite view, which is as much that of the narrator of the *Lune* as it is of Bacon, is always the result of the interchange between mind and particulars.

The desire to find out the true nature of the moon is appropriate, therefore, only if, as here, it leads to a question that can be resolved by showing, through "works," that the hypothesis produced by the desire corresponds with facts: might the moon not have attributes in all ways similar to those of the earth, since it has similar outward appearance? As Bacon had put it: "For to form judicious wishes is as much a part of knowledge as to ask judicious questions" (VIII.329: *NO,* II.xlix). Only the narrator obeys this stricture, all the others "flying off" to those imponderable "generalizations" which Bacon so condemns.

In Cyrano's novel, as in Bacon's or Descartes's philosophy, the new discourse gets under way by showing that the familiar discourse(s) are all negative instances of a true knowledge. What makes the discourse of experimentalism the only one suitable for a true knowledge is precisely what also enables its particular truths to be received as parts of such a knowledge: the assumption that the discourse has exhausted all the negative instances. In such a way all the ambiguities—the relation of discourse to its recipients, the relation of discourse to its objects, the relation of discourse to its enunciation, the relation of discourse in process to the axioms making possible that process—are laid to rest at once, and in the same way: by excluding all nonverifiable assertions and all negations or contradictions of its own assertions, once the assertions have been verified. It is assumed that particulars will verify (or falsify) an assertion once and for all, and it is then more or less clear what is and what.is not permissible in the discursive space of experimentalism. It must be susceptible of being said to be 'true' or 'false' in terms of facts outside discourse, and it must be in accordance with a system of axioms which have themselves supposedly been verified by the same means. Once again, the difficulty is to get all this under way.

At the end of this second element in the first experimental sequence we are examining, the *Voyage* underscores the importance of the *elaboration* of this discourse. That it should choose to do so is not surprising, for it is apparent that this first sequence is not simply an example of the order of experimentalism but also the performance in miniature of the establishment of the whole class of the analytico-referential. The narrator insists on the relation of interior and exterior, emphasizing not only the observation of particulars but also the interiority of the process that seeks to perceive their order: "notion," "humour," "lodged so deeply in my mind," the metaphor of pregnancy and birth. These are themselves set into a further relation with a third term which, as we have seen in Bacon, subsumes and 'validates' (by its 'method' and axioms once verified) the other two: that of discourse itself.

For there occurs at this point in the novel the rather interesting aside to the reader that concludes the long quotation above. The Paris manuscript of the novel is even more explicit that the passage is indeed an aside to the reader: "I remained pregnant with a thousand definitions of the moon of which I could not be delivered; and as a result of upholding this burlesque belief with serious arguments, I almost persuaded myself. But listen, reader, to the miracle or accident used by Providence or fortune to convince me of it."[9] Still, in the printed version the "on" of "on nommera" (translated as "will be called") is evidently an appeal to the reader's consideration, though it is made more apparent in the text just quoted by the words "listen, reader" ("écoute lecteur"). In the same way, the phrase "burlesque belief" ("croyance burlesque") forms a commentary by the narrator on what he regards as the evident opinion of the reader toward the suggestion he has made concerning the moon. It will be the same as that of his companions for the very simple reason that the reader, too, occupies an older and more familiar discursive space. By the aside the reader's attention is drawn not only to the clash of discourses but also (and possibly more important at this point) to the fact that he is reading a writing in the process of its elaboration.

An integral part of this aside is a 'heretical' lumping together of miracle and chance, of providence and fortune, which sends us back to the myths of which we have already been reminded: the Christian, the pagan, the animistic. It sends us back, that is to say, to the content of the familiar discouses used in the novel's initial discussion. So far as the narrator is concerned, one might as well ascribe his finding Cardano's book open at the very page that treats of inhabitants of the moon to any one or all of these agencies ("peut-être ce qu'on nommera . . . si on veut"), implying that none of them is responsible, and that the attempt to find such causes is irrelevant. In a way the reference to miracles and providence—both of them notions tending to reflect that universe of analogies where everything is linked and works toward the 'ultimate meaning' which is God Himself—by opposing the reference to chance and fortune resumes at another level the dispute between the narrator and his friends.

9. Cyrano de Bergerac, *Voyage dans la lune (L'autre monde ou les états et empires de la lune)*, ed. Maurice Laugaa (Paris, 1970), pp. 31–32; Lachèvre, ed., *Oeuvres libertines*, I.6. The translation is my own, using Strachan as a base.

The irony of the terms "vision," "fiction," "chimera," and "madness" ("folie") in the published version draws the reader's attention to the very writing of the novel before him; it emphasizes that what is in question is the very process of discovering thinking and then writing down that thinking. For the textual *on* ("on nommera") these terms refer to an idea (that the moon is a world) whose falsity is opposed to the truth of those others which preceded it and which are the mythologies of fixed systems. For the narrator, on the contrary, the idea suggested by these terms signifies a possibility of truth, an attempt to remove from the moment of observation all that is not essential to it (I see the moon; the moon looks *like* what we may suppose the world to look like if we could view it from an analogous vantage point), and to relate that observation to some testable hypothesis (since they look alike, perhaps moon and earth *are* alike). The ironic commentary will be taken further yet, for the narrator will imply that his first journey is the result of a dream, and even perhaps that it *is* a dream: "In order to make an end of it, I shut myself away in a comparatively isolated country house where, having gratified my *daydreams* with some practical measures appropriate to my design, this is how *I gave myself to* the sky" (F 13; E 5, my italics).

"Fiction," "madness," "dream" are simply the means that permit the undertaking of a voyage which the narrator intends will terminate in the real and true knowledge of a verified hypothesis concerning the factual world. "Fiction" it is, in the sense that Bacon's or Galileo's or Descartes's invention of a new discourse is also a fiction. Not for nothing does the last of these refer to *Le monde* as a *fable* at the outset, only to conclude that it corresponds precisely to the real world. "Madness" it is, because the use of any discourse that is unfamiliar will necessarily be so classified by those whose familiarity is with another. "Dream" it certainly is, if by that one wishes to mark the fulfillment of a desire. What these terms indicate above all is that the discourse is a new invention (fiction), that it is different (madness), that it seeks a particular goal (dream).

In Cyrano's novels, the voyage will always, as in this first experimental sequence, mean a 'passage' through an accumulation of images (here, the mythologies) that will have to be discarded before the goal can be achieved. We have seen how this can be done: by making experience literate. This, it seems to me, is the final implication we can draw from the aside to the reader: the fact that this is a *writing*. And this is evidently reinforced by the very event which inspired the aside: reading Cardano's *written* autobiography. Knowledge progresses, as we have seen Bacon affirm, only when writing makes order and clarity possible, when writing performs the exclusion of superfluities, when it—and it alone—makes possible a legitimate experimental follow-up.

The first two elements of the sequence, observation and discussion leading to hypothesis, are now followed by the third: the experiment to test the hypothesis. In the present case it consists of the narrator's first attempt to fly, achieved by binding dew-filled flasks around himself. To be sure, to the extent that it does not succeed in taking him to the moon this flight is a failure, yet it does respond partially to the hypothesis. Because his ascent and descent are supposedly vertical and because he nonetheless returns to earth not in France but in New France (F 15; E 7), he believes he has successfully demonstrated that the earth turns on its axis. Like the possible similarity of the earth and moon, this is one of the consequences of the heliocentric hypothesis (which will be the matter of the second experimental sequence). Knowledge has therefore been advanced by his experiment, while his own particular hypothesis receives a resounding boost, even though the particular form of this result is more or less 'accidental.' Still, Bacon's method covers this eventuality as well: "in the whole collection of this history of arts it is especially to be observed and constantly borne in mind that not only those experiments in each art which serve the purpose of the art itself are to be received, but likewise those which turn up anyhow by the way."[10]

Here, then, the fourth element in the sequence has been supplied: the full or partial verification of the hypothesis. This will in turn be bound directly to a new observation. It will even overlap with it. The sequence remains in that way entirely open-ended, leading immediately—and always—into a following sequence. Before showing how this occurs in Cyrano's novel, however, it might be as well to make an aside of my own, to suggest that the system which is becoming the structure composing the novel is not limited to what we have found in Bacon.

For this structure, not only in the symbolism of the first element of this first sequence (the observation of the moon) but also in the precision of the sequence of elements, reflects very closely what I have been suggesting is also the Galilean experimental method. This begins with what may be called an *intuition* of truth following upon

10. Francis Bacon, *Description of a Natural and Experimental History* (aphorism V), in *The Works*, ed. James Spedding, Robert Leslie Ellis, and Douglas Denon Heath, 15 vols. (Boston, 1861–64), VIII.364.

the isolation of a given phenomenon which it is then necessary to resolve into elements capable of mathematization. From these it would be possible to deduce, by *demonstration*, certain generalizations which themselves were taken as a matter of purely mathematical calculation. These two stages correspond, of course, to the first two elements—observations and discussion leading to hypothesis—that we have found formally in Bacon and 'performatively' in Cyrano, though it is only to be expected that the emphasis on mathematics would be altered in them to an emphasis on the elaboration of 'ordinary' discourse.

In Galileo, the exactness of the generalizations which have been elaborated will now be illustrated by "works," by *experiments*. In the case of the Italian scientist we cannot really speak of a 'testing' because in his view the rigor of the mathematical demonstration dispenses with the need for practical proof.[11] Nevertheless, even for Galileo experiment leads to a *public verification* of the hypothesis (generalization). Thus the sequence is the same in Galileo and Bacon, whatever may be its implications for the scientist or philosopher making use of it. In Cyrano, and in the novel in general from now on, these implications will be incorporated in the very structure of its composition.

In the novel, it is probably needless to say, such structure needs disinterring. Still, it is worthy of note in passing, because we are after all speaking of what seems to occur in the 'literary' text, that this 'experimental' sequence will become systematically 'visible' much later as the structure of the detective novel. According to Claude Brémond's analysis of the genre, for example, the detective novel is composed of three basic sequences: the statement of the problem, the investigation, the clearing-up of the mystery. The investigation itself is divided into a further sequence, though it might be clearer if one admitted that the first and last elements in that investigative sequence in fact correspond to the moments of statement and clearing up. That admitted, the investigative sequence is precisely that at which we have been looking: examination of observed facts, elaboration of hypothesis, experimentation, verification of hypothesis.[12]

Almost contemporaneously with Poe's invention of the genre of the detective novel in just these terms, certain 'serious' novelists were

---

11. For this résumé of the Galilean method I am indebted to Edwin Arthur Burtt, *The Metaphysical Foundations of Modern Physical Science* (Garden City, N.Y., 1954), p. 81. See also my "Espaces de la pensée discursive: Le cas Galilée et la science classique," *Revue de synthèse*, no. 85–86 (Jan.–July 1977), pp. 5–47.

12. Claude Brémond, "Le message narratif," *Communications*, no. 4 (1964), pp. 4–32.

attempting a similar systematic experimentalism, whose object was the grasping of truths about psychosociological or politicohistorical situations and events: one thinks of Balzac or Dickens, of Tolstoy perhaps or Turgenev, above all of Zola. In the 'serious' novel such a visibility of the experimental system cannot last for long because the 'truths' will soon sink beneath the accusation that they are 'contrived.' One might say that the "responsibility of enunciation" has been readmitted to discourse: and in the neoclassical episteme what could then be called its 'objectivity'? It is therefore symptomatic that on the one hand the detective novel heads speedily into the domain of what is now being called 'paraliterature,' where few serious questions are asked of the material of fiction, while on the other such novelists as Stendhal or Flaubert, Dostoevsky or James, appear to be heading elsewhere—toward Proust or Joyce and beyond. The names of Maxwell and Marx, of Peirce and Frege, mentioned already in connection with this new 'crisis,' may be recalled here as well.

It may be that the 'openness' (to use Umberto Eco's term) of such texts as are represented by the last novelists named was not possible until what had become a structure in the seventeenth century had once again been avowed as a system, a visible discursive means of grasping and situating the world of phenomena and of organizing all the objects of our knowledge. It may be that there could be no place for any new class of discourse until the analytico-referential proved to be nothing but a particular form taken by human ordering, and was therefore no longer privileged as the only possible place of truth. It could no longer be the dominant discursive class once this had been made clear, since the introduction of such 'discursive relativism' assumes one is already 'outside' the discourse thus relativized. My Chapter 12 will argue at greater length that we now find ourselves, indeed, at the nether end of the development of the analytico-referential. Other kinds of discourse seek to accompany, if not to displace, it. Yet it remains present and in use. Analytico-referential discourse has controlled the forms of Western knowledge (and action) from the period we are discussing down to the present day. Not to seek to understand its operation in all types of discourse, then, is to cripple the development of other discourses (of other "knowledge").

Cyrano marks a point at the other end of this time scale, the moment when the experimental order is becoming dominant, and the first sequence of the *Voyage dans la lune* is a kind of general methodological introduction. It is not only that, however, for it is also where the familiar discourse of patterning is dismantled, the only remains being the bits and pieces we have seen dismissed by the narrator as "ingenious fancies." I have further suggested, and the matter will be dealt with at greater length in Chapter 8, that the mythological elements that do remain will themselves be adjusted to the experimental order (which implies that Bachelard's notion of a prescientific mind, recognizable essentially by its use of myth, is far too simplistic).

The experimental structure, it is apparent, reveals itself as a succession of sequences that can be given no foreseeable term: they could come to an end only when the last bit of true knowledge had been found. But no one inside the discursive space in question could know when that goal had been achieved. Indeed, the assumption of having arrived at that point would mean that a different space was now occupied: a space in which such terms as 'knowledge' and 'truth' would be defined within a quite different set of elements and discursive 'assumptions.' The end of the experimental series, then, would be, not complete knowledge, but silence. Cyrano does not shy away from this consequence, as we will see in Chapter 9.

The second sequence overlaps with the first and begins as the other comes to an 'end.' The experimental flight with the dew-filled bottles leads straight into another observation or, rather, series of observations. The first of these concerns once again celestial bodies in their relation with the earth: "I perceived that the sun was now at its highest point from the horizon, and that it was midday" (F 13–14; E 5). It is also at this point that the first tentative evidence of the partial verification of the hypothesis is presented: "it seemed to me that, having gone straight up into the air, I should have come down in the place I had left from" (F 14; E 5). As in the first sequence, the observations are multiple and reciprocal. In the first, it was a question of the entire company looking at the moon and of the narrator's idea that someone on the moon might be looking back at them; here the narrator is himself surrounded by men: "j'aperçus," "je me vis entouré," "qu'ils eussent jamais vu," "ils voyaient," "à leur vue." Indeed, the concept and activity of seeing takes over the entire situation: "un moment les vit" (F 14).

The second element, as before, is the attempt to seize the observed phenomenon in a first explanation: here occurs the first material image, the image to which Bachelard has given the name "obstacle." It is this moment in this second stage of the sequence that Galileo himself sets aside as useless, by means of the character Simplicio, in the *Two Chief World Systems*. In the *Lune*, the narrator uses many of the same techniques. As a consequence there will be less emphasis on the first obstacle hereafter, with the result that *the role played by discourse in the knowledge of phenomena will also be less emphasized, as though the act of enunciation itself were unimportant.* This consequence is yet to come, however, and for the moment the second stage of the sequence remains highly verbalized.

The narrator now turns to one of the "stark naked men" who have met him and attempts to find out where he is. He is unable to understand the reply: "He mumbled between his teeth for a long time but I did not notice that he was articulating anything and took his talk [*langage*] for the husky babbling of a mute" (F 15; E 6). This same lack of comprehension is in evidence between himself and the soldiers who come for him immediately afterward. Only after the narrator has met the Viceroy (called "M. de Montmagny" in the Paris manuscript—as in reality) will the further perfecting of his hypothesis occur.

It is as though the immediate "flying-off" to generalization in the terms of a familiar discursive class had been replaced by a kind of suspension of belief which will allow the new discourse to have its say, as though there were now a space of ignorance waiting to be appropriately filled. Little by little that filling will be achieved in conversations with the Viceroy and in response to the latter's questions and proposals. The perfecting of the hypothesis is based on two kinds of evidence now, and the narrator's choice is significant: (1) the experiment of flight that he has already performed, and (2) the arguments advanced by Galileo himself in order to show the 'relativity' of the human mind. Indeed, one might suggest that the form of the discussions between the Viceroy and the narrator echoes that of the *Two Chief World Systems,* the former playing Sagredo to the latter's Salviati. We even have a Simplicio represented by the Jesuits who take the narrator for a "sorcerer" (F 16; E 7) and the Father who, dismissing Copernicus, is said to have suggested that the turning of the earth is due to the movements of the damned in Hell who climb around inside to escape the flames (F 18; E 9).[13]

In the same way the narrator, following Galileo (and others), emphasizes how ridiculous it is to believe that the sun is placed in the sky merely to serve mankind:

> For it would be as ridiculous to believe that this great luminous body revolved round a speck which is useless to it, as to imagine when we see

13. See Galileo, "Letter to the Grand Duchess Christina," in Stillman Drake, ed., *Discoveries and Opinions of Galileo* (Garden City, N.Y., 1957). Galileo notes here his admiration for Copernicus, who never, he writes, confuses mechanistic and religious arguments.

a roast lark, that the hearth has been revolved about it in order to cook it. Otherwise, if the sun had to perform this task, it would seem as if the medicine needed the sick man, the strong should yield to the weak, the great serve the small and, instead of a ship sailing along the shores of a province the province would have to be navigated round the ship. [F 17; E 8][14]

From Vergil to Oresme and Cusanus, from Galileo to Cyrano, from Copernicus to Pascal, from Bernier to Fontenelle, the ship/earth image had a fortune all its own. The narrator himself uses it here a second time to dismiss just this sort of hasty generalizations, too-familiar ways of speech, illiterate experience: "Sir, I replied to him, the majority of men, who only judge things by their senses, have allowed themselves to be persuaded by their eyes, and just as the man on board a ship which hugs the coastline believes that he is motionless and the shore is moving, so have men, revolving with the earth about the sky, believed that it was the sky itself which revolved about them" (F 19; E 10).[15] Another dispute recalled by the narrator had become virtually the symbol of the struggle between the old and the new, between biblical exegesis and natural philosophy: the debate around "Joshua's sun"; it is repeatedly in the same sources.[16]

14. And a little later: "No, no, if this visible god lights man's way it is by accident, as the King's torch accidentally gives light to the passing street-porter" (F 19; E 10). Most of the arguments and images concerning the 'relativity' of the human mind are to be found in the Third Day of Galileo's *Dialogue Concerning the Two Chief World Systems— Ptolemaic and Copernican*, tr. Stillman Drake, 2d ed. (Berkeley and Los Angeles, 1970), esp. pp. 367–68. They are to be found also in Campanella's *Apologia pro Galileo* (Frankfurt, 1622), and in John Wilkins's *A Discovery of a New World. . .* (London, 1638), among many other places.

15. See, e.g., Galileo, " Letter to the Grand Duchess Christina," pp. 170, 200–202; *Two Chief World Systems* (Second Day), pp. 115 ff., 255. Diodati, translator into Latin of some of Galileo's material, was a close friend not only of Galileo himself but of Gassendi as well, in whose learned circle Cyrano himself moved (not to mention, among others, Thomas Hobbes). Many of the arguments used here by Cyrano's narrator had of course become commonplace by this time and no particular acquaintance was necessary in order to pick them up. Gassendi's own works are full of them— a fact to which the Viceroy refers ("I have read several books by Gassendi on this subject," F 18; E 9). The fact remains that the terms of the critique recalled by the narrator are those constantly used by Galileo himself to buttress his experimental system. Still, what is of interest here is not the search for sources but the increasing familiarity of a discourse that had been new for Galileo and Bacon. On the particular image of ship:shore::earth:sun, see Erica Harth, *Cyrano de Bergerac and the Polemics of Modernity* (New York, 1970), p. 144.

16. E.g., most notably, in the "Letter to the Grand Duchess Christina." Foscarini, one of Galileo's less cautious supporters, wrote an entire volume around the subject: his volume was placed on the Index soon after its publication. Says the narrator of the *Lune*: "I was insolent enough to imagine God had favoured my daring by once more nailing the sun to the heavens" (F 14; E 5).

The narrator extends his hypothesis in a perfectly coherent way, and one which is again susceptible (in time) of experimental proof. Beginning the second sequence with a partial verification of one of the implicit conditions of his hypothesis (that the earth turns upon its axis) achieved by the first flight, he has gone on to affirm that the earth turns about the sun, that therefore the sun is a star like any other, and that one may therefore conclude with the hypothesis that there is an infinity of habitable worlds (F 19–20; E 10). In all this he is merely repeating the more audacious hypotheses of those who were carried away by the new discoveries, and it might seem that we are here confronted with those same overhasty generalizations of which we have seen Bacon so critical. However, the point of these hypotheses in the novel is that they set forth an experimental program—of which only certain parts will have actually been 'accomplished' by the 'end' of the *Voyage au soleil.*

Clearly the hypothesis has been considerably broadened and extended, and the trip to the moon will now serve to verify only a part of a far more ambitious program. The scheme could only be formulated 'legitimately' *after* the first experiment had proved partially successful. In this the novel is following exactly the precepts laid down by Bacon and carried out by Galileo. For this reason it is rather striking that the narrator should stress as a third stage in this sequence an experiment that recalls the point of departure both of the novel and, in the sense stressed at the very outset of this volume, of the order of analytico-referential discourse itself. He suggests that just as he and his companions had watched the moon, so the Viceroy should emulate Galileo's second series of telescopic experiments and study sunspots: "if ever I have the honour of seeing you in France, I will have you observe by means of a most excellent spyglass, how certain obscurities which look like spots from here are worlds in formation" (F 22; E 12). At this point discourse as such ceases, as one might expect: "My eyes were closing as I finished this speech and the Viceroy was obliged to leave me" (F 22; E 12).

It is nevertheless not *this* experiment which is now carried out (though the hypothesis behind it is 'verified' on the flight to the sun in the novel's sequel). Rather, it is almost as though we ourselves traveled up the telescope: from this sleep we pass directly into the next experience of flight. This is carried out (accidentally) by means of rockets and, when these fail, by the suction effect of the moon on the animal marrow with which the narrator had smothered wounds received in a fall when testing his flying machine. Clearly this is the third element of the second sequence. And it immediately verifies his initial hypothesis. For he lands on the moon in the midst of the luxurious vegetation of the "earthly paradise." Luckily for him he lands in the "tree of life" and some of the juice of its fruit runs into his mouth; otherwise, as he observes, he might not have survived (F 25; E 15). A completely new knowledge is now possible, in a new world; a different world, certainly, but a world nonetheless.

That this knowledge is possible is, then, the result of the experimental verification of an hypothesis "educed," as Bacon calls it, from particulars, and as the result of posing "judicious questions." In the second stage of the two sequences we have so far examined, the narrator gave pride of place to discourse as the means of organizing reality and producing works. From now on this will no longer be the case.

Knowledge will increasingly be achieved when—and because—discursive awareness disappears, for, far from being a conscious organizing principle, it has been made 'transparent.' Little by little, as I have indicated, the evidence of the role of discourse as making possible and organizing all knowledge is being obliterated, *as though the act and responsibility of enunciation were themselves being occulted*. On the contrary, the use of language *per se* will be proffered as the chief obstacle to true knowledge and true communication, and it is in those terms that the philosophical discussion of language will henceforth take place (and not only in the novel), up to and including, for example, Saussure. As we will see in Chapter 9, the treatment of language in Cyrano's two *Voyages* is increasingly in the form of concern over an *obstacle* to experimental knowledge. This is a principal mark of the passage to domination: the disappearance of the 'conscious' discursive ordering of what is spoken of.

Two full sequences have now been completed in the *Lune*.

I. First sequence
  1. View of the moon
  2. Discussion and hypothesis concerning what it is or is like
  3. Flight to "New France"
  4. The earth turns (one element of the new cosmology verified)
II. Second sequence
  1. View of the sun and of New France
  2. Discussion and further hypothesis concerning the world, the solar system, and the universe
  3. Flight to the moon
  4. The moon is a world (another element in the new cosmology and the narrator's initial hypothesis verified)

As expected, we are taken right away into the next sequence. That the moon is a world has actually been only partly verified, for the narrator's landing in the "paradis terrestre" would appear to provide equal evidence for the suggestion of his companion who sought to fit the moon into the order of a Christian myth. The third sequence, while following the same order as the first two, appears to seek falsification rather than verification. In this way two aims are to be accomplished. First, one alternative general theory of 'true knowledge' will be excluded (the Christian); second, the experimental 'theory' will be reinforced in accordance with the Baconian dictum concerning the exclusion of contradictory instances.

In the earthly paradise, then, the first stage of the sequence becomes unreliable. The narrator looks around, but is not able to trust his eyes: "stones were neither hard nor uneven ["except to the eyes," adds the Paris manuscript] and they were careful to soften themselves when one walked on them" (F 25; E 16). The senses no longer support one another; rather they dispute each other's evidence—in direct contradiction to the atomistic explanation of the senses that will be developed later (F 101–5; E 83–86). Indeed, it is evident that if the senses could not be trusted experimental knowledge of any kind whatsoever would be beyond human powers. Since the first two experimental sequences have already been shown to work, we are at liberty to doubt the case where experimental proof would be axiomatically impossible: the case, that is, whose first axiom would be that the senses cannot be trusted. This would lead us to blind faith: "it is to God that you owe this homage!" cries Elijah (F 28; E 18). That, of course, would be to return to a position of no *knowledge* at all in any scientific sense.

In the earthly paradise the first stage of observation cannot even give rise to a meaningful second stage. The narrator looks at the enormous trees that appear to grow there: "Letting my eyes wander from the roots to the top, and then fall from the summit to the foot, I began to wonder [*je doutais*] whether the ground supported them or if they did not themselves carry the ground suspended from their roots" (F 26; E16). This observation, or anti-observation, can lead only to attempts at description. Whereas in the first two sequences observation gives rise quite naturally to the development of a hypothesis, here it cannot because it is itself far too uncertain. Even 'simple' description, unburdened of some firm basis, unladen of *any* theory whatever, proves a chimera: "One *would even take* this plain *for* an ocean, since it is *like* a sea which offers *no* shore, so that my *eye*, *terrified* at having run so far *without discovering* the edge *quickly sent my thought after it*; and my thought *unwilling to believe* it was the end of the world, *wanted to persuade itself* that the charms of the place had *perhaps* compelled heaven to join on to the earth" (F 27; E 17).[17]

Preciosity is itself, perhaps, no other than a different discursive means of ordering reality. But why is it necessary to bring in such a passage here (and what is quoted is only a small part of a very long passage of description in the same vein)? The negatives, the conditional, the subjunctive, verbs of doubting and of fearing, all accumulate to reveal the failure of description and observation. The mind has recourse immediately to generalizations. It goes with all speed from failed observation (*"mon oeil épouvanté"*) to overweening imagination and reasoning by analogy—and tautological analogies at that: the plain was like an ocean because it was like a sea; because it was a sea with no visible edges it was like the end of the world, and so on. What is being presented here, in burlesque form, are the worst elements of the very kind of thinking that the narrator is seeking to replace. And things go from bad to worse.

It is at this point that the narrator comes across Elijah. The prophet proceeds to translate Genesis into a series of voyages between the earth and the moon (F 28–40; E 18–28). Needless to say, all this fails the first test of the experimental discourse: it is untestable by means of reference to particulars—though the narrator does meet Enoch, one of those who is supposed to have made the trip. The narrator dismisses these tales first with obscenity (F 36; E 25) and then with blasphemy (F 39–40; E 28). Not only does the place itself give rise to contradictions, quite apart from its being the "earthly paradise" on the moon,[18] but Elijah, who now affirms that he has the "perfect philosophy" of the old Adam (F 33; E 22), is given to making claims whose only 'proof' is their own assertion (that the narrator's blasphemy, for example, would not go "unpunished if the All-Wise God did not wish to leave you to the nations as a famous example of His mercy," F 40; E 28), and statements that are contradicted by experience. In this way he asserts that eating the skin of the

17. "On *prendrait même* cette prairie *pour* un océan, à cause qu'elle est *comme* une mer qui n'offre *point* de rivage, en sorte que mon *oeil épouvanté* d'avoir couru si loin *sans découvrir* le bord y *envoyait vitement ma pensée*; et ma pensée *doutant* que ce *fût* l'extrémité du monde, *se voulait persuader* que des lieux si charmants avaient *peut-être* forcé le ciel de se joindre à la terre" (my italics).

18. When he lands in paradise the narrator's hunger disappears completely because of the place; however only a short while later he complains of being famished, and twice at that: "if I had been in a state to die of anything else but hunger," "my hunger tormented me so violently" (F 40; E 28, 29). No doubt this can be explained on the grounds that he first ate the tree of life, while later he is to be punished by Elijah. But this is simply one hesitation or contradiction among several.

fruit of the Tree of Knowledge will lead to complete ignorance (F 36–37; E 25), but when the narrator does so later on it does nothing of the kind. For this contradiction the narrator tries to find some explanation, but it will remain as unverifiable as Elijah's original claim ("I have surmised," F 41; E 29).

The narrator eventually passes out of the earthly paradise exactly as though he were leaving some kind of dream: "a thick cloud enveloped my mind: I no longer saw anyone beside me, and my eyes could not discover a single trace of the road I had taken anywhere on this side of the horizon, but for all that, I did not fail to remember everything that had happened to me" (F 41; E 29).[19] It is as though a further journey (for he now finds himself in the midst of an unknown country) had *demonstrated* the meaningless—indeed burlesque in the telling—nature of whatever kind of knowing might derive from the Christian mythology.

At the same time, this experiment further confirms the original hypothesis of the moon as a world. All he has learned from the earthly paradise is the evidence provided by his first landing there and finding things growing just as on earth. All the rest is a mockery of the knowledge he is seeking. Now the learning process can continue once again: the narrator shortly sees people coming toward him and will soon be taken to his first lunar town (F 42; E 29). We may call this an 'experiment' because, as in *New Atlantis,* the 'journey' and the 'experiment' have become virtually synonymous. In the *Voyage au soleil,* indeed, they become so quite explicitly. Thus the "atomic tree" in its human form tells Dyrcona that his people spend their time journeying about in order to achieve "a certain science of what is" ("une science certaine de ce qui est," F 189; E 160), and Campanella informs him that he travels for just the same reason (F 240 ff.; E 205 ff.). Earlier in the same novel Dyrcona will beseech one of the talking trees to "deign to enlighten someone who had only risked the perils of so great a journey in order to learn" (F 225–26; E 192).

As before, the journey both concludes and begins a series: "In vain I cast my eyes about me and scrutinized the landscape" (F 41; E 29). The narrator recommences his observation, at the same time proving two previous hypotheses: (1) that the Christian myth is a

19. "Une épaisse nuée tomba sur mon âme; je ne vis plus personne auprès de moi, et mes yeux ne reconnurent en tout l'hémisphère une seule trace du chemin que j'avais fait, et avec tout cela je ne laissais pas de me souvenir de tout ce qui m'était arrivé." No doubt one could argue that this "passage" corresponds exactly to his blasphemous remark concerning the ascension of St. John the Evangelist, and that it therefore "bears out" the Christian myth.

fantasy so far as the winning of knowledge is concerned (F 11; E 3), and (2) that the moon is like the earth: for clearly there are several different countries, of which some appear to be unknown to others. He also discovers that the moon is occupied by people who "had bodies and faces like ours" ("avaient la taille et la figure comme nous") but who walk on all fours (F 41; E 29).

From now on, indeed, it is no longer necessary to *state* any hypothesis: all experiments and experience from now on in the novel will set out to fill in the particulars of the general hypothesis that the moon is like the earth. In a sense 'mere' experience is now just as useful as experiment, for it henceforth occurs in the context of the initial hypotheses; it is now always literate; it is "theory-laden."

Nevertheless, the reader is presented at the same time with what amounts to a refutation of the other mythologies. If the earthly paradise is revealed in its essential uncertainty and aimlessness, then the first part of the narrator's stay with the lunarians is virtually a demonstration of the flaws in any way of knowing other than through experience. The lunarians are at first likened to "sirens, fauns, and satyrs" (F 41; E 29), and we discover little by little that they suffer from all the errors that the experimentalists are trying to overcome. The exception to this rule is the "demon of Socrates" who sets out to teach the narrator, just as he says he had taught Socrates, Epaminondas, Cato, Cardano, Agrippa, Campanella (especially), La Mothe Le Vayer, Gassendi, and the rest (F 43–44; E 31–33). The demon explains that he is a native of the sun and that he is here because the people of the moon "are lovers of truth. There is not a pedant to be seen. Philosophers only permit themselves to be persuaded by reason, and neither the authority of a scholar nor that of the majority can outweigh the opinion of a thresher on a farm, provided he reason with sufficient force. In this country, briefly, only sophists and rhetoricians are considered to be mad" (F 46; E 34).

Such is the demon's ideal. It is not generally borne out, however, by the narrator's experience on the moon, which tends to demonstrate rather the prevalence of a more common attitude: "There is a common herd here as there is there [on earth], who cannot tolerate the thought of anything to which it is not accustomed" (F 43; E 31). This remark corresponds to Gonzales's later criticism to the effect that on earth "whatever fine things you may say, if they are against the principles of the doctors of the cloth, you are an idiot, a madman, and something more besides" (F 58; E 45). Like the narrator, the inquisitors of the moon reject the authority of an Aristotle (F 69;

E 55); but when the narrator is on trial for having suggested that he is human, that their "moon" is a world, and so on (F 66–70, 74–79; E 53–55, 59–62), they show themselves every bit as closed to unfamiliar notions as had his companions on the road to Paris, as will Dyrcona's accusers at the beginning of the *Soleil* (F 132–43; E 109–19) and the birds later on in the same novel (F 201–15; E 170–82).

When they do not understand something the lunar populace, like the narrator himself at the end of the first experimental sequence, close their ears: those who hear him and Socrates's demon conversing together in Greek take that language "for inarticulate grunting" ("un grognement non articulé," F 48; E 36). The narrator himself has learned from his experience and rapidly gets to know his hosts' languages (F 67; E 54)—with disastrous results. For it leads to just those arguments concerning reason and instinct, animal nature and human, the privilege of the human world over the other realms, which are to place him before the lunarian inquisition.

In fact the narrator learns relatively little from the lunar people, with the exception of some information about their customs from a girl at the court who takes a liking to him. What he learns he learns from Gonzales, another representative of the new experimentalism; from Socrates' demon, who argues from his own experience but more from what he can demonstrate on material present to the senses; and from the "host's son" in the latter half of the *Lune*, whose status is dubious since he may be the Antichrist!

In this way the narrator makes acquaintance with an atomistic theory of all matter (F 58–63, 99–105; E 45–49, 80–86), with the consequent unity of matter and "spirit" (F 63–66; E 49–52), with the notions of the infinity of worlds (F 92–94; E 75–77) and the eternity of the universe (F 75, 95; E 59, 77). All this, deriving from an atomistic theory, provides in turn an explanation of the reason why the senses, though fallible in man, are nevertheless adequate to a 'comprehension' of material things: the senses and all material things are merely different configurations of the same basic atomic forms (F 102–5; E 85–86).

Certainly the demonstration of much of this is peculiar, to say the least. But that is not the point. The point is that demonstrations *are always made* by means of material particulars. Some of these will be carried to further fruition in the *Soleil*. There it is demonstrated that the earth turns (F 166–67; E 140–41); the hypothesis of the infinity of worlds, if not proved, is at least provided with the strong evidence of the "several earths like ours" which Dyrcona leaves to right and left on his trip to the sun (F 167; E 141); the order, motion, and physical composition of the planets is suggested by the waxing and waning of Venus and Mercury (F 167; E 141); that sunspots are worlds being created is 'proved' by his landing upon one (F 169; E 143); atomism is verified by the well-known episode of the tree of precious metals and stones which dances itself into a vast number of people, then into one person, and finally into a flock of birds which flies away (F 184–97; E 156–67).

Indeed, Dyrcona's initial landing on the sun may be viewed as a specific correction of the failure of the earthly paradise. When he finds himself on the "plains of day" his immediate feeling is that they are not solid:

> My very body was bewildered and sought the support of my eyes, but since this transparent land through which they penetrated could not hold them up my instinct became master of my thought in spite of myself and drew it towards the hollow depths of a bottomless light. However, my reason gradually disabused my instinct; I left firm and untrembling tracks upon the plain, and I measured my paces so proudly that if men could have seen me from their world they would have taken me for the great god who walks upon the clouds. [F 183; E 155]

It might be suitable to conclude this chapter on such a note: the experimental scientist as the godlike bringer of knowledge, the new Prometheus. That aspect of the *Lune* is indeed the subject of the next chapter. However, in addition to demonstrating how to verify hypotheses by experiment, how to use material particulars so as to provide at least evidence for, and not seldom proof of, a given hypothesis,[20] another aspect of this novel is particularly revealing: it appears to include certain elements of a theory of probability. Such a theory, of course, is tied in with the whole matter of experiment and evidence in the sense of which I have just been speaking. It is an essential witness to the power of analytico-referential discourse. On occasion it becomes an explicit concern of the novel, where its presence is profoundly significant.

Ian Hacking has placed the emergence of a mathematical theory of probability in a broad "conceptual space" (not, that is to say, as it may have appeared as an isolated instance in the work of a Cardano) squarely in the decade around 1660. The key figures are Pascal and the authors of the Port-Royal *Logic,* though Hacking quotes a pas-

---

20. The existence of the different worlds the narrator passes on his journey is *evidence* for the theory of the infinity of worlds; that he actually *sees* the lands of the earth passing around its surface is *proof* that the earth turns.

sage from Hobbes in which he spots the first emergence of probability "in all but name," and he emphasizes at the same time the importance of Gassendi in this matter.[21] It is a matter of historical record that from 1641 on Cyrano was very closely associated with Gassendi and the circles in which Hobbes was a familiar. Where Cyrano may have 'obtained' such elements of probability as occur in the novel is, I feel, of no greater interest than may be the 'precise' source of the Galilean elements which have been mentioned. For the point is—and Hacking makes it repeatedly and well—that the emergence of the modern theory of probability is directly tied ('discursively,' as I have been saying here) to the developments we have been considering. It is, that is to say, *an integral part of this new class of discourse,* and an exemplary case of its use of abstract systems as true descriptions of the concrete.

"Probability," writes Hacking at the very outset of his work on the subject, "has two aspects. It is connected with the degree of belief warranted by evidence, and it is connected with the tendency, displayed by some chance devices, to produce stable relative frequencies."[22] Both of these aspects appear explicitly in Cyrano's first novel, though evidently not in precise mathematical terms.

As to the second, the narrator recounts, toward the end of the *Lune,* how his host's son likens the atoms of nature to just such a chance device: he points out how, when we play with three dice, the possible permutations are such that any given configuration of the dice considered singly may appear to require explanation in terms of law. He observes that this is nonsense and that what is significant is the totality of possible permutations:

> When you throw three dice upon a table and a triple two comes up, or three, four, five, or two sixes and a one, you will say: "Oh, what a miracle! The same number has come up on all the dice, although so many numbers could have done!" "Oh, what a miracle! Three consecutive numbers have come up!" "Oh, what a miracle! Just two sixes have come up and the opposite side of the other six!"
>
> But no, I am sure that being a man of intelligence, you will never make such exclamations, since the numbers on the dice are limited and it is impossible for one of them not to come up. [F 100; E 81–82]

21. Ian Hacking, *The Emergence of Probability*, pp. 48, 46–47. The work of Hobbes in question is *Humane Nature, or the Fundamental Elements of Policie* (London, 1650), IV.10; probably written around 1640.

22. Hacking, *Emergence*, p. 1. He goes on to say that "neither of these aspects was self-consciously and deliberately apprehended by any substantial body of thinkers before the time of Pascal."

Problems of chance in dicing, as Hacking observes, had been around for some time and remained a matter of lively, if playful, interest to mathematicians; more significant is the connection that is then made with the atoms of nature. Hacking notes a certain passage in the Sanskrit *Mahábarata* (c. 400 A.D.) in which a similar connection is made between dicing and the estimation of the number of leaves and fruit found on the branches of a tree, and he remarks on "the degree of sophistication" that is implied in the making of such a connection. It is clearly not at all evident that a calculus of probabilities applicable to problems in dicing can be transferred to particulars in nature. That is why Hacking adds: "Even after the European invention of probability around 1600 it took some time before any substantial body of people could comprehend that decisive connection."[23]

The manuscript of Cyrano's novel was circulating from around 1649–50 (though the passage in question was cut by Le Bret when he published the novel in 1657). Madeleine Alcover argues that while the *terminus ad quem* of the completed *Lune* was certainly 1650, it seems probable that the novel was fairly well along as early as 1642.[24] The significance of these dates is not merely anecdotal. The applicability of an abstract calculus of probabilities to concrete phenomena was in the air, a clearly integral part of the development of the new analytico-referential discourse.

Certainly, nothing here indicates the possibility of a mathematical law capable of describing the relative frequency of the occurrence of each permutation. Yet when the connection is made with atoms in nature there do appear some hints of ideas moving in the same space. For the host's son proceeds to explain the increasing infrequency of increasingly complex configurations of atoms on the grounds of the increasing number of possible permutations, so that the 'right' one (for the creation of a human, for example) turns up only rarely, whereas simple configurations turn up very frequently because the possible permutations are so much fewer (F 100–01; E 82). Thus he explains the bottom-heavy nature of the ladder of creation. What we may think of the argument in itself is a matter of indifference, and it may be that the "probability calculation" gets little beyond common sense. What remains noteworthy is the application of probability to nature.

This is not the only example of probability theory. The other aspect noted by Hacking, the question of warranty for belief, also occurs. Very interestingly it appears in the form of an abbreviated

23. Ibid., p. 7.
24. Alcover, ed., *L'autre monde*, pp. xxxv–xl.

and simplistic version of what is now known as Pascal's wager.[25] Cyrano's version retains more than a tinge of the older meaning of probability as authoritative opinion, and many of the limitations Pascal placed on the context of his wager are lacking,[26] but it is striking that it should occur here in any form at all.

The host's son flatly denies the existence of God. Unlike Pascal, the narrator sets out to offer an attenuated choice between the act of belief and that of disbelief: while it may not be possible to decide to believe, it is possible to decide as to the *wisdom* of belief. Pascal sets out to bring an agnostic into a state where belief becomes possible; it is not simply a matter of advantage, but one of probable correspondence with a divine reality. The narrator of the *Lune* seeks to bring an atheist to a state where belief may be seen to be advantageous. Although with less force than Pascal,[27] the narrator leads up to the wager by deliberately setting aside arguments from probable authority (though such authority tinges the argument about God Himself): "'I will not amuse myself,' I said to him, 'by reciting to you the clear demonstrations by means of which the philosophers have established this, for I should have to repeat all that reasonable men have ever written'" (F 122; E 100–01). The wager itself follows immediately:

> I will only ask you what inconvenience you find in believing it, and I am certain you cannot claim a single one. Since it is impossible to derive anything but benefit from it, why do you not convince yourself [*que ne vous le persuadez-vous*]? For if there is a God, apart from the fact that in not believing this you will be wrong, you will have disobeyed the precept which commands us to believe in Him. While now, even if there is none, you are still no better off than us. [F 122; E 101]

The argument here seems to be that which Hacking analyzes as the argument from dominance.[28] The choice is between two states of the world (there is no God; there is a Christian God),[29] and two courses of action (disbelief and belief). Each implies different benefits.

25. For the chronologically minded it is perhaps worth recalling here that Pascal's discussion does not appear in print until 1670, though a version of it was printed at the end of the Port-Royal *Logic* in 1662. A form of it will be included in 1690 in Locke's *Essay Concerning Human Understanding*, II.xxi.72.

26. *Emergence*, pp. 18–30, 65–69.

27. See, e.g., ibid., p. 71.

28. Ibid., pp. 64, 67.

29. That the God is the Christian God is, of course, one of the restrictions in Pascal's wager. It may appear unclear here that such is the choice, but as soon as the argument of authority of the word is invoked (the precept which commands us to believe in Him), it is clear that this restriction is intended. Actually the *context* of the wager in the novel is in any case a discussion about a Christian God, though the way the wager itself is presented lacks some clarity.

The argument is clear enough: if there is no God then neither belief nor disbelief will make any difference; if there is a God disbelief will bring damnation (the necessary result of disobedience), while belief can bring only "*utilité*." Since it is obvious that the latter is preferable to the former in the second state, while in the first conditions are precisely even, then the wager in favor of the premise "there is a Christian God" dominates.

Underlying this is the assumption that two different life-styles are at stake. The atheist is able to reply: "Indeed I am better off than you, . . . for if there is none, you and I are evenly matched [*à deux de jeu*]: but if on the contrary there is one, it will be impossible for me to have offended something which I did not believe existed at all, since in order to sin, one must either know it or wish it" (F 122; E 101). This argument amounts to saying that if there is a God belief will bring salvation (the theme underlying the term "utilité"), but disbelief can bring nothing less because a Christian God could not possibly hold this lack of belief against me, once the premise of the wager is accepted. The atheist then proceeds to embroider at some length on this theme, affirming that damnation because of ignorance would contradict the narrator's premise as regards the nature of a Christian God. On the other hand, if there is no God, then disbelief makes me "better off than you." This assertion is possible only if disbelief implies that a different life-style follows from it: otherwise it would obviously make no difference at all.

Pascal would presumably be able to answer this objection by affirming that the Word is an integral aspect of the Christian God and that therefore if there is a God the argument of ignorance is automatically invalid. Quite clearly the wager as it appears here is more than a little defective, and bears small comparison with Pascal's logical machine so admirably analyzed by Ian Hacking. Yet, once again, the important point is that the discursive scheme throws up these aspects of probability *as an integral part of its space*: and Locke will base an entire concept of the human upon them.

The narrator himself finds that he is unable to answer the atheist's arguments except by a "fit of shuddering" in the face of such "ridiculous and diabolical opinions" (F 123; E 102). He is forced back on a burlesque of the Church's response to such positions: the holder of them is the Antichrist and will go to Hell, dragged in the devil's wake—with the narrator clinging to his heels (F 124; E 102–3).

This conclusion reaffirms the ambiguity in the novel. I said earlier that the discourse represented by Elijah had been discredited by that of experimentalism. And yet the narrator, who has previously been accused by the Prophet of skirting such blasphemies (F 40; E 28), *does* get back to earth on the heels of the devil, who *does*, it would appear, continue on down to Hell inside earth with the host's son (named as the Antichrist). Elijah *had* said that the narrator would be left alive as an example of God's mercy, and it is according to Christian eschatology that the prophet Elijah is to be one of the witnesses (with Enoch) against the Antichrist at the Day of Judgment.

On the other hand, the narrator escapes condemnation (Elijah's claim being unverifiable), and he does come to a landing in Italy, the country of Galileo, in what amounts to yet one further reminder of the scientist whose abjuration had earlier been parodied: "Such is what the priests deem it good for you to believe!" (F 78; E 62). At the end of the *Lune* the success of the narrator's return to the very cradle of experimental science seems to indicate the dismissal of both church and the devil, and their replacement by the triumphant narrator, repeating the practice of Galileo, Bacon, and others. Yet the ambiguity is maintained, for the novel concludes on a note of piety which we are free to take as ironic or not, as the fancy suits us.

It is as if the narrator were finally leaving us with a choice of a rather different kind from that expressed in the wager, though the implications are inextricably linked: given that the world exists, does that necessitate the existence of God? Of course, in a sense the very fact of proposing the wager presupposes a negative answer, because it makes the matter of God's existence one of probability, while to be in a position to propose the wager makes the existence of the world axiomatic. This being so, is it possible to propose a way in which the world could exist without God? The answer in the *Lune* leans toward the affirmative. It is sought in the very terms of probability I have been indicating.

If God did not create the world, whence did it come and how does it "keep going"? The answer provided in the novel assumes first the eternity of the world (an assumption which, like that of the Creation, is neither verifiable nor falsifiable—the world in this case meaning the 'universe'). The novel then goes on to consider whether the evidence is sufficient to permit a nondivine explanation of the existence of such things as different material bodies, motion, the animal senses, intellect, 'soul,' emotion, and so on. This evidence is sought in terms of the random movement of atoms combining with sufficiently stable relative frequencies to account for the recurring existence of these things (Bacon's "letters of the alphabet," his "seeds of things").

In the *Lune* the answer is perhaps tentative. It may be a novel which is also in part 'about' the *formation* of a discourse. In the *Soleil* the narrator gathers sufficient further evidence to provide a resounding "yes" for an answer. But by then the question is only partly about the existence and nature of things *per se*. It has come increasingly to focus on *communicating our knowledge of that nature.*

At this point it would seem useful to diagram the experimental structure of the *Voyage dans la lune* that we have been exploring. This will provide a few more details in answer to the problem raised at the end of Chapter 4, where I suggested that by the time of Cyrano's novel the structure (of "thought") that has developed is composed of an open-ended series of experimental sequences beside which no other kind of discursive ordering remains. I use the same diagram as before (see facing page).

As before, the nomenclature of these columns is of no particular importance. What the plan indicates is that any suggestion we may make of a single overall order is precisely the same as that of each sequence taken individually. More significantly still, we will see in the following chapter that this is the case even when we consider the 'material of myth.' It is thus quite different in its ordering from a text like Kepler's *Dream*. No longer is there an alternative class of discourse available for even a suggestion of use—and thus, too, a Bachelardian 'psychoanalysis' is unacceptable.

It is no doubt the triumph of this order which gives the narrator confidence enough toward the end of the *Voyage au soleil*, after the rejection through falsification of the other mythologies that we have seen, to undertake the beginnings of a criticism of that 'other' modern method, that of Descartes. This novel has been universally considered an affirmation of Cartesianism, but it certainly contains a criticism of that discourse's most apparent contradictions with the discourse of experimentalism (for, as I have implied, they are in many ways similar).

Campanella informs the narrator that on the sun Descartes is considered the philosopher's philosopher, with a mind so subtle that only the "true and consummate philosopher" can hope to understand his work (F 251; E 214). He finds himself obliged to make this assertion after the narrator has suggested that Descartes's theory of the origin of the universe contradicts his other notion that there can be no vacuum in nature. Since this notion is also contradicted by "geometry" (F 250; E 213), Campanella is reduced to referring the narrator to the Frenchman himself, whom he is later to meet (F 271–72; E 232).

The Italian then goes on, in a discussion that becomes increasingly

OBSERVATION	DISCUSSION AND HYPOTHESIS	EXPERIMENT	VERIFICATION
View of moon	Presentation of mythologies; hypothesis that moon is a world	Flies to "New France"	Earth turns
View of sun and of New France	Discussion and hypotheses of new cosmology	Flies to moon	Moon is a world
View of earthly paradise	Confusing description	Eats fruit/displacement in space	(1) Christian myth is useless for knowledge; (2) moon is made up of several lands
View of moon people	Necessity for interpretation	Travels to lunar town	People live in society as on earth
	Discussions with the demon of Socrates	Travels to court	Political institutions are as on earth
	Discussions with Gonzales; inquisition	Travels to house of demon of Socrates' pupil	False method is dismissed; people think like those on earth
	Discussions with host's son, etc., about atomism, infinity of worlds, eternity of universe, nature of senses, existence of God, etc.	Returns to earth on heels of the Antichrist borne by the devil, lands in Italy	[Ambiguous]

ironic in tone, to relate how the philosophers on the sun use Descartes's principles in their discussions because they are "certainly so clear, and seem to satisfy everything so well" (F 251; E 214). Unfortunately this clarity is not borne out by example, and what follows ends up in a contradictory confusion:

You will well remember how he says that our understanding is finite. Thus, since matter is infinitely divisible, one cannot doubt that this is one of those things that our understanding can neither understand nor imagine, and that it is far beyond it to explain.

But, he says, although it cannot be observed by the senses, yet we can nonetheless conceive that this is so by the knowledge we have of matter; and we must not hesitate, he says, to base our judgement on things we conceive. [F 251; E 214][30]

Descartes is said here to argue two things: (1) we can neither understand nor imagine the infinite divisibility of matter because the understanding is finite; (2) yet we do "conceive" it by the "knowledge" we have of matter. To this there are several obvious responses. First, what is "conception" if it is neither understanding nor imagination? If it means "to have a concept in the mind," it is close to either these first two or to judgment itself: the first are both denied, and if it is the last the argument is tautological ("fix our judgment on things we judge"). If it means "conceive" in the sense of "perceive" then the argument is contradictory since it denies the action of the senses.[31]

We are not concerned here with what Descartes may really have said but only with the use that is made of his name in the novel. If "conceive" is taken to refer simply to the "so clear principles" (as it presumably does), then the narrator has already resolved the question 'externally' (the other matters all being internal to Campanella's relating of Descartes's arguments). For the entire structure of the novel denies any claim that knowledge is based on such principles, having asserted that the only way to obtain *any* knowledge about matter is through the senses (see F 101–5, 204, and passim; E 83–86, 205). This 'answer' on the part of the narrator is confirmed when Campanella follows up the passage just quoted with a question whose answer he takes to be negative: "Can we actually imagine the manner in which the soul acts upon the body?" (F 251; E 214). To this the narrator would have been able to answer "yes we can, because the material which composes both is the same, being merely different combinations of atoms" (see, for example, F 120–21, 179–81,

30. "Vous vous souvenez bien qu'il dit que notre entendement est fini. Ainsi la matière étant divisible à l'infini, il ne faut pas douter que c'est une des choses qu'il peut comprendre ni imaginer, et qu'il est bien au-dessus de lui d'en rendre raison. Mais, dit-il, quoique cela ne puisse tomber sous les sens, nous ne laissons pas de concevoir que cela se fait par la connaissance que nous avons de la matière; et nous ne devons pas, dit-il, hésiter à déterminer notre jugement sur les choses que nous concevons."

31. I discuss the question of the meaning of *concevoir* and its role in Descartes's epistemology in "The *concevoir* Motif in Descartes," in *La cohérence intérieure*, ed. J. Van Baelen and D. L. Rubin (Paris, 1977), pp. 203–22.

193–95; E 99–100, 152–53, 164–65). But at this point Campanella sees that Dyrcona is not following Descartes's reasoning as he relates it and he remarks that this is because the latter cannot purify his mind of his body, it having sunk so low that it now needs the senses for any kind of knowledge. For Dyrcona mind and body, as I suggest, are the same basic substance, and this remark obviously calls for a response on his part. Just as he is about to make one, however, Campanella abruptly changes the subject (F 251–52; E 215). In one way, the 'failure' of the method of Descartes is emphasized at the end of the novel, where silence falls as he and Campanella start to exchange their ideas (F 272; E 232).

None of this has anything to do with the narrator's admiration for the French philosopher—if it matters. It is a question of the best method for the production of a knowledge of nature. Socrates's demon affirms, "I should like to show you *by experience* that this is so" (F 52; E 40), while in Colignac's dream at the beginning of the *Soleil,* Nature, seeing the persecution of Dyrcona, cries out, "Alas! . . . he is one of my friends!" (F 138; E 114). It is to Nature, or chance her agent, that the narrator himself constantly turns for guidance (see, for example, F 41, 179; E 29, 152). Yet perhaps this contradiction between what is the right method for Bacon or Galileo on the one hand and for Descartes on the other only seems to be a contradiction, which is why the narrator's admiration is undiminished.

The aim in all is possession and control of nature, by the *I* of enunciation, by means of a discourse adequate to concepts and things; the method in all involves the same elements. The difference is the respective weight given to each and to their order. It is here that the narrator's ambiguity toward Descartes comes into ironic play. Descartes elaborates a method and its axioms *before* experimentation, and there is little play between ordered experiment and 'first' principles—although there certainly is between *experience* (as opposed to 'experiment') and the setting into order of such principles, undertaken initially out of dissatisfaction with and to overthrow the false knowledge passed on by his teachers' authority. This is not excessively different from what we find in Galileo, though there some play between *experiment* and theory continues later 'down' the sequence. In Bacon this play, this 'dialectic of knowing,' continues even further down the sequence. This, it seems to me, is the essential difference and why it is possible for the narrator to praise them all (though the name of Bacon is not actually mentioned).

The "father" has been overthrown and replaced by the son, and rightly, say the lunarians. For the father blocks the son's liveliness, the manifestation of his courage, of his strength, of his quickness of mind and imagination, of his virile relationship with nature (F 79–84; E 63–68). The son, then, is at liberty to "walk upon the belly of the father that begot" him ("sur le ventre du père qui [l']engendra," F 81; E 65). The son(s) has given birth to an open-ended, developing method: a potentially endless repetition of the same structure, each time filled out with different and sequential variables, and leading to an unlimited expansion of knowledge (though Bacon and Descartes, at least, both suggest a distant future when there will no longer be any available new variables, when all will be known). The *Voyages* of Cyrano de Bergerac are the novels of the son. After *New Atlantis* itself, they are the first fictional evidence of the "masculine" birth.[32]

32. A recent thesis has sought to assimilate the novels to "the tradition of the Menippean satire" and is of course quite dissimilar to the analysis just presented in this chapter: Judy Carol Walker, "The Unity of Cyrano de Bergerac's Imaginary Voyages" (Ph.D. diss., University of Kentucky, 1974; Ann Arbor, 1975), p. 172. Such an assimilation strikes me as ignoring the historical specificity of the novels, even though her argument that they each follow a threefold ordering of "demystification," "chastisement," and subsequent "re-education" may seem to bear some slight resemblance to my discussion of experimentalism. But her discussion deals only with the gross ordering of the texts, so as to be able to align them with the literary tradition of the Menippean satire. That she can only deal with such "macro-organization" seems to be a consequence of trying to assimilate all "literary" texts to "their own" tradition seen as in some sense outside history—a matter to which I will return in Chapter 12. A more subtle attempt to see a novel contemporary with Cyrano's as Menippean satire, and at the same time to insert it into its specific historical context (following Bakhtin, therefore, rather than Frye), is Joan De Jean, *Scarron's "Roman comique": A Comedy of the Novel, A Novel of Comedy* (Berne, Frankfurt, and Las Vegas, 1977).

8 · *The Myth of Sun and Moon*

Up till now I have not emphasized a very remarkable characteristic
of the Prometheus myth: *namely that it is an entirely masculine one.*
— Karl Abraham, *Traum und Mythos*

We propose, then, to place together under the name of the *Prometheus complex* all those tendencies which impel us *to know* as much
as our fathers, more than our fathers, as much as our teachers,
more than our teachers.
— Gaston Bachelard, *La psychanalyse du feu*

When the narrator of the *Lune* returns from his conversation
with his friends on the road back to Paris, he finds open upon his
table a book by Cardano. It is open at a passage in which the philosopher recounts how he spoke to some spirits from the moon. It
suggests, then, that the moon may be inhabited. As we have seen,
this incident confirms the narrator in his idea of making a trip there
to find out: "'But'—I added—'how can I resolve this doubt without
going the whole way up there?'—'And why not?' I answered myself
at once. 'Prometheus went to heaven long ago to steal fire there. Am
I less bold than he? And have I any reason not to hope for an equal
success?'" (F 13; E 5).

From the beginning of the novel the narrator invites us in this way
to be entertained by a particular 'translation' of his cosmic voyages.
It will be a translation whose principal elements are drawn from the
material of myth. It suggests that there is an element in this otherwise experimental discourse which turns aside from the kind of
knowledge implied there and seeks to reflect a different space of
discourse (or of conceptualization): a discourse of 'dream,' a 'fantasy'
or 'associative' thinking, a discourse that would have more in common with patterning than with analysis and reference. For Prometheus would be the universal consciousness finally achieving that kind
of "divine Unity" at which we glanced earlier in connection with
Bruno. He would be the symbol of fire in all its forms: fire as divine

spirit, actual earthly fire, fire as life, fire as love.[1] In fact we will see that though the material is different, the discursive relation is the *same* as what we discussed in Chapter 7—and this is an important sign of dominance.

In the novel Prometheus is also Adam, and the latter seems to represent, according to Jung's researches, the universal soul.[2] Elijah explains to the narrator: "The Hebrews knew him under the name of Adam and the idolaters under that of Prometheus. The poets made up the story that he had stolen fire from heaven, because he begot descendants endowed with souls as perfect as the one with which God had filled him" (F 29; E 19). Adam, needless to say, is depicted here as possessing the "perfect philosophy" (F 33; E 22). This side of the Promethean myth would be favored by that theory of signatures in which man and the world, objects and words, signs and things, are all linked as one within the divine fire (proclaimed, for example, by the alchemists and by Bruno). That is the unity which seems to be maintained in the writing of Kepler or Campanella. It is not surprising that in the novel it is chiefly upheld by Elijah in the earthly paradise.

There is another side to Prometheus: it is he who breaks up that union. He is perhaps the myth of the destruction of myth. He *steals* fire and brings it to those who do not have it; he is the sole *master* of fire, the possessor of a secret previously unknown, the generous purveyor of knowledge to the ignorant, bearer of the word. Galileo writes, "it seems to me most reasonable for the ancients to have counted among the gods those first inventors of the fine arts, since we see that the ordinary human mind has so little curiosity and cares so little for rare and gentle things that no desire to learn is stirred within it by seeing and hearing these practised exquisitely by experts."[3]

Galileo does not, so far as I know, have Prometheus especially in mind in this passage. That is not my point. The scientist, like the narrator of the two novels we are considering, is clearly making 'mythology' out of 'myth': what is here being said is that the gods and their doings are no more than colorful representations of events

1. Karl Abraham, *Traum und Mythos: Eine Studie zur Völkerpsychologie* (Leipzig and Vienna, 1909), p. 56.

2. Carl Gustav Jung, *Mysterium coniunctionis: An Enquiry into the Separation and Synthesis of Opposites in Alchemy*, tr. R. F. C. Hull, in *Collected Works*, vol. 14 (London, 1963), 382–456.

3. Galileo, *Dialogue Concerning the Two Chief World Systems—Ptolemaic and Copernican*, tr. Stillman Drake, 2d ed. (Berkeley and Los Angeles, 1970), p. 406 (Third Day).

in human history. The material of myth is being *explained* in terms of the new rationality. In *De sapientia veterum*, Bacon had done the same.

In Kepler I suggested that two classes of discourse were functioning side by side; in Cyrano this is no longer the case, for the elements of the Promethean 'myth' he selects in effect *analyze* it into the very order of experimentalism. Faust was seen as a new Prometheus; here Prometheus appears as a Bacon or a Galileo of ancient times. He becomes the very symbol of the new science. It is not the aspect of universality that is emphasized, but rather that of the *ego*—in all its individuality.[4]

If the narrator sees himself as a Prometheus it is because he envisages himself in a particular role. The fire stolen by the mortal Prometheus, the fire that was a part of Adam's new knowledge upon leaving the Garden, was not simply a spiritual one: it was also carnal. The narrator of the *Lune* is surprised by the sight of men naked except for "the image of a virile phallus" which hangs from their belts. On one occasion, having questioned his host about it and learned it to be the distinguishing mark of noblemen, he exclaims that a sword, as on earth, seems a less extraordinary sign of nobility. To this his host replies:

> Oh, indeed, my little man! So the great ones in your world are frantic to parade an instrument which designates the executioner and is only forged to destroy us—in short, the sworn enemy of all living things, and on the contrary to hide an organ without which we should be among the ranks of the non-existent, the Prometheus of every animal and the tireless repairer of the weaknesses of nature! [F 113; E 93]

The Promethean hero, remarks Bachelard, feels "a need to penetrate, to get to the *interior* of things."[5] This is, as a matter of fact, the very kind of image that occurs constantly in the writings of a scientist like Galileo: nature there is a woman to be penetrated.[6] In the first epigraph to this chapter, Karl Abraham remarks on the "purely masculine" nature of the Promethean legend: need we be reminded of the "masculine birth of time" that forms so constant a theme in Bacon's writings? of the son who will replace the father and seize nature as his own? The elements which compose the Promethean sequences in the novel seem selected to present this aspect of the 'hero.' And the internal order of those sequences corresponds exact-

4. On Adam in this sense see Jung, *Mysterium*.
5. Gaston Bachelard, *La psychanalyse du feu* (1949; rpt. Paris, 1969), p. 70.
6. See, e.g., Reiss, "Espaces de la pensée discursive: Le cas Galilée et la science classique," *Revue de synthèse*, no. 85–86 (Jan.–July 1977), pp. 15–16 and passim.

ly to the discursive order of experimentalism: whatever 'meaning' we may desire to provide (Bachelardian, Jungian, or whatever) is indifferent. The point is the way the elements are organized.

I suggested that the end of the *Lune* seems rather ambiguous. This same ambiguity is given its appropriate mythological rendering. In view of what I have just said, it is not unexpected that the narrator's first journey should be to the moon, the virgin goddess floating in the darkness of space (writes Bachelard) to be the passive victim of the narrator's fiery rocket, in an attack that does end in a kind of (re)birth. But the moon is also, if we follow Bachelard and others (not to mention astrological and alchemical lore), the symbol of death and inaccessible sexuality. The fire is, so to speak, quenched in the waters on which floats the lunar goddess. In Jungian terms, we might say, the fire of Logos comes up against the cold of Eros, logical thought against associative thinking. It is indeed the case that much of the narrator's sojourn is taken up with arguing against the Christian and pagan discourses of Elijah and the lunarians, as though this conflict were being acted out in less esoteric terms.

After the moon journey the narrator is "forced" to come back to earth, and he does so by going "up the chimney" and returning to "a mountain in flames" (F 124; E 102–3). He *comes back,* that is to say, to the fire *by means of which* he left. *To leave the fire* constituted a mistake for Prometheus, and he must return. This flawed departure matches the ambiguity with which the *Lune* concludes in so far as experimental knowledge is concerned. In going to the sun, Prometheus is going toward fire. And there, too, we find the resounding affirmation of experimentalism suggested in the previous chapter.

The first 'mistake' of the Promethean narrator—a partial one to be sure—occurs, however, before he gets to the moon. It is the error of a Prometheus who attempts to tame not fire but water. Nevertheless, although the flight with dew-filled bottles does not raise the narrator to the moon, it does lead to a kind of shamanic 'apprenticeship' and a return of some importance. For when he comes down he finds himself in a more or less primitive world, "surrounded by a large number of stark naked men" (F 14; E 6), who do not appear to possess an articulate language—with whom therefore he cannot communicate. He is in fact in *New* France (F 15; E 7). It is as if he had gone back in time to wipe himself clean of all the obstacles and habits of civilization.

The narrator, however, passes very swiftly out of this state of deprivation, for he manages to seize one of the naked men before he can escape: "The man to whom I was speaking was an olive-skinned ancient who first of all threw himself at my knees and then clasped his hands in the air behind his head, opened his mouth and closed his eyes" (F 14; E 6). The narrator appears to have been put in the position, if not of a god, at least of an intermediary before whom the posture of prayer is normal. "I saw a company of soldiery arriving with beating drums" (F 15; E 6). In this primitive world (whose first and most immediate mark is the loss of the function of his native language) he can easily become a messenger of the devil,[7] or a "sorcerer" (F 16; E 7).

As we will see very soon, the whole sequence, including the drum beating, is quite akin to a shamanic ritual, in which a 'stripping' and 'election' will be followed by a kind of 'apprenticeship,' a preparation taking the form of conversations with the Viceroy in which a project of knowledge is laid forth. In turn this leads to a more physical kind of preparation; one which is at the same time a solitary contemplation and which terminates in an annointing prior to ascension: "As soon as [the moon] rose I would go off through the woods, dreaming of the conduct and success of my enterprise; and, finally, one Eve of St. John, when a council was being held at the Fort to determine whether help should be given to the local savages against the Iroquois, I went off all alone behind our house to the top of a small hill and here is what I carried out" (F 22; E 13).

He builds a "machine" which he supposes capable of getting him to the moon. Unfortunately it fails and he emerges "covered with bruises," which he soothes by smothering himself with "marrow of beef" from head to foot. Experimentally this is a failure, but it turns out to be an essential preparation for the eventual success of his journey. In the meantime we may perhaps venture a few questions appropriate to the mythic material (if quite inappropriate to the experimental): how better to pursue the lunar goddess and huntress, Diana, than by going off alone into the woods? And when better, as in Kepler's story, than at the time of the summer solstice, when Apollo is soon to be at his farthest from earth and moon and when a Prometheus may perhaps steal in more successfully?

We have earlier noted as well the fire ritual that accompanied the Feast of St. John and its resemblance to the shamanic techniques which facilitate entry into another world: "A shamanic session generally consists of the following items: first, an appeal to the auxiliary spirits, which, more often than not, are those of animals, and a

---

7. The question "what devil has put you in that state" is interpreted literally: "the devil had certainly not put me in that state I was in" (F 15; E 6). At the end of the novel, the devil will indeed have put him in a state!

dialogue with them in a *secret language*; secondly, drum-playing and a dance preparatory to the mystic journey; thirdly, the trance (real or simulated) during which the shaman's soul is believed to have left his body." The first stage of this session, adds the historian of religions, is a return to the primitive. The whole affair is performed by a shaman whose particular marks are "mastery of fire," powers of "ascension, magical flight, disappearances." The shaman is capable of breaking loose from the fetters of the human condition.[8]

I have already mentioned how linguistic communication was not immediately possible for the narrator upon his arrival in New France, and how this is just one aspect of a general 'return' to the primitive. One may maintain, without splitting too many hairs, that his conversations with the Viceroy, the only other person in the land "capable of lofty reasoning" (F 15; E 7), constitute a "secret language": for what they say is either not understood or rejected by everyone else. The soldiers whom the narrator first meets "with beating drums" are encountered anew after they have "cut wood to build a fire for the feast of St. John" and after they have attached rockets to his flying machine "in the middle of the square in Quebec" so that it might be taken for "a fire dragon" (F 23; E 13). The narrator remarks that he is so excited by seeing this (the French verb used is *transporter*), that he snatches the lighted fuse from one of the soldiers and leaps "furiously" into his machine. It is unnecessary perhaps to emphasize the etymology and cognates of the verb *transporter* or the adjective *furieux*. He now finds himself "borne up into the blue" ("enlevé dans la nue," F 23; E 13).

After this new Prometheus has run the risk of "leaving [his] crown upon that of some mountain" (F 23; E 14) and of thereby suffering the instant separation of body and soul, the marrow with which he has annointed his wounds is sucked up by the moon and carries him with it. The result of this timely intervention of the moon's power is that he "fortunately" (*par bonheur*) lands on the moon in the midst of the earthly paradise, and only then does the separation of body and soul start to occur: "the vital juice of the fruit [of the tree of life] which had trickled into my mouth must have recalled my soul before it had gone far from my corpse, while this was still warm and disposed to the functions of life" (F 25; E 15).

8. Mircea Eliade, *Myths, Dreams, and Mysteries*, tr. Philip Mairet (London, 1960), pp. 61, 63–66, 93, 94. Compare a passage from Dom Anselme Stolz, *Théologie de la mystique*, 2d ed. (Chevetogne, 1947), quoted by Eliade, p. 69: "only he who has been purified by fire can thenceforth enter into Paradise. For the way of purgation comes before the mystical union, and the mystics do not hesitate to put the purification of the soul on the same plane as the purifying fire on the way to Paradise."

This forms, then, in the 'Promethean analysis' of the tale, the end of a second sequence. The first appears to be incomplete, unless we can assimilate the concern with the moon and the narrator's subsequent isolation with a 'return to the primitive.' Nevertheless, the subsequent stages are all to be found: the linguistic aspect is present in the clash of different discourses, the ritualistic element is the 'appeal' to Cardano and to Prometheus (whom the narrator will 'become'), the flight itself corresponds to the trance, the translation of the narrator to another world. All these elements seem to follow a fairly distinct order, which is repeated with increased clarity in the second sequence: the return to the primitive is the landing in New France and the encounter with the "stark naked men"; the linguistic experiences are now double in so far as, first, the narrator cannot communicate at all and, second, he later does so in a "secret" discussion meaningful only to an elite of those "capable of lofty reasoning." The element of purification and the sign of the narrator's 'mastery' of fire lies in the ritualistic Feast of St. John and the use of rockets to achieve flight, not to mention the narrator's "furious transports." The trance may once again be identified with a flight that transports the narrator to another world.

I earlier referred to the Feast of St. John as unique in the Christian calendar because it celebrates a saint's nativity. In the novel the completion of the narrator's flight is indeed a birth or, rather, a rebirth: that of the Promethean narrator himself. He discovers in Eden (and we may well recall here Elijah's assimilation of Prometheus and Adam) a perfection of the body that has no physical needs to be supplied (he loses, for example, his feeling of hunger, F 25; E 15). He can hope, too, for some kind of immediate and perfect knowledge of nature (though this is mistaken in the event, as we have seen). All this is marked by a kind of 'communion' with nature whose sign is a visual admiration providing evidence of a 'purifying' and 'vivifying' of all his senses. They are assailed by a nature entirely fresh and exemplary in the experience of the observer: "On all sides there the flowers, which have no other gardener than nature, exhale a breath so sweet, though they are wild, that it both pricks and satisfies the nostrils. There, neither the crimson of a rose on the briar, nor the brilliant azure of a violet beneath the brambles leave me any freedom of choice, for each enforces the judgement that it is lovelier than the other" (F 26; E 16).

Between "New France" and the "earthly paradise" stretches, in a sense, the distance that lies between an 'apprenticeship' and an unparalleled achievement. The return to the primitive involved in the first of these can now be seen as a preparation for the birth of a 'real,' if unlikely, Prometheus. Apparently he has stolen his fire and completed some kind of 'rebirth':

> I must confess to you that at the sight of so many objects of beauty, I felt myself tickled by those pleasant pains which the embryo is said to feel at the infusion of its soul. My old hairs fell out and gave place to a new head of hair, finer and more luxuriant. I felt my youth rekindle, my face become ruddy, my natural warmth gently mingle once again with my bodily moisture; in short, I went back on my age some fourteen years. [F 27–28; E 17]

I say "apparently" because we will see very shortly that this is not the case: he cannot stay in the earthly paradise. His continual departures make of the Promethean series just another open-ended set on the same model as those we saw in the previous chapter. On the moon, I proposed earlier, the thief of fire cannot succeed. As though to confirm this, the Spaniard, Gonzales, will say to him rather later, when speaking of the unity of the vital material of all phenomena (atoms): "we lack a Prometheus to draw from the bosom of nature and make perceptible to us what I would call *primary matter*" (F 66; E 52).[9] Like Adam, before he departs from the earthly paradise the narrator will eat of the fruit of the Tree of Knowledge (F 40–41; E 29). Again, like Adam, he will bring back to earth *some* knowledge, even if it may be incomplete and unsatisfactory.

For the present, however, the sequence in the earthly paradise continues along the order already indicated: the return to the primitive (rebirth) is accompanied by a miraculous comprehension ("a stranger who speaks my own language," F 28; E 18), and the narrator almost goes so far as to adopt the same posture of adoration before the "youth" Elijah as the old man in Canada had before the narrator himself. For Elijah remains a kind of experienced precursor, himself come to the moon in search of Adam's perfect philosophy as an earlier Prometheus, himself having a certain link with the sun because of his name: "You have not, I think, forgotten that my name is Elijah [*Hélie*] for I told you that just now" (F 32; E 22).[10]

9. The Paris MS reads here: "mais il nous manque un Prométée pour faire cet extrait" (Laugaa ed., p. 73; Lachèvre ed., I.52).

10. The French for Elijah is Elie, spelled Hélie in the originals of the novels as everywhere else at the time (= Helios). Elijah is not the only precursor: he had been preceded on the moon by Enoch, who ascended by means of fire (F 29–30; E 19–20), and by Achab (F 31–32; E 20–21), who, as befits the female element, had been borne to the moon on the waters of the flood.

Like the narrator himself, Elijah, before his departure from the earth, had been content with a knowledge that came to him from authority: "There among my books I lived a life pleasant enough" (F 33; E 22). It is only after a dream that he becomes a kind of technician and, by means of a fiery furnace, makes himself the means to ascend to the moon where he would "find the Tree of Knowledge in Adam's paradise" (F 33; E 22). And it is in fire that he departs from the earth: "It was truly a most astonishing spectacle to behold, for the steel of this flying house, which I had polished with great care, reflected the light of the sun so vividly and brilliantly from every side that I thought I was all on fire" (F 34; E 23).

Since Elijah claims to have acquired "universal philosophy" by eating the fruit of the Tree of Knowledge (F 37; E 26), it may seem that the remark I made concerning the narrator's 'mistake' (as Prometheus) in departing from (and by means of) fire to make a journey toward 'water' does not hold true for Elijah. It is as though he *has* accomplished the shaman's goal of overcoming the nostalgia for Paradise and of reestablishing that *communication* between Heaven and Earth taken to have existed *in illo tempore,* in that time when man had not yet been splintered off from the Divine.[11] And yet we have already been able to suggest some of the contradictions in Elijah's discourse, and he falls back eventually on defending it to the narrator not in terms of his supposed "universal philosophy" but through an appeal to authority. When the narator makes a mockery of the story concerning the ascension of St. John the Evangelist, Elijah is no longer the second Adam, but rather "an outraged prophet" (F 40; E 29). It is as though he has fallen anew—together with the narrator.

After relating all these fiery ascensions, the narrator bites into the rind of a fruit from the Tree of Knowledge, so hungry is he. This "eating of the gods" (for Adam's sin was that of acquiring a knowledge previously only divine) leads to an immediate further translation: "a thick cloud enveloped my mind" (F 41; E 29). He has made another journey and finds himself once again at the beginning of a new sequence: "I remained surprised to find myself alone in the middle of a country I did not know at all. In vain I cast my eyes about me and scrutinized the landscape; they could pick out no creatures to console them" (F 41; E 29).

What the narrator eventually sees are the animals with "bodies and faces like ours" (F 41; E 29) but who walk on all fours. He is quick to view them in terms of human babies who move about in the

11. Eliade, *Myths, Dreams, and Mysteries,* pp. 63–66. He adds that the shaman was always believed to have ascended to Heaven and met with God (pp. 66, 68).

same way, arguing that the machines provided by civilization to make them walk upright make it 'natural' for adults to walk on two legs. The connection here once again with notions of primitiveness, of childhood and birth, is quite apparent, as is their opposition to the 'flaws' of civilization. Then, too, communication disappears, for these people speak to him in a language which he will come to understand only much later. He is himself taken for the mate of his predecessor in the moon, called the "Queen's animal" (F 42; E 30), whom, it turns out, the lunarians believe to be a monkey. Subsequently the narrator will speak to the "demon of Socrates" in a language which, as we have seen, is a secret so far as the lunarians are concerned. Later still he is taken to the court, learning on the way how the demon can transform himself to youthfulness (F 50–51; E 38), how he himself may be nourished merely by scenting aromas of food, how the people sleep on flowers appropriate to their constitution, and how verses of poetry replace money (F 51–56; E 39–43).

We can see here how the sequences composed from the material of myth are coming more and more to coincide with those which are more strictly experimentalist. Indeed, after his journey to the court the narrator 'becomes' a monkey (F 56; E 44). At that time he not only discusses many 'philosophical' questions with his "mate" in a language which the lunarians take for "a grunting which the joy of being reunited made us give voice to by natural instinct" (F 57; E 44), but he also learns the lunar languages (F 67; E 52–53). This knowledge in turn leads directly to the ritual of his inquisition, out of which he emerges successfully but as a result of which he is obliged to leave the court and go to the home where the demon is also staying. Here he becomes a kind of pupil in philosophy and acquires all kinds of novel ideas. This last sequence concludes with the flight up the chimney and the return to earth in Italy.

At the end of Chapter 7 I sought to diagram the experimental sequences of which the *Lune* is composed. In Kepler's *Somnium* we saw that the analytical discourse and the discourse of patterning do not mesh with one another—as though they reflect different structures of knowing or as though one kind of knowing must be enveloped in another, of which the first is then merely but one element. In Cyrano's *Lune*, on the other hand, the elements which formed the pattern in Kepler have been selected and lined up differently: they now form a mythology, a *reading* of myth which repeats the order of analysis. If we here line up those elements as we did for the *Somnium* we will find that just *one* order is repeated continuously; that the elements of the analysis itself are repeated in each sequence: that the order produced by lining up the sequences is exactly that of each sequence taken individually. We will find that the sequences are open-ended, so that we feel the later incompleteness of the *Soleil* to be, in a way, an *internal* necessity of structure (though it may or may not be an accident of history), whereas the *Somnium* pattern is a closed one, even though, once again, an accident of history may have intervened before it was actually 'finished.' It is, needless to say, quite different in the case of the *Somnium*'s notes, which could (and did) continue to accumulate. The nonending of Cyrano's *Voyages* is in every way comparable to that of *New Atlantis*.

As before, the nomenclature of the columns in the plan is little more than simply indicative, using terminology already suggested. The elements of the experimental sequences are also given, to show that the ordering is indeed identical.

PRIMITIVITY	PREPARATION (LANGUAGE)	RITUAL	TRANCE (TRANSLATION)
Moon	Battle of discourses	Appeal to Cardano and Prometheus	Flight with dew-filled bottles
New France; stark-naked men	Lack of communication	"Secret language" of discussions with Viceroy; fire ritual	Flight with rockets and by lunar suction of marrow
Earthly paradise; no hunger, hair renewed, etc.	Miraculous comprehension of Elijah; "universal philosophy"	(Story of fiery ascensions); eating of fruit	"A thick cloud enveloped my mind"
Unkown country, men on all fours (like babies)	No communica-tion (until later)	Discussions with the demon of Socrates	Journey to court
"Becomes" monkey	Acquisition of lunar languages	Inquisition abjuration	Trip to demon's host's house
"Pupil" of philosophers	Learned discussions	Up chimney; fiery mountain	Trip to and landing in Italy
Ignorance of whereabouts	Discovery of where he is	Cleansing of lunar "bad air"	Journey to France
OBSERVATION	DISCUSSION AND HYPOTHESIS	EXPERIMENT	VERIFICATION

Each of these sequences (reading across the diagram), contrary to those picked out in the *Somnium*, (1) leads 'naturally' and 'necessarily' into a subsequent one, and (2) is 'explained.' By 'explained' I mean that whereas the elements of each sequence in the *Somnium* (though 'sequence' is there the wrong word) formed each one a kind of nucleus around which there accrued a body of material of which it formed the center, in the *Lune* each element is fitted into a series of events which provides it with meaning: the biblical stories of Adam, of Enoch, of Elijah, say, are 'explained' as versions of the Promethean myth; the Promethean myth is 'analyzed' as a prescientific history of experimentalism. There is no longer any question as to which class of discourse dominates.

I suggested that the ascent to the moon by means of fire represents an erroneous decision on the part of Prometheus, and that he is condemned to return to the earth from the outset. This error is echoed 'experimentally' in the ambiguity of the knowledge the narrator has gained. His next successful flight occurs in the *Soleil* and takes him toward fire and away from water (the dampness of his prison in Toulouse, F 155; E 130). Indeed, his movement toward knowledge *comes from* fire itself, and the icosahedron that powers his flying machine is made of "crystal," the material of the philosopher's stone, key to the universe, which comes from the very material of the heavens.[12] It is there *sucked up* by the fires of the sun whose rays it concentrates, just as the marrow had earlier been sucked up by the moon.

The fires which bore the narrator to the moon, by contrast—the bonfire in Quebec, the exploding of the rocket stages which project him toward Paradise—come from an earthly source and a human one: in a sense, from himself. And he lands, after all, in the *earthly* paradise. No knowledge is produced *there* that he does not already possess. That this fire brings him back toward the flames of Hell, where it would represent not happiness but misery, is the natural symbolization of this nonproductivity, perhaps. It is only by letting go of the "Antichrist" that he manages to save himself from the fate of Empedocles in falling into the interior of the volcano (F 124; E

12. Eliade notes the idea in many primitive societies that the sky is composed of "rock crystal," this being thought of as the source of meteorites, of aeroliths. He adds that the oldest word meaning "iron" is the Sumerian word AN.BAR whose pictographic signs separately mean "sky" and "fire." The philosopher's stone, he writes, impure because it is mingled with the earth, is also taken as coming from the sky (*Forgerons et alchimistes* [Paris, 1965], pp. 17–21, pp. 172–73). Jung remarks in *Mysterium coniunctionis* that in alchemy Adam is often the symbol of the philosopher's stone.

103). He also, of course, avoids the fate of Prometheus at the same time. Yet that he does avoid that fate is itself a testimony to the doubtful value of the knowledge he has 'acquired.' It is as though no reprisal were needed. For how can a new knowledge be achieved when the means presume that they already contain that knowledge (a fire *already* possessed)? This, too, is the situation of Elijah, who finally remains the "enraged prophet," not the universal philosopher.

None of this is to say that the *experimental discourse* is revealed, through the Promethean myth, to be merely solipsistic, or to be but a different form of the old familiar discourse supposedly caught up in the discussion of its own verbalization. The Promethean series is not a *commentary* on the experimental. The two run parallel to one another, just as do the various sets of notes in Kepler. It is just precisely this parallelism that is at issue: in the *Somnium*, we found it impossible to align the discourse of patterning (making use of much the same mythical material as here) with those of analysis and referentiality (themselves much more fragmented than here). Now the parallel forges itself. The Promethean error finds its precise complement in the ambiguous and incomplete success of the experimental discourse, as we find it in the *Lune*. Our Prometheus lives, after all, to fly another day.

The Promethean winner of knowledge, it is implied, will be he who goes after it without preconceived ideas. He will not backtrack upon himself. The discourse which will achieve it for him is to be found in nature, say Galileo and Bacon, even though some part of this discourse is *also* to be found in the mind. It is as if Prometheus reacts *passively* to the fire: the mind may find some part of the right means (the icosahedron of crystal), but only nature can complete and fulfill them (the fire itself). The way the mythic material is used manifests (for us) the very same occultation that we observed in the experimental order.

The narrator of the *Soleil*, Dyrcona, does not set out to go to the sun. His intention is to make a flying machine which will get him from prison in Toulouse to his friend's estate at Colignac (F 160, 163; E 135, 137), but the power of the sun's rays on his crystal icosahedron proves too great and he is taken inexorably toward its fire. Prometheus becomes Phaeton. Yet he does not fail for all that: "I am still following Phaeton's example, in the midst of a chariot race which I cannot abandon and in which, if I make one false move, all nature together cannot save me" (F 166; E 140). He has a limited responsibility, he can keep on track, so to speak, and there remains something of Prometheus in this Phaeton: but it is essentially nature now who directs the course.

Phaeton, of course, disappears into the fire. For others he has gone, he is dead. Nature, for him, is no longer communicated through its signs, for he has become one with it—and that is inexpressible. The new knowledge has almost no connection with what preceded it. To those familiar with the old, it is all but incomprehensible. Phaeton burns up and disappears:

> Then a moment later I became aware that I could see directly behind myself. As if my body had no longer been anything but an organ of sight, I felt my flesh, purged of its opacity, transmitting straight through itself, objects to my eyes and my vision to objects. . . . I discovered that, through some secret law governing the light near its source, we had become transparent, my cabin and I.   [F 178; E 50–51]

As Prometheus, however, he is simply purged of those obstacles to feeling and knowing which the very clumsiness of the human organs places in the way of their exact functioning. The demon of Socrates had already pointed this out to the narrator during his stay on the moon, and had remarked at the same time that the solar inhabitants do not suffer a like disability (F 47–48; E 35–36).[13] To those who have not made the journey, then, Prometheus has disappeared from view, but he remains visible to himself and to those who *have* made the same journey. As Prometheus, perhaps, he has found Logos in the sun, symbol of the power of discrimination, judgment, and intellectual understanding; behind him he has left Luna and Eros. Others have made the same trip. The minds of the philosophers in the sun become transparent to one another, so that linguistic communication is no longer necessary. As Bachelard puts it, "Death in the flames is the least solitary of deaths. It is truly a cosmic death in which the entire universe is consumed with the thinker. The stake is a companion of the thinker."[14]

Dyrcona will not return from the sun, anymore than will the spir-

---

13. "Except by an act of faith, you men could no more attain to such lofty conceptions—because you lack the senses proportionate to such marvels—than a blind man could imagine what makes up the beauty of a landscape, the colouring of a picture, or the nuances of a rainbow, unless he imagined them as something palpable like food, as a sound, or as a scent. In exactly the same way, if I sought to explain to you what I perceive with the senses which you do not possess, you would picture it to yourself as something which can be heard, seen, touched, smelt or tasted, and it is, in fact, none of these things" (F 48; E 36).

14. Bachelard, *La psychanalyse du feu*, p. 39.

its of Campanella or of Descartes. Knowledge is truly secret, for those who possess it have passed beyond the ken of those who do not. Moreover, only those who possess the means to communicate it can enjoy it. But in the sun the perfect knowledge of the philosophers involves the union of subject and object: in that sense there can be no consciousness of it.[15] Nor can there be communication, for language presupposes what we might term the distance and difference of transitivity. For the reader or listener the result can be only silence, the ellipsis which marks the incompleteness of the *Soleil.* Small wonder that this text also contains an ironic commentary on the philosophy of Descartes, placed in the mouth of Campanella: this silence will demand a solution.

The problematic of the discourse of experimentalism is thus brought full circle. Communication of knowledge and mediation of nature are its presuppositions. If language and the use of language fail or are unreliable, then its knowledge is impossible. This is no doubt the further significance of the appearance in these texts of the material of the Prometheus myth: for in all mythologies fire is also speech and the Word.

The problem for Cyrano, as for his contemporaries, becomes that of finding the right discourse to make possible the right order of knowledge. The nonending of the *Soleil,* its falling silent, seems to present just four possibilities of interpretation: either (1) the achievement of complete knowledge will be marked by silence, or (2) the Cartesian method (if it is the only one possible) leads into contradiction and produces only this silence, or (3) the right knowledge can make no use of language as an instrument of communication (or of anything else) and silence follows of necessity, or (4) writing and experiment are two complementary components of experimental knowledge, both necessary each insufficient by itself, but writing comes to a temporary halt when it is time for experiment. This last would imply that the significance of the end of the *Soleil* is closely akin to that of the end of *New Atlantis.*

The first of these alternatives is a matter of indifference, because at this time experimental discourse assumes it will not achieve any

15. Jung has noted how the direct understanding of "the language of nature" forms a kind of myth of the preconsciousness (so-called): a blending with nature as a union with the mother before a subsequent separation of subject and object and the birth of consciousness (*Symbols of Transformation: An Analysis of the Prelude to a Case of Schizophrenia,* tr. R. F. C. Hull, in *Collected Works,* vol. 5 [London, 1963], 324 ff.). Dyrcona risks going in the opposite direction as he speaks with birds, trees, and so on. Eliade notes this as an attribute of the shaman, who is also of course going 'back from' consciousness.

complete knowledge for some centuries. The second two alternatives imply a failure in knowledge. Equally evidently, they contradict both the claims of the narrator himself and what is implicit in the experimental structure of these novels. The implications of the last alternative yet remain to be demonstrated by the discourse of experimentalism. The difficulties suggested by all four interpretations are considerable: they were for Bacon, they were for Descartes, they were for the entire century, and, indeed, have remained so ever since. It is not, therefore, a cause for surprise to find that the two novels, particularly the *Soleil,* pay enormous attention to the status of language and the problem of communication.

9 · *The Difficulty of Writing*

> In Yana the noun and the verb are well distinct, though there are certain features that they hold in common which tend to draw them nearer to each other than we feel to be possible. But there are, strictly speaking, no other parts of speech. The adjective is a verb. So are the numeral, the interrogative pronoun . . . , and certain "conjunctions" and adverbs. . . . Adverbs and prepositions are either nouns or merely derivative affixes in the verb.
>
> —Edward Sapir, *Language*

> The world for them is not a concourse of objects in space; it is a heterogeneous series of independent acts. It is successive and temporal, not spatial. There are no nouns in Tlön's conjectural *Ursprache*, from which the "present" languages and dialects are derived: there are impersonal verbs, modified by monosyllabic suffixes (or prefixes) with an adverbial value. For example: there is no word corresponding to the word "moon," but there is a verb which in English would be "to moon" or "to moonate." "The moon rose above the river" is *hlör u fang axaxaxas mlö*, or literally: "upward behind the onstreaming it mooned."
>
> —Jorge Luis Borges, "Tlön, Uqbar, Orbis Tertius"

It is a fundamental tenet of Edward Sapir's book on language—as it is of virtually everything written on the subject since the European seventeenth century, at least in the West—that language is the sign of, as well as the setting into signs of, thinking in concepts. This notion in turn is based upon a "prerational" fund of images "which are the raw material of concepts."[1] Such a model supposes a clear separation between three stages of the functioning of mind: storing images, ordering concepts, and using language. These correspond respectively, for example, to the first book of the Port-Royal *Logic* (Conception), to the second, third, and fourth books of the same volume (Judgment, Reasoning, Order), and finally to the

1. Edward Sapir, *Language: An Introduction to the Study of Speech* (1921; rpt. New York, 1964), p. 38.

Port-Royal *Grammar*. Between these stages there is, of course, considerable overlap, even though theorists are able to distinguish between them with relative ease.

Even supposing we can accept such a model, we are still faced with the enormous difficulty that follows upon the assumption that using language enables us to express and communicate not only concepts but also the things themselves that the images 'behind' such concepts and 'in front of' language are thought to indicate in some way or another. For Sapir the "latent content of all language is the same—the intuitive science of experience."[2] Such a claim, if it can be upheld, suggests that the difficulty is superficial, for in this "intuitive science," in its very universality, would lie the 'proof' of its adequacy to our experience of things: otherwise why should it be everywhere the same?

Unfortunately, Sapir's use of the word "science" here is something of a cheat, for it certainly cannot have the meaning that it has usually had since the European eighteenth century. His usage implies that the latent content *is* common to all mankind: it seeks, if you will, to dispense with the necessity for proof. Certainly no evidence exists to date of the universality of such content. Frege's researches propose rather that at the level of images (*Vorstellungen*) 'thinking' is absolutely individual (and would, perhaps, not be 'thinking' in any normally accepted usage of the word), and that the setting into concepts is the level at which any 'communal' order comes into question (the terminology is not Frege's). But at this level the role of language is *already* of manifest importance, as the third book of Locke's *Essay Concerning Human Understanding* had made resoundingly clear in 1690.

Sapir's "intuitive science" is akin to Descartes's *conception*, whose ramifications I have explored elsewhere. It assumes indeed that the problem of representation is resolved at the moment of the formation of 'images,' because such an image is a direct sign of the object in the world and immediately associated with it. We must not suppose that the clear and distinct idea in Descartes is simply and entirely intellectual, lacking all connection with a material exterior: the beginning of *Le monde* would alone suffice to dispel that notion. If representation is resolved at the level of images (whatever one may choose to call them), then language *can* be an adequate means of communication. It will be so whenever it succeeds in provoking just the same set of images in the mind of the hearer as produced the

2. Ibid., p. 218.

particular enunciation in the speaker: for at this level, it is said, we are dealing with an "intuitive science," with a "*common* sense." And that is the same in everyone.

Such a claim runs into the obvious difficulty that in languages "the manifest form . . . is never twice the same, for this form, which we call linguistic morphology, is nothing more nor less than a collective *art* of thought, an art denuded of the irrelevancies of individual sentiment."[3] The neoclassical search for universal grammar or the more contemporary quest for a deep structure of language may be seen as the attempt to make that "art" reflect precisely the "science" taken as preceding it and making it possible.

But what enables us to presume that such a common science underlies the speech of Borges's Tlönian, who expresses his conceptualization of reality entirely in verbs? or that of Sapir's Yana, who is obliged to choose between things that have real existence in the world (nouns) and those whose nature depends on the relationship of the speaker *with* the world (verbs)—or some such choice, at least? or that of the Indo-European speaker who divides up reality into even smaller slices? The answer lies fundamentally in the assumption that man's reason, together with his capacity for language (the 'voice' of reason), is part of the very definition of 'human'—and a principal part at that. This being given, it becomes relatively automatic to take the 'faculty' of reason for some thing singular and itself definable as some sort of circumscribable 'object.' One begins to search for the precise *location* of the "reason," just as one had sought for the "seat" of the soul. What then becomes variable is not the faculty of reason itself but the way it is put to use. This, of course, is the entire theme of the *Discours de la méthode* (1637): it is this use which must be made methodical. Only in this way can we be sure that the reaction of the hearer's reason to an utterance will be the same as that which provoked it in the speaker.

Toward the end of 1629, Marin Mersenne wrote to Descartes concerning what the latter, in his reply, calls a "proposition for a new language." Of this we know nothing whatever except Descartes's response, which is adverse. He does oppose to the proposition in question his own idea of what such a perfect human language (as that sought in the proposition) would be, if it were possible to create one:

> I consider that one could add to this a discovery [*invention*] both for the composition of the basic [*primitifs*] words of this language and for the

3. Ibid.

letters composing them, such that it could be taught in a very short time. This would be by means of order, that is to say by establishing an order among all the thoughts that can enter into the human mind, just as there is one established naturally among numbers. And just as to count all the numbers up to infinity can be learned in a day, as well as to write them in an unknown language, even though this is an infinity of different words, so, too, one could do the same with all the other words necessary to express all the other things which occupy the minds of men.[4]

This challenge will be taken up some forty years later in precisely the form suggested by Descartes, most notably by John Wilkins in his *Essay Towards a Real Character and a Philosophical Language* (1668). Descartes is in fact suggesting here an intellectual language whose relationship with thought (taken to be universal in humans and, potentially at least, the same everywhere) is entirely analogous to the relationship that exists, he writes to Mersenne a month later, between "natural language" (as spoken) and the natural language of emotions caused by sensation. *This* natural language *is* universal, he affirms. It is constituted by human reactions to pain, surprise, joy, and the like—almost what today one might call "body language," a language composed essentially (though not entirely) of gesture.[5]

Unlike the optimistic Wilkins, Descartes acknowledges in the earlier letter that such an intellectual language as he suggests (the term is not his) has yet to be made possible. He avers, indeed, that it may never be commonly or universally possible because it depends on the prior discovery and ordering of "all man's thoughts" according to "the true philosophy." If this condition were achieved, such a language would virtually formulate itself. Unfortunately, few people are capable of such disciplined discovery and order.[6] Most, like Cyrano's Elijah, are "fallen." Indeed, Descartes himself, I will suggest in a moment, assumes the general impossibility of such discipline—unlike many of his successors who fondly believe all difficulties to have been overcome.

Instead of proposing a universal intellectual language, Descartes will leave the expression of the interaction between mind and matter to "the conventional and arbitrary particularity of representational languages" (though he does so only provisionally, perhaps, and as a temporary stopgap, like his *morale*). "Words," he writes in the more

4. Descartes, letter to Mersenne of November 20, 1629, in *Oeuvres philosophiques*, ed. Ferdinand Alquié, 3 vols. (Paris, 1963–73), I.230–31.
5. Letter to Mersenne of December 18, 1629, ibid., p. 234.
6. Ibid., p. 231.

or less contemporaneous *Monde*, "signify nothing except conventionally, and yet suffice to make us conceive things to which they bear
no resemblance."[7] At this point, Descartes compares the convention-
ality of language to the sensation of light, which, he affirms, is a sign
having no necessary resemblance with what causes it and yet does
not fail to give us a correct conception of the nature of light.[8] The
assumption that there is a similar semiotic relation in the functioning
of language with respect to concepts and in the functioning of objects and events in nature with respect to the images we have of
them corresponds exactly to the claim of which we were speaking
earlier: that of the relationship between language and a science of
experience on the one hand, and between the latter and the world
on the other. It also appears to pick up once again the identity of
functioning depicted by Bacon and Galileo between letters, words,
and sentences, and the "alphabetical" seeds of things and the written
book of nature.

Later on Descartes himself seems to lose the optimistic hope of the
earlier affirmations, both as they concern a universal intellectual
language and as they concern a conventional but adequate *langage
représentatif*. It may be that the comparative failure of his own 'practical' scientific work is partly responsible for that, but whatever the
cause, toward the end of his life he tends increasingly to imply that
language is less useful as communication than simply as the manifestation of thought itself. While language is certainly unique in man
and linked to reason, he implies that these facts by no means urge
that language is any simple help in 'getting outside oneself.' Language, and the use of signs in general, is sufficient proof of the
existence of reasonable thought in mankind, but beyond that we
cannot go with much ease. In a letter to the Marquis of Newcastle at
the end of 1646, Descartes links "reflective consciousness of self and
of the object of thought" to the use of language, while in a letter of
early 1649 to Henry More, he remarks that the use of language and
other signs is certainly the principal reason for distinguishing men
from beasts.[9] Language is an evidence of reason, that is to say, but
that fact is of little help in its use as a methodical tool of knowledge,
for that use will depend on a prior discovery of their relationship
with one another.

7. Ibid., p. 234; *Le monde ou traité de la lumière*, ibid., p. 317.
8. On all this see Reiss, "The *concevoir* Motif in Descartes," in *La cohérence intérieure*,
ed. J. Van Baelen and D. L. Rubin (Paris, 1977), esp. pp. 206–12.
9. *Oeuvres philosophiques*, III.694–95, 886. The paraphrase is quoted from Leonora
Cohen Rosenfield, *From Beast-Machine to Man-Machine: Animal Soul in French Letters
from Descartes to La Mettrie* (New York, 1941), p. 15.

Today we would perhaps prefer to say that such use depends only on a *definition* of such relationship, that any knowledge is reliable (as well as its expression and communication) provided the axioms which control its 'shape' be clearly laid down. The seventeenth century did not yet have this possibility before it. For Bacon and his contemporaries, thought and things occupied their particular places and language had to fulfill a function of mediating between them, of rendering possible a knowledge and a communication of knowledge whose two sides were constituted by human concepts in their expression of things and their order on the one hand, and by the things themselves in the world on the other. If, as Bacon and others have it, writing is essential to the expansion of the new knowledge, then language must be made the 'transparent' bearer of the thought whose evidence it is: "languages have only been invented to express the conceptions of our mind," writes the Abbé Bouhours in 1671.[10]

Such transparency can only be achieved if a correspondence of some specifiable kind may be supposed to exist between language, thought, and things. If this correspondence can be demonstrated then language no longer intervenes as an obstacle, and the three-way division between image, concept/thought, and language is effectively reduced to a dichotomy consisting only of the first two. This is why the occultation of enunciation itself is so important. Such a reduction is one of the main purposes of the logical and grammatical researches of Port-Royal, and its intention will be picked up by many. We can see it at work equally clearly in the development of scientific theory.[11] "Fine language resembles a pure, clear water with no taste," writes Bouhours. And Valincour adds, a little later: "the conformity of a language with the function it is to fill is its precellence."[12] The function it is to fill is the precise expression of thought, which is in turn the result of the discovery of an intellectual system whose order also controls that of the world. As far as a Bouhours is concerned the French language has already achieved such expression: "In my opinion only [the French language] is able to paint after nature and to express things precisely as they are."[13] With regard to both English and French such claims are rampant in this period.

10. Le Père Dominique Bouhours, *Les entretiens d'Ariste et d'Eugène* (1671), ed. Ferdinand Brunot (Paris, 1962), p. 32.

11. See, once again, Reiss, "Espaces de la pensée discursive: Le cas Galilée et la science classique," *Revue de synthèse*, no. 85–86 (Jan.–July 1977), pp. 31–41, esp. pp. 30–33, 38, 40–41, and n. 84.

12. Bouhours, *Entretiens*, p. 37; Jean-Baptiste-Henri du Trousset de Valincour, *Avis sur les occupations de l'Académie* (Paris, 1714). This kind of remark is absolutely typical of the period, of course.

13. Bouhours, *Entretiens*, p. 34.

Needless to say, these ideas are picked up without ado in the utopias of the period. Thus, for example, Gabriel de Foigny in *La terre australe connue* formulates a rather simplistic idea of a language intended to overcome all difficulties by *being* at once the thing and the thought capturing it: "The advantage of this way of speaking is that you become a philosopher as you learn the first elements [of the language], and you can name nothing in this land without explaining its nature at the same time [for, he has just observed], they form their nouns so perfectly that upon hearing them you conceive immediately [*aussitôt*] the explanation and definition of what they are naming." Foigny continues his description of the Australian language by observing that when a child is taught the meaning of the elements of the written language and when he joins them together, "he learns at the same time the essence and nature of all the things he puts forward."[14] More's Utopians would have loved this language! But it is not to be confused with the old notion of signatures: Foigny's traveler is quite clear that humans *form* their language.

Whatever may be the hesitations and ambiguities of the developing notions about the functioning of language, clearly any search for a language that 'corresponds adequately,' if not 'exactly,' to the thought it expresses presupposes that there is *in fact* a separation of the function of 'thinking' from the function of 'enunciating'—and that the latter is by nature a visible or audible articulation of the former. It presupposes that thinking *comes before* any linguistic system, and that it is therefore possible to conceive of one 'language' which *would* correspond exactly to that thinking and would underlie all particular languages. In Cyrano this one language occurs as the *langue matrice*; it is the Australian language of Foigny, the universal intellectual language suggested by Descartes and elaborated by Wilkins in the *True Philosophical Language*, and perhaps it is Chomsky's deep structure: certainly he himself has claimed that it is.[15]

No discursive (or simply linguistic) model of the type suggested by the aforegoing is initially available to Cyrano. He is, as we have seen, in the midst of the developments which lead to these later concep-

14. Gabriel de Foigny, *La terre australe connue* (1676), in Frédéric Lachèvre, ed., *Les successeurs de Cyrano de Bergerac* (Paris, 1922), pp. 130, 131.
15. In *Cartesian Linguistics* (New York and London, 1966). An apparent exception is Denis Veiras's *L'histoire des Sévarambes*, in which the philosopher Seromenos makes a remark hearking back more to the early Bacon than to Descartes, though the latter seems to approach it late in life: language and discourse are the foundation and cause of thought and knowledge. If men "did not have the use of speech, they would have scarcely more light [than animals]. They communicate their thoughts to one another by means of discourse, and most of the arts and sciences owe their origin and progress to the art of expressing oneself by speaking" (Lachèvre, *Successeurs*, p. 197).

tions of language: indeed, he helps 'create' the structure that eventually makes analytico-referential discourse possible. This is a very far cry from being able to rely on the certainty of the model. The many discussions of language that occur particularly in the *Soleil* sometimes seem, therefore, to contradict the reliance of the experimental method on writing and discourse in general. Certainly, the narrator is unable to rely from the outset on a singular discursive model whose domination would never be in question (this, of course, despite its domination throughout at a different level of the novel—hidden, as it were, from the narrator himself). Nor does the narrator in fact conclude with such a sure model, though he travels a long way toward it.

A rather interesting 'encounter' between one element of Cyrano's text and a brief passage in the writings of Bertrand Russell (though it is long in its implications) emphasizes Cyrano's inability to rely on any already constructed model. For Russell the model in question goes back by and large to the Greeks. I argued the contrary in Chapter 2, but whether it does so or not is here beside the point, for we are concerned with a particular discursive class and the way in which its inception functions *for us*: and *this* inception occurs during the period we are examining.

Russell writes:

> The influence of language on philosophy has, I believe, been profound and almost unrecognized. . . . The subject-predicate logic, with the substance-attribute metaphysic, are a case in point. It is doubtful whether either would have been invented by people speaking a non-Aryan language; certainly they do not seem to have arisen in China, except in connection with Buddhism, which brought Indian philosophy with it. Again, it is natural, to take a different kind of instance, to suppose that a proper name which can be used significantly stands for a single entity; we suppose that there is a certain more or less persistent being called "Socrates," because the same name is applied to a series of occurrences which we are led to regard as appearances of this one being.[16]

'This' very example is 'used' by Cyrano to put into question in the *Lune* the very logic with which Russell is here preoccupied, as it also was by Locke in the long discussion (related to Cyrano's) of "personal identity" in chapter 27 of the second book of the *Essay*. The narrator first meets the demon of Socrates—who is not, to be sure,

16. Bertrand Russell, "Logical Atomism," in *Logic and Knowledge: Essays, 1901–1950*, ed. Robert Charles Marsh (1956; rpt. New York, 1971), pp. 330–31.

the "being called 'Socrates'"—as an old man whose material existence puts no habits of thought or their expression into question, despite the fact that he has been 'present' through the ages to a variety of sages. He is, that is to say, a "more or less persistent being called '[the demon of] Socrates.'" It comes, therefore, as a considerable shock to the narrator, even though he had been warned (F 46; E 34), to meet a "very young and tolerably handsome man" who greets him most familiarly and says he is the demon of Socrates: "my amazement was so great that I now believed that the whole globe of the moon, all that had happened to me on it and everything I could see there must be nothing but an enchantment" (F 50; E 38). He is the more amazed because he had by this time been traveling for some way on the lunarian's back without realizing it to be Socrates' demon. The experience will be repeated later, when the demon becomes the advocate who saves him from the "inquisition," and the narrator will be only a little less "astonished" by this second transformation (F 78; E 62).

As we can see from the passage quoted from the first metamorphosis of the demon, the inability to rely on the constancy of the relationship between, in this case, name and material manifestation throws into doubt for the narrator the very reality which he is living, which he is experiencing. That doubt will result from the destruction of the one-to-one relationship between nominal meaning and single entity is, broadly speaking, one of the implications of Russell's remark. Yet what is indicated here is that after an initial "amazement" a name *can* be used significantly *without* standing for a single entity: for, after all, the narrator does continue to treat the demon of Socrates as though it remained always the same being. In a way it is the name that makes the entity significant, rather than the reverse: "I brought my mouth close to his and went in through it like a breath of air" (F 51; E 39), explains the demon.

The narrator is not offering a 'serious' choice, but rather discovering that discourse does not function in any self-evident way and that it does not follow any *necessary* sets of relations. Why indeed should the model of which Russell is speaking be dependent upon some "intuitive science of experience" rather than the reverse (except that, then, the "science" would no longer be intuitive)? Further, why should we suppose not only that such a science exists but that it is singular and underlies such diverse linguistic (let along discursive) forms as those of the Yana or the Tlönians, the lunarians or Paracelsus, Russell or the Solarians? If one cannot make such assumptions, then recourse must be elsewhere: to the use of language itself, not to what it might or might not cover up, block, represent, signify, and so on. Again, in just these terms, the problem was to be posed formally and at considerable length by Locke in the third book of the *Essay*.

We have already seen the several occasions in the *Lune* when the narrator finds himself involved in some way in the utterance of apparently inarticulate sounds: first in New France when he cannot comprehend the old savage; second in the moon when the lunarians cannot understand his and the demon's Greek; third at the lunar court when his and Gonzales's Spanish is likewise incomprehensible to the lunarians. Those whose language is not understood are referred to as "mutes" or "animals." And indeed as soon as communication is impossible one is effectively mute. The encounter of two mutually incomprehensible languages merely serves to pose the difficulty of *any* discursive communication in a more acute manner.[17]

In this light we may consider perfectly 'justified' the narrator's astonishment when he and Elijah understand one another without the slightest difficulty. And it is in connnection with the difficult question of communication that the narrator first introduces what *may* be a version of two of Descartes's languages—the universal natural (gestural) and the particular conventional: "I did not know their language and they did not understand mine and you can judge now what similarity there was between the two. For you must know that only two idioms are used in this country, one which serves the great and the other which is peculiar to the common people" (F 48–49; E 36). One of these languages is a kind of "natural" language consisting of gestures and body movements, though it is, the narrator affirms, not quite as simple "as you might imagine it." The description is in fact very similar to the way one might characterize the use of gesture on the oriental stage. The other language, the superior one, consists of music (an idea Cyrano may well have obtained from Godwin's *Man in the Moone*).[18] Actually it is unclear whether this superior language corresponds to Descartes's conventional one, or to the universal intellectual one he proferred once as a possibility, for the narrator goes into no details except to mention briefly the questions debated in it (F 49; E 37). That particular aspect is of small importance. What is more interesting is that this language seems to re-

17. Saussure has observed that the Greek word *bárbaros* apparently implied a speech flaw, while the Russian word for Germans is *Nêmtsy*, meaning "mutes." Everyone, he adds, believes in the superiority of his own language: Ferdinand de Saussure, *Cours de linguistique générale*, ed. Tullio de Mauro (Paris, 1972), p. 262.

18. Francis Godwin, *The Man in the Moone: or, A Discourse of a Voyage thither, by Domingo Gonsales, The Speedy Messenger* (London, 1638). The French translation was published in 1648.

spond to the very difficulty posed each time speakers of different languages meet one another: the difficulty of recognizing the artic-ulation of words.

We have already seen the way in which, through the metamor-phoses of the demon of Socrates, the relation of verbal significance and material entity is put into question—suggesting perhaps that the relation of mediation does not depend on the stability of the mate-rial entity, and that the contrary is just as possible (that is, that the stability depends on the name). Words have meaning and can be used meaningfully regardless of any constant anchor in 'reality.' The demon of Socrates is, in a sense, an idea, not a material being. Language is related to that idea, while the relation of that idea to the 'entity' in question is no concern of language as such at all. The latter relationship is to be *carried out* and composed by the structure of the experimental discourse that we examined in the previous three chapters. It is on *that* supposition that the language used in the experimental structure may be conceived of as a transparent me-dium, or potentially so. Language will *have* to be viewed as though it played no role in the performance of that structure.

It is only to be expected, therefore, that the next element of natu-ral language to become a concern is articulation itself: the superior language of the lunar people "is nothing else but a variety of non-articulated notes—more or less like our music when the words are not added to the melody" (F 49; E 37). Such an idea would appear to eliminate the incomprehension that follows whenever an articulate language cannot be made out by the hearer of the sounds of an unfamiliar tongue. Lack of articulation would appear, in fact, to do away with *language* completely and, at this stage, the narrator has yet to learn what makes this language meaningful (F 67; E 53). Actually, even this language is far from transparent, for the narrator implies that its aesthetic virtues are, indeed, far above its power to commu-nicate meaning: "sometimes a company of as many as fifteen or twenty will meet together and dispute a point of theology or the intricacies of a lawsuit in the most harmonious concert one could possibly devise to charm the ear" (F 49; E 37). Furthermore, this musical language, or something very like it, will be used by the 'inferior' nightingale on the sun (F 87, 190–91; E 158, 161–62) and will be replaced by two attempts to 'situate' language more satisfac-torily. The musical language would not, therefore, appear to have had much success in overcoming the obstacle posed by the mere fact of articulation.

While the narrator is still on the moon he encounters at least two other indices of such an attempt to 'place' language. The first is the suggestion that the contamination of writing may be removed from language, as though writing were no more than a representation of speaking and thus at a further remove from thinking, as though one more form of linguistic obstacle could be done away with.[19] I am referring to the episode of the "talking books," those boxes in which one simply "turns the needle to the chapter he wishes to hear" (F 108; E 89). This, writes the narrator, removes a considerable block to knowledge: "I am no longer astonished to see how the young men in that country possessed more understanding at sixteen or eighteen than the greybeards do in ours, since, knowing how to read as soon as they can talk, they are never without reading matter" (F 108; E 89).

The notion of referential mediation, the need for articulation, the role of writing have now all been placed in doubt. All these elements concern the use of language as an obstacle to thought and its communication, as a barrier to knowledge. In the *Lune*, therefore, one further matter remains to be considered: the idea of discursive—or linguistic—meaning. It is true that the matter is raised only briefly and in an oblique fashion. Perhaps it could be brought up in no other way.

Traveling to the court, the narrator's party stops at an inn. When the time for departure arrives the next day the narrator learns from his demon that the bill is paid in poetic verses (F 55–56; E 42–43). Such a valorization of discourse as currency would appear in a way to remove all meaning from language as the mediator of ideas: its 'meaning' becomes its 'value' as an object permitting the exchange of other objects. We may argue that this valorization symbolizes, or carries out in a different medium, the exchange of ideas. If it does so, then language has effectively become a counter devoid of any weight in itself: it has become a neutral counter between, in this case, service given and service received. Writing *can*, it is thus asserted, be made into a transparent mark of exchange involving quite different 'things.' The 'meaning' of language, its *value* in exchange, is then assessed by a "Jury of Poets of the Realm" (F 55; E 42). It is given its place in a process of exchange simply by convention, by the public decision of a particular elite.

---

19. This view of the relationship between the spoken and written language has, one need hardly be reminded, a long and hoary tradition backing it, from Plato to Saussure and beyond. It does not appear to be the unreserved opinion of Bacon, who, as we saw when examining certain of his writings, views *writing* as essential to the development of the *right* experimental method.

This writing 'works,' of course, in a rather limited arena of sense, and the episode of the verses being used as currency precedes the episode of the talking books, which appear to propose the complete rejection of writing. Indeed, though the poems are apparently written on paper, they would presumably be written in some form of musical notation (since the lunarians possess only the languages of gesture and of music), and would therefore appear as a kind of offshoot of the talking books. In that way their very form may be a devalorization of the writing which composes them. But the relative status of these incidents is of small interest. These questions are merely raised here, not solved. The point is just that they *are* raised, in connection with all the other matters discussed in the previous two chapters, as part of a nexus of problems whose solution is essential to the functioning of discourse (thought).

The *Voyage dans la lune* seems concerned with language almost by the way: its main preoccupations are aimed rather at the possibility of an (experimental) knowledge of physical reality—with the order of the solar system, with the infinity of worlds and the eternity of the universe, with an atomistic theory of matter (and of the human senses as matter), with the existence of God. The *Voyage au soleil*, on the other hand, gives a greater place to matters 'spiritual,' psychological even: the rationality of animals, the nature of justice, of love and friendship, the relationship of knowledge, language, and communication. Certainly, I am speaking of emphasis, not exclusivity, for there is considerable overlap between the two novels: we are not, after all, concerned with learned treatises.

The major preoccupation of the *Soleil* seems to be with language and the communication of knowledge—from the primary language to the voice of reason as animator of the body, from the language of birds to that of trees, to the disappearance of language between Campanella and Descartes and the consequent disappearance of communication. This, clearly, states the final difficulty: if a perfectly 'transparent' language were available, one in which concepts 'sent' and concepts 'received' were identical, one for which concepts and their referents were perfectly adequate to one another, then it would no longer be available for purposes of communication. By very definition, it would no longer be a medium and could carry no message. The result would be silence.

On his trip to the sun, Dyrcona, as the narrator is now calling himself, lands on one of the "little earths" circling the sun, and soon comes across "a little man, stark naked" (F 169–70; E 143–44), who speaks to him in a language he has never heard before yet which he understands perfectly. This time Cyrano does indeed appear to be echoing the third kind of language we saw in Descartes—the universal intellectual one:

> he addressed me for three solid hours in a language which I am perfectly sure I had never heard before and which had no connexion with any in this world, but which, none the less, I understood more readily and more clearly than my mother tongue. He explained, when I asked him about this marvel, that in the sciences there is a truth, outside of which nothing is easy. The more a language departs from this truth, the more it falls short of the concepts it seeks to express and the harder it is to understand. . . . A man who discovers this truth in letters, words, and their sequence can never fall short of his original conception in expressing himself: his speech is always equal to his thought. It is ignorance of this perfect idiom that makes you falter, knowing neither the order nor the words to explain what you have in mind. [F 170–71; E 144]

The little man explains that with this language one could be "universally understood," because it is "the instinct or voice of nature" ("the intuitive science of experience"?).

How this language (as communication) is bound both to reason and to the material world is expressed later, in a picture. The King of the "tree people" (who first appeared to the narrator in the form of a tree composed of precious stones and metals), once his people have transformed themselves into the shape of a young man, goes in through its mouth. It is as though the mode of transformation of the demon of Socrates were here being repeated. Only after the young man has absorbed the talking King through its mouth does he come to life (F 189; E 160). What is this but speech transforming mechanical existence into reasonable existence? Indeed, when the King comes forth once again from the young man's mouth in the shape of a nightingale, "the great man collapse[s] at once" (F 197; E 166).

Here, then, is a kind of utopian solution to the problem of winning and communicating knowledge. The hint is perhaps to be found in Bacon when he claims that the order of experimental discourse conforms both to nature and to the mind (though this claim is a cliché of the period). On the moon the narrator had learned that material things, the human senses, and the rational soul itself are simply differing organizations of the fundamental atomic forms which compose the entire universe. Here on the sun he *sees* the material and apparently senseless tree disgorge a speaking man, prior to its further metamorphoses. He *sees* the talking trees and the rational birds. He learns from Campanella that to understand someone else perfectly it suffices to adopt "the same body": "I observed that he was imitating my carriage, my gestures, my expression, . . . my reflection in relief would not have counterfeited me better." Campanella tells him: "I arranged all the parts of my body in a pattern similar to yours. For, being disposed like you in all my parts, I arouse in myself, by this arrangement of matter, the same thoughts that it produces in you" (F 240–41; E 205).

The physical and the mental, says all this, are merely different arrangements of the same material. Sounds, the narrator was told on the moon, are simply the effect of atoms in movement striking upon the ear (F 103; E 84). Speech, too, is therefore nothing but a different arrangement of the same material. And if all this is the case, then language *naturally* functions simultaneously in the conceptual and the material, it *is* the same as what it transmits. Language would then be capable of communicating not so much particular 'things' as the continual flux of thinking and the world: it would be the "successive, temporal" language of the Tlönian in Borges. Of course, if all this were so, neither verbal nor written language would any longer be necessary at all.

In the land of the philosophers to which Dyrcona is being guided by Campanella on the sun, language is part of the opacity of which the philosophers divest themselves whenever they wish to communicate their thoughts. Language has finally become quite indifferent in this atomistic fantasy world:

> We can, however, make ourselves diaphanous by a vigorous effort of willpower, when the fancy takes us, and it is even true to say that the majority of the philosophers do not use their tongues for talking. When they wish to communicate their thoughts, their flights of imagination purge them of the sombre vapour, beneath which they generally keep their ideas hidden. . . . Similarly, when he is communing with himself, one can clearly observe the elements, that is to say the images of each thing he contemplates, imprinting or projecting themselves and presenting to the eyes of the observer not an articulate speech, but the story of his thoughts in pictures. [F 261–62; E 223–24]

Does this mean that in relation to experimentalism, once any utopian solution has been excluded, any 'truthful' and accurate communication is finally a failure? that the search for an appropriate speaking or writing is ultimately a vain one? These would, I think, be false conclusions.

The operative phrase in this complete effacement of the instrument of mediation is undoubtedly "a vigorous effort of willpower" ("une vigoureuse contention de la volonté"). Experimentalism did indeed *will* the disappearance of the double-edged instrument of language as the only possible means to achieve perfect knowledge and perfect communication *of* knowledge. The occultation of enunciation of which I have spoken several times is one result of this. Cyrano invents an impractical 'solution' that is a fantasy. What is significant is that it should have been necessary to do so, and that its achievement results in the silence of the interrupted novel.

This ideal language (or, rather, nonlanguage) has no relation with earlier notions concerning language and discourse. For Cyrano, no possible criticism of analysis could lead to its replacement by some kind of equally illusory 'language of origin,' a 'pre-Babel' discourse installing some kind of immediate communication. The discourse of analysis and reference may be 'insufficient,' and all linguistic mediation imperfect, but, suggest the *Voyages*, it is the only one which carries any hope of an efficacious knowledge. The rest—anything beyond an exchange of arbitrarily and conventionally meaningful signs—is silence. The very order of experimentalism is embedded in the structure of the novels, or their structure in the order of experimentalism. It is perhaps not simply an accident of history that brings the *Soleil* to an abrupt silence when dialogue between Campanella and Descartes remains unheard by any third party and breaks off when it risks becoming audible. It is as if Cyrano had raised a problem he is as yet unable to resolve.

If we align Descartes and Bacon, as we have with certain important reservations, then the silence that falls between the former and the philosopher of the sun is not simply sign of the impossibility of immediate and perfect communication; it is also the mark of the impossibility of any mutual reading by one another of two different classes of discourse. In the novel, indeed, Descartes is criticized in much the same way as the philosophers of the moon mock Aristotle. In the narrator's view, that is to say, *both* Campanella and Descartes may be reduced to silence. Dyrcona plays Bacon at the level of content, as Cyrano does in the construction of the form.

Together they suggest that in a sense the final silence has *no meaning*; it bears the trace of the mere *possibility* of meaning. It is the end of a discourse that has been effaced (the philosophers in the sun are *all* from the past). But it is also the place of a new instauration, because this silence on the sun has its *observer*. And this very observer, 'learning' a new discourse, passing through the moment of silent noncomprehension accompanying such learning, has *already* written down the knowledge won in his journeys by the time we, the reader, reach it. Indeed, it is already contained in the *Lune*, where the demon had left with him to read a volume entitled "The States and Empires of the Sun" (F 107; E 87). The silence is an invitation to the reader/observer: an invitation perhaps to continue writing, to extend ever further the open-ended series.

It is in response to the establishment of such a discursive order that a Defoe and a Swift will write, and not as participants in the establishing of it. Later still, a Rousseau will view the discourse of analysis as essentially vicious (despite his admiration for *Crusoe*), the cause, for example, of oppressive societies. But on the other hand, the same thinker—as the epigraph to Chapter 3 suggests—finds the mythical discourse of plenitude sought by the Utopians to be no more than a nostalgic delusion. For Rousseau silence is a *solution*, and we can understand in these terms Derrida's remark to the effect that the *Essay on the Origin of Languages* is a *praise of silence*.[20]

This seems to confirm the analysis I have been making of Cyrano's novels: Rousseau's pessimistic response to the optimism of Cyrano and his contemporaries. For the late seventeenth century the silence at the end of the *Soleil* must be viewed as a preliminary, a space pregnant with the *cogito* and the "works" of the discourse of exper-imentalism.

20. Jacques Derrida, *De la grammatologie* (Paris, 1967), p. 202.

10 · *Crusoe Rights His Story*

"What is required is a passion for the truth."

"A passion for the truth," said Henrietta meditatively. "Yes, I can see how dangerous that might make you. Would the truth satisfy you?"

He looked at her curiously.

"What do you mean, Miss Savernake?"

"I can understand that you would want to *know*. But would knowledge be enough? Would you have to go a step further and translate knowledge into action?"

—Agatha Christie, *The Hollow*

Robinson Crusoe is for classical political economy what the statue, the first man, will be for the theory of knowledge.

—Pierre Macherey, *Pour une théorie de la production littéraire*

Robinson Crusoe starts out upon his long, weary, and solitary journey to ultimate prosperity with a thoroughgoing rejection of family, and particularly of father. His mother, indeed, is included in that rejection only inasmuch as she functions as his father's deputy. Crusoe sets out, as he later remarks, "*in order to* act the Rebel to their Authority."[1] The rebellion is, then, conscious and deliberate.

This beginning is, of course, exceedingly well known, and it has had to withstand the commentary of almost all those who have written on the matter of *Robinson Crusoe*. For reasons which previous chapters will already have made clear we, in turn, cannot pass by without comment. For *Crusoe* is written in the light of and in response to a discursive order which is now *already established*.

We may say, indeed, that that is what *Crusoe* is 'all about.' The

---

1. Daniel Defoe, *The Life and Strange Surprizing Adventures of Robinson Crusoe, of York, Mariner*, ed. J. Donald Crowley (London, 1972), p. 40 (my italics). Though I have used the Everyman edition for *The Farther Adventures*, I have referred to this Oxford edition for *Crusoe* because it maintains, by and large, the capitalization, spelling, and punctuation of the first edition of 1719, and these will occasionally be necessary to the discussion.

novel is not a tale of origin; nor is it the story of the creation of a new type of society or economic order, an allegory of "natural man" or the "fortunate fall," a revelation of "the miracle of a new view" of things, as Pierre Macherey puts it.[2] *Crusoe* elaborates *the place of the individual (as it will be known) in an already familiar order; it is the story of the legitimization of that elaboration and of that place.*

Crusoe's sojourn on the island is generally recognized to occur in the context of journeys to and from the Mediterranean, Africa, Brazil, England, and Portugal. It has also been noticed that this sojourn is enclosed within the 'story' of his Brazilian plantation: its purchase and ever increasing value (not to mention sale).[3] But Crusoe's *entire* situation and behavior is enclosed in a context which is indicated only a little less clearly than the context of the island episode within that entirety. If the first forty or so pages are given over to the creation of this latter context, the first ten or so, the last pages, and much of *The Farther Adventures* provide the former context. For what has been but little remarked upon (indeed, I have found it nowhere: but reading the mass of Defoe criticism would be almost a life's work) is that Robinson's father appears to have acted in a way very similar to that in which his third son will also act. This provides an indication, that is to say, of the discursive context.

Crusoe tells us that his father was a "Foreigner of *Bremen,* who settled first at *Hull,*" that there he made himself "a good Estate by Merchandise, and leaving off his Trade" moved to York to settle down and marry (p. 3). His father, then, has also left his family and

2. The quotation is from Pierre Macherey, *Pour une théorie de la production littéraire* (Paris, 1966), p. 267. All the views just mentioned are, of course, linked, and represent in one form or another the main lines of Defoe criticism. From Rousseau to Marx, from Moore to Watt, Tillyard, Novak, Hunter, and so many others, these represent the underlying thematic interpretation, whether made in economic, religious, moral, or sociopolitical terms: Jean-Jacques Rousseau, *Emile, ou de l'éducation;* Karl Marx, *Kapital,* I; John Robert Moore, *Daniel Defoe and Modern Economic Theory* (Bloomington, 1934); Ian Watt, *The Rise of the Novel: Studies in Defoe, Richardson, and Fielding* (Berkeley and Los Angeles, 1957); E. M. W. Tillyard, *The Epic Strain in the English Novel* (London, 1958); Maximillian E. Novak, *Economics and the Fiction of Daniel Defoe* (Berkeley and Los Angeles, 1962), and *Defoe and the Nature of Man* (Oxford, 1963); J. Paul Hunter, *The Reluctant Pilgrim* (Baltimore, 1966). Certainly there are disagreements: Tillyard views *Crusoe* in terms of an allegory of the "fortunate fall" (as do many others); Hunter's views are similar, though more reliant on specifically Puritan views of the religious progress of the individual; Moore views the book as a praise of *laissez faire,* while Novak sees in it a violent criticism of the new economic attitudes in favor of mercantilism. Watt is more circumspect: Crusoe, like Defoe's other heroes, is the very embodiment of "economic individualism," an attitude which is in their very blood (p. 63), and this is quite apart from Defoe's own views on the matter. In this sense, though very differently expressed, Watt's views are akin to my own.

3. See, e.g., Pierre Macherey, *Pour une théorie,* p. 274.

native country for the sake of trading elsewhere, and has cut himself off to a greater or a lesser degree from any 'authority' but his own (the reason why he might have done this is never given: the fact remains that his past activities stand, as such, as part of the context of his son's future activities). Crusoe's two older brothers have taken similar measures on their own account: the eldest has been killed fighting the Spanish after going off against the express advice of his father (p. 6), while of his second brother, Crusoe writes, "I never knew any more than my Father and Mother did know what was become of me" (p. 3).

Crusoe's entire family, then, as its behavior is related by him, supplies a very particular context for his future. It appears as one whose successive generations deliberately set out to cut themselves off from what preceded them, as one in which the individual is accustomed to seek entire responsibility for his actions, as though each were entirely at liberty to make his own path through life. It is not just Robinson who is the epitome of "economic individualism" (see the writings of Moore, Watt, Novak, and others). That is the nature of the very context out of which he springs, though his father may not only have settled down to trading by the time the story begins but have already given it up in favor of a settled life of leisure. Indeed, that his father has now given up trading suggests that the time he spent as a merchant was simply a stage on the way to respectability. Nor does he suggest that his son take up trading: on the contrary, he affirms that the latter need not be "embarass'd with the Labours of the Hands or of the Head," that he can "in easy Circumstances [slide] gently thro' the World," and that he is "under no Necessity of seeking [his] Bread" (p. 5).

The father started by traveling, continued by trading, and is ending by settling down in ease. He wants, indeed commands, his son to maintain that 'ending.'

From the outset, however, Crusoe views his own life as a series of journeys ("my Head began to be filled very early with rambling Thoughts") whose foundations, if we may so call them, are to be found nowhere but in *forward movement itself,* in the mere idea of process: they do not look toward any specific goal, and they are preceded by *nothing* (says Crusoe). He is "not bred to any Trade," he has a "competent Share of Learning" but nothing more, his family is of small account to him, he has no possessions *of his own* of any kind.

It is as if Crusoe wishes to see himself as coming from a kind of void, so that responsibility for what he does, for what he *can* do, and for what he becomes will be all his own (though this will, as we shall see, have to be concealed): "[Defoe's and Crusoe's] impulse is toward process rather than end, toward unfinished life endlessly in the making rather than the simple illustration of a predetermined and fixed pattern."[4] So writes Donald Crowley. He is speaking of the end of the novel and of its continuation in *The Farther Adventures*, but he might just as well have been speaking of its beginning: Crusoe desires to make his own roots. And so he will, with a vengeance.

His father will beseech Crusoe "not to play the young Man" by heedlessly going off traveling, almost as though he wished to see in his son the image of his own now "ancient" self (p. 5). Crusoe, at this time, is eighteen. His father sees him as *certifying*, so to speak, the station of life to which the family has been brought, and desires to make a lawyer of him (p. 3). But this law of the father is repudiated by the son who will be satisfied "with nothing but going to Sea," and there follows a clash of wills and desires, or at least of words, whose resolution marks a rupture of authority: "I continued obstinately deaf to all Proposals of settling to Business, and frequently expostulating with my Father and Mother, about their being so positively determin'd against what they knew my Inclination prompted me to" (p. 7). In order to follow his penchant he must set himself "strongly against the Will, nay the Commands of [his] Father" (p. 3), he must contradict his "Father's Desire" (p. 6).

Certainly Crusoe refers to this repudiation of paternal authority as the "fatal" result of "that Propension of Nature" (his desire to travel) which will lead, says he, "directly to the Life of Misery which was to befal" him (p. 3). I will return to this "misery" shortly, because I believe its implications have been largely misunderstood. But let us also note that this reflection precedes the well-known praise of "the middle State" of life, a state which his father affirms is envied by all who do not themselves occupy it. Criticism does not appear to have taken overmuch notice of the fact that this praise is sufficiently contradictory as to undercut both Crusoe's attempt here to suggest that his future "misfortunes" are caused by his refusal to occupy this middle state and his much later, and celebrated, remark to the effect that this refusal is his "ORIGINAL SIN" (p. 194).

Crusoe, then, relates how his father tried to convince him of the foolishness of his impulse to wander: "He ask'd me what Reasons more than meer wandring Inclination I had for leaving my Father's House and my native Country, where I might be well introduced, and had a Prospect of raising my Fortunes by Application and In-

4. J. Donald Crowley, "Introduction," ed. cit., p. xxi.

dustry, with a Life of Ease and Pleasure" (p. 4). How is one to reconcile this "Application and Industry" with a "Life of Ease and Pleasure"? Indeed, as certain quotations have already indicated, we soon find his father arguing that he will be able to enjoy, quite simply, a life of idleness and pleasure, with no question of work. As Crusoe's story unfolds it becomes more and more certain that he abhors such an attitude toward life: for him, as the episode of the mutineers on the island make quite clear, idleness and criminality are natural and necessary companions.

Here, then, is the first contradiction to which I have alluded. The praise is contradicted, too, at a slightly different level ('externally' rather than 'internally'). We may not know what were his father's reasons for doing just exactly what he is now counseling his son against (leaving his father's house and his native country), but the fact remains that his father's advice runs directly counter to his own life's experience and to his own actions. Since he considers his own present situation to be entirely admirable and enviable, there can be no question of this advice being a warning to his son to avoid errors he himself might have made: clearly he has made none. What he rather appears to be demanding is that his son continue a visible success in the exact terms provided by the father: "he would do well for me, and endeavour to enter me into the Station of Life which he had just been recommending to me" (p. 5)—his own.

Indeed, the father's ties with his son depend entirely upon the son's submissiveness. He will, he says, provide for his son if the latter will stay, but he will give him nothing if he chooses to leave. By warning his son he discharges "his Duty," after which he is able to affirm that he has "nothing to answer for" (p. 5). We might do well to remember this when Crusoe praises the Portuguese captain who picks him up off the coast of Africa and refuses to accept any of his money in payment on the grounds that if he did so Crusoe would be left destitute upon landing in Brazil (pp. 33–34), or when Crusoe later finds himself in the same position with regard to the members of the burned French ship out of Quebec and makes his nephew refuse such payment so that those victims would not find themselves destitute either when put ashore. For, writes Crusoe, "if the Portuguese captain that took me up at sea had serv'd me so, and took all I had for my deliverance, I must have starv'd, or have been as much a slave at the Brasils as I had been in Barbary."[5] His father does just

5. Daniel Defoe, *The Farther Adventures of Robinson Crusoe*, in *Robinson Crusoe*, ed. Guy N. Pocock (1945; rpt. London and New York, 1969), p. 238 (cited hereafter in the text as *FA*).

that to him on the grounds that he will not encourage his folly by giving him anything.

Crusoe's father leaves him destitute on life's shore, because he refuses to accept that father's authority, will, and desire; because he will not agree to become his father's image. That father then goes on to threaten him with another authority by affirming that if he does leave home "God would not bless" him (p. 6). In order to impose his authority the father finds himself not only in contradiction but in excess—for this is surely to take the name of the Lord in vain: save, possibly, inasmuch as duty to father and duty to God may be taken as following naturally the one from the other.

Robinson Crusoe, then, cuts loose from and is cut loose by his father. He will undergo experiences that both 'repeat' those of his father and go far beyond them. The repetitions happen as though the father's experiences had never been: the son's are a complete replacement. By and large the father is forgotten, save only when Crusoe finds himself afraid of something and once in *The Farther Adventures* when he reacts to Will Atkins's regret for having mistreated his father: "I murder'd my father as well as you, Will. Atkins, but I think for all that, my repentance is short of yours too by a great deal" (*FA*, 319).

The father's advice is a kind of sealing off. It is as though a process had come to an end and the father wished to make that 'end' permanent: to seal his son forever in his image. This is, indeed, made quite clear in the text: Crusoe writes that his father is to be found in "his Chamber, where he was confin'd by the Gout" (p. 4).

Robinson seeks to begin the process afresh and on his own behalf. He wishes to write *his own* story and to make it 'right' within a process that, as far as he is concerned, is permanently underway, but in which his story will have to be inserted and justified. I will argue that his cries of "misfortune" and the like, the story of his "conversion," are a necessary part of the legitimization of his story. Certainly we cannot otherwise take his talk of "misery" too seriously. While a third of his life is indeed spent alone on the island he is very far from being miserable the whole time he is there. On the contrary, he is able to take particular pleasure in his privilege of kingship, power, and authority, in the mechanical and agricultural arts which he gradually masters and makes productive, in the taming of the island and the bending of nature to his will. Afterward, of course, the island will become a part of his very considerable wealth, and something of whose ownership he will boast even after he has confessed his failure to take proper care of it and has stated he will no longer speak of it.[6]

We may well be tempted to ask why, in the light of this, Crusoe so constantly deplores his life? And that from the very moment when its process gets under way: he left Hull, he writes, "in an ill hour, God knows" (p. 7). Soon he is remarking: "never any young Adventurer's Misfortunes, I believe, began sooner nor continued longer than mine" (p. 8). There is a constant harping on the subject. It may be granted that he does get into a storm immediately upon leaving the mouth of the Humber, but storms in the North Sea in September are scarcely unknown. The main point, however, is that Crusoe is writing his story after it is over (indeed, after what is related in *The Farther Adventures* is over, too, for he speaks of this at the end of the first novel) and that he *knows* this first departure to be the first step on the way to wealth and fortune. He will constantly imply that actions can be judged only by their results, and the result of his "misfortune" is ultimate success both in wordly and, he affirms, in spiritual terms.[7]

This success militates against our accepting his regrets at their face value. And in that case then "the Breach of my Duty to God and my Father" (p. 8), so regretted during Crusoe's first experience of a storm at sea, should not be taken at its face value either; indeed, at the time, he is himself very quick to forget it: "we went the old way of all Sailors" (p. 9). Besides, we may well ask, what is his duty? To sit on what he is given and do nothing, as his father seems to advise? Or to go out and work? By the end of his story we can be in no doubt as to the answer. Indeed, in *The Farther Adventures* the answer becomes one more way of rejecting the father, who, it will be recalled, has given up trading so as to live at York in ease. After the

6. To the Russian nobleman, for example, in *The Farther Adventures*: "First, I told him, I had the absolute disposal of the lives and fortunes of all my subjects; that notwithstanding my absolute power, I had not one person disaffected to my government or to my person, in all my dominions. . . . I told him that all the lands in my kingdom were my own, and all the subjects not only my tenants, but tenants at will: that they would all fight for me to the last drop; and that never tyrant, for such I acknowledged myself to be, was ever so universally beloved, and yet so horribly feared by his subjects" (*FA*, 415). Of course, there is a certain amount of irony in his retelling of this conversation, for he has already told his readers that things are no longer going quite so well on his island (see note 8, below). This irony seems to correspond to the self-criticism that just precedes his admission of failure.

7. By the *outcome* of his various "mishaps" he will constantly judge that God is showing him His mercy: in religion, too, the proof is in the eating. For he might equally well lay the satisfactory outcome, when it occurs, at the feet of reason—as on occasion he does and as the praise he often gives to reason suggests is the right place to put it.

death of his own wife, Robinson becomes increasingly restless and leaves the country to go up to London. But even there he finds that living off the fruits of his labors is not for him: "I had no relish to the place, no employment in it, nothing to do but saunter about like an idle person, of whom it may be said, he is perfectly useless in God's creation; and it is not one farthing matter to the rest of his kind whether he be dead or alive" (*FA*, 229).

In suggesting that we cannot accept at face value the exclamations of misery and the like, I am not speaking of 'sincerity' or 'honesty' or of any such moral judgment that the critic might make upon the novel and Crusoe's attitudes. I am proposing rather that their meaning lies elsewhere than on the surface, where they appear to encounter a number of contradictions. We are given a clue as to where this meaning might lie at the very outset of Crusoe's life's process.

What is related in the first few pages of the novel is a clash of will and refusal, of desire and counterdesire, of command and disobedience. It is all very deliberate. Yet Crusoe's departure from home is, he would have us believe, distinctly *accidental*, scarcely, he affirms, his fault at all: "But being one Day at *Hull*, where I went casually, and without any Purpose of making an Elopement that time; but I say, being there, and one of my Companions being going by Sea to *London*, in his Father's Ship, and prompting me to go with them . . ." (p. 7).

It is as though his launching out upon his own 'process' were entirely *passive*. I spoke in earlier chapters of an '*occultation*' of the enunciating subject, of the *disappearance* of the 'responsibility of enunciation.' It seems to me that by this time this is the form these take: no longer are they the gradual result of the invention of a class of discourse, as we saw them to be in the texts examined previously. The discourse *has been* invented, it has been established, and this occultation and this disappearance are two of its essential characteristics.

What is remarkable in *Robinson Crusoe* is that every important moment or aspect of its hero's path through life is marked *discursively* by this very same passivity, this very same lack of responsibility: the departure from Hull, the landing on the island itself (continued process), the first growing of seeds and the discovery of how to fire pottery (acquisition of knowledge and power), the growth of his Brazilian estate (acquisition of property and capital), even elements of possession and authority in quite general terms, as we will see. I say 'discursively' because, of course, all these things demand that Crusoe 'do' *something*: the point is that when they are related, they are related as though he had done nothing—*as though he were caught up in a process, in a discourse, for which he is not responsible.* His passivity is occulted activity.

Such an operation implies the necessity of two kinds of 'activity':

(1) In order to deny responsibility for the process he and all others are "caught up in in spite of themselves," he must show that such responsibility lies elsewhere, because the discourse occurs and because he *does* have the power and authority he will constantly claim. The appeal to God, the exclamations of misfortune, the passiveness of the subject are the result. The discourse, the process, is not organized by any particular subject of enunciation: that subject is merely inserted into an already existing discourse. So, at least, the narrator will imply.

(2) If Crusoe then wishes to claim any authority, power, or *right* of possession (as he puts it), he cannot utterly deny such responsibility. To do so would be to lose the authority, power, and possession he is claiming, as indeed he admits risking in the *The Farther Adventures*.[8] He is obliged, therefore, to find some way of legitimizing such claims. This he can do by the various affirmations that he has worked for them, suffered for them, and, finally, that God has granted them to him by His favor. He can also do it by allowing the discourse, so to speak, to work for him, though it may appear not to do so. He can 'do' this by means of the various occultations which are now inscribed in analytico-referential discourse—it is certainly not Crusoe or Defoe who invents them.

It must be shown, then, that the discursive order we have been discussing does in fact control the text of *Robinson Crusoe*, that it does aim toward certain goals, that it does "replace" another('s) discourse but 'acts' as though it did not, that legitimization is therefore necessary. I must also show, more generally, that all this corresponds to what has been suggested with regard to a dominant class of discourse.

Many critics have claimed that Crusoe's "original sin" lies in his refusal of trade and his "breach of duty," in his repudiation of a

---

8. "Yet even this, had I stay'd there, would have done well enough; but as I rambl'd from them and came there no more, the last letters I had from any of them was by my partner's means; who afterwards sent another sloop to the place, and who sent me word, tho' I had not the letter till five years after it was written, that they went on but poorly, were male-content with their long stay there; that Will. Atkins was dead: that five of the Spaniards were come away, and that tho' they had not been much molested by the savages, yet they had had some skirmishes with them; and that they begg'd of him to write to me, to think of the promise I had made to fetch them away, that they might see their own country again before they dy'd" (*FA*, 342).

wealth of whose increase he should have been the steward (indeed, Crusoe himself is the first to suggest this), in exchange for the pursuit of a will-o'-the-wisp. No doubt all this is the case. But we must never forget that his story is an afterword: Crusoe is relating it *after* he has won out at the end. His talk of "sin," his laments of "misfortune," "miseries," and "woe" are precisely akin to his father's precautionary counsel: do not do as I have done, do as I say I would do now. Now Crusoe himself is the figure of authority seeking to seal off the process whose continuation would be the replacement of *his* authority by another's. Indeed, at one extraordinary point in *The Farther Adventures* at which we will look later, Crusoe undertakes that very continuation on his own behalf: a kind of self-criticism that might have started his story all over again.

If the father had been obeyed all future gain and knowledge, all authority, would have been the father's: just as, later on, the island, its inhabitants, and its produce are all considered to be Crusoe's—by himself and by his "tenants." This is why Crusoe cannot follow his father's counsel. He could not but repudiate it in the light of his story, whose entire 'point' is what he has achieved through undertaking a forward-looking process on his own behalf. And in all worldly and material terms he is eminently "successful." What he has, he has a "*right*" to have.

He succeeds *because* of the way he goes about it, not in spite of it, as Crusoe himself would have us believe and as so many critics have argued. The way he goes about it is by following the path we have seen established by the writing of Bacon, Galileo, Cyrano, Hobbes, to some extent Descartes. The same path is followed by economic writers like Petty, by philosophers such as Locke, not to mention others. That is why *Robinson Crusoe*, and others of Defoe's writings, have been considered illustrations of economic or possessive individualism. But capitalism, scientific positivism, and puritanism or Calvinism are not linked to each other as cause to effect, or, at least no evidence can show that they are. It is not one or the other that is preponderantly important in *Robinson Crusoe*, for example, as so much recent criticism seem to suppose, following the work of Max Weber and his successors: so that the novel would become the story of the new individualistic capitalism, or a criticism of it, or a relation of a (the) fall and redemption. That is not to say that the novel does not make use of such themes. But they are simply the *material* of discourse, just as particular 'myths' may be (as we saw of Prometheus in Cyrano's novels). The form of discourse is what provides them with a particular 'meaning,' their discursive *relation*. What I am suggesting is that a general process of change in the use of signs (here, linguistic signs) is taking place—by now, *has taken* place. The result of this change is called "puritanism" in one type of discourse, "capitalism" in another, in another "positivistic science," in yet another "neoclassical literature," elsewhere "modern" philosophy, and so on and so forth: all these are parallel types of a single class of discourse, the product of Kepler's notes to the *Somnium*, if you will.

The *order* of this discursive class shines out through the text of *Robinson Crusoe*. All particular interpretations are readings in terms of one or other of the parallel types of discourse. They are not 'wrong' but rather in a way superfluous, for once the order is apparent then clearly its correspondence to any particular inflection is relatively easily demonstrable. Certainly a pattern of fall and redemption lies somewhere in the background, but it is carried along in a new class of discourse as a kind of 'remnant,' ready to be placed in a whole new set of relations. No longer is it dominant; it is part of the material out of which this new discursive class has been made, as certain theological beliefs are of 'Puritan' science. For "sin" there is not; rather there is a process of learning, of acquisition, of making, of coming to power and authority.

Knowledge is made and found in a variety of different domains: meteorological, navigational, and geographical; agricultural and mechanical; economic; political and social. As Crusoe himself puts it at one moment with regard to the second of these: "I improv'd my self in this time in all the mechanick Exercises which my Necessities put me upon applying my self to" (p. 144). What he has particularly in mind and has already demonstrated by this time are carpentry, candlemaking, pottery, basketmaking, tanning, butchering, baking, hunting, farming. It is scarcely surprising that in *The Farther Adventures* the inhabitants of the island "could not name any thing that was more useful to them" than the Jack-of-all-trades brought by Crusoe (*FA*, 298). That Crusoe should use the word "thing" when writing of this "general mechanick" (*FA*, 231), and that this man can do considerably fewer things than Crusoe himself (*FA*, 231–32), is equally revealing.

Underlying and accompanying the acquisition of these domains of knowledge, indeed making it possible, is a gradual process of learning what 'knowledge' is in a more general sense. This process is performed in the particular order of which I have been speaking (the class of discourse itself) and it is the end product of that order. Crusoe insists upon it, and *Robinson Crusoe* is, first of all, the story, the *history*, of that all-important acquisition. Francis Bacon had long before spoken of just this knowledge in terms of which *Robinson Crusoe* could almost be the illustration:

> if my judgement be of any weight, *the use of History Mechanical* is, of all others, the most radical and fundamental towards natural philosophy; such natural philosophy I mean as shall not vanish in the fumes of subtle or sublime speculations, but *such as shall be operative to relieve the inconveniences of man's estate. For it will not only be of immediate benefit, by connecting and transferring the observations of one art to the use of others, and thereby discovering new commodities; a result which must needs follow when the experience of different arts shall fall under the observation and consideration of one man's mind* [and follow, let us add, the same discursive order]; *but further, it will give a more true and real illumination concerning the investigation of causes of things and axioms of arts, than has hitherto shone upon mankind.*[9]

In the same chapter of the *De augmentis*, Bacon makes the link between the terms "mechanical" and "experimental": they refer to the reasoned production of "works" in nature, made possible by a particular discourse. "History mechanical" is the writing of that production, of experiments in nature: it is their "literacy," so to speak.

That is what Crusoe learns, and the *The Life and Strange Surprizing Adventures* is the history of that learning:

> I must needs observe, that as Reason is the Substance and Original of the Mathematicks, so by stating and squaring every thing by Reason, and by making the most rational Judgment of things, every Man may be in time Master of every mechanick Art. I had never handled a Tool in my Life, and yet in time by Labour, Application, and Contrivance, I found at last that I wanted nothing but I could have made it.   [P. 68]

He becomes, he writes, "a compleat natural Mechanick" (p. 72). Once order is established, experiment becomes "literate." In this way Robinson acquires a knowledge of planting and harvesting: "by this Experiment I was made Master of my Business, and knew exactly when the proper Season was to sow" (p. 105).

"Mastery" is important, and Crusoe *says* here that it is an acquisition, not something he started out with. We will see that such a claim represents an occultation much like the one we saw with regard to the responsibility of enunciation: they are clearly linked. We will see that this mastery is inscribed in the very order of the writing of his story.

9. Bacon, *De augmentis scientiarum*, II.2, tr. Spedding, *The Works*, VIII.415 (my italics).

Crusoe goes on to argue, following Bacon, Descartes, and the rest, that reason and language define man, that every human can therefore enjoy the same powers provided only that he learns *the right way* to use them ("he" only, because women for Crusoe are definitely possessions and could never enjoy the same powers). Indeed, the castaway ties this argument to a criticism of the divine ordering of things. He wonders why God has given to all men the "same Powers, the same Reason, the same Affections, the same Sentiments of Kindness and Obligation, [etc.] that he has given to us" (p. 209), and yet He has deprived some (others) of the possibility of using these abilities and capacities. He wonders indeed why He allows us to make so "mean a use . . . of all those" even when we are not so deprived. Above all, *reason* and the *right method* for the use of reason are all-important. Crusoe discovers this 'formally' on the island, but we may say that he knew it 'intuitively' from the time of his first desire to wander (that is, "very early") and from his mere repudiation of paternal authority.

Certainly Crusoe appears to check, at the moment we have just been talking about, his doubts concerning divine justice with the traditional assertion that it is impossible for humans to know the divine "Light and Law," but he does not do so before admitting that he "sometimes was led too far to invade the Soveraignty of *Providence*" (p. 210). He cannot go too far in what amounts to a repudiation of divine authority, because this would *reveal* where the true responsibility of enunciation lies. So he makes confession.

The matter of legitimization enters into account, then, at the very moment when the narrator is concerned with *teaching* the right use of reason, and thus of overcoming the disability that is due to an apparent flaw in divine justice, a flaw that would deny man his humanity. For to deny him right use of reason is to deprive him of the very faculty which (with language) defines him. So Crusoe, in setting out to correct the divine plan, must do so with what amounts to a longish apologetic. But the absolute sway of the new discursive order is such that no sense of criticizing the divine plan can prevent Crusoe from instructing Friday in accordance with what he himself has been doing, from teaching him the right use of reason and the right idiom for its use:

> I was greatly delighted with him, and made it my Business to teach him every Thing, that was proper to make him useful, handy, and helpful; but especially to make him speak, and understand me when I spake, and he was the aptest Schollar that ever was, and particularly was so

merry, so constantly diligent, and so pleased, when he cou'd but understand me, or make me understand him, that it was very pleasant to me to talk to him. [P. 210]

In light of what was said in the previous chapter, it is interesting to note that Crusoe should be teaching Friday "especially" to "speak." For in relating his rescue of the Indian he had written that the latter "spoke some Words to me, and though I could not understand them, yet I thought they were pleasant to hear, for they were the first sound of a Man's Voice, that I had heard, *my own excepted,* for above Twenty Five Years" (p. 204). It is as though Crusoe, in teaching Friday to speak his language and his way of using it, were introducing his servant to language as to something entirely new. But for Friday, what is new is English and analytico-referential discourse.

Before Crusoe can properly achieve this introduction (as he says), he must 'reinvent' the Indian, he must 'place' him in his own discourse: "first, I made him know his Name should be *Friday,* which was the Day I sav'd his Life" (p. 206). Friday is to be *named* in terms of Crusoe's activities (though we could note that Friday has at least as much part in saving his own life as Crusoe has) and as a consequence of Crusoe's needs: "now was my Time to get me a Servant, and perhaps a Companion, or Assistant" (p. 202). Not for nothing does Crusoe write "I made him know"; or continue with "I likewise taught him to say *Master,* and then let him know, that was to be my Name."

It is a form of discourse that Friday is learning here, for "Master" has no social meaning for him: it is but a name, as Crusoe says, like his own. For Crusoe, however, it inscribes a particular order in their relations with one another long before that order corresponds to anything in an external 'social reality.' The latter, in fact, derives from the former.[10] The naming will produce the fact, as in the case of

10. See also Gilles Deleuze, *Logique du sens* (Paris, 1969), p. 63: "it is clear that Robinson on his desert island can only reconstruct an analogue of society by providing himself all at once with all the rules and laws that mutually imply one another, even when they have as yet no objects." Deleuze goes on to suggest that there is a lack of commensurability between the existence of such a social structure and what he calls the gradual "conquest of nature." In Crusoe's case there is, then, a paradox between the simultaneous and immediate existence of all social rules ("juridical, religious, political, economic, of love and work, of kinship and marriage, of slavery and freedom, of life and death") and the necessary but progressive winning of knowledge about nature—equally essential to societal existence (pp. 63–64). I do not feel there is any paradox here, and it is 'ahistorical' to suppose that the constitution of the laws in question is "instantaneous." That is part of a fad for 'rupture.' That there is change is hardly in question, but the discursive change is itself a gradual "conquest," as I am

the demon of Socrates, where the meaning of the name does not depend on the object but rather the reverse. The fact produced is an object 'viewed' in a way which is entirely dependent on the discourse which will have produced the fact. "Friday" as "servant" is just such a fact. Once an object has been inserted into discourse as a fact, the instruction can begin. Of course, and necessarily, this insertion is not treated as though it were entirely dependent upon Crusoe's use of language: on the contrary, Robinson treats the whole matter as though it were a natural part of an existing social order. "Friday" is inserted in just precisely the way Crusoe himself had refused to be inserted at the outset of his story. Friday is *seized* by a particular discourse, at once Crusoe's and not Crusoe's (because it is not that of a single individual, he seems to suggest).

The process of learning and teaching is a joyful one because it is involved with the *right* order. And Crusoe can affirm that it is a *natural* order, indeed *the* natural one, for it merely confirms in use what is already part of the definition of man. Thus there is no longer any question of establishing a discursive class: it has become the natural and familiar order. And *Robinson Crusoe* is its story. Rousseau is not slow to acknowledge this:

> Since we must have books, there is one which, to my thinking, supplies the best treatise on an education according to nature. This is the first book Emile will read; for a long time it will form his whole library, and it will always retain an honoured place. It will be the text to which all our talks about natural science are but the commentary. It will serve to test our progress towards a right judgement, and it will always be read with delight, so long as our taste is unspoilt. What is this wonderful book? Is it Aristotle? Pliny? Buffon? No; it is *Robinson Crusoe*.

Lord Macaulay was to echo the sentiment in an official document on education in 1835: "Give a boy *Robinson Crusoe*. That is worth all the grammars of rhetoric and logic in the world."[11]

The book provides the essential order of discourse: processive, sequential, emphatic of 'thing' and of action upon things. This is certainly why the preface announces that the "Editor believes the thing to be a just History of Fact" (p. 1). Such is the discursive ideal:

---

seeking to show. As to the paradox, given process it no longer exists: the "conquest of nature" will be made in terms of the gradual imposition of discursive rules and laws. In turn it affects them. This is Bacon's 'dialectic of knowing'; it is also a dialectic of acting.

11. Jean-Jacques Rousseau, *Emile*, tr. Barbara Foxley, intro. P. D. Jimack (London, 1974), p. 147; *The Life and Letters of Lord Macaulay*, ed. George Otto Trevelyan, 2 vols. (London, 1876), I.408.

literature is a 'natural' system ("History") which at the same time provides an analysis of the order of the real ("Fact"). *Robinson Crusoe* gives us nature still, but nature methodiz'd, to use Pope's phrase. It is, then, an ideal instrument; it is at once equal to reality and able to be studied by scientific metadiscourses just as reality itself can be (which is Rousseau's declared intention), and at the same time it is a denotative representation of reality (the "Editor's" claims). As such it is an almost archetypal example of neoclassical 'literature.'

Still, this entire process is, as already indicated, an entirely open-ended one. Crusoe deprives himself of an origin. He comes from a kind of 'void' he has created for himself, and he proceeds through a series of never-ending journeys. Even at the end of *The Farther Adventures* a cliché is used to prevent closure of any kind: "And here, resolving to harrass myself no more, I am preparing for a longer journey than all these" (*FA*, 427). Rousseau, then, is entirely wrong in affirming that the important part of *Robinson Crusoe* is its hero's sojourn on the island, the rest being a mere *fatras*.[12] The process of power, of acquisition, of learning and authority begins before Crusoe's marooning and never ends—much as it does for Rousseau's pupil, for whom the novel itself is but a single stage in a longer process.

Crusoe is never confined to his island in the broadest of senses. All his tools come from the ship; the kind of life he envisages is that with which he is already quite familiar in terms of productivity and labor: even its solitude is not something to which he is unaccustomed. It is perhaps small wonder that he leaves up to the reader the choice of viewing his sojourn as part of a whole over which he has control or as something unfamiliar to him and separated from the controlled process (and that he leaves it to the reader is again a means of displacing responsibility): "in the sixth Year of my Reign, or my Captivity, which you please" (p. 137). There will be no doubt as to how Crusoe himself views it. His life on the island is in every way part of a longer—indeed an unlimited—process that began in the novel with his father (and before him with his, and before that with . . .) and continues after the novel with *The Farther Adventures,* with the "longer journey" to come, and, equally important, with the readers whom Crusoe is constantly conscious of addressing: a process which Crusoe now conducts.

If there is any "sin" at all, we are forced to conclude, it is that

12. Ibid., pp. 147–48. Crusoe has already 'made' a kind of visionary journey out of the world which will later be recounted in *His Vision of the Angelick World*. Ostensibly he had had the vision on the island, though it will not be told till after the *Serious Reflections* (see below, note 21, for full reference).

Crusoe constantly *belittles* that desire to travel whose result will be less misfortune than rewarding labor and wealth. Crusoe, writes Maximillian Novak, "does not disobey his parents in the name of free enterprise or economic freedom, but for a strangely adventurous, romantic, and unprofitable desire to see foreign lands."[13] If there is one thing his desire is not, in terms of its outcome, that is "unprofitable." Crusoe constantly recounts how he doubles, triples, quadruples his capital. Again, as before, there is a kind of occultation here: he acquires possessions without having to admit that he ever *intended* to do so. Crusoe becomes victim of an inexplicable providence, he proposes.[14]

If there is any "sin" it is an extraordinarily fortunate one: it makes the entire future possible as an organization of acquisitive knowledge, power, and authority in the face of which exclamations of misery and misfortune lose any literal significance. They become a kind of white ground upon which to outline his felicity the more clearly, at once part of the 'void' from which he has come and the mark of a possibility of displacing responsibility: for they provoke the inference that his discourse is not isolated, that it is part of a familiar and communal scheme, that what is done by its means is therefore supported by the discursive reality of an entire society. Only thus can the individual make his own place: to choose a quite different discourse would be the choice of madness (perhaps not possible, as a *choice*); to adopt what is provided would be the choice of servitude (Friday's "choice," but also that of Robinson's "tenants"). Crusoe goes a middle way by means of the ruses I am collectively calling a 'legitimization.'[15]

Talk of "misery" and "misfortune," then, is Crusoe's obeissance to the discourse of the father (whether biological or divine) and the eventual justification for his reentry, so to speak. It marks a point of departure and return that must be both affirmed and rejected: the latter cannot occur without the former, but nor, without it, could he insert his own discourse into society's. At first this talk of woe is

13. Novak, *Economics and the Fiction of Daniel Defoe*, p. 48.
14. The presence of this 'intention' depends, needless to say, on the presence of the structure of experimentalism which creates it and in which it is embedded. That it is present will be shown at length in a moment.
15. These discursive ruses have their physical counterpart in various of Crusoe's activities on the island: the way in which his "fortress" and his goat pens are made to look like woods, the covered pits he makes as traps, his disguises while tricking the mutinous sailors, the trick taken from *The Tempest* by which the sailors are lured off into the island, and so on. The same point is made in a slightly different context by Pierre Macherey, *Pour une théorie*, pp. 273–74.

classified as that of a "young Sailor" who had "never known any-thing of the matter" (p. 8); later it will be the sign of making his way back. At first the "Vows and Resolutions" (p. 8) he makes to go home to his father if he survives the storm are a mark of fear, and fear is closely allied with the authority of another. Later, fear will be divorced from misfortune and will become something he, Crusoe, will inspire in others.

For authority depends on fear—fear of deprivation, fear of pun-ishment, fear of divine wrath (as when the Father says he will with-hold God's blessing). As soon as Robinson Crusoe begins to be "a little inur'd to it" (in the form of the stormy sea, at this point) this aspect of the father's argument fades away to nothing and there is a kind of liberation: "the Sight was, as I thought, the most delightful that ever I saw" (p. 9). Part of the story of *Robinson Crusoe* will be the tale of the rejection of an authority and the growth of a new one. That rejection, that process of growth, the open-endedness of that growth and its story, are all major aspects of the structural order of experimentalism.

It is time to take a look at that order as it occurs in *Crusoe*:

1) Family	Father's counsel against departure, etc.	Repudiates father's counsel; sets sail	Storm off mouth of Humber (pp. 3–8)
2) Fear of storm	Thoughts of father's counsel, of going home	Storm abates; forgets "Vows and Resolutions"	Storm in Yarmouth Roads (pp. 8–11)
3) Fear of storm, "Horror of mind"	After rescue, might have gone home; father would have "kill'd the fatted calf for me"	Notes process as passive: "my ill Fate push'd me on now with an Obstinacy that nothing could resist"	Decision to go to London instead of back to Hull (pp. 11–14)
4) Captain's advice that R.C. go home; likens him to Jonah: "you will meet with nothing but Disasters and Dis-appointments till your Father's Words are fulfilled upon you" (p. 15)		Travels to London "by land"	Goes "on board a vessel bound to the Coast of *Africa*" (pp. 15–16)

The beginning of the novel contains a quite clear series of se-quences which, taken together, appear to perform the gradual re-pudiation of the bourgeois authority represented by father and family, of the "upper Station of *Low Life*" (p. 4), which I have considered at some length. Each sequence matches each of the others, and they illustrate precisely the form rather elaborately indicated for Cyrano's *Voyage dans la lune*. Using one naming of the experimental sequence previously recalled, we might separate the elements as follows: problem posed (observation); discussion and hypothesis; experiment performed; original problem, or aspects of it, verified or otherwise 'resolved.'

The repudiation is gradual, and these four sequences are almost alike even as to the content of their four stages (the variables). In each sequence, especially the first two, the last stage confirms the first (authority and fear), but only partly: Crusoe does, after all, survive to repeat his rejection. With the third sequence, Crusoe admits for the first time to a specific decision to go on, only to be confronted in the fourth sequence with the advice of the captain, who stands almost as a surrogate for the father. His traveling "by land" may be viewed as a commentary on the advice of the seaman— a minor mark of repudiation. For the fifth sequence inaugurates something utterly different, something that produces an even clearer echo of the sequences of experimental discourse:

> I first fell acquainted with the Master of a Ship who had been on the Coast of *Guinea*; and who having had very good Success there, was resolved to go again; and who taking a Fancy to my Conversation, which was not at all disagreeable at that time, hearing me say I had a mind to see the World, told me if I wou'd go the Voyage with him I should be at no Expence; I should be his Mess-mate and his Companion, and if I could carry any thing with me, I should have all the Advantage of it that the Trade would admit; and perhaps I might meet with some Encouragement.
>
> I embrac'd the Offer, and entring into a strict Friendship with this Captain, who was an honest and plain-dealing Man, I went the Voyage with him, and carried a small Adventure with me, which by the disinterested Honesty of my Friend the Captain, I increased very considerably. [Pp. 16–17]

Certainly all question of "sin" has so far disappeared that even his "Father, or at least [his] Mother" (p. 17) contributed something to his journey: as though the son were beginning to draw some authority to himself. In the same way, the elements of the sequence now look forward, instead of backward. Not only do they lead into new sequences whose variables do change considerably, but the end of each sequence marks a particular acquisition of a knowledge or capacity that Crusoe did not previously possess or declare:

5) Meets captain, wants to "*see* the World"	Will be taken on free because of ability in "Conversation" (discussion)	Makes trip to Guinea	Great success
Acquisitions: Increase in capital by 750%; knowledge of mathematics and navigation; status of a sailor and a merchant (p. 17)			

Just as Friday will later, he finds he takes "Delight to learn" (p. 17). To be sure, once he is home again he can speak of "those aspiring Thoughts which have since so compleated my Ruin," upon which we have perhaps commented sufficiently. But it is worth remarking that this time he chooses to support his clamors of "ruin" with the claim that even this voyage was not free of misfortune, as though he were no longer quite sure that his reader will believe him. For he writes that he had suffered a bad fever (p. 17). Clearly, such a "misfortune" was a normal part of sailing at the time: he might as well have lamented that he caught a cold from going out in the rain.[16] The implication seems to be that the writer feels a need to indicate that his activities are part of a larger whole, but that he no longer takes it very seriously. Lamentations are no longer necessary. Crusoe is beginning to feel self-sufficient.

From now on the sequences repeat what we have just seen in the fifth, and the completion of each represents what one might call an increasing command over the order: each one concludes with an increase of some kind, even when he has reason to lament his "misfortune." He becomes increasingly self-possessed, increasingly the director of his discourse:

6) Decides to become "a *Guiney* trader"	Discussion of new wealth	Sails	Is captured by pirates and made a slave
Acquisition: Learns to cope with solitude; learns to fish; learns to operate a small boat			
7) Prepares for escape in Moor's boat, stocks it with provisions, tools, weapons	Throws Moor overboad, makes peace with Xury	Sails, and notes fear of wild beasts and humans	Anchors safely in creek
Acquisition: Learns to overcome his own fear, even though others may be fearful			

16. Charles Gildon, indeed, argues that the case is similar for *all* of Crusoe's misfortunes: *The Life and Strange Surprizing Adventures of Mr. D—— D——, of London, Hosier*

This last acquisition is, of course, as important as any other possession: it marks the changing of authority. After dark had fallen in their anchorage in the creek, Crusoe writes, they were assailed by such dreadful animal noises "that the poor Boy was ready to die with Fear, and beg'd of me not to go on Shoar till Day; well *Xury* said I, then I won't, but it may be we may see Men by Day, who will be as bad to us as those Lyons" (p. 24). Not only does Crusoe show in this 'passive' way that his fear is defeated, but he *overcomes* his fear deliberately, first by fighting off the animals when they attack and then by going ashore. Fear is no longer directly associated with authority and, in addition, he has learned to resist it by a deliberate *act of will* (not simply, as before, by affirming the disappearance of the cause).

The defeat of fear in himself is quickly followed by his inspiring of fear in others:

8) Decides to continue along coast to find English boats		Hugs barren coast hearing "nothing but Howlings and Roarings of Wild Beasts" (p. 27); continues trip	Shoots lion; meets natives; talks to them "by Signs" (p. 29); shoots leopard, inspires fear in natives (p. 34); considers Xury to be his possession

Acquisitions: Inspiration of fear in others; "ownership" of other men

9) Is to leave "*my* friendly Negroes" (p. 31)	Tries to decide where to make for	Makes for Portuguese ship	"They bad me come on board, and very kindly took me in, and all my Goods" (p. 33)

Acquisitions: Confirmation of ownership of men (Xury is among his goods); bargaining—he offers to make exchange of all his goods with captain in payment for rescue (p. 33), as earlier he had thought of doing with "his" negroes (p. 30)

(London, 1719), pp. 8–9. Peter Earle also remarks on the overwhelmingly common nature of the supposedly special mishaps that befall Crusoe: "People were not shipwrecked or captured quite so often in reality [as they are in all of Defoe's novels] but these were fairly common hazards of the sea," and he adds, "never can there have been so many ships at sea whose sole function was to seize or destroy other ships" as there were in the years just before and during those which see all of Defoe's activity as a writer (*The World of Defoe* [London, 1976], pp. 65, 59).

10) To go to the "*Brasils*"	Discussion with Portuguese captain about his belongings; sells Xury	Voyage to Brazil	Goes ashore

Acquisitions: Money, and his plantation; learns the arts of planting and sugar production; regrets the settling down which before it was his "misfortune" not to have accepted (pp. 35–36); obtains his money from London and quadruples "the Value of [his] first Cargo" (p. 37); acquires a slave and two servants

11) Plans other "Projects and Undertakings" (p. 38)	Considers advantage of staying where he is; discussions with other acquaintances; will not have to contribute money to project	Sets sail	Is wrecked on "a sand"
12) Takes to ship's boat	Boat overturns: "Confusion of Thought" (p. 44)	Swims to shore	Lands on island
13) "I was now landed, and safe on Shore, began to look up" (p. 46)	Joy at being saved; explains his faintness	Goes out to ship	Shifts effects to shore

Acquisition: Mechanical knowledge (makes raft, p. 49)

14 Goes to top of hill and *looks* about him	Finds he is on uninhabited island, no civilization "since the Creation of the World" (p. 53)	Brings cargo on shore	Barricades himself
15) Decides to make another trip to ship	"I call'd a Council, that is to say, in my Thoughts" (p. 54)	Sets out to ship	Brings them all safe on shore" (p. 54)
16) "I found no sign of any Visitor, only there sat a creature like a wild Cat upon one of the Chests" (p. 54)	Makes "friends" with cat	Brings things to encampment	Further barricades himself and heaps up "the biggest Maggazin" that ever was "for one Man" (p. 55)

He makes, of course, several trips more out to the ship, but we may perhaps say that the disappearance of the ship in the next storm, after he has completely unloaded it, marks the end of an episode in his life. Rousseau says we should begin reading the book at this point, and it is certainly the life on the island that chiefly comes to mind when the reader thinks of *Robinson Crusoe* (not surprisingly, since it composes five-sixths of the book). It is here too, I think, that the enumeration of sequences may be concluded. It is quite possible to continue with it, but the main purpose has been to show how the experimental series guides the story of Crusoe. Before we do leave it, however, I would like to note one rather remarkable passage that comprises an entire sequence in itself. It is remarkable because of its position in the story and because its object is money.

On his last trip out to the ship, Crusoe discovers some coins he had previously overlooked:

> I smil'd to my self at the Sight of this Money, O ['observation']
> Drug! Said I aloud, what art thou good for, Thou ['discussion' etc.]
> art not worth to me, no not the taking off of the
> Ground, one of those Knives is worth all this
> Heap, I have no Manner of use for thee, e'en remain
> where thou art, and go to the Bottom as a Creature
> whose Life is not worth saving. However, upon
> Second Thoughts, I took it away, and wrapping [performance
> all this in a Piece of Canvas, I began to think of of action =
> making another Raft, but while I was preparing experiment]
> this, . . . the Wind began to rise . . . : Accordingly
> I let my self down into the Water, and swam cross
> the Channel. . . . ['problem'
> But I was gotten home to my little Tent, where I resolved—home
> lay with all my Wealth about me very secure. [P. 57] safe with wealth]

We might remark (as others have) that throughout the story financial acquisition and possession form a kind of 'model' for all other kinds of acquisition (for example, as a particular part of sequences 5, 6, 9, 10, 11). The usefulness of money obviously depends, as Crusoe remarks here, on the presence of other people, on a market. It is therefore significant that Crusoe should devote a full sequence to the matter at the very moment when that usefulness is lost. It is almost as though he is assuring himself (and us) that there will remain with him the sign of a process which has brought him to the island and, above all, whose future continuation is already foreseen.

The passage is actually considerably longer than my quotation from it, and there is no break in the first paragraph stronger than a colon once the "Second Thoughts" have begun. The sequence is really complete by the end of that paragraph because at the beginning of the next he has *already* "gotten home." Crusoe shows a kind of breathless haste to note down that he remains in the context of an ongoing process, that all he has done till now and all he will have done by the 'end' of his story is a part of the *same* story.

Nor does he neglect to remind us later that he has this money: "I had, as I hinted before, a Parcel of Money. . . . There the nasty sorry useless Stuff lay" (p. 129). In view of what we have just been saying the understatement of that "hinted" is a masterpiece. As Peter Earle remarks: "Fine thoughts, but Robinson Crusoe found plenty of business for his money once he got off the island."[17] Indeed; and that, once again, is just the point: constantly writing of the money maintains a discursive link with the past and the future of the process along which Crusoe is traveling in terms of the very paradigm of the acquisition, possession, power, and authority which are inscribed in the process of the discourse of experimentalism. There are, needless to say, other links: Crusoe notes, for example, that he has "a tollerable View of subsisting without any Want as long as [he] liv'd" because, having saved so many useful things from the ship, he does not have to start at the beginning (p. 63).

Yet it is precisely the apparent paradox of his insistence on keeping a store of "useless" money that marks his reminders to the reader as having a *purpose* different from his comments on things that are obviously able to become an integral part of his life on the island: "all the good Things of this World, are no farther good to us, than they are for our Use" (p. 129). Saying this does not prevent him from taking a particular pleasure in the "glorious Sight" of his cave, partly at least because he decides that its sparkling is due to nothing other than gold ("which I rather suppos'd it to be," p. 179). Nor does it prevent him, more significantly yet, from repeating the money sequence again on the occasion of the wreck of the Spanish ship when, having removed two sea chests to the shore, he finds in one of them a considerable amount of coin and uncoined gold: "as to the Money, I had no manner of occasion for it: 'Twas to me as the Dirt under my Feet; and I would have given it all for three or four pair of *English* Shoes and Stockings." This time Crusoe goes even further than before in his reminders of a link with past and future—perhaps because he has been so many years longer on his island.

17. Earle, *The World of Defoe*, p. 68.

The incident of the Spanish ship is enclosed in such reminders. Before he tells us of removing anything, Crusoe remarks that if the ship had not broken up so rapidly, he "might have made a good Voyage" because he believes she "had no doubt a great Treasure in her; but of no use at that time to any body" (pp. 191–92). At the conclusion of the incident the link becomes specific:

> Well, however, I lugg'd this Money home to my Cave, and laid it up, as I had done that before, which I brought from our own Ship; but it was great Pity as I said, that the other Part of this Ship had not come to my Share; for I am satisfy'd I might have loaded my *Canoe* several Times over with Money, which if I had ever escap'd to *England*, would have lain here safe enough, till I might have come again and fetch'd it. [P. 193]

Money, then, forms a discursive link with the social and economic order out of which he presently finds himself but into which he foresees his 'reinsertion.' Upon that occasion it will be necessary that he not appear to organize that order himself but that he be merely a part of an order *objectively* existent, exterior to any desires and wishes of his own. Already I have suggested that 'mastery,' 'responsibility of enunciation,' and 'intention to possess' are occulted. I would add that the very *act* of acquisition is also: the money, which will be his 'passport' back into a market society, is virtually a *gift*, for which he does nothing other than bring it to shore; an "act of God" gives it to him, not an act of Crusoe. Indeed, not only was it perfectly useless to him at the time of the gift, but he did not even obtain all he might have done.

The culmination of this discursive passivity comes at the end of the novel, when on inquiry in Portugal he finds himself a very wealthy man—again, not through any activity of his own but because the value of his Brazilian plantation has increased *all by itself*. He has become a "Master" of property "all on a Sudden" without having acted as one and, indeed, without doing so now: "And in a Word, I was in a Condition which I scarce knew how to understand, or how to compose my self, for the Enjoyment of it" (p. 285).

Monetary possession, he insists, then, comes to him "by accident." He is not responsible for it. The same is true of power and authority of a political kind. We saw in earlier chapters that such political power and authority are inscribed in the very order of analytico-referential discourse, at the outset overtly so. What is clear is that that very *same* order, as the basis of the story of Robinson Crusoe, is now far less overt as to this inscription. Indeed, had we not seen that it *is* the same order, it would be possible to argue that they are not present at all, and certainly not as the 'attributes' of an individual subject of enunciation. That, of course, is the point: the discourse *has* become general, though at the outset it marked the imposition of a 'particular' subject of enunciation.

If the individual is to reinscribe himself in that discourse it must be surreptitiously and by ruse, in such a way that the order is not threatened. Power, authority, willful possession, and acquisition are the *result,* not the 'origin,' of discourse now. The several occultations to which I have referred are *the means of reconciling this discourse as it composes the episteme of an entire society with that 'same' discourse as the expression of an individual within that society.* The general and the particular are then no longer in conflict. *The 'ideal' social contract has been forged in discourse* some time before it is formally expressed by a Rousseau.

It goes without saying that I am not claiming *Robinson Crusoe* to be unique in reconciling social and individual discourse, simply that it is exemplary of the way that reconciliation occurs *in its time.* It is apparent that any and all discourse, in order to function, must find a way to reconcile enunciation and communication. The point is that those activities are not necessarily the same in all times and places. A Plato, a St. Augustine, a Rabelais, or a Dante (to recall some of those mentioned earlier) a Mallarmé, a Joyce, a Proust, or a Musil in our own times may also be exemplary of such an achievement: but their ways of doing it are incomparable—so far apart indeed that the kind of reconciliation we might be talking about seems quite different. There are worlds between that achievement as it might occur, for example, in a discourse of patterning, in a discourse of analysis and referentiality, and in one of mediation. As there are worlds between the use to which the 'material of myth' is put in the *Somnium* and what happens to it in the *Voyages à la lune et au soleil.* Or between the operator *anima* of medieval discursivity and the individualized possessive self of a later discursive class. The entire mode of conceptualization is different, and with it all relations, all social or other practices, the very conception of action in the world or of human intercourse.

What I have been trying to show in *Robinson Crusoe* is not simply the consolidation of analytico-referentiality (already achieved, by and large, from the time of Bacon and his contemporaries), but what makes it so powerful an instrument not only for scientific knowledge and technique, but as a class of social praxis and as a means of giving meaning to all human activities (not merely some). I suggest that its fundamental efficacy is the reconciliation of enunciation and communication, achieved by a series of 'discursive discoveries' and their accompanying occultations. In *Robinson Crusoe*, political power and its growth go the same way as monetary acquisition and possession, as ownership of whatever kind. Obviously these diverse aspects are closely allied with one another. At the beginning of his stay on the island, Crusoe tells of his isolation in a rather ironic tone. The irony is composed nonetheless in terms of power, and it is this ironic authority that little by little gives way to a real authority. And it will indeed *be real*, however much the reference to power may have begun in irony:

> it was a great Pleasure to me to see all my Goods in such Order, and especially to find my Stock of all Necessaries so great. [P. 69]

> I descended a little on the Side of that delicious Vale, surveying it with a secret Kind of Pleasure, (tho' mixt with my other afflicting Thoughts) to think that this was all my own, that I was King and Lord of all this Country indefeasibly, and had a Right of Possession; and if I could convey it, I might have it in Inheritance, as compleatly as any Lord of a Mannor in *England*. [P. 100]

> I fancy'd now I had my Country-House, and my Sea-Coast-House. [P. 102]

> In this Season I was much surpriz'd with the Increase of my Family [his cats]. [P. 102]

> I was Lord of the whole Mannor; or if I pleas'd, I might call my self King, or Emperor over the whole Country which I had Possession of. There were no Rivals. I had no Competitor, none to dispute Sovereignty or Command with me. [P. 128]

> in the sixth Year of my Reign, or my Captivity, which you please. [P. 137]

> It would have made a Stoick smile to have seen, me and my little Family sit down to Dinner; there was my Majesty the Prince and Lord of the whole Island; I had the Lives of all my Subjects at my absolute Command. I could hang, draw, give Liberty, and take it away, and no Rebels among all my Subjects.
> Then to see how like a King I din'd too all alone, attended by my Servants, *Poll*, as if he had been my Favourite, was the only Person

permitted to talk to me. My Dog . . . sat always at my Right Hand, and two Cats. [P. 148]

This irony, which is in any case scarcely an irony at all on some occasions (in the second quotation, for example), begins to disappear as the island gradually becomes populated by humans: of Friday Crusoe is soon remarking that "his very Affections were ty'd to me, like those of a Child to a Father" (p. 209), and increasingly his authority comes to resemble that very authority he started out by repudiating:

> My Island was now peopled, and I thought my self very rich in Subjects; and it was a merry Reflection which I frequently made, How like a King I look'd. First of all, the whole Country was my own meer Property; so that I had an undoubted Right of Dominion. *2dly,* My People were perfectly subjected: I was absolute Lord and Law-giver; they all owed their Lives to me, and were ready to lay down their Lives, *if there had been Occasion of it,* for me. [P. 241]

By the time Crusoe has arrived at the temporary conclusion of his story, there is no longer any question of irony: "I visited my new Collony in the Island. . . . I shar'd the Island into Parts with 'em, reserv'd to my self the Property of the whole, . . . and engaged them not to leave the Place. . . . The Fellows prov'd very honest and diligent after they were master'd, and had their Properties [as "tenants"] set apart for them" (pp. 305–6).

These last remarks lead directly into the matter Crusoe will relate in *The Farther Adventures.* I am not really concerned with that text here, although I might note that two further occultations are suggested there: that of authority itself ("*they told me* I was a father to them . . . and they all *voluntarily* engag'd not to leave the place without my consent," *FA,* 298—my italics), and that of the *achievement* of possession (the young man and the maid ask "to be enter'd among *my* family, *as they call'd it,*" *FA,* 299—my italics). Toward the end of the second novel, Crusoe will boast of his authority in just these terms.

Before this last boast there occurs a rather remarkable passage, to which I referred earlier. In it Crusoe achieves two objectives: in the first place it is a further occultation of his *use* and *ordering* of power and authority by means of a self-criticism that seeks to put himself in the wrong (and which the later boast contradicts, in the order of our reading of the novel); in the second, this very self-criticism permits him to repeat the activity that began the first book. Crusoe repudiates his own authority as he had there repudiated his father's—

and implies at the same time a condemnation of those who accept such authority, since they do so "at will." For if we read the novel from the point of view of the narrator's *writing* of it, the self-criticism *follows* the aforementioned boast and coincides rather with Robinson's talk of a further and longer journey: it coincides not with the moment when Crusoe actually leaves the island but rather with the moment when he relates the event, with *its writing down*. The self-criticism offers a kind of 'release' from the position of authority at which he has arrived; it permits the 'experimental' process to continue. But it is, too, a denial of authority, and so a further 'righting' of his story:

> I was possest with a wandring spirit, scorned all advantages; I pleased my self with being the patron of those people I placed there, and doing for them in a kind of haughty majestick way, like an old patriarchal monarch; providing for them as if I had been father of the whole family, as well as of the plantation. But I never so much as pretended to plant in the name of any government or nation, or to acknowledge any prince, or to call my people subjects to any one nation more than another; nay, I never so much as gave the place a name; but left it as I found it, belonging to no man, and the people under no discipline or government but my own; who, tho' I had influence over them as father and benefactor, had no authority or power to act or command one way or other, farther than voluntary consent mov'd them to comply. [*FA*, 341–42]

No doubt this also forms a kind of *mea culpa* akin, at one level, to his clamors of misery: an admission that the status of his discourse has not been legalized. In that case, his authority is in conflict with no one's, because it is not a 'real' authority. This self-criticism, that is to say, most 'legitimizes' his authority because it 'effaces' it. At the same time, I affirm, it opens up process once again. We return then to that 'ideal' social contract we saw before: the individual composes his place within the discourse of society without threatening that discourse.

As far as the story of *Robinson Crusoe* itself is concerned, power is most 'legitimized' by referring it, as I have suggested several times, away from 'self' to divine authority, or societal authority. This is truly where Crusoe rights his story. He does so first of all as a *commentary* upon his journal.

Like the naming of Friday, the *recounting* of events presented in the journey is a way for Crusoe to *make* a factual story. Friday was inserted into a discursive order immediately upon his rescue. By means of his journal Crusoe is able to relate one part of his story three times: first, we are reading a history of his life beginning with his birth and ending with his second return to England, as a part of which he tells of the shipwreck and events on the island during the time he was writing the journal. Second, the journal itself retells the story of his landing and initial activities upon the island—up to the time when he starts running out of ink. Third, he comments upon what is said in the journal. He has, in a way, three opportunities to write his story, two chances to rewrite it. It is in the *commentary*, which, like his later self-criticism, coincides with the actual writing of the 'history,' that he first undertakes to recount a religious 'conversion,' that he justifies his present authority and possession (that is, at the time of writing) in terms of the Divinity. God is named as Friday is named, and He is named as part of the discursive order.

Crusoe tells us that he first thought the growth of the barley to be a miracle, but then he realizes it was due to his having shaken out the "Husks and Dust" from a seed bag (p. 77) and notes that his "religious Thankfulness . . . began to abate" (p. 78). He then adds, in his commentary, that he "ought" to have continued thankful, since growth from so unpromising material was no less a miracle than if cereal had sprung up from nothing, especially considering it could have landed anywhere at all. This "ought" continues to be his comment on his behavior in the earthquake and at other times. And we might note that this "ought" (among other indications) marks the commentary as occurring afterward: at the time of writing, in fact.[18] Finally, Crusoe falls sick and has a delirious dream of divine punishment (p. 87).

At this point he tells us that he underwent a conversion, though he "had alas! no divine Knowledge" (p. 88). Now here, it is worth noting, he is no longer writing as if it were his journal but rather his later commentary upon it: that is to say, the full weight of the Divinity presses not upon the journal written at the time but upon the history Crusoe writes later: "No-one that shall ever read this Account" (p. 88) becomes "In the relating of what is already past of my Story" (p. 88), and this in turn becomes "Even when I was afterwards" (p. 89), and finally, "The growing up of the Corn, as is hinted in my Journal" (p. 89). The whole description of this conver-

18. In that sense it occurs *after The Farther Adventures* and may be said to be contemporary, as to its role with regard to the story, with the *Serious Reflections*. It is of small matter whether Defoe was himself 'conscious' of these various levels or not: that is beside the point, for I am speaking of a discursive *order* (class) over which, as such, neither Defoe nor any other writer (or speaker) has very much, if any, control.

sion is concluded with the avowal that we are dealing with a narration far removed from the actual occasion: "This was the first Prayer, if I may call it so, that I had made for many Years: But I return to my Journal" (p. 91).

Now, too, he returns to lamentations of "a dreadful mis-spent Life" (p. 92) and feels that he should have been drowned, and so on (p. 93). All this occurs while he is sick, and he notes: "when I awak'd I found myself exceedingly refresh'd, and my Spirits lively and chearful" (p. 95). He remarks that he continues to think of God during his recovery. The remark occurs as though it were a part of his recounting of the occurrences of a specific day (July 3), but it is quite clear that it is part of the commentary: "I miss'd the Fit for good and all, tho' I didn't recover my full Strength for some Weeks after" (p. 95). He could hardly have written such a sentence just a week after the original onslaught of his illness. In the same way he talks, under the date of July 4, of how he now reads the Bible daily—until he brings himself up short in order to write: "But leaving this Part, I return to my Journal" (p. 97). Whether the "conversion" occurred or not is, of course, a pointless and irrelevant consideration. Crusoe says it did, and that is sufficient. My point has to do with *the way in which he 'chooses' to tell it within his story*, though 'choose' may be the wrong word (see note 18).

He is in fact writing down his later reading and interpretation of his journal, and doing so in a way that suggests that the events of the interpretation occurred at the same time as the activities on the island, as carried out and then first written into the journal. From now until he leaves the journal account altogether the two levels are increasingly mingled, until he leaves it by the way—almost as an afterthought: "A little after this my Ink began to fail me, and so I contented my self to use it more sparingly, and to write down only the most remarkable Events of my Life, without continuing a daily *Memorandum* of other Things" (p. 104). The journal has, however, served the very useful purpose of giving legitimacy to Crusoe's discourse of authority: it is a mark of divine favor, a reward, even, for a repentant sinner. Nonetheless, the divine word is never allowed fully to replace the secular discourse, and it is constantly put in question.

Thus Crusoe remarks that his conversion made him look "upon the World as a Thing remote" (p. 128), and we may well find ourselves asking what this has to do with piety: since he has now been on the island three years, without a sign, near or far, of humans, he might well consider the world "remote." It is. And we may find ourselves tempted to remember that all his "repentances" have taken place during sickness and fear. Later, as we saw, he shows some skepticism as to God's just use of human reason. Again, when he is teaching Friday the rudiments of Christianity Crusoe finds he is unable to answer some of the Indian's more perspicacious questions concerning the supposed behavior of God, and he reacts as did Cyrano's narrator to the questions of his host's son on the same subject, and as did Campanella to Dyrcona. He changes the subject: "I therefore diverted the present Discourse between me and my Man, rising up hastily, as upon some sudden Occasion of going out" (p. 219). Later still, in *The Farther Adventures,* after his ship's crew have massacred the majority of the inhabitants of a village in Madagascar, they lose five men "in the Gulph of Persia" and Crusoe maintains that this loss is a divine retribution. But the claim is immediately put in doubt, chiefly because the five men had not been on shore in Madagascar—so God must be either unjust or indifferent (*FA*, 355).

Other occasions of the same kind of thing are very many. Divine support and reward are thus brought into account but are not allowed to overwhelm Crusoe's discourse. Indeed, again in *The Farther Adventures,* Robinson becomes a 'stand-in' for God: he names Will Atkins's soon-to-be wife "Mary," because he "was her godfather" (*FA*, 326), and gives her away in marriage "as I was her father at the altar" (*FA*, 328). The 'social' contract holds.

Pierre Macherey considers that *Robinson Crusoe* relates the rejection of various "manifest and apologetic myths": myths of Providence, of God (who becomes a parrot calling Crusoe's name, pp. 142–43), of good and evil (the impossibility of making any more judgment upon the cannibals), and finally of the idea that there might be "a state of nature."[19] What I have been saying will suggest rather that one cannot so much consider these rejected as made use of. The appeal to these "mythologies," as Roland Barthes might call them, is the means of rendering 'harmless' the discourse of analysis and reference.

We have seen that their inclusion in the discourse, or rather the appeal to them, results in the 'disappearance' of the enunciating subject, except as the humble user of another's discourse: this appeal 'legitimizes' the individual's occupation of the particular order of discourse and his constitution of *his own* 'piece' of it by disguising the fact that the occupation and the constitution occur at all. It is accompanied by the signs we have seen of a whole group of occulta-

19. Macherey, *Pour une théorie*, p. 274.

tions: responsibility of enunciation, mastery of discourse, acquisition of knowledge as controlled by discourse, the intention, act, and achievement of possession, power, and authority, and so on. It is as though Crusoe were saying: "I have the authority of *my* discourse but I am not responsible for that authority and its manifestations because the discourse is actually all of yours."

That, too, is why it is so important to be able to claim that the discourse is *factual* and owes nothing whatever to the particular speaker. The factual detail and its accuracy is no doubt a commonplace of Defoe criticism. Peter Earle puts it as well as anyone:

> If we concentrate, we can learn an immense variety of things, from the direction of the flow of the rivers of Siberia to the best way to salt penguins in the South Atlantic, from the relative prices of gold and brass in West Africa to the length of the summer night in Nova Zembla. Nothing is more characteristic of Defoe['s novels] and nothing is more vital in the build-up of his realism than his detail, whether it is the coordinates of a fictional South Sea Island or the bill of lading of a ship seized by one of his pirates. Much of the information supplied is quite accurate.[20]

Like the other surface manifestations of discourse this factual detail conceals the machinery that makes it function, machinery that corresponds to the Baconian mechanism announced in *The New Organon*. It is a machinery that is itself hypostatized into a different kind of '*object*,' in such a way that discourse can now grasp and speak of its own machinery as though it were not discursive at all, as though it were not the result of a particular organization of discourse. It can be treated as though it were itself reducible to an analyzable referent: "The World, I say, is nothing to us, but as it is more or less to our Relish: All Reflection is carry'd Home, and our Dear-self is, in one Respect, the End of Living."[21] This self corresponds to a particular European rationality, and it may be opposed, says Crusoe, to non-European (and non-Christian) "ideas," which are "most *unmanly*, inconsistent with Reason."[22] The masculine birth has been fulfilled. We may note that this notion of *self*—'individualistic,' 'psychological,' 'possessive,' and the willful image of God in man— did not exist before. It has now been born.

Self and *reason* go together. They are given to us as the *origin* of all

20. Earle, *The World of Defoe*, pp. 47–48.
21. Daniel Defoe, *Serious Reflections during the Life and Surprising Adventures of Robinson Crusoe: with his Vision of the Angelick World, Written by Himself* (London, 1720), p. 2.
22. Ibid., p. 135 (my italics).

right discourse. We may perhaps be forgiven if after the foregoing discussion we see them as in fact the *product* of a particular and specifiable discursive organization, a product that has been hypostatized as a new object for analysis.

The 'individual' now makes a place for 'himself' within an order 'he' shows and uses as if it had existed from all time and had been established for all time. Crusoe acquires his power and authority—and all his property—*'passively'* because he follows that order (even though he needs must 'activate' it). It is the order itself that is important, and Crusoe makes this very clear: the 'reasons' for it, its particular 'aims,' are whatever interpretation and analysis wish to make them.

11 · *Gulliver's Critique of Euclid*

> Our imagination, dominated as it is by our modes of visualizing and by the familiar Euclidean concepts, is competent to grasp only piecemeal and gradually Lobachévski's views. We must suffer ourselves to be led here rather by mathematical *concepts* than by *sensuous images* derived from a single narrow portion of space. But we must grant, nevertheless, that the quantitative mathematical concepts by which we through our own initiative and within a certain arbitrary scope represent the facts of geometrical experience, do not reproduce the latter with absolute exactitude. Different ideas can express the same facts with the same exactness in the domain accessible to observation. The *facts* must hence be carefully distinguished from the *intellectual* constructs the formation of which they suggested.
>
> —Ernst Mach, "Space and Geometry from the Point of View of Physical Inquiry"

Galileo had been condemned for claiming that what his accusers called a mathematical fiction capable only of satisfying the appearances was in fact the true picture of the way things work in the world. We have seen that for Bacon and for Descartes the order of concepts, whether systematized mathematically or not, can indeed be claimed to provide such a true picture. Whatever the manifold differences between these two thinkers, at its core that is what their use of the word 'method' signifies.

For both these philosophers, as for the vast majority of their successors certainly until the end of the nineteenth century (ignoring relatively minor variations as to viewpoints and overlapping as to period), there is just one *right* method. There is, in other words, just one method in which conceptual order, sense perception, and world order correspond: it may be referred to in shorthand as 'Euclideanism.' Apart from its use of an analytico-referential discourse, it involves the claim that a Euclidean plane geometry of parallel and right angle *is* the order of 'common sense,' and that this order of common sense (though we may make obvious, and corrigible, mistakes) is the order of objective reality. This order is the *right* ('legitimate') one and it is the *only* one.

This does not mean that other orders are inconceivable. On the contrary, as the epigraph from Ernst Mach indicates,[1] it is possible to compose other orders that do 'correspond' to the 'facts' and that can provide us with some other kind of usable knowledge of them. Such orders do not 'reproduce' the *facts*, however. Rather they give us an intellectual 'construct' suggested *by* the facts. No longer are *these* 'facts' themselves thought of, as they still were to some degree by Galileo, Bacon, and Descartes, as a construct of the interaction of human system and the world. They precede any such construct and they are discoverable by common sense ('Euclidean') without any particular mathematical construct we may be able to compose in order to 'account for' such facts, to make them in some way useful. We may say, then, that there is one right order (the dominant one of 'common sense'), but any number of usable constructs. Such a construct is no more than a *transcript* of nature into the coherence of a particular (and "arbitrary," writes Mach) language. "What the scientist aims at," says Albert Einstein, "is to secure a logically consistent transcript of nature. Logic is for him what the laws of proportion and perspective are to the painter."[2]

By the time Einstein's remark was recorded, of course, the notion that there is only one 'natural' order but several possible transcripts of it was considerably blurred—though not so much for Einstein himself, who remained largely faithful to his early belief that Mach's view was correct in all essentials. Nor by this time would such a natural order be thought of as Euclidean, in any case. The main point here, though, is not so much the claim concerning the particular order of Euclid as the claim that there is *just one right order*. Furthermore, since this order is taken as reproducing the facts *before* they are intellectually 'constructed,' its common sense is no longer (and not yet again) assumed to be "theory-laden." The order is 'transparent.'

That order is repeated in all the discourses of knowledge, which, as we have seen, form parallel and 'different' interpretations of a single reality, 'starting' (here) with Kepler's notes to the *Somnium*.

1. From an essay originally written, together with two others, especially for *The Monist* and published there in English in 1903. All three are available in Ernst Mach, *Space and Geometry in the Light of Physiological, Psychological, and Physical Inquiry*, tr. Thomas J. McCormack (1906; rpt. La Salle, Ill., 1960); the quotation is from p. 132.

2. Quoted in Max Planck, *Where Is Science Going?* tr. and ed. James Murphy (London, 1933), p. 211.

These parallel interpretations do not meet except in a 'cross-section' that might be made through them. In a discussion of a 'literary' text, whose order may be viewed at one level as in every way comparable to the order of nature, such a cross-section would be the 'meaning' of a particular moment of the text: in one way such a 'meaning' would be unlimited, because one could always compose a new parallel and thereby add 'more' meaning (as in the various critical interpretations of Crusoe, the 'reasons' given for his story); in another it is strictly limited, because the 'logic' of any parallel is the same as that of all the others. More generally, the cross-section that might be taken of all the discourses of knowledge would represent the totality of the real at the moment it is taken; the 'real' being simply the accumulated meanings of the various "types" of discourse whose sum is the discursive class characterizing our episteme.[3]

Because these various discourses (the "types") run parallel to one another, such a cross-section will make possible the "connecting and transferring [of] the observations of one art to the use of others" of which we saw Bacon write. The cross-section gives us the 'content' of the real, the variables, so to speak, which are its events and objects; while the order of the real, its process in time and its 'motion,' are given by the constants of the logic that alone underlies all the various 'interpretations.' These constants appear to correspond, in a general way, to the model of what I am calling the "discourse of experimentalism" or "analytico-referential discourse."

Thus, for example, John Stuart Mill will be able to admire what he considers the Continental method of history and, while criticizing its "Cartesianism," to view its methodological order as essentially cor-

3. I need hardly add that such a cross-section is what I have sought to take with regard to Kepler, Cyrano, and Defoe, of which the 'lists' of sequences form the résumé. It is what Lévi-Strauss has sought to do, in a very different way, with regard to myth. Such an attempt to discover "meaning" is what I have had in mind in the various references to Wittgenstein's lion and when, at the beginning of Chapter 3, I spoke of the "betrayal" due to the "Euclideanism of the textual critic." Clearly such an activity *necessarily* views the text (*any* discourse indeed) in terms of forms of knowledge which have become habitual to us yet which we are showing even here to be but the outcome of developments in discourse. This outcome has already been put into question from many points of view: as to its epistemological 'reliability,' its social utility, its moral and political desirability. The only alternative to this *for us*, in so far as *our* present is concerned (it is a mighty difficult task to escape a heritage, as Bacon constantly acknowledged), is possibly the deconstruction of the very models which the seventeenth century built up for us. Such at least is the claim of Derrida and his followers, though it may be doubted whether such 'deconstruction' can be undertaken save in terms of the very models it seeks to undo. If that is so, one may wonder whether it can escape them: is this the position of *Gulliver's Travels?* In any case, we may be permitted to use such models to examine the texts which created them— understanding that our use of these models is put into question by, among other things, the series of occultations that proved necessary for their installation.

rect. He criticizes its absolutism, its apriority, and its 'self-contained' nature, but is able to suggest a way to adjust the method so that it will become the right one: for what is above all important is the kind of order it conceives and the kind of relation it sets up between historical facts and that order. It is the latter, not the former, which Mill corrects. This adjusted method, then, "consists in attempting, by a study and analysis of the general facts of history, to discover . . . the law of progress; which law, once ascertained, must . . . enable us to predict future events, just as after a few terms in an infinite series in algebra we are able to detect the principle of regularity in this formation, and to predict the rest of the series to any number of terms we please."

Mill disagrees with the assumption of the Continental philosophers that the "order" of these facts will produce a "law of nature," but he does affirm that it would produce "an empirical law," itself dependent on "psychological and ethological laws" and on "the concilience of deduction *a priori* with historical evidence."[4] Still, the aforementioned "empirical law" *will become* "scientific law" once the more fundamental "psychological and ethological laws" and the agreement ("concilience") of method and fact ("evidence") have been properly taken into account. Though Mill would limit the extent of the predictions made possible by such scientific law, nevertheless the basic concept of methodical praxis remains that of which I have been speaking. The Cartesian cast of the Continental notion of history and law has been readjusted, so to speak, to fit in with a Baconian-style empiricism, but the relation of fact and law remains the same, save that the 'dialectic of knowing' has been added. What is the case for the "method of history" is likewise the case for all other discourses.

Like the parallels of Euclid, then, these various types of discourse never meet (though one may bisect them with the line of a 'cross-section'). They are separated into what were to become quite rigidly compartmentalized 'disciplines.' They are objective and perfectly 'general,' in the sense that no individual need, or indeed can, take responsibility for them: they are institutions. For on the one side of these discursive types lies their common referent, the real, while on the other is their common ordering: that of analysis, the experimental order. They are, then, both true and right. They depend on no one; they 'just are.'

By the time Defoe and Swift are writing this episteme is consolidated. But even in a Cyrano a new departure is signaled by the very

4. John Stuart Mill, *A System of Logic* (1843), bk. VI, ch. X, § 3, in *John Stuart Mill's Philosophy of Scientific Method*, ed. Ernest Nagel (New York, 1950), pp. 343–44.

opening lines of the novel ("The moon was full . . ."), abrupt and 'realistic,' already representative of what Valéry was eventually to criticize in the 'traditional' novel ("La marquise sortit . . ."). The beginning of romance, and even of such parodies of romance as Sorel's *Francion,* was considerably more 'Homeric' in tone and provides the reader with a much more deliberately fictional entrance to his matter.[5] Of course, realism within the story itself will be abetted by claims made in prefaces and introductions by "editors" and "friends" of the "real" author/protagonist of the story, and similar devices.

The beginning of the *Lune* marks an overt claim to be a representation of reality, an empirical ordering of time, place, and substance. It is a challenge to traditional prose fiction; but at the same time such a claim puts in question *any* discursive rendering of the real, even though such a rendering, as any novel says, is all we have. At one level, Cyrano's two novels seek to deal with that problematic. Eventually it will have been dealt with, and a Defoe can get on with telling things as they really are. This, too, is the case with Swift. The difficulty posed here is that how things are, at least as far as humanity is concerned, is rather unpleasant. This being so, the most suitable course of action is that which will best permit us to put up with the unpleasantness: both Gulliver and Candide will decide to sit things out in their gardens.

For Swift the discourse of experimentalism may be no more than the best road to knowledge available to us, and we should not rely on it too heavily: that way madness or foolishness lies, an excess of pride or an exaggerated horror of humanity. Thus, in Glubbdubdrib, Lemuel Gulliver, that typical representative of the English middle classes, comes face to face with Aristotle, the essential philosopher of common sense (though he would doubtless not have been so considered by most of Gulliver's contemporaries). The two of them together meet with Gassendi and Descartes, those two archetypal philosophical adversaries of the seventeenth century, and Aristotle finds himself obliged to remark "that new Systems of Nature were but new Fashions, which would vary in every Age; and even those who pretend to demonstrate them from Mathematical Principles, would flourish but a short Period of Time, and be out of Vogue when that was determined."[6]

5. This is true, too, of the pastoral tradition, but not of the Spanish picaresque novels or, come to that, of *Don Quijote* itself.

6. Jonathan Swift, *Gulliver's Travels, 1726,* ed. Herbert Davis, intro. Harold Williams (1941; rpt. Oxford, 1965), p. 198. All quotations are from this edition and will be indicated in the text by page reference.

Of course, Aristotle's views may not be too reliable either: he is old and stooped, his face is "meager, his Hair lank and thin, and his Voice hollow" (p. 197). Aristotle's own system may be as hollow as all others are said to be. Swift appears to underscore the permanent inconclusiveness of method, but in a rather different spirit from the open-endedness which is inscribed in the very discourse itself. To be sure, Gulliver's voyages *could* well become as unlimited as those we saw earlier. They could be an echo of Bacon's explicit progression, of Crusoe's espousal of the whole process from base to product with its achieved goal of possession and authority, of utility and power. This does not happen: they are brought to a halt, and there is a kind of stock-taking, a suggestion that improvements *may* be possible even now, though it is not clear how they may be undertaken.

There lies the point, however. We are not being forced to choose between Yahoo and Houyhnhnm; nor are we pushed to select the middle way of Pedro de Mendez, or even of Gulliver himself at certain moments. But nor are we shown that humanity is irredeemable. The degenerate behavior of the Yahoos is abhorrent in all ways (as is that of their European counterparts), but the point surely is that it *is* a degeneracy, and recognized as such by all: it started out as something better, and that something was not the innocence of the Garden but the civilized experience of the first European couple to have appeared in the land of the Houyhnhnms. The behavior of the Houyhnhnms is usually admirable—there can surely be no question about that, and only a willful misreading could claim that either Gulliver or Swift saw it otherwise. Admirable as it is, however, it is by no means as perfect as some criticism has sought to suggest.

I will seek to show that this behavior follows the discourse of experimentalism, and that its flaws are those of that discourse. The stock-taking of the conclusion suggests that this discourse with all its flaws is the best we have and we must make do with it. These flaws can even be reduced in their effect: the Houyhnhnms will stay in their own country, Gulliver will enjoy his "own Speculations in [his] little Garden at *Redriff*" (p. 295), and later still will live "retired" in the country "near *Newark,* in *Nottinghamshire*" (p. 9). Presumably others could also keep to their own affairs.

Swift suggests that the 'absence at the centre,' of which I have spoken earlier, is to some degree reducible. Morally man cannot be perfected, but he can be made relatively sociable; epistemologically some kind of knowledge of the real is available, but it is neither infinite nor, perhaps, unlimited. The goal of completeness, in any domain whatsoever, may be unrealizable, but that does not provide a

reason for looking upon *Gulliver's Travels,* and especially the concluding "Voyage to the Country of the Houyhnhnms," as entirely 'pessimistic.' Man may be fairly revolting on the whole, but he can learn
from the Houyhnhnms: as they have 'learned' from him, for the
order of all such learning is now that of analysis and referentiality.
Perhaps this is one reason why the eighteenth and nineteenth centuries gradually came to treat Swift as such a pariah. In an age that
believed in unlimited progress and the perfectibility of man, he has
taken the discourse of that progressive man and shown not so much
its flaws, its lack of perfection in its present state of development
(which might be supposed corrigible), as its absolute lack of perfectibility.

Nevertheless, neither for Gulliver nor for the Houyhnhnms nor, it
would seem, for Swift himself, is there ever any question as to the
necessity of the discourse they use. Imperfect it may be, but it is all
we have. That discourse is always supposed to have a precise referent and a precise signified whose quality may vary according to the
society using (and used by) it but which is certainly representative of
a more or less readily definable reality—social, ethical, historical,
physical, and so on. There is never any question as to the way in
which discourse means or as to the way in which it controls what it
grasps.

Gulliver always learns a new language by first learning the names
of things. Those who can 'reason' by speech are quite naturally the
rulers: speech, reason, and power are naturally concomitant. As the
"master" Houyhnhnm puts it: "if it were possible there could be any
Country where *Yahoos* alone were endued with Reason, they certainly must be the governing Animals" (p. 242).[7] In Brobdingnag the
King had taken Gulliver for "a piece of Clock-work" until he discovered that what Gulliver "delivered" with his "Voice" was "regular
and rational" (p. 103). The master Houyhnhnm is "astonished at
[his] Capacity for Speech and Reason" (p. 237).

These are commonplaces, reminiscences of much that we have
already seen. But it is precisely as commonplaces that they are important. There is no question at all but that the Houyhnhnms' notion of reason and its relation with speech on the one hand (for they
"have not the least Idea of Books or Literature," p. 235) and with
facts on the other is that of analysis and reference, is that of experimentalism.[8] This will be considered at greater length when I come to

7. And, e.g., "the Ship was made by Creatures like myself, who in all the Countries
I had travelled, as well as in my own, were the only governing, rational Animals" (p.
238).
8. This orality and the fact that they do not use money (p. 251) are two of the very

speak a little later of the Houyhnhnms' idea of what constitutes knowledge. Let us content ourselves for the moment with one very minor example that occurs shortly after Gulliver has landed in the country of the Houyhnhnms and when he is being examined by the first two horses: "They were under great Perplexity about my Shoes and Stockings, which they felt very often, neighing to each other, and using various Gestures, not unlike those of a Philosopher [natural scientist], when he would attempt to solve some new and difficult Phaenomenon" (p. 226).

Although Gulliver does eventually land in a country where a particular order is maintained, the beginning of his fourth voyage can scarcely be thought overly auspicious. Man's capacity for control might reasonably be wondered about. Of two captains, the one, "Captain *Pocock* of *Bristol*, . . . an honest Man, and a good Sailor," succeeds only in losing his own life and those of his entire crew "but one Cabbin-Boy," because, says Gulliver, he was "a little too positive in his own Opinions, which was the Cause of his Destruction, as it hath been of several others" (p. 221); the other, Gulliver himself, is overwhelmed by his crew, "debauched" by the buccaneering recruits picked up in the West Indies (p. 222).

Rational systems which oppose civilized man to the state of mere nature and which propose the supremacy of the individual (both over nature and over mankind) are cast into doubt: the first by nature itself (for Pocock perished in a storm), the second by Gulliver's overthrow. In a conflictual system it is apparent that only one participant can come out on top: there will always be those who rule, those who have and who use knowledge and power, and those who are ruled, who are used by knowledge and power. *Crusoe avoided this difficulty by means of now generalized ruses and occultations, thus making the system appear not to be conflictual at all.* At the beginning of Gulliver's fourth voyage the roles of ruler and ruled are reversed when

---

few ways in which the Houyhnhnms resemble More's Utopians. Gulliver twice remarks on the nonwritten nature of the Houyhnhnms' literature: in the passage just quoted and again when he writes that the "*Houyhnhnms* have no Letters, and consequently, their Knowledge is all traditional" (p. 273). Gulliver himself follows the strictures of Bacon. As he learns a language, it acquires its full meaning only when written down: "I pointed to every thing and enquired the Name of it, which I wrote down in my *Journal Book* when I was alone" (p. 234). Indeed the pronunciation of such words appears more as an aid to the written than the other way around, and it is only when they are written and ordered that they become useful to him; to this end he compiles a Houyhnhnm-English dictionary (pp. 234–35). The superiority of the written to the oral is perhaps not surprising in Gulliver's case, when we consider that the voyage 'itself' is necessarily subordinated to its written, reported form. But neither perhaps is the lack of this mark of experimentalism surprising in the Houyhnhnms: essential to get that discourse "under way," it is no longer so once its dominance is assured.

the buccaneers seize power, and this conflictual aspect of things is laid bare once again in a kind of degeneracy which prefigures those others of which so much will be made: that of the Yahoos, and that of the Europeans.

The process is not laid bare in order to be replaced by something else, however, or even reworked in any way. On the contrary, Gulliver will find himself in a situation that reconfirms the familiar structure of discourse. In his analysis of the all too well known "excremental" nature of the voyage to the Houyhnhnms (starting with Gulliver's near "stifling" with excrement at the hands of the Yahoos, p. 224), and in particular of the passage where Gulliver describes European medical practices to his Houyhnhnm master (pp. 253–54), Jacques Ehrmann associated (as others have) the "reversal" of the "natural" functions of the body's orifices with a symbolic attempt to overcome the "distance" introduced between interior and exterior by the advent of civilization, with the search for a way to express the "interior" in the familiar terms of an exterior perception: this reversal would mark a kind of despairing attempt to experience once again that proximity with nature, that participation in the life of nature, broken forever by civilization. *Man* is supposed to have made a break from *nature*, civilization to have made a beginning by means of a rupture from the brutish and nasty life of the beasts—or, alternatively, to have broken the bonds of sympathy which united him with nature in the idyll of the Garden. Ehrmann remarks: "This origin (the birth of the individual, of 'civilization') consecrates—according to this tradition of thought—the beginning of interiority (of the 'inside'). Death marks its end. 'Art,' 'culture,' thus represents a desperate attempt to utter interiority and so to oppose death taken as an expulsion towards exteriority."[9]

Gulliver's critique of European medical practices would therefore be a critique of the whole tradition of thought underlying it. For themselves, of course, the Houyhnhnms would not need to worry, for the harmony of their way of life with nature is such that they are never ill. The Houyhnhnms themselves would thus be the inhabitants of a utopia in which the difference of interior and exterior has never been made, in which the rupture has never occurred—which does not prevent them from applying an improved version of the European medical practice to the Yahoos, who *have* experienced that rupture (at one time).[10]

9. Jacques Ehrmann, "Le dedans et le dehors," *Poétique*, no. 9 (1972), p. 34.
10. Which is why they are 'degenerate' and not simply brutes in a state of innocence: otherwise there could be no explanation for their difference from the Houy-

I do not believe this to be the case: Gulliver does not find himself in a country that enjoys the state of innocence—even though "Houy-hnhnm" may mean "in its Etymology, *the Perfection of Nature*" (p. 235). He finds himself in a country in which a particular discursive 'logic' has found its least unsatisfactory extension. As far as Gulliver is concerned man cannot escape his brutal instincts *unless* he follows that extension. The European way of life does not give evidence of a 'false' use of reason, according to the Houyhnhnm, it gives evidence of a *degenerate* use: in effect the inhabitants of Europe do not use reason at all. The Yahoos may be physically degenerate, but Euro-peans are morally so, because "instead of Reason, [they] were only possessed," says Gulliver's master "of some Quality fitted to increase [their] natural Vices" (p. 248). Or, as Gulliver says a little later, the Houyhnhnm "looked upon us as a Sort of Animals to whose Share, by what Accident he could not conjecture, some small Pittance of *Reason* had fallen, whereof we made no other Use than by its Assis-tance to aggravate our *natural* Corruptions, and to acquire new ones which Nature had not given us" (p. 259). But this is to deprive Europeans of all reason whatsoever, because, as will be repeated several times, a rational creature *cannot* act irrationally, and vice is irrational; therefore a vicious person cannot be rational.

Houyhnhnmland does not give us a picture of a state of inno-cence: left to itself nature is vicious, corruption is 'natural.' Gulliver's view is entirely that of Hobbes. There is no return to a prelapsarian condition and Gulliver does not make one. What he finds is a right use of reason—so, at least, the Houyhnhnm (and Gulliver) never tires of implying. Since there cannot be a 'false' use of reason, for that would be contrary to reason and therefore excluded by defini-tion, the Houyhnhnm is obliged to argue that Europeans have some other quality instead of reason. But this argument does not change the structure and organization of what may be considered reason: it simply opines that Europeans have yet to learn to follow it. It is this that Gulliver will come to find in Houyhnhnmland, not its denial.

It is true that the voyage starts with the apparent defeat of the institutionalized rational system, at least in the use to which it is put. Pocock's navigational skill is incapable of saving him and his crew from drowning. Gulliver's leadership cannot prevent him from being reduced to the solitude of his cabin and then to the "desolate condition" of his being cast away in an unknown country in an

---

hnhnms. This *degeneracy* is given as the reason for "the violent Hatred the *Houyhnhnms,* as well as all other Animals, bore them" (pp. 271–72).

unknown part of the world. Yet Gulliver is not entirely destitute: he has on his "best Suit of Cloaths," he has "a small Bundle of Linnen," he has a weapon, some money, and "some other little Necessaries" (p. 222). All this may be a parody of Crusoe, but the effect is the same, however reduced. He remains bound to his past, and as he sets out to "advance forward" (p. 223), it is with a view to buying his way back to civilization.

Ehrmann has sought to equate metaphorically Gulliver's ejection out of European civilization with excrement, remarking that he is at this moment symbolically dead.[11] But Gulliver is not completely ejected; he does maintain certain physical ties. He may be 'outside,' but he is not cut loose from, European rational art and culture. He is not to advance in complete 'freedom' (whatever that might be). He goes to find a more finished example of the ideal of that culture. Gulliver himself is already closer to that ideal than are the contemporary doctors and lawyers, politicians and statesmen whom he will describe to the Houyhnhnm, and that is why the latter will treat him as he might a more lowly Houyhnhnm (indeed, the "Sorrel Nag" becomes virtually Gulliver's servant). Gulliver is treated in this way from the outset, so that this proximity to the ideal is not the result of a learning process—at least, not in the eyes of his master Houyhnhnm.

Indeed, the other Houyhnhnms will resent this grand treatment of Gulliver by his master:

> the Representatives had taken Offence at his keeping a *Yahoo* (meaning my self) in his Family more like a *Houyhnhnm* than a Brute Animal. . . . He was known frequently to converse with me, as if he could receive some Advantage or Pleasure in my Company: . . . such a Practice was not agreeable to Reason or Nature, nor a thing ever heard of before among them. [P. 279].

Gulliver, like Crusoe, has lost none of his predisposition to the systems of European rationality: it is just that which the Houyhnhnm approves of, which he finds principally attractive in Gulliver, and why no doubt he concludes Gulliver's stay in his country with "so great a Mark of Distinction" as to raise his hoof so as to permit Gulliver to kiss it without prostrating himself (p. 282).

In fact Gulliver will never question the discursive ideal, any more than will the Houyhnhnms. His very admiration for the horses proceeds from their having achieved that ideal, not from any rejection

11. Ehrmann, "Le dedans," p. 36. Cf. Norman O. Brown, *Life against Death: The Psychoanalytical Meaning of History* (1959; rpt. New York, n.d.), pp. 179–201.

of it on their part. Gulliver's rejection of the Yahoos is based upon a perfectly habitual rationalistic judgment; and so, too, is the disgust the Houyhnhnms feel toward them. The Houyhnhnms have achieved a more entirely satisfactory practice of the moral, social, and political discourses of Enlightenment man—at least in Gulliver's eyes. There are all kind of indications.

When the traveler first meets with the horses he records the gradual dawning of his recognition of this achievement. The horses greet one another in "a very formal Manner" (p. 225), their behavior is "orderly and rational, . . . acute and judicious" (p. 226), their furnishings are "not unartfully made, and perfectly neat and clean" (p. 229), they eat "with much Decency and Regularity" (p. 231). Certainly all this is Gulliver's initial impression, as the smug and condescending tone serves to indicate (and, again, we must remember that this is written *after* Gulliver's return to Europe). Yet the general interpretation he is able to make of their activities is only confirmed by the passage of time, and if Gulliver ends up by condemning the Yahoos and humanity as a whole it is not because a rational system has failed. It is rather because it has not been permitted to function, because man has allowed degeneracy to set in.

First of all, the Houyhnhnms' language is very close to that ideal transparent mediator which we have seen to have become the ideal expressive instrument of European rationalism. When Gulliver first hears it, he notes: "I plainly observed, that their Language expressed the Passions very well, and the Words might with little Pains be resolved into an Alphabet more easily than the *Chinese*" (p. 226). As he comes to know it better he is able to remark that "their Language approaches nearest to the *High Dutch* or *German*, of any I know in *Europe*; but is much more graceful and significant" (p. 234). This combination of aesthetic pleasure in the order of a language with meaningfulness in its expression of true knowledge is precisely what constitutes, for the European seventeenth and eighteenth centuries, the perfection of a language, its precellence.

Such perfection is achieved when a language is composed of the fewest words possible necessary to communicate *all* the concepts lying behind language. For this reason Gulliver further admires the Houyhnhnms: "their Language doth not abound in Variety of Words, because their Wants and Passions are fewer than ours" (p. 242). If he speaks of "our barbarous English" (p. 245) it is chiefly because it lacks this one-to-one correspondence between words and their denotata. Words are multiplied to so great a degree that the excess of signifier *creates* new signifieds, which no longer correspond to anything real and give rise, therefore, to extensive falsehoods: in this way European lawyers, for example, are bred up "in the Art of proving by Words multiplied for the Purpose, that *White* is *Black*, and *Black* is *White*" (p. 248). Even in poetry the Houyhnhnms do not make this error, and Gulliver can note there "the Minuteness, as well as Exactness of their Descriptions" (p. 273),[12] and he is able to record in like manner their "Conversations, where nothing passed but what was useful, expressed in the fewest and most significant Words" (p. 277).

Gulliver apparently doubts whether so perfect a language could in fact have been achieved, and his (or Swift's) praise of it is tinctured with irony: "The Emperor *Charles* V. made almost the same Observation when he said, That if he were to speak to his Horse, it should be in *High Dutch*" (p. 234). Worry over the perfectibility of language for use as an instrument to communicate and gather knowledge was a general critical and philosophical preoccupation before and during the time Swift is writing. He himself in the *Tatler*, in 1710, "announcing that the corruption of English was in full career, pointed to recent usages 'altogether of a *Gothick* Strain,' and to 'a natural Tendency towards relapsing into Barbarity, which delighteth in monosyllables . . . when we are already overloaded with monosyllables.'"[13]

In Lagado Gulliver had already seen two projects that were intended to overcome the lack of correspondence between signifier and signified and this "barbarity" in general. One of these involved the reduction of all polysyllables to monosyllables and the rejection of all parts of speech but nouns, "because in Reality all things imaginable are but Nouns." The other was the more drastic scheme "for entirely abolishing all Words whatsoever" (p. 185). For us this may be a reminder of Cyrano's conclusion. If so, the Houyhnhnms' language is the response. As it is also Swift's response (and that of Enlightenment Europe as a whole) to the general corruption and degeneracy of vulgar tongues.

Since the Houyhnhnms' language has attained the sought-after coincidence of word and concept there is no danger of falsehood or disguise, at least in theory. They have achieved John Wilkins's universal language. They have, in a sense, overcome the dichotomy interior/exterior because their language mediates perfectly. And not only language, one might add. In a similar way their 'code' of man-

12. This "even" is not really necessary, of course, for poetry is just as much governed by the laws of analysis and referentiality as any other type of discourse.

13. Emerson R. Marks, *The Poetics of Reason: English Neoclassical Criticism* (New York, 1968), p. 18.

ners (another type of the same class of discourse, though using a different medium from language) does not rearrange or reform nature: it strives to make social phenomena a perfect 'representation' of nature. Thus, when Gulliver is to show the Houyhnhnm that he is a Yahoo, he writes: "I would give him immediate Conviction, if he pleased to command me; only desiring his Excuse, if I did not expose those Parts that Nature taught us to conceal. He said my Discourse was all very strange, but especially the last Part; for he could not understand why Nature should teach us to conceal what Nature had given" (pp. 236–37).[14]

The "strangeness" of the discourse here concerns the apparent lack of coincidence between its own order and the order of nature: the Houyhnhnm cannot comprehend why they should differ. This assumption of automatic correspondence between words and things also applies, needless to say, to language use in general. It is covered by the Houyhnhnms' use of the phrase *"the thing which was not"* (p. 235). The absence of the very idea of lying that is claimed of the Houyhnhnms' discourse asserts that coincidence of exterior and interior, of language, concept, and referent on which we have been remarking. We might note right away, however, that the use of a paraphrase is hardly proof that the idea is absent: on the contrary, it suggests rather that the idea is being concealed for some reason, and the particular paraphrase selected is more than a little revealing.

Let us note, too, that the concealment of Gulliver's real appearance, acquiesced in by his master, is no less a falsehood for its not being called such. And the reason for the concealment itself is Gulliver's correct awareness of the contemptuous and superior pride native to the Houyhnhnms, even if they do not admit it—though the mistress of the house did in fact make it obvious right away (she "gave me a most contemptuous Look," p. 229). While we are speaking of similarities between the Houyhnhnms and Gulliver, we might add that there is little obvious difference between Gulliver's astonishment at their rationality and theirs at his (p. 238).

Some kind of false-speaking does, then, exist in the Houyhnhnms' discourse: indeed, the very use of the phrase "the thing which was not" may be thought of as a falsehood. It is hardly surprising, therefore, that the search for coincidence (rather, its claimed achievement) between sign and referent should be expressed in terms identical to those which the European discourse of rationality likewise

14. This coincidence is also revealed in the Houyhnhnms' 'code' of food, which is why they are never ill. Gulliver notes that his adoption of a similarly "natural" diet had the same effect on himself (p. 232).

seeks to impose: it is entirely a matter of the ordered expression of referential *truth*. *Reason and knowledge exist only to the extent that discourse expresses such truth*. The Houyhnhnms manifest a kind of Cartesian optimism, and Gulliver's master put it in terms that might well have come from Montaigne (e.g., *Des menteurs*):

> And I remember in frequent Discourses with my Master concerning the Nature of Manhood in other Parts of the World; having Occasion to talk of *Lying*, and *False Representation*, it was with much Difficulty that he comprehended what I meant; although he had otherwise a most acute Judgement. For he argued thus; That the Use of Speech was to make us understand one another, and to receive Information of Facts; now if any one *said the Thing which was not*, these Ends were defeated; because I cannot properly be said to understand him; and I am so far from receiving Information, that he leaves me worse than in Ignorance; for I am led to believe a Thing *Black* when it is *White*, and *Short* when it is *Long*. And these were all the Notions he had concerning that Faculty of *Lying*, so perfectly well understood, and so universally practised among human Creatures. [P. 240]

What is "altogether past his Conception" is, for example, the idea that anywhere in the world a Yahoo could be the governing animal (p. 240): the Houyhnhnm is therefore led to believe that this is a falsehood. The "thing which was not" is, quite simply, the expression of anything that the discourse itself excludes (an expression the horses hold to be impossible by definition): the Houyhnhnms are the rational, governing creatures, and the expression of any other notion will be contrary to the truth. This repeats the legitimization of analytico-referential discourse we saw in Bacon and Cyrano: by the exclusion of nonverifiable assertions, or of negations and contradictions of its assertions.

Montaigne implies something similar in the essay "On Cannibals" when he remarks (as we saw at the end of Chapter 3) that not only are the natives of Brazil without "name of magistrate" or "of politike superioritie," but that they have no words to express the typical vices of European men: "The very words that import lying, falsehood, treason, dissimulations, covetousnes, envie, detraction, and pardon, were never heard of amongst them." In Montaigne, however, the argument avowedly concerns the visible limits of conceptual space. (He remarks that his interpreter was unable to express his questions adequately—and presumably also the answers given by the three natives of Brazil; thus an authentic incomprehensibility is in question.)[15] In Swift, we are dealing with an occultation by the Houy-hnhnms of an activity that certainly continues to function, albeit in a concealed manner. Thus, just as various evils are always expressed by the epithet "Yahoo" (which, again, does not mean the idea of 'evil' is absent), so too the Houyhnhnm finds it necessary to translate Gulliver's explanation of the relation between man and horse in Europe into that which his self-esteem requires between Houyhnhnm and Yahoo (pp. 241–42). But the comparison is erroneous, and in making it the Houyhnhnm, too, is guilty of saying "the thing which was not." He can do nothing else.

For the Houyhnhnms *presuppose* an identity of discourse and concept (and indeed of thing); they have built into the system an a priori assumption of an absence of falsehood. What is not true cannot, they argue, be said at all: no concept corresponds to a false assertion, and since all words correspond to concepts (as we saw in Gulliver's remarks about their language), a false assertion is not only impossible to make but is literally *inconceivable*. During a later period of crisis in the dominance of this discourse, Wittgenstein will be saying nothing else: "We cannot think what we cannot think; so what we cannot think we cannot *say* either." But for Wittgenstein (not altogether unlike what I suggested of Montaigne), such a proposition is presented within the context: "*the limits of my language* mean the limits of my world."[16] Wittgenstein is asserting that we are necessarily bound within the limits of a specifiable "logical space," and that whatever is outside it can neither be thought nor said: though we can always say *how* things are in relation to a certain way of grasping the world, we can never say *what* they are.

Like others we have seen and will be seeing, Wittgenstein is writing as analytico-referential discourse attain *its* limits. This is obviously not yet (or no longer, if we think of a Montaigne, for example) the case for the Houyhnhnms—or Swift himself, or his contemporaries. The limits of logical space have already been hypostatized into the objective *place* of the real world. In their case, therefore, the notion of inconceivability leads to certain difficulties, because it provokes the dubious assertion that what cannot be conceived does not exist—in any sense whatsoever. They neglect the "how" and believe they

15. Michel de Montaigne, "On Cannibals," in *Montaigne's Essays*, tr. John Florio, intro. L. C. Harmer, 3 vols. (1910; rpt. London and New York, 1965), I.220, 229 (I.xxx).
16. Ludwig Wittgenstein, *Tractatus logico-philosophicus*, tr. D. F. Pears and B. F. McGuinness, intro. Bertrand Russell (London, 1961), §§ 5.61, 5.6

are concentrating on the "what." As Wittgenstein remarks once again: "The whole modern conception of the world is founded on the illusion that the so-called laws of nature are the explanations of natural phenomena." Like Heisenberg, Wittgenstein insists, rather, that laws are about descriptive models in their relation with the "how" they are describing, not about "what" is described.[17] The Houyhnhnms are hardly at this stage. Even Gulliver's (apparently somewhat emancipated) master has difficulty understanding the existence of a country beyond his experience,[18] and the "inferior" Houyhnhnm, the "Sorrel Nag," never does: the island which Gulliver can *see* remains for him only "a blue Cloud" because "he had no Conception of any Country beside his own" (p. 881).

In much the same way Gulliver's disquisition on the marvels of European warfare is cut short by his master because "he found it gave him a Disturbance in his Mind, to which he was wholly a Stranger before. He thought his Ears being used to such abominable Words, might by Degrees admit them with less Detestation" (p. 248): for words may make concepts and concepts facts. He is afraid of losing, so to speak, his own discourse, and the answer here is to stop up his ears. Cremonini refused to look through Galileo's telescope because, while he did not doubt the scientist's assertion as to what he would see, he felt that there was no way of measuring and allowing for the distortions to sight that the use of such an instrument would necessarily entail. The Houyhnhnm closes the circle in similar terms: there is one right discourse; what is not familiar to it cannot be said and no way can be found in that discourse for saying it. Therefore it is not.

Still, Gulliver's master does eventually come to admit new concepts, and this acceptance implies a considerable change in his very idea of reason and knowledge and an 'expansion' of language to deal with it. The inferior sorrel nag cannot rise to such heights any more than could the vast majority of Galileo's or Bacon's contemporaries: as Bacon and Descartes had said, it requires a return to zero and a learning of the lion's tongue. In fact, as we saw, such a

17. Ibid., §§ 6.371, 6.35. One could argue that the first aphorism of the *Philosophical Investigations*, though ostensibly referring to an Augustinian description of language, is in fact reducing the *Tractatus* itself to the same status: it is not a description of the way in which all language and any logical space must work, but a description of one such (a stricture that applies not simply to the content of the *Tractatus*, but its very existence as a description).

18. Actually the Houyhnhnm seems to remain dubious concerning such existence until he finds an idea he can use: that of castration for the purpose of exterminating the Yahoos. As we will see, this idea is a perfectly logical extension of certain aspects of the class of discourse we are examining.

feat is also beyond any of the other Houyhnhnms, who order Gulliver's master to treat him differently or to get rid of him. Among them he is unique.

The rejection of all that cannot be contained in their received discourse is evident, too, in their idea of reason as carrying "immediate Conviction; as it must needs do where it is not mingled, obscured, or discoloured by Passion and Interest" (p. 267). But the only concepts that can carry any conviction are those which are provided with a means of expression: one might say that they carry "immediate Conviction" because they are ruled over by precisely what Gulliver criticized in his family's and friends' (or his own) behavior upon his return from Brobdingnag: "the great Power of Habit and Prejudice" (p. 149). Any other concepts are not simply not real; they do not exist at all, and to say them is offensive.

Certain other ideas have no word in the Houyhnhnms' language, and, as in the case of falsehood, this lack is more a sign of the same occultations we saw in earlier chapters than it is of the absence of the concepts involved: "Power, Government, War, Law, Punishment, and a Thousand other Things had no Terms, wherein that Language could express them" (p. 244). The use of the phrase "the thing which was not" implies that their discourse is *complete*: it can utter all there is to utter. In the same way, the Houyhnhnms may have no word for "power," but the reaction of the Yahoos whenever a Houyhnhnm approaches is indicative enough of their wielding of it. In any case, as we saw, the Houyhnhnms always put reason and governing together. As for "government" as such, what else can one call the "Representative Council" which meets "every fourth Year, at the *Vernal Equinox*" (p. 270), a moment which also forms a pleasant pun? They themselves do not engage in "war," but certain of the Yahoos' activities recounted by the Houyhnhnm come quite close to it. And so on. I suggest that the omission of such terms merely permits the presence of the practices they signify in rather more surreptitious form and that it corresponds in many ways, therefore, to what we saw in *Crusoe*.

In the meantime the Houyhnhnms can be said to enjoy in their own minds the advantages of a certain 'Cartesianism.' Samuel Monk has observed that the concepts which strike with immediate conviction are a "version of Descartes' rational intuition of clear and distinct ideas."[19] We may add that they bask in that identity of language, concept, and object viewed as perfection by Descartes in the letter to

19. Samuel H. Monk, "The Pride of Lemuel Gulliver," *Sewanee Review*, 63 (1955), 67.

Mersenne of November 20, 1629, and dismissed by him immediately as likely to be put into use only in "a terrestrial paradise" of "a fictional world."[20] That is why Gulliver is able to admire "the Justness of their Similes" in poetry and "the Minuteness, as well as Exactness of their Descriptions." These are, he affirms (and Descartes would certainly agree) "inimitable" (p. 273).

For the Houyhnhnms such accuracy of description confirms the complete adequacy of their discursive structure. Our world may be "a broken and twisted version of the truth" and man "less capable than once he had been of penetrating beyond it to what is eternally valid" in the eyes of Swift himself,[21] but for the Houyhnhnms there quite simply *is* no other true and rational knowledge but what they themselves can express. That is why the Houyhnhnms cannot consider Europeans rational. That judgment is confirmed by the Europeans' lack of virtue. Gulliver records how his master condemns the existence of European "Institutions of *Government* and *Law*" as due only to "our gross Defects in *Reason*, and by consequence in Virtue; because *Reason* alone is sufficient to govern a *Rational* Creature; which was therefore a Character we had no Pretence to challenge" (p. 259).

Virtue is the sign that the Houyhnhnm system of discourse has been adopted. Virtue and reason are indeed synonymous: "They will have it that *Nature* teaches them to love the whole Species, and it is *Reason* only that maketh a Distinction of Persons, where there is a superior Degree of Virtue" (p. 268). But reason has another sign. For as virtue is marked by living according to the way of life established by the Houyhnhnms, so reason is marked by a submissiveness to that system: what most astonishes them in Gulliver is his "Teachableness, Civility and Cleanliness" (p. 234), just as what is most deplored in the Yahoos is their "unteachable" (p. 235), intractable (p. 241), and "indocible" (p. 271) nature. Reason is essentially *teachable*, and docility is a principal evidence of its presence.

The idea of reason as marked by submissiveness to right thinking is what separates the "natural" from the "rational," though that distinction should not be too greatly emphasized, because reason is itself a product of nature: there is a *natural* superiority built into the Houyhnhnms' discursive structure. The reasonable naturally imposes itself. This is why Gulliver and the first Houyhnhnm he meets

20. Descartes, *Oeuvres philosophiques*, ed. Ferdinand Alquié, 3 vols. (Paris, 1963–73), I.232.

21. Kathleen Williams, *Jonathan Swift and the Age of Compromise* (Lawrence, Kan. 1959), p. 40.

fall automatically into the master/servant relationship that is demanded by the individualist structure and will last until Gulliver
leaves the country. Here the Houyhnhnm's superiority is as "natural"
as was Gulliver's as captain of his ship or as lord and master within
his family, as was Crusoe's over Friday and eventually over the
other "tenants": "For they looked upon it as a Prodigy that a brute
Animal should discover such Marks of a rational Creature" (p. 234).
In a way Gulliver's debased copy of this stance upon his return home
may be Swift's retort: a plague on all their houses, but what have we
better?

This treatment of reason as power is echoed throughout the entire
society over which Houyhnhnms like Gulliver's master are the lords.
Within it not only is there no social mobility of any kind whatsoever,
but there is what amounts to a caste system:

> He made me observe, that among the *Houyhnhnms*, the *White*, the *Sorrel*,
> and the *Iron-grey*, were not so exactly shaped as the *Bay*, the *Dapple-grey*,
> and the *Black*; nor born with equal Talents of Mind, or a Capacity to
> improve them; and therefore continued always in the Condition of
> Servants, without ever aspiring to match out of their own Race, which in
> that Country would be reckoned monstrous and unnatural. [P. 256]

In this way, while the race of masters practices a kind of zero-growth
regime (they allow themselves one colt and one foal per couple), "the
Race of inferior Houyhnhnms bred up to be Servants [is] allowed to
produce three of each Sex, to be Domesticks in the Noble Families"
(p. 268). Now here we certainly have "Power, Government [and]
Law" in practice, whether or not they are named as such.

With regard to the Yahoos this practice is taken yet further. Gulliver had told his master of the behavior of men toward horses in
Europe. The master views his servant's revelation with the utmost
horror: "But it is impossible to express his noble Resentment at our
savage Treatment of the *Houyhnhnm* race; particularly after I had
explained the Manner and Use of *Castrating* Horses among us, to
hinder them from propagating their Kind, and to render them more
servile" (p. 242). At this point in Gulliver's knowledge of the Houyhnhnms we might be inclined to believe that this horror is not a
reaction simply to the treatment of the master's own race but to a
distortion by reason of nature—one more sign that the Europeans
are not endowed with reason but merely with a means to encourage
their vices. For here the teachableness of reason is not in harmony
with nature, docility is in fact *un-natural*. However, this is certainly

not the reason why the Houyhnhnm reacts with horror to Gulliver's revelations. For the activities of European rationality are rapidly improved upon by the Houyhnhnms.

Some time after this Gulliver's master is able to tell him of the debate ("the only Debate that ever happened in their Country," p. 270) concerning the final solution for the Yahoos, in which Gulliver's hint about castration is taken up as the ultimate expedient. The Houyhnhnm recounts how he told the assembly "that the Operation was easy and safe; that it was no Shame to learn Wisdom from Brutes. . . . That this Invention might be practised upon the younger *Yahoos* here, which, besides rendering them tractable and fitter for Use, would in an Age put an End to the whole Species without destroying Life" (p. 273). We might note that the speciousness of this last argument comes at least close to a falsehood, and certainly stretches meaning somewhat.

Whether this genocidal project is ever to be carried out we are not told, because Gulliver is obliged to leave the country shortly after it has been proposed (luckily for him). The Houyhnhnms are, however, "exhorted" to develop the necessary alternative workers ("the Breed of Asses," p. 273), and that, Gulliver will explain, is tantamount to "a Decree of the general Assembly" (p. 280). We may suppose the plan would be carried out, for, as it is implied, the expedient is a natural extension of the rationalistic process of control, possession, and utility, and the Houyhnhnms insist that "no Person can disobey Reason, without giving up his Claim to be a rational Creature" (p. 280). The Yahoos upset the smooth running of the Houyhnhnms' society; they are considered "the most filthy, noisome, and deformed Animal which Nature ever produced, . . . the most restive and indocible, mischievous and malicious" (p. 271). What more 'reasonable' than to get rid of them once and for all?

Still, whether the final solution is actually applied or not is as indifferent to our present discussions as it is to *Gulliver's Travels* itself. My point is that the Houyhnhnms' discourse simply reproduces what we have seen being developed. It places it under a clearer and more pitiless light. The Houyhnhnms make this discourse uncompromising, and what is opposed to it is not an alternative—we do not have to choose between the Houyhnhnms and the Yahoos of Europe—but *a debased version of the very same class of discourse*. Gulliver and Don Pedro are marks on the scale that goes from the discourse as it is used in Europe to the same discourse as it is applied in Houyhnhnmland.

Gulliver claims that the Houyhnhnms are free of greed, ambition, and lust, the vices of progressive individualism. But to the extent that they *appear* not to be present one is tempted to suggest that it is due to lack of obvious opportunity. For the same logic that dictates the use of genocide—convenience, superiority, utility—is also behind the seeming lack of the vices just mentioned: "He was wholly at a loss to know what could be the Use or Necessity of practising those Vices" (p. 244).

The elements of power and utility so pervasive in the Houyhnhnms' social practice are exactly those of European rationality, and of Gulliver as its representative: one need only look at his attitude toward his family, of which the example occasioned by his return from the Houyhnhnms at the end of the fourth voyage is but an exaggerated version of what we have read at the beginning and end of earlier voyages. Such similarities are everywhere to be found.

So the very same assumptions of dichotomy (interior/exterior) and reversal (mouth for anus, ingestion for expulsion) which govern European medicine as scornfully related to the Houyhnhnm by Gulliver (pp. 253–54) also govern the practice of the Houyhnhnms themselves in their treatment of the Yahoos' diseases (the horses being free from illness of any kind): "the Cure prescribed is a Mixture of *their own Dung* and *Urine* forcibly put down the *Yahoo*'s Throat" (p. 262). This treatment, with the greater excremental purity of the medicine involved, shows the same improvement over the European method as we have already seen in the discussion leading to the expedient of genocide (for, after all, the Europeans had no mind to exterminate horses).

Gulliver praises the Houyhnhnms' lack of pride, saying that they "have no Name for this Vice in their Language" (p. 296), but it is hard to see how else one can consider their attitude toward the inferior Houyhnhnms, toward the Yahoos, toward Gulliver himself. It accompanies a sentiment of superiority which had so often been Gulliver's own in earlier voyages. Then, too, Gulliver rejects the use of precedents in English law as pernicious nonsense and as justifying "the most iniquitous Opinions" (p. 249), but this does not prevent the Houyhnhnms from arguing that Gulliver's master should get rid of him because, among other reasons, the keeping of a Yahoo was not "a thing ever heard of before among them" (p. 279). One might reasonably ask, in like manner, whether the Houyhnhnms are any less 'positive' in their opinions than was poor Captain Pocock, drowned for just that reason.

All this, of course, is in the name of that expression of truth we saw claimed for their language by Gulliver. All else becomes justifiable provided only that the assertion of "truth" is possible: "I had likewise learned from his Example an utter Detestation of all Falsehood or Disguise; and *Truth* appeared so amiable to me, that I determined upon sacrificing every thing to it" (p. 258). *Truth* is the standard; its place and measure is the discourse of analysis and referentiality.

It is not, therefore, the efficacy of the Houyhnhnms' discourse that is put in question: there can be no question but that it works—and effectively. Nor is Houyhnhnm society held up for admiration as the perfection of innocence (if the two terms can be put together at all): they, too, like everyone else, have come out of a past, and if the derivation of the word "Houyhnhnm" is *"Perfection of Nature,"* now it merely means *"Horse"* (p. 235). The efficacy of their discourse is due to three essential factors: that its functioning necessitates a series of what I am calling "occultations"; that it never questions itself by stepping outside its own assumptions; that it supposes the nonexistence of anything which escapes its own order ("the thing which was not").

What Swift's attitude to this discourse ('way of thinking'—and of acting) may be must remain unknown; or so the violence of the critical disputes on that subject would seem to encourage us to believe. My point has been that while the Dean may criticize or praise the discourse he places before us, his readers (depending on the *interpretation* we wish to give his text), he has no choice at all as to *which* discourse it is: experimentalism is dominant. Its use may be criticized, but its premises and the way it functions are now inviolate.

12 · *Emergence, Consolidation, and Dominance of a Discourse*

> In the third chamber, two books were found. One was black, and it set forth the properties of metals, the use of talismans, and the planetary laws of the days, as well as the preparation of poisons and antidotes. The other book was white, and although its letters were quite clear, no one could decipher its teaching.
>
> —Jorge Luis Borges, "La cámara de las estatuas"

By the time a critique of discourse is no longer able to affect the premises or the functioning of that discourse, it seems safe to say the discourse in question has become dominant. Swift's critique 'makes use of' the same occultations, the same (functionally necessary) closed logical space, and the same principle of exclusion of contrary instances that are essential to the very imposition of analysis and referential truth. By the time the Dean is writing, the discourse of patterning (or any other) has yielded completely to that of experimentalism—willful, possessive, authoritarian.

In this sense the results of the preceding analysis agree entirely with the general view expressed in a collective volume published for Swift's tercentenary in 1967. The Dean there appears as fundamentally supportive of Church and State authority, albeit not uncritical of certain aspects of it. He is considered as holding an essentially Hobbesian opinion of humanity. conceived therefore as in constant need of correctives (this last being a view Rousseau will also maintain). He is basically critical of all extremes and of all that departs from a customary norm. Though he appears frequently to parody Bacon, he is not at all averse to approving him at other times. One could well argue that the "ambivalence" of Swift's attitude toward the Chancellor, the mere fact that he has "covered his tracks so well," as Brian Vickers puts it, referring to the Dean's satire on Bacon, that the attack has barely even been noticed before in its

351

detail, is further evidence that the critique is in terms of the new discursive space itself.[1]

Here too, then, the evidence tends to show that Swift is attacking less Baconianism *per se* than certain extreme opinions within it, and this position is entirely consonant with my own analysis of *Gulliver's Travels*. That text and the views indicated above are expressions for a time of stability. The argument of the foregoing chapter has been, precisely, that the discourse of analysis and reference is by now confirmed in its dominance. It has overcome crisis and doubt. It is the stable discourse of order. It is the "Euclideanism" of a *right* discursive order already expressed, perhaps, in the angular layout of the capital city and chief model of *Utopia*: "Amaurotum . . . is almost four-square in outline. The breadth is about two miles" (p. 64).

Here is born a signal of mathematization, a kind of leitmotiv expressing the calculated mechanization of *factual* reality. From Dom Juan's expression of faith ("I believe that two and two make four, Sganarelle, and that four and four make eight") to the affirmation made by Turgenev's materialist Bazarov ("What really matters is that two and two make four, the rest's all fiddlesticks"), we find ourselves confronting a dominance of which Dickens's Gradgrind is one of the most exemplary literary manifestations:

> Now, what I want is Facts. Teach these boys and girls nothing but Facts. Facts alone are wanted in life. Plant nothing else, and root out everything else. You can only form the minds of reasoning animals upon Facts: nothing else will ever be of service to them. . . .
>
> Thomas Gradgrind, sir. A man of realities. A man of facts and calculations. A man who proceeds upon the principle that two and two are four, and nothing over, and who is not to be talked into allowing for anything over.[2]

These are but shorthand versions of Laplace's celebrated assertion that if he knew the present facts of the material universe in sufficient detail, he could predict its future to all eternity: such prediction being the exact equivalent of a mathematical projection.

It is not surprising, therefore, that, like Dickens in 1854, Lautréamont in 1869 uses the same motif both to represent and to reject

1. Brian Vickers, ed., *The World of Jonathan Swift: Essays for the Tercentenary* (Cambridge, Mass., 1968). I refer here particularly to the first four essays in the collection, by Pat Rogers, Basil Hall, W. A. Speck, and Brian Vickers. The quotations are from Vickers's "Swift and the Baconian Idol," pp. 100, 117.

2. J. B. P. Molière, *Dom Juan*, III.1; Ivan Turgenev, *Fathers and Sons* (New York, 1962), p. 54; Charles Dickens, *Hard Times* (New York, 1961), pp. 11, 12.

the dominant order of discourse. In the *Chants de Maldoror,* he writes:

> Two enormous towers could be seen in the valley; I said so at the outset. Multiplying them by two, the product was four ... but I could not really make out the need for this arithmetical operation. I continued along my way, my face all feverish, and I shouted endlessly: "No ... no ... I cannot really make out the need for this arithmetical operation!" I had heard the clanking of chains and agonized groans. As he goes through this place, may no one be able to multiply the towers by two, so the product be four! Some suspect I love humanity as if I were its own mother and had borne it nine months in my sweet-scented womb. That's why I no longer go through the valley where the two unities of the multiplicand are raised![3]

Others before had certainly entertained and expressed similar doubts. That is not the point. Dickens, Lautréamont, Peirce, Marx, and others mentioned in this connection are all contemporaries. They are, I suggest, the mark of the limits *ad quem* of the truly efficacious functioning of the analytico-referential. Subsequently will follow a long period of crisis, similar to what obtained between Machiavelli and the third or fourth decade of the seventeenth century.

The euphoria of late Victorianism is likewise marked by increasingly widespread and savage wars, striking ever more closely home to their principal participants (instead of being fought out, though not exclusively, over others' land). This is not entirely dissimilar to what happened in the second half of the sixteenth century and in the early seventeenth. In 1648 the Thirty Years' War came to its official end with the Peace of Westphalia (1659 for France and Spain, with the Peace of the Pyrénées), and it is not coincidental that Brecht's perhaps best-known play, *Mother Courage,* written in the year of the outbreak of an equally savage war in our own time, should be set in that earlier war. I have suggested elsewhere that Renaissance and neoclassical tragedy was importantly instrumental in the performed creation of analytico-referential discourse, and that Brecht's theater may have participated in an analogous performance for our time—though that creation is not yet clearly consolidated. I am not, of course, trying to suggest a new instauration of analysis and reference, but an analogous elaboration of a movement toward a new discourse.

3. Isidore Ducasse (comte de Lautréamont), *Les chants de Maldoror,* in *Oeuvres complètes,* ed. Maurice Saillet (Paris, 1963), pp. 224–25; my translation.

We may perhaps say that the discourse of patterning 'sought' only to place its user in a context, whether divine or human. It employed the 'images of things' not for the sake of a knowledge and use of things in themselves, not to gain power over them or so that they might become the manipulated objects of the master of discourse, but simply to make possible the utterance of intrahuman relationships and a certain relation within a totality of which man himself was but a part. Such discourse sought what has been termed a "conjunctive" reality. In Kepler, Bruno, or Campanella, for example, the 'human condition' was a closed one of "heart and eyes, intellect and soul" (*anima*), tending toward a 'unity' of all knowledge and a 'fullness of being,' culminating ideally in some kind of quasi-mystical 'absorption' into the light proceeding from the Divinity—whether such culmination is conceived primarily in terms of knowledge (Kepler), or in those of Being (Bruno or Campanella).

The achievement of some kind of 'wholeness of being' seems to have been the principal role played by such discourse. The kind of conjunction in question may differ from what is expressed in a medieval discourse coming mainly out of St. Augustine, or what may be indicated through examples taken from Greek Antiquity. But however "disjunctive" Renaissance discourse may have become, its goal is to overcome such disjunction. Kepler demonstrates such a strain just as much as Thomas More. Yet where More can offer no solution but that of a passage out of this world (the *Dialogue of Comfort* being perhaps as much a response to a conceptual as a physical constraint), Kepler's discursive explorations provide a passage of development.

An intention to 'understand' the world as external to the space of discourse would have been a later product of that discursive practice, destined to take on a life of its own and become dominant at a certain moment in history. This intention accompanies a new *use* of language, a new class of discourse, new forms of knowledge and society. For Galileo, Bacon, or Descartes, the human condition is not closed. It is the arena of an ongoing and ever-open dialectic between particulars, axioms, predictions, and "works" (the production of new facts and particulars), between knowing and doing, being and willing, that will enable an endless spiritual and material 'improvement' for all the individual members of the human race.

Through certain of the texts considered here, we can spot an interesting progression in a particular *topos* that both 'summarizes' these developments in some way and shows how the 'meaning' of specific discursive material (such as the motifs of 'soul' and 'self,' of the Prometheus myth or the Great Chain) changes according to the discursive class in which it appears. The *topos* of the two Delphic sayings, "Know thyself" and "Nothing in excess," has already been mentioned, but it merits discussing in slightly more detail. F. M. Cornford long ago suggested that these sayings are an early sign of the individual's breaking away from his full participation and absorption in a divine order. He asserts that Apollo's dicta reveal the full ambiguity of the human relation with the Divine, the uncertainty of the individual's status in respect of the Olympians.[4] Individuality is marked, but its standing remains indefinable. In view of what was said in Chapter 2 concerning the absence in any discourse 'available' to the ancient Greeks of such concepts as 'will,' 'person,' 'subject,' and so on, we may well be inclined to think the matter beyond ambiguity. And such would have been the situation predominant until certainly as late as the high Middle Ages.

In Chapter 3 I recalled Colin Morris's reference to the Delphic "Know thyself" and to the passage in the *Song of Songs*: "If you do not know yourself, go forth." Morris remarked that throughout the European twelfth century these were "the two foundation-texts of the movement for self-exploration."[5] What he emphasizes less is the clear fact that such 'self-knowledge' was primarily a mediatory passage to 'organic' union with and in the 'divine whole.' Society itself, in which the baptized *fideles* were largely unindividualized integral elements, was simply the earthly manifestation of such union. In a sense, I suppose one could say that the "Know thyself" permits the participant in totality to identify his 'personal-ness,' while the "Nothing in excess" insists that he is such a participant. The epigraph to Chapter 2 taken from Aquinas's *Summa contra Gentiles* is a brief example of such a view.

In More's *Utopia*, the two Delphic sayings are 'replaced' by two others that I believe mark Hythlodaeus's "residence in the infinite": "He who has no grave is covered by the sky," and "From all places it is the same distance to heaven" (*Utopia*, p. 13). They indicate that the ambiguity of the Delphic sayings could have been overcome by the retrieval of something one might call an 'integrated' participation in the Divine, the rediscovery of a 'unity' in which the latent individual would disappear altogether, and where discourse of any kind would be superfluous. More relates that these two dicta "are constantly on [Raphael's] lips," as though this were the sum total of all knowledge

4. Plato, *Charmides*, 164d–165b; Francis Macdonald Cornford, *From Religion to Philosophy: A Study in the Origins of Western Speculation* (1912; rpt. New York, 1957), p. 119.

5. Colin Morris, *The Discovery of the Individual, 1050–1200* (New York, 1972), p. 78.

that matters. This attempt, in *Utopia*, is rendered impossible by the very existence of the text itself, and by the time Gulliver appears on the scene the 'total' will have been torn to shreds.

The Enlightenment surgeon replaces the Apollonian sign of a search to situate the 'individual' in his relation to the Divine with the sign of his material situation in the order of nature: ambiguity and query are replaced by complete confidence in the certainty of his situation, even in his control over that situation despite apparent obstacles. The sign of the search for a difficult equilibrium between social man and man as participant in an order that surpasses all possible comprehension ("Nothing in excess") gives way to a complete confidence in man's technical ability to bend nature to his will and needs: "No Man could more verify the Truth of these two Maxims, *That, Nature is very easily satisfied*; and, *That, Necessity is the Mother of Invention*" (*Gulliver's Travels*, p. 276). Gulliver's certitude is, of course, just one place on the scale that runs from the practice of discourse in Europe to that of the same discourse in Houyhnhnmland, and while it may be dominant the discourse of analytico-referentiality will never be entirely free of ambiguity.

Gulliver's terms, however, correspond entirely to Rousseau's similar claim to the effect that natural man lives in a state of minimal requirements, acceding to socialization only under the impulse of necessity. Such is the fundamental reason behind the social contract, as he observes at the outset of the chapter on the "social pact" in the first book of the *Contrat social*. For Rousseau it is in a sense these two maxims that permit the creation of human society to be conceptualized. In his earlier *Discourse on the Origin of Inequality*, he comments at one point that "a wise providence saw to it that the faculties potentially possessed by man should only develop when the occasion demanded their use, so that they should be neither superfluous nor burdensome ahead of time, neither late nor useless when needed."[6]

Gulliver's scale is transformed into a different gamut, running from a kind of zero state of humanity in nature, the very equivalent of Condillac's statue, through the gradual increase in felt needs that for Rousseau corresponds to the decadence of advancing socialization. The passage from isolated savage man, "alone, idle and always close to danger," endowed only with the "passion" for self-preservation and the simplest of needs, to the actual realization of his socialized

6. Jean-Jacques Rousseau, *Discours sur l'origine de l'inégalité*, in *Du contrat social ou principes du droit politique* [and other political writings] (Paris, 1962), p. 56.

potential in will, reason, thought, and language requires the intervention of necessity. To mere savage man "difficulties soon presented themselves," and their solution is first of all through a diversity of *techniques*: war and venery, agriculture and metallurgy.[7] For Rousseau as for Gulliver, for Emile's tutor as for Crusoe, necessity (demand) and technique (supply) become the very essence of socialized humanity. The reasoning of the *Discourse on Inequality* explains the admiration for *Crusoe* expressed in *Emile*, not to mention the educational project we saw urged by Lord Macaulay, that grand later exponent of the Enlightenment and the so-called Whig interpretation of history.

In Rousseau, the ambiguities already seen as inherent in analytico-referential discourse are clearly visible, but in a rather different and more concrete manner than in *Gulliver's Travels*. I have twice referred to the fact that the works of such sixteenth-century writers as Fabri, Palsgrave, and Tory can be taken as indicative of a discourse in crisis: the multiplication of levels of signification suggests an attempt to resolve the contradictions inherent in theologico-feudal discourse. Like Thomas More's, it was an attempt doomed to failure; and these writings, too, are exactly contemporary with Machiavelli's. From Hobbes to Montesquieu to Rousseau, one can easily see an analogous multiplication of such levels of mediation. This time it takes the form of a historical linearity that matches the concept of progress (process) built into analytico-referentiality (both as regards its description in the texts themselves, and as to the chronological passage from Hobbes to Rousseau).

For Hobbes there are but two levels of humanity: that of brutish and always warring natural man, and that of the socialized individual living under the monarchical state. Confronting certain obvious contradictions (for example, that the founding contractual covenant assumes, indeed demands, a legal system by definition absent from the state of nature), Montesquieu seeks to resolve them by installing a third level: the timid man of an original peaceful state of nature, the individual of the "first associations" characterized by inequality and strife, and the socialized member of advanced societies of diverse types (though the ideal is that of a kind of liberal monarchism). Unsatisfied with the many logical problems that still exist, Rousseau puts humanity through four levels: a happy state of nature, primitive egalitarian societies, gradually decaying societies based on the inequality of property and constant struggle, the eventually ideal

7. Ibid., pp. 48, 67; more generally on the techniques, pp. 50, 67–68, 73–74.

egalitarian (and highly controlled) society of the contract that combines natural equality with "moral and legitimate equality."[8]

Rousseau, of course, constantly refers to the "immense gap" that lies between nature and any form of society whatsoever. He is well aware that that gap would ultimately demand an infinity of different mediatory levels in the familiar bad regression. For "nature" is at once the point of origin and the atemporal utopia in which process (here, "society") cannot be inscribed that I discussed at the beginning of Chapter 3 on *Utopia*. It is Kepler's contradiction, once again, between entropy and process. The leitmotiv of "two and two are four, and nothing over" marks a kind of desperate belief that such contradictions have been finally overcome.

The multiplication of mediatory levels seems indicative, then, of contradictions within analytico-referential discourse that will culminate in Hegel's attempt to resolve them in a new dialectic. *Aufhebung* is not simply a 'practice' *within* that dialectic; it is the response to an entire discursive history. The contradictions that became ever more apparent in the theologico-feudal episteme met with the beginning of a response in the writings of Machiavelli, as forms of dominant practice within that episteme started to become tools of analysis. As I suggested before, it seems apparent that Marx performed a similar role after Hegel. In a sense Darwinism also 'overcomes' the divisive multiplication of levels by creating an unbroken set of developmental moments between the most primitive state of nature and the most advanced condition of culture imaginable. In another way, of course, one could argue that the notion of the "descent of man" is simply a more sophisticated means of overcoming the contradictions in question (an argument dramatized by the continuing belief in and search for the celebrated "missing links"). The advantage of Darwin's 'solution' is that it overcomes the circular effect of the others, proposing an ever-open system. Its very clear disadvantage is that to do so it inscribes violence in society as a necessary and forever inevitable element.[9] Freud's arguments in the fourth essay of *Totem and Taboo* and in the third section of *Moses and Monotheism* are a direct (and avowed) result of that inscription: and there the violence is at once internalized and exorcized by a displacement into the realm of the symbolic (*aufge-*

8. Rousseau, *Du contrat social*, p. 249.

9. All of these matters, both as regards the theoretical model of the development of discursive classes and epistemes in general and with regard to the development of Western political theory in particular, are being explored in detail in work currently in progress.

hoben, as Hegel might have said, were it not for the symbolic nature of the displacement).

Still, though I will return later to the problem of Freudianism, that particular outcome of these ambiguities and contradictions remains some distance away, even if it is the direct consequence— indeed an aspect—of the various occultations, ruses, and traps of analytico-referential discourse that I will recall very shortly. For the present Crusoe, Gulliver, and the Houyhnhnms are triumphant. Discourse has established the status of an individual self out of the mere mark of enunciation, and it has established it as essential to denotative meaning. In its turn, such a form of meaningfulness (of the ascription of *sense* to *practice*) was essential to the kind of activity that henceforward was to be at once possible and necessary. The egalitarian individual is as essential a part of the kinds of perfect society indicated by the names just mentioned, as the willful self is to the forms of knowledge and action that accompany them. Though it is by no means the only, or even perhaps the most important, element of this class of discourse—as the preceding analyses have made clear—Roland Barthes has captured well the network of discursive relations that surround this element in particular:

> Denotation would be a scientific myth; that of a "true" state of language, as though every sentence contained an *etymon* (origin and truth). Denotation/connotation: this dual concept has a value only in the domain of truth. Whenever *I* need to test a message (to demystify it), *I* subject it to some exterior instance . . . which forms its true substratum. The opposition is useful therefore only in the framework of a critical operation analogous to a chemical analysis: whenever *I believe* in truth, I need denotation.[10]

Two plus two equals four, and the facts add up.

This network of utterance, self, truth, denotation and reference, subjection of the exterior, and analysis are the discursively formed elements of analytico-referentiality. This status of the individual and its consequences was not to be created until some two thousand years after the heyday of Athens, and some three hundred or so years after the summit of Scholasticism.

Analytico-referential discourse was produced out of patterning as a kind of attempt to represent the contradiction between process and entropy in discourse, a contradiction proceeding from a concept of an eventually complete knowledge as the goal of a search for

10. Roland Barthes, *Roland Barthes par lui-même* (Paris, 1975), p. 71 (my italics).

truth that by definition would be ever ongoing: the discourse thus contained a radical contradiction within its own functioning. But it was itself a response to the contradiction of that earlier patterning discourse (as we saw in *Utopia*), and the difficulty was to find a way of 'resolving' such contradictions. The problems and its potential solution had been presented with particular acuity by Kepler. Bacon and his contemporaries were able to turn the contradiction of the potentially new discourse into a simple epistemological difficulty—which could then be viewed as resolvable.

The means of achieving such a resolution was essentially to place the stasis of complete knowledge at a different level from the ongoing quest for truth. (It may be worth observing here that at the end of the period of analytico-referential dominance, Bertrand Russell was to use an identical technique to 'solve' the paradox of the so-called Cretan liar: by placing the general assertion of mendacity and this particular instance of it in two different 'languages' of a potentially infinite hierarchy of such languages—a discursive 'repetition' not perhaps dissimilar in its implications to Freud's 'internalization' and hypostatizing of, among other elements, the telescope metaphor, as I will show in a moment.) For Bacon, the stasis of complete knowledge was to correspond to the order of facts in nature (reference). The ongoing search for truth was simply the *process* of human reasoning and discursivity, manifesting the limitations inescapably present in any human activity but potentially perfectible on the one hand by 'method' and on the other by the very 'progressiveness' inherent in such 'forward' movement (analysis). For such limitations were indeed only temporary. First, they could be provided with the counterproofs of "works." Second, they could be terminated by the axiomatic exclusion of contrary instances. The exclusion of nonverifiable assertions or of assertions that negated or contradicted its own was the affirmation of the complete power of this discursive class. The Houyhnhnms' discursive practice was not after all so extreme. What it cannot "*know*" does not exist.

The production of discourse, its objects, and its relations by the *I* of enunciation that originated it, in secret, in power, and with the complicity of a knowing elite, was gradually occulted: discourse became the common, transparent, and objective property of all, while the enunciating *I* was hypostatized as individual will. Discourse was infallible because it corresponded to "common sense," while will could control it only with the assent of all potential users (it was said). A discursive contract was born through a series of occultations: discursive mastery (which was also a responsibility of enunciation), the possessive intention and the acquisitive act (of knowledge, of power, and so on), the use and ordering of power and authority. These diverse occultations legitimized the individual's presence in and use of a discourse for whose dominion he was no longer responsible.

By this series of ruses, by these occultations, that discourse was able to lay claim to referential meaning and truth. It was able to perform 'objectively' while allowing the individual power and authority to control 'his' discourse and possess 'his' knowledge, which, because it was objective, was also everyone else's. This could be seen most clearly no doubt in *Robinson Crusoe*. But that text is only an end result of a complex development, and is perfectly representative of what can be seen not only in other literary texts but also in other types of discourse: science, philosophy, political and economic theory, law and juridical practice, criticism, and so on. The "possessive individual" (all users of analytico-referential discourse with a greater or lesser degree of success) was now able to put his stamp on the "other," conceived as exterior to the space of discourse. He was able to put a value on that other, whether "person," "object," "concept," "event," or whatever. At the same time he could cede responsibility to the discourse itself as the institution of society.

Thus in *Crusoe* a 'private' practice is embedded within a societal one and succeeds because the one does not pose any threat to the other. *How* it succeeds is what I sought to show. The private and public prove essential to one another if the discourse is to function as a transparent mediator of true knowledge, of useful power. That is what I meant by the term "already formed social contract" of discourse. Recent discussions around Locke's semantic theories suggest that a similar problematic is central to them. On the one hand words are signs for ideas, and both the signs and the ideas must be sufficiently institutionalized for mutually comprehensible communication to take place; on the other, at the moment of utterance signs can express only those particular ideas entertained by the user of language who is making the utterance. That is to say that what the words *mean* in a particular utterance *can* only be the result of an *intention* which is the speaker's. Language in use must therefore provide the crossroads between the public and the private: discourse must *be* the social contract.[11]

11. Reference here is to the third book of Locke's *Essay Concerning Human Understanding* (1690), though it can clearly not be discussed in detail. Norman Kretzmann in particular has considered Locke's theories from this standpoint in "The Main Thesis of Locke's Semantic Theory," now collected in I. C. Tipton, ed., *Locke on Human*

The same thing exactly applies to *concepts* as they are received through communication. And I think one could equally well show that a notion such as that of *taste* as it is elaborated in eighteenth-century aesthetic theory corresponds to the same function. (The government inspector of *Hard Times* will take the matter a step further, equating fact and taste: "you are not to see anywhere what you don't see in fact; you are not to have anywhere what you don't have in fact. What is called Taste is only another name for Fact.")[12] Certainly the concept of scientific language functions contractually as it is presented by a writer such as Lavoisier (out of Condillac) in the introduction of his *Traité élémentaire de chimie*.[13] It is this consolidation that had been 'finalized' in a text like *Robinson Crusoe*, as both Rousseau and Macaulay recognized in their educational advice. But the need for its elaboration was clear from the very 'beginning' of the development of the analytico-referential. Human discourse had been inadequate to reality, merely an ordering of its diverse manifestations. Now it is the measure of reality. Out of need has come a means.

That particular discursive measure of reality, I have been suggesting, remains by and large our own, even though the limits of its efficacious functioning appear to have been revealed long since. Now, such revelation is at once the résumé of a discursive history and the indication of a new need. At this point the implications of a specific example merit some exploration, not only because it is one that our own time has endowed with quite exceptional weight, but because it has at the same time been taken as in fact *responding* to such need by a passage into a new discursive space—falsely, I believe. The case is exemplary, though for obvious reasons it cannot be dealt with here at the necessary length. I refer to Freudian psychoanalytical theory and practice, and its conceptual context.[14]

I spoke earlier of the "euphoria of late Victorianism," implying thereby its self-image of having arrived at some summit of human endeavor. One cannot but be aware at the same time that it was a period

Understanding: Selected Essays (Oxford, 1977), pp. 123–40. There is a most useful summary of Kretzmann's views, with considerable further discussion, in Stephen K. Land, *From Signs to Propositions: The Concept of Form in Eighteenth-Century Semantic Theory* (London, 1974), pp. 6–20.

12. Dickens, *Hard Times*, pp. 15–16.

13. See my "Espaces de la pensée discursive: Le cas Galilée et la science classique," *Revue de synthèse*, no. 85–86 (Jan.–June 1977), esp. pp. 30–34, 38–40.

14. The following brief interpretation of psychoanalysis and of the human psyche, its 'object,' as the hypostatization of a particular discursive history will be explored at greater length in another writing.

of intense self-criticism in any number of domains: Dickens, Peirce, Marx, Frege, Maxwell, Lautréamont, Helmholtz, Mach, and others have already been mentioned as exemplary. In literature one might make the obvious addition of Mallarmé; in the physical sciences, the consequences of the Michelson-Morley experiment and its invalidating of certain aspects of classical mechanical theory, or the theorizing of Lorentz, Planck, and others, as it seemed to be leading toward some quite new 'alternative'; in biology, the development of a scientific genetics; in mathematics, the development by Lobachevski and Riemann of non-Euclidian geometries. And so forth. These developments were accompanied by neo-Kantianism, social Darwinism (Peirce remarked of Darwinism that it was but the transference of "predatory capitalism" to the domain of nature, while Russell, less dramatically, speaks of laissez faire economics being thus applied to the animal and vegetable world), and other seemingly "conservative" reactions. These apparently contradictory movements—or, rather, the forms they take—are witness that some kind of discursive limits have indeed been reached. Freudianism is exemplary.

Little more than a year before the death of Queen Victoria, Freud published what has since come to be considered a "scientific classic" and a foundation-text of psychoanalysis, *The Interpretation of Dreams* (1899–1900). At the end of Chapter 4, I referred to an apparent similarity between his and Kepler's approach to science, in seeming opposition to Galileo's, though I suggested how he in fact 'disagrees' with both (for the limits his work reveals are not, of course, those performed by Kepler's, and if it points the way to a new inception it cannot be Galileo's). I also mentioned his particular use of the telescope metaphor. Just because psychoanalysis has become in many ways an exemplary scientific theory and practice for our time, it is useful—and even urgent—to show to how considerable a degree its founding texts repeat the specific history of analytico-referentiality and how its establishment is exemplary of the particular dominance with which we are by now familiar. At the same time, by its incorporation of discursive elements earlier occulted (remaining unidentified and unidentifiable, then), it reveals the limits of the analytico-referential.

In the *Interpretation* the telescope is used not only to explain the psychology of dreams but to set forth the relation obtaining between the mind and the world 'outside' it. Frege had 'demystified' and resuscitated the telescope as a metaphor of meaning in 1892. In 1900 Freud recomposes it as a representation of the real relation between mind and world, the former being a "reflex apparatus."

The telescope is at least partly explanatory of a concrete reality, the human psyche itself ("concrete" not in the sense that it is fixed and singular, but that it can be understood as a real process, as an actual functioning of the mind):

> Accordingly, we will picture the mental apparatus as a compound instrument, to the components of which we will give the name of "agencies" [*Instanzen*], or (for the sake of greater clarity) "systems" [*Systeme*]. It is to be anticipated, in the next place, that these systems may perhaps stand in a regular spatial relation to one another, in the same kind of way in which the various systems of lenses in a telescope are arranged behind one another [*etwa wie die verschiedenen Linsensysteme des Fernrohres hintereinanderstehen*]. Strictly speaking, there is no need for the hypothesis that the psychical systems are actually arranged in a *spatial* order. It would be sufficient if a fixed order were established by the fact that in a given psychical process the excitation passes through the systems in a particular temporal sequence.[15]

The mental apparatus in question starts with "perception" (stimuli), runs through systems where memory traces are deposited, and arrives at a motor stage where occurs a consequent mental action. The force of the telescope metaphor can readily be seen, though the presence of "memory traces" implies complications (explored especially by Jacques Derrida), which tie the image to the widespread metaphor of the mind as a camera. We will shortly see the enormous extent of the telescope 'metaphor' and its implications: they go very far indeed.

The earliest use of the metaphor in Freud appears to be the one just quoted. But the notion of the "dream image" (*Traumbild* as a *reflection* of experience retained in the memory) that is the result of such an apparatus seems to have preceded the literal elaboration of the specific metaphor—though it implies the elaboration of some such. The telescope was itself preceded by the use of a more general mechanistic model to describe the same "mental" or "psychical" ap-

---

15. Sigmund Freud, *The Interpretation of Dreams*, vols. 4 and 5 of *The Standard Edition of the Complete Psychological Works*, ed. James Strachey, 24 vols. (1953–66; rpt. London, 1975) [*SE*], V.536–37; *Die Traumdeutung*, in *Studienausgabe* (Frankfurt, 1972), II.513. I am indebted to Chantal Saint-Jarre and Marielle Baillargeon for forcefully reminding me of this text. I am particularly grateful to the former, who also pointed out the significance for many contemporaries (though I think it is incorrect) of the 'passage' from the visual to the linguistic in Freud, and who brought to my attention certain writings concerning the matter. She has herself drawn conclusions from these texts (though quite different from mine) in her "Le concept d'inconscient chez Freud" (M.A. thesis, Université du Québec à Montréal, 1981).

paratus (*seelischer* or *psychischer Apparat*). In the *Project for a Scientific Psychology* of 1895, Freud writes: "In the first place there is no question but that the external world is the origin of all major quantities of energy, since, according to the discoveries of physics, it consists of powerful masses which are in violent motion and which transmit their motion."[16] It goes without saying that the motion in question here is transmitted to the psychical receptor system: the telescope of 1900. This system itself then continues the transmission of energy, sometimes with interruptions (caused by the "contact barriers" corresponding to the lenses), sometimes more easily. Hobbes had also found a way to equate mass and movement in the material world both with the way in which the individual functions and with the organization of social man. This 'similarity' is very far from indifferent, as we will see.

Freud never dropped this optical manner of viewing his new science. The telescope is less a metaphor than an identification permitting "psychology to take its place as a natural science like any other." This remark does not come from an early text but from what may well be the penultimate text of his life, the *Outline of Psycho-analysis* (1938). He asserts:

> We know two kinds of things about what we call our psyche (or mental life): firstly, its bodily organ and scene of action, the brain (or nervous system) and, on the other hand, our acts of consciousness, which are immediate data and cannot be further explained by any sort of description. Everything that lies between is unknown to us, and the data do not include any direct relation between these two terminal points of our knowledge.[17]

These sentences lead directly to Freud's restatement of what he calls his two fundamental hypotheses. The first is that the psyche or mental life "is the function of an apparatus to which we ascribe the characteristics of being extended in space and of being made up of several portions—which we imagine, that is, as resembling a telescope or microscope or something of the kind." Yet it is much more than a merely "imaginary" conceptual aid: "the consistent working-out of a conception such as this is a scientific novelty."[18] It isn't of

---

16. Sigmund Freud, *Project for a Scientific Psychology*, SE, I.304. The passage from the *Project* to the *Interpretation* has been the subject of a useful discussion by André Green, "De l'*Esquisse* à l'*Interprétation des rêves*: Coupure et clôture," *Nouvelle Revue de Psychanalyse*, 5 (Spring 1972), 155–80.

17. Sigmund Freud, *An Outline of Psycho-analysis*, SE, XXIII.158.

18. Ibid., pp. 144–45.

course: the working-out of precisely this model ("conception") is the very foundation of the analytico-referential.

Freud's second hypothesis is to the effect that it is just this apparatus and its functioning that is to be termed the "unconscious." It is indeed this view, he remarks, that enables psychology to become "a natural science like any other." For, he writes, consciousness could only be a matter of "broken sequences" (as it is experienced), whereas the psychology of the unconscious becomes a matter of identifying the logical "laws" "obeyed" by the processes of the apparatus itself. Such a psychology is enabled to follow the "mutual relations and interdependences [of unconscious processes] over long stretches —in short, to arrive at what is described as an 'understanding' of the field of natural phenomena in question." The only difficulty then is the fact that while "every science is based on observations and experiences arrived at through the medium of our psychical apparatus . . . *our* science has as its subject that apparatus itself." This does not prevent him from asserting in *The Future of an Illusion* that psychoanalysis is "an impartial instrument, like the infinitesimal calculus, as it were" (a rapprochement not entirely without interest, in the light of earlier remarks). An analogous problem was being dealt with almost simultaneously by quantum mechanical inquiry. Here Werner Heisenberg and Niels Bohr in particular were exploring the philosophical and scientific consequences of the input of the experimental instrument of knowledge into the observation, experiment, and knowledge it made possible. These researches appear today as similar marks of a discourse at its limits.[19]

One might well assert that the very concept of the psyche as principally the functioning of unconscious processes is itself derived from the telescope as used by Freud. From the first he affirms that it is a means to describe the mental apparatus in question while avoiding "the temptation to determine psychical locality in any anatomical fashion." In this regard, the identification of the optical instrument with mental processes is extremely precise, and, as for Galileo, provides a description of a (mental) "apparatus" as well as a metaphor for its processes. It provides a way, says Freud, of understanding "psychical locality" as corresponding "to a point inside the apparatus at which one of the preliminary stages of an image comes into being.

19. Ibid., pp. 158–59; *The Future of an Illusion, SE*, XXI. 36. On Heisenberg's explorations and some of their implications in this very regard (as confronted especially with Wittgenstein), see my "Archéologie du discours et critique épistémique: Projet pour une critique discursive," in *Philosophie et littérature* [ed. Pierre Gravel] (Montreal, Paris, and Tournai, 1979), pp. 143–89.

In the microscope or telescope, as we know, these occur in part at ideal points, regions in which no tangible component of the apparatus is situated."[20] The unconscious is precisely a process apparently independent of such tangible components. The ideal points, of which the entire apparatus is composed so far as its functioning between the two "terminal points" is concerned, *are* the unconscious —likewise only indirectly accessible.

The precautions Freud takes against a too-literal understanding of the telescope 'metaphor' ("imperfections," "only intended to assist . . . ," "it would be sufficient . . .") are themselves suggestive of the very "defense mechanisms" he will also be exploring. Furthermore these precautions are in fact denied by the very detailed manner in which the 'image' *will* serve "to make the complications of mental functioning intelligible by dissecting the function and assigning its different constituents to different component parts of the apparatus." One is tempted to say that rather than making mental functioning intelligible, it makes mental functioning.

Yet the precautions are not only denied by the detail. As I have suggested, they are denied by the structure Freud ascribes to all mental activity as its very foundation: "All our psychical activity starts from stimuli (whether internal or external) and ends in innervations."[21] Now, whether any given instance of the process be viewed as entirely external or as a combination of external/internal stimuli, it is clear enough that the mechanistic model first indicated in the *Project* of 1895 and the division world/'subject' (stimuli/innervations, perception/judgment) are both a priori. That is so even if the concept of 'subject' here needs some redefining. The dual hypotheses of unconscious mental functioning and of the mind as a telescopic apparatus themselves correspond to the division in question (that is, in so far as they are a means of conceptualizing the psyche, they correspond to the dualism of internal/external, process/stasis, and so on).

To such a degree is this a priori the case that it holds even though the process itself may on occasion be conceived as entirely 'internal.' The *Project* makes it quite clear that Freud is seeking the mechanism of *identification*: "The aim and end of all thought-processes is thus to bring about a *state of identity*." In the case of *cognition* this is with the outside; in the case of "*reproductive* thought" it is with the psyche itself. Freud repeats here the analysis of the very problematic whose resolution was essential to the instauration of analytico-referentiality

20. *The Interpretation of Dreams, SE,* V.536.
21. Ibid., pp. 536, 537.

—the necessity of 'discovering' and then explaining the adequacy of the internal/external relationship. The telescope, then, is not simply metaphorical. The psychical apparatus is identical with it: "Reflex processes remain the model [*Vorbild*] of every psychical function."[22] One might say that one starts with the *Vorbild* and ends with the *Traumbild*, as reality becomes concept or event-in-the-mind, or as the 'fiction' of the material telescope becomes the 'reality' of psychical process. The movement is identical to Descartes's fabulous passage in *Le monde*, as he proceeds from his modeling "story" (*fable*) of the material world to its concrete reality. *Vorbild* is neither 'model' nor 'reality.' Like the Baconian *writing* examined in Chapter 6, it is taken as *preceding* in some sense and as enabling the discourse that can (then) make such a distinction. The same is the case for Descartes's *fable*. Once the discourse has been created, however, it can redefine that *Vorbild*, as model or as reality in accordance with its need. In the first case it is simply an explanatory device whose arbitrary and conventional relation to "reality" is emphasized—a saving of the appearances. In the second, it involves the "illusion," as Wittgenstein put it, of real identity between "the so-called laws of nature," "natural phenomena," and the functioning of the human mind. That is what I mean to imply when I suggest that psychoanalysis repeats in its elaboration a particular discursive history.

Inasmuch as this very process corresponds to the inception of the analytico-referential during the European Renaissance and neoclassicism, it is relevant to observe that when Freud is writing about how the blocking mechanisms, as which the "ideal points" of the apparatus also function, can lead to the forgetting of dreams, he chooses to refer to just that period. The reference is in the same chapter of the *Interpretation of Dreams* as the introduction of the telescope. In the previous section, Freud compares "the forgetting of dreams" (a consequence of a psychical "proscription" or "resistance") to "the state of things . . . after some sweeping revolution in one of the republics of antiquity or the Renaissance." The analogy is pursued at some length with regard to the Renaissance (and perhaps implicitly to Machiavelli, since it concerns in particular the proscription of nobles left over from the previously dominant state power structure).[23]

The political analogy had been pursued earlier, when Freud was discussing dream distortion and the systematic interpretation of it—a phenomenon closely associated with the forgetting of dreams. He used the analogy of *political* censorship. Again, as in the case of the

22. *Project, SE,* I.332–33; *Interpretation, SE,* V.538; *Traumdeutung,* p. 514.
23. *Interpretation, SE,* V.516.

telescope, it is rather a matter of identity than mere analogy: "The fact that the phenomena of [political] censorship and of dream-distortion correspond down to their smallest details justifies us in presuming that they are similarly determined."[24] The implications of such later texts as *Civilization and Its Discontents* are similar. Once again: the discussions of Bacon and later writers have already shown us just to what extent the political reference was an essential means of consolidating and developing the analytico-referential. Indeed, referring to Machiavelli, I suggested that it may well have been his analysis of a particular political practice that provided essential elements leading into the development of that discourse. I have already had occasion to mention Hobbes in relation to Freud. So it is significant, too, that in 1914 Freud should have added a footnote to his definition of the dream process as a regression (a kind of traveling backward up the telescope), referring not only to Albertus Magnus but, more to my purpose, to Hobbes's discussion of dream regression in *Leviathan*.[25]

Taken together these diverse elements suggest the argument (I can do little more here) that not only the psychical processes as a whole, but also such of their particular functionings as regression, forgetting, resistance, association, and so on are hypostatizations of the discursive history the present volume has been following. Thus, for example, the "work of displacement" and the "work of condensation," which permit "representation" in dreams, seem to take up rather exactly Tesauro's *versabilità* and *perspicacia*, respectively. They are now processes internalized as unconscious functionings, the inverse of conscious ones. Thus hypostatized they can be reincorporated in a history that had had to occult them as processes of reason. Freud's 'purpose' here is not dissimilar to Galileo's (or that of Kepler's notes to the *Somnium*): to reduce overdetermination and multiplicity to an identifiable (not necessarily singular) meaning.[26]

These things are all aspects of the *way in which* dreams function. Even more revealing is the *purpose* ascribed to dreams. Dreams,

24. Ibid., IV.142–43.

25. Ibid., V.542. The *Leviathan* reference is to pt. I, ch. 2. I will be exploring the political theoretical establishment of discourse in the writing already referred to several times (see above, note 9). It is worth noting here that when speaking of the absence of civilization in *The Future of an Illusion*, Freud affirms that the individual would find himself in a "natural" state exactly like what Hobbes pictures (*SE*, XXI.15). *Totem and Taboo* had somewhat complicated a view similar however in its main lines, and the matter is taken up again at length in *Moses and Monotheism*. The Hobbes/Freud relation is, of course, rather a commonplace: see, e.g., Jean Roy, *Hobbes et Freud* (Halifax, N.S., 1976), for a detailed discussion, and Philip Rieff, *Freud: The Mind of the Moralist* (1959; rpt. New York, 1961), passim.

26. *Interpretation*, *SE*, IV.277–338.

writes Freud, are wish-fulfillments. Their manner of functioning is by regression: "In regression the fabric of the dream-thoughts is resolved into its raw material."[27] Both Bacon and Galileo had rejected "raw material" as unusable for knowledge. In their view such raw material ("brute experience," said Galileo) was useless. Only already ordered experience (experiment, or even perhaps *Vorbild*) was of any epistemological use. Nonetheless, the ideal of analytico-referential discourse was eventually direct access to such immediate concrete reality. The fulfillment of *its* most ardent wish would have been immediate knowledge of the raw material of nature. Again, a major problem confronting the inception and progress of the discourse of analysis and reference is absorbed into the psychical mechanism. The *use* of raw material in dreams corresponds perhaps to the wish for scientific knowledge of such material (for utility and knowledge are one, said Bacon). Such "a wish from the unconscious," remarks Freud, is "invariably and indisputably" the "capitalist" providing the "outlay" that a dream may occur to satisfy it.[28] Once again, one is constrained to affirm, this analogy is surely not indifferent and certainly corresponds to the fact that this telescope, the unconscious, is completely at the service of the *I* that corresponds to that "capitalist" wish: "Dreams are completely egoistic."[29]

We have already seen that this hypostatization holds for the case of the unconscious itself. But the centrality of the concept (to understate the case) makes it bear repeating. The unconscious corresponds precisely, Freud suggests, to the intangible system of places within the optical apparatus. Cremonini refused to look up the telescope because he claimed (so it is said) that his acceptance of what he would see depended on his prior acceptance of an extrapolation from the functioning of the whole instrument. It depended, that is to say, upon an acceptance of the implications of Baconian "writing," of Galilean "mathematical language," of Cartesian "method"— or of Freudian "*Vorbild.*" For in a similar way, "access" to the unconscious is the consequence of an extrapolation from what is taken as the functioning of the entire apparatus. It may be that Freud's assimilation of ontogenesis to phylogenesis, of individual development and functioning to that of "the human race,"[30] would better be seen as the theoretical hypostatization of a historically situatable discursive

27. Ibid., V.543.
28. Ibid., p. 561.
29. Ibid., IV.322. This view will be somewhat modified in 1925.
30. Ibid., V.548. *Totem and Taboo* is doubtless the most exemplary text in this respect.

'birth' into the form of permanent human mental processes, just as the psychoanalytical theory that contains it may be viewed as the hypostatization of that discursive history itself.

It goes without saying that the telescope is not an entirely accurate or self-sufficient model. For at each ideal stage of the apparatus, as we saw, is left an imprint that may be described "as a 'memory-trace' [*Erinnerungsspur*]."[31] This aspect of the matter was also destined to a great future, not only in the work of Freud himself but also in that of many of his most recent successors. It involves the question of psychical processes as *writing*, or at least as the production of signification in a manner strictly analogous to the functioning of natural languages. Some contemporary writers have sought to ascribe a special importance to a *passage* in Freud's own writings from the 'optical' to the 'linguistic.' These writers can then play down the 'positivistic' side of psychoanalytic theory and practice, just so as to be able to offer that science as a form of 'knowledge' (or 'praxis,' or "athesis") of a quite different order from that of the 'traditional' experimentalist form—as though, far from being a mark of discursive limits, it was already in a new space of discourse. Thus Jacques Derrida can assert that the metaphor of text precedes that of machine, though he in fact shows the former as developing between the time of the *Project* and that of *The Interpretation of Dreams* (in the correspondence with Fliess). Similarly, he affirms that "the mechanical models will be tested and discarded," though the telescope is still essential in 1938. And he tries to underplay the kind of significance I am here drawing from the optical 'metaphor' by asserting that in any case the telescope in Freud is not to be understood as "a simple, homogeneous structure"—a fact that is indicated, he says, by the diverse refractions of light (excitations) as it passes through the lens systems (ideal points), and by the changes in medium contained in the system.[32] This last point is undoubtedly correct. But it had never been otherwise from the first. That is precisely why Galileo (for example) remarked that to change the length of the telescope was to change both the 'object' and the observation involved. Perhaps that was why Cremonini refused to look up it.

Such writers as Jacques Lacan, Derrida, and others (whatever their

---

31. *Interpretation, SE,* V.538; *Traumdeutung,* p. 514.

32. Jacques Derrida, "Freud and the Scene of Writing," in *Writing and Difference,* tr. and ed. Alan Bass (Chicago and London, 1978), pp. 206, 200, 215. Derrida has constantly returned to Freud—e.g., in *La dissémination* ("Hors livre" and "La double séance" especially) and the entire second half of *La carte postale, de Socrate à Freud et au-delà* (Paris, 1980), pp. 277–549.

manifest differences) have thus sought to emphasize the 'linguistic' side of things, by picking up on Freud's other favorite 'metaphor.' Here the very concept of interpretation becomes more important than what is to be interpreted. A different kind of reading of the *Traumdeutung* is emphasized, along with such texts as *Jokes and Their Relation to the Unconscious, The Psychopathology of Everyday Life, Beyond the Pleasure Principle, The "Uncanny,"* and the "Note Upon the 'Mystic Writing Pad.'" The view that such an interpretation of psychoanalysis is a discursive way to the future is quite widespread—however diverse may be the interpretation involved. But as we saw in the earlier quotation from the *Traumdeutung,* the optical metaphor and that of the *trace* were in fact simultaneous, a part of the very same description. They are simultaneous here as they had been at the inception of analytico-referential discourse. We saw in Chapter 6 that the identification of a capacity for knowing and doing, and the characterization of coherent social *being* in terms of writing and ordered use of language, was essential to the Baconian instauration— just as the telescope was to the Galilean version of the *same* instauration. John Wallis was quite correct, we would say, to name the two as co-founders of the modern science and the new knowledge. Derrida refers to these metaphors as "apparently contradictory"; if they are, then it is a contradiction from the very outset of this discursive history.[33]

It is just when he speaks in the *Traumdeutung* both of the optical instrument and of the "written" trace that Freud starts speaking of "association." It is surely not simply a play on words to point out that such association is made possible by the *simultaneous* functioning of the telescopic perceptual apparatus and the 'writing' that accompanies it: "Our perceptions are linked with one another in our memory."[34] The association of the two is thus just as essential to Freud's analysis as it had been to the inception of the particular discursive history leading toward it. Freud himself never dropped either schema, though he seems to insist upon the visual one. Even so, we may recall that Frege (not to mention Galileo and Tesauro) has shown how that visuality is *also* a particular elaboration of the signifying process, at the same time as it *is* that process. Both are hypostatizations from *the same singular discursive history.* Derrida appears to

33. Derrida, "Freud and the Scene of Writing," p. 216. We should observe here that Derrida has viewed Lacan's reading of Freud (through Poe in this case) as a 'rediscovery' of singularizable truth and a 'misuse' (my term) of both Freud and Poe. See "Le Facteur de vérité," in *La carte postale,* pp. 441–524.

34. *Interpretation, SE,* V. 539.

view the two as opposed, contradictory. He argues that the conflict would finally have been erased by (in) the writing machine of 1924. One wonders, however, whether such 'oppositions' as unconscious *process*/memory *trace* (in the form of a *fixed* imprint) or telescope/writing, which are so constant and permanent in Freud, and such 'contraries' as the 'readable' trace/"deferral" combination in Derrida are not once again efforts to overcome the process/stasis contradiction we have seen as endemic to analytico-referential discourse, and which a Bacon (for example) had already 'resolved' in his own way. The very notion of the psyche as both an "apparatus" and a "process" is exemplary of the same opposition.

The same duality is played out and provided with a certain stability in a more significant way in diverse writings of Freud dating from the early 1920's. We can see it in such texts as *Beyond the Pleasure Principle* (1920), with the introduction of two fundamental instinctual urges: not simply the familiar sexual impulses (an urge to life and conservation), but also the new urge toward death (the "death-wish," the tendence toward dissolution and inertia). In this case, life itself, and not simply the organization of the unconscious, becomes the place where the process/stasis conflict is played out. In *The Ego and the Id* of 1923, Freud appears to make this quite explicit: "The emergence of life would thus be the cause of the continuance of life and also at the same time of the striving towards death; and life itself would be a conflict and compromise between these two trends. The problem of the origin of life would remain a cosmological one; and the problem of the goal and purpose of life would be answered dualistically."[35] Here the central conflict of a particular discursive history is with a vengeance hypostatized into the principle of all human life, whenever and wherever it be found. The discursive elaboration is analogous to what has already been seen, though we are here concerned with later texts, more or less contemporaneous with that of the writing machine—of which too much should surely not be made. The life/death duality is not yet to be found, for example, in the *Metapsychology* of 1917 (where only the urges to life are conceived). The *ongoing* discursive elaboration is therefore precisely in the terms set for it by a particular discursive history: it does not change fundamentally.

Furthermore, speaking of the combination of the impulse to death and the urge to life, we might also wish to take a cue from Pope's *Essay on Man* (1733–34):

35. *The Ego and the Id, SE,* XIX.40–41.

As Man, perhaps, the moment of his breath,
Receives the lurking principle of death;
The young disease, that must subdue at length,
Grows with his growth, and strengthens with his strength:
So, cast and mingled with his very frame,
The Mind's disease, its RULING PASSION came.   [II.133–38]

No doubt, Pope's concepts are not Freud's. Nonetheless I urge that such as these are not simply thematic resemblances, that Pope's debt to Locke is also Freud's, and that though the terms may indeed differ what is indicated here is a common conceptual framework.

Freudian psychoanalysis may thus be seen as an entertaining translation of the discourse and discursive history of a particular moment in the West: a version of Cyrano's "Promethean analysis," translating the course of analytico-referential discourse, hypostatizing it into a universal human "psyche." We have seen that such functions as displacement and condensation, regression, forgetting and association, such factors as the *I* of the unconscious, such purposes as wish-fulfillment, such processes as the unconscious itself and indeed the very concept of life provide us with a complete repetition of the discursive means by which analytico-referentiality was installed. Small wonder that it is often translated into experimentalist, possessive economic, or individualist political terms by Freud himself. Indeed, these very terms may provide access to another set of complex relationships, which again can only be briefly indicated here.

Locke's assertion that man may suspend action until his desires are elevated above baseness, "till he hungers or thirsts after righteousness,"[36] is perhaps not so very far structurally from the Freudian concept of sublimation—though the process is obviously a conscious one for Locke. Nonetheless, human freedom (here, to elevate or sublimate base desire) as the manifestation of some absolute notion of moral inclination is close to the operational function ascribed to the Superego: in Locke, of course, it could not be presented as a constraint (since it is "human freedom"), though it *is* given as an avoidance of "unpleasantness." Now, if we look closely at this notion, we see immediately that we are not at a very great distance from the Hobbesian argument concerning the free cession of individual power (possessed in the state of nature) to the singular authority of the state. Both in Hobbes and in Locke society functions as a con-

36. John Locke, *An Essay Concerning Human Understanding*, ed. Alexander Campbell Fraser, 2 vols. (1894; rpt. New York, 1959), I.335 (bk.II.xxi.35).

sequence of the individual's urge to find the best way to do good for himself in a context of others' requirement to do good for *them-selves*. Both assert that individual freedom implies the individual's self-restraint on behalf of himself and his good: self-restraint and social authority are in fact at one. The economics of *laissez faire* depends on no other assumption.

Freud inverts the very same process, arguing that this urge is in fact an internalization of restraints imposed by society—society of a certain form, one could add. It is indeed just such a mechanism as this that allows a theoretical assumption of individual equality to conceal a practice of inequality. At one level, Freud's analysis shows how it does so. The association of rational and moral freedom with a particular concept of social constraint (called "civil liberty" by the liberal philosophers, and made into a form taken by the mind's functioning by Freud) was available from the outset. In 1707, Shaftesbury could write that what essentially elevates man above the beasts are "*Freedom of Reason* in the Learned World, and good Government and *Liberty* in the Civil World."[37] The eighteenth century could argue that rational and moral freedom in the individual coincide with the concept of civil liberty as a certain kind of socialized order and constraint, and that the combination was the essential characteristic of the human. Freud demystifies this conception by reversing it: the liberal concept of individual freedom is the consequence of a particular order of society. The limits of a particular class of discourse may have been reached and *shown* to have been reached, but the process that does the showing is just the same: we are still, though more radially, with Swift.

Derrida asserts that "the Freudian concept of trace must be radicalized and extracted from the metaphysics of presence."[38] In view of what has been argued here, one wonders whether that is possible, whether the attempt is not bound to end up in just the same discursive space. Both of our central images, the optical instrument and writing, had been important in Locke's analysis of human understanding. The mind may be supposed, writes the English philosopher, "a white paper, void of all characters, without any ideas." Experience will write on that paper, through observation of "external sensible objects" and through consideration of the mind's "internal operations." Freud was to remark that all "major quantities of

37. Anthony Ashley Cooper, 3rd Earl of Shaftesbury, *Several Letters Written by a Noble Lord to a Young Man at the University* (London, 1716), p. 8 (letter of May 10, 1707).
38. Derrida, "Freud and the Scene of Writing," p. 229.

energy" proceed from "the external world" into the mind. At the same time, psychoanalysis itself is engaged in understanding the mind's internal operations, that mind being obscure and unconscious in its functioning. Just thus had Locke viewed it as a kind of *camera obscura,* illumined only by "external and internal sensation":

> These alone, as far as I can discover, are the windows by which light is let into this *dark room.* For, methinks, the understanding is not much unlike a closet wholly shut from light, with only some little openings left, to let in external visible resemblances, or ideas of things without: would the pictures coming into such a dark room but stay there, and lie so orderly as to be found upon occasion, it would very much resemble the understanding of a man, in reference to all objects of sight, and the ideas of them.[39]

On the appearance of the *Essay,* John Norris had taken Locke to task for refusing to admit the possibility of unconscious elements in the mind, an idea that Locke had indeed rejected outright. In his view, individual will and judgment order ideas in a perfectly comprehensible manner, however complex it may sometimes be. Nothing in the mind is hidden. Freud simultaneously brings back, or creates, the occulted 'subject' and thrusts it even deeper beyond reach of inspection: its functioning can be known only through such manifestations as analysis may bring to the 'surface.' Nonetheless, it is now *there.* As such, it is a revelation of limits.

I have mentioned the question of psychoanalytic discourse at some length here, though only indicatively, because of its exemplary character for us. But it is important, as we explore a discursive inception, to become cognizant at the same time of its present ramifications for us *and* of the potential consequences of ignoring discursive history. Of course, psychoanalysis would affirm that this partial analysis has merely indicated the world-historical validity of its scheme, at least for the past three hundred years. I am affirming the reverse: that it is 'merely' the hypostatization of that history. That achievement and its internalization cannot but be seen as an ideological effort at maintaining the discourse in question, an effort quite similar to that of logical atomism, for example, to provide a new and more 'acceptable' foundation for an empirical science in logical and epistemological trouble. As here, Bacon had already explored that foundation in detail, if less formalistically than Whitehead, Russell, or Wittgenstein would do three centuries later. Russell's solution to the "Cretan liar"

39. Locke, *Essay,* I.121–22, 211–12 (bk.II.i.2; xi.17).

paradox had been provided in essence from the very beginning; so, too, had the elements of psychoanalytic theory. Ignoring the history in question may well lead only into further traps: such as a repetition of the same process, mistaking a given discourse for something quite new and unfamiliar, deluding ourselves that we hear the voice of the lion. As Freud himself put it at the beginning of *The Future of an Illusion* (1927): "the less a man knows about the past and the present the more insecure must prove his judgement of the future."

The internalization of a particular history, so apparent in psychoanalytic theory, was put in a different and more concrete way by Theodor Adorno, but with similar implications:

> Perhaps from very early on in the bourgeois era the experiment became a surrogate for authentic experience. . . . The cruelty, shrinking back from nothing, not even cruelty against oneself, is intimately connected with it—seeing how a person handles himself under such and such conditions, for example, when he is castrated or murdered, or how one himself reacts. The new anthropological type has become internally what earlier was true only of the method: the subject of natural science —of course also the object.[40]

Despite Adorno's own adoption of aspects of Freudian thought, and despite the extreme nature of the Nazi practices referred to here, the quotation takes us very precisely from Galileo's and Bacon's rejection of raw ("authentic") experience, through the hypostatization of Method into objective Fact, to the internalization in psychoanalytic theory (for example) of the discursive history in which the original rejection was an essential element.

The retreat of patterning discourse is evidently not immediate. A hint of a lack or of an excess of meaning remains to vex the consolidation of the new discourse. As patterning fades before the elaboration of the analytico-referential, as it is occulted there together with the very elements that make the latter discourse possible, there still remain indications of a 'sense' that would escape the (intentional) meaningfulness of this new discourse. Kepler's dream can never be adequately circumscribed by the marginal analyses; there is always some excess. Cyrano is unable to conclude except with a complementarity of discourse, experiment, and reality that always remains am-

40. Theodor W. Adorno, "Notizen zur neuen Anthropologie" (Frankfurt, Adorno Estate, 1942), p. 6, quoted in Susan Buck-Morss, *The Origin of Negative Dialectics: Theodor W. Adorno, Walter Benjamin, and the Frankfurt Institute* (New York and London, 1977), p. 177. The previous Freud quotation is from *The Future of an Illusion, SE,* XXI.5.

biguous. Bacon never ceases to emphasize the threat of the 'old' to the 'new.' The transparent discourse recorded in the second of Borges's two books of this chapter's epigraph poses a problem of decipherment: it is at worst impossible, or made possible at best by the imposition of an entirely arbitrary logic.

Within the functioning of the dominant discourse of analysis and reference, some such indication must necessarily persist. It is the consequence of such contradictions as that between stasis and process. That indication will be a kind of permanent ghost in the machine, posing a latent question to the signifying, denoting intentions of that discourse. It is the mark of a potential meaninglessness of discourse because it would be the contradiction of the logic of the dominant discourse in which it lies more or less hidden. That is not to say, of course, that a discourse of *patterning* could ever function again as such for us. The indication in question does not refer to any particular *other* discursive class. it is simply the index of the limits of discursive space: Wittgenstein's lion. Indeed, it is not impossible that texts such as Wittgenstein's *Philosophical Investigations,* Derrida's *Dissémination,* or Joyce's *Finnegans Wake* are the uncovering of such an index and the consequent attempt to expand or even go beyond the limits in some way: the result so far has been a 'marginal' discourse problematizing into a kind of regressive infinity the function of signs and the production of meaning.

To discover limits is not to go beyond them. It is significant in this regard that the principle 'elements' of Derridian discourse (again, for example), "margin," "supplement," "*différance,*" "deferral," "athesis," and so on can all be subsumed under a paradigm of "between" (*entre*). This is avowedly the case, of course. It is as though this discourse wished to expand the 'space' of the limits themselves, to enlarge indefinitely those "ideal points" in Freud that are also the "contact barriers" simultaneously preventing and allowing the operation of the 'discourse of the unconscious': preventing, because they obstruct, proscribe, censor; allowing, because it can function only by the differentiation that refraction and the change of medium make possible. 'Space' is of course the wrong term. "Between" is a better indication of the attempt.

The marginality is owing to the fact that while such texts may uncover the limits of discourse, they do not go beyond such uncovering ("deconstruction," as Derrida has it)—indeed they claim that it is impossible to go beyond or to escape our habitual discursive space, because we are necessarily limited to questioning such 'space' in its own terms. Logic and history appear to be in some disagreement on that point. Bacon, Descartes, Galileo, and their contemporaries had no hesitation in ascribing what they understood as a profound crisis in all spheres of human activity to a discursive enigma, to a problem of sense and meaningfulness. And they succeeded in creating, in what they understood as a new "logic" (or "method," or "reason"), the conceptual space of the modern West. That was a momentous achievement, entirely justifying the exultation of its creators. If it has now arrived at the apparent limits of its efficacy, it is a problem for our time not at all dissimilar in its implications to those of the early seventeenth century. This is why we need to understand what made possible the foundation of what still remains the dominant discursive class. That conceptual sphere should be neither a cause for shame nor an object of scorn. While it worked, it did so superlatively. That it should have given rise to misuse was inevitable and is obviously endemic to any such system. That it should have reached the limits of its useful and progressive action should only encourage us to undertake a work parallel to that of its founders.

The development of analytico-referential discourse meant that it gradually came to oppose the discourse of patterning. It could not simply occlude it, because the discourse of experimentalism functions by the Law of the Excluded Middle, and whatever could not be accommodated to the 'true' was necessarily 'false,' and must be shown to be so: Bacon's law of the exclusion of contrary instances. By that time patterning was no longer a practice but an 'object' classified as a 'form of thought': "ancient," "primitive," "mythical," or later even, as we saw, "pathological." Thus hypostatized it is no longer what was to be found in Kepler and his predecessors: it has become an *object* fit for analysis. Kepler's 'attempt' to maintain the simultaneous functioning of both (the one now already partly residual, the other already visibly developing) was doomed to failure, because the one puts the practice of the other fundamentally in question: what analysis cannot understand it must exclude. Patterning, for it, is the voice of the lion. Patterning could accept, indeed precariously absorb, experimentalism—as Kepler's attempt suggests. Experimentalism could not reciprocate. To adopt a metaphor whose prevalence we have seen: the father can accept the son, but the son quite rejects his progenitor.

Patterning itself becomes distanced as "mythical," "primitive," or "prescientific" thought. But some other indication of insufficiency in the visible dominant discourse model responds to the hegemony of the analytico-referential: perhaps what I referred to in Chapter 2 as the occulted dominant discourse practice. As a mark in discourse it is the potential destruction of analysis. Like the residual mark of patterning, it was perhaps also present in Kepler's *excess,* in Cyrano's (and to some extent, Defoe's) *ambiguity,* in Bacon's *threat.* In our time it has become increasingly apparent. The simple imposition of dichotomy by which the analytico-referential eclipsed the discourse of patterning, naming it as an object of abuse, is increasingly impossible in our modernity—or post-modernity as some would have it, with something just like that impossibility in mind. Nor is it indifferent that the analytico-referential itself has increasingly become a similar object of abuse. Tesauro's critique has come into its own again, and the immanent questioning of the very possibility of making (any) sense (not of *intending* a particular meaning), which is the mark of the fallible limits of all discourse, has become a problem whose urgency has increased as the premises of experimentalism itself have been cast into doubt—and first of all in the very discourse of science from which the model was supposed to have been taken.

When Freud asks the question, at the beginning of chapter 7 of *The Future of an Illusion,* whether most if not all our cultural activities may not be "illusions" (beliefs motivated by wish-fulfillment), we have genuinely come full circle. We might well say that the question was hinted at but avoided three hundred years earlier ("occulted," as I have been calling it): to the effect that all knowledge and belief, all human activity and social functioning may be but the creation of a discursive "space" providing, as Bacon put it, "a new face of things." To pose the question clearly, as to incorporate the very occultations essential to the discursive inception, is to reveal the limits of that discourse—if the question can be answered (as it is by Freud) in the affirmative. Whether or not the "illusions" may be 'correct,' may correspond to a 'reality,' is both indifferent and unanswerable, because from within that discourse there would be no way of 'knowing' it, while from within some other discourse the concept of reality would be different. Whether or not the incorporation of occultations already proposes a passage into another discursive domain, only history will show. Freud may be right when he asserts at the end of the text just mentioned that the rule of "*Logos*" (a kind of science of which psychoanalysis would be exemplary) will indeed be "for a new generation of men" and foreseeable. The time is not yet that we could know it. But it is most certainly time to recognize the development of and a vital need for a new instauration—a matter the present volume has several times asserted. As Noam Chomsky has put it, perhaps with more vivacity and assuredly more contentiously:

Predatory capitalism created a complex industrial system and an advanced technology; it permitted a considerable extention of democratic practice and fostered certain liberal values, but within limits that are now being pressed and must be overcome. It is not a fit system for the mid-twentieth century. It is incapable of meeting human needs that can be expressed only in collective terms, and its concept of competitive man who seeks only to maximize wealth and power, who subjects himself to market relationships, to exploitation and external authority, is antihuman and intolerable in the deepest sense.[41]

We cannot yet know whether a new instauration has occurred or is in the process of occurring. That is indeed for history to show. Still, it is of some interest to note that at the same time as Lewis Carroll was basing much of the nonsense of *Alice* on games with the law *tertium non datur*, C. S. Peirce was seeking to constitute a semiotics on the basis of a tertiary relationship replacing the stasis of the true/false dichotomy with a continuous process of the production of sense. Nor is it an accident that both Peirce and Carroll use the paradox of Achilles and the Tortoise in order to argue process over discontinuity, the latter performing an infinite regression of sense that concludes with the deconstruction of the very property of the name according to which it is in a relation of denotation with the thing. We saw that this matter had had to be questioned during the very development of a discourse whose terms were supposed to be made meaningful by their denotation of objects all of whose properties were taken as independent of the names applied to them. We saw the "amazement" of Cyrano's narrator when confronted with the idea that this might not be the case, and the use to which it was put by Crusoe. The question becomes crucial in Locke's discussion of identity and his analysis of the functioning of words and concepts. Humpty Dumpty pours scorn on Alice for her belief in such denotation: "When *I* use a word . . . it means just what I choose it to mean—neither more nor less." It is, as he puts it, merely a question of mastery: "They've a temper, some of them—particularly verbs: they're the proudest—adjectives you can do anything with, but not verbs—however, *I* can manage the whole lot of them! Impenetrability! That's what *I* say!"[42]

41. Noam Chomsky, *For Reasons of State* (New York, 1973), pp. 403–4. The preceding references to Freud are from *The Future of an Illusion, SE*, XXI.54.

42. Justus Buchler, ed., *The Philosophical Writings of C. S. Peirce* (New York, 1955), p. 304; Lewis Carroll, "What the Tortoise Said to Achilles," in *The Works*, ed. Roger Lancelyn Green (Feltham, Middlesex, 1965), pp. 1049–51; the Humpty-Dumpty cita-

Like others already mentioned, Peirce and Carroll represent a moment when the analytico-referential is itself being put in question. In 1898, the former made an analysis of mechanistic causal relations that undermines the accepted order of cause-effect much as quantum-mechanical principles were to do some thirty years later. In this regard it is a matter of some interest that the same passage in *Through the Looking-Glass*, where Alice is unable to fix the position of the "large bright thing" as it ascends from shelf to shelf in the Sheep's shop to pass finally through the ceiling, should have been used to speak both of the fleeting frontier of discursive sense and of the impossibility in quantum mechanics "of pinning down the precise location of an electron in its path around the nucleus of an atom."[43] If some unfamiliar kind of discursive class is emerging here, it has yet to do so with any clarity. Perhaps it would involve the movement of what one might call a processive communicational network, where fixity, discrete denotated objects of knowledge, analytical knowledge itself, discursive transparency, objective grasp, absence of the 'subject' would all be strangers. How that could be translated into political and social terms remains to be seen. Be that as it may, the future of any such practice is itself problematical and, as in Freudianism and its avatars, the attempt must be in the nature of a wager with (and in) history.[44]

The indication within discourse of an unfamiliar discursive class may be thought of as a 'potentiality,' not as anything like 'an entity in its own right,' even if it were only a conceptual one. It would be a mark of 'displacement' within the discourse where it occurs, and therefore not a 'sign' at all for that discourse. It is *non-sensical* because what it would signify (were it able to do so) could never 'fit' the other signifieds of the discourse, or *how* it would signify could not do

---

tion, p. 174. These questions have received an excellent treatment in Gilles Deleuze, *Logique du sens* (Paris, 1969), pp. 27–29, 37–38. With respect to the interpretation of Peirce, see my "Peirce and Frege: In the Matter of Truth," *Canadian Journal of Research in Semiotics*, 4, no. 2 (Winter 1976–77), esp. pp. 25–31, and to these questions more generally, my "Archéologie du discours."

43. Martin Gardner, ed., *The Annotated Alice* (New York, 1960), p. 253 n. 9. The Peirce reference is to the fourth lecture in the series "Detached Ideas on Vitally Important Topics: Causation and Force," in Charles Sanders Peirce, *Collected Papers*, ed. Charles Hartshorne, Paul Weiss, and Arthur W. Burks, 8 vols. (Cambridge, Mass. 1931–58), VI.46–66 (§§ 66–87). Gilles Deleuze is the author who uses the *Looking-Glass* passage to discuss problems of sense: *Logique du sens*, p. 56.

44. I think here especially of certain of Michel Serres's essays, in *Hermès* (5 vols., Paris, 1968–80); *La naissance de la physique dans le texte de Lucrèce* (Paris, 1977); *Le parasite* (Paris, 1979). Even if it eventually 'fails,' the attempt itself, with all the risks it entails (of becoming, for example, but an *effet de style*, a new mysticism or a kind of escapism), is admirable.

so. It thus becomes *excessive*. It can never be more than the *possibility* of meanings beyond the exclusive limits of the space of analytico-referential discourse. It would break the logical space that constitutes the class of discourse within which it occurs. It is just the mark of a potentiality of sense that escapes particular utterance in discourse. But while it *may* be able to develop 'on its own' into some other discourse, it can be nothing more *within* analytico-referential discourse, and those who dwell on it there will remain within the marginality of carnival questioners of the authority on which they depend. In the nature of the case the disappearance of the discourse of order will entail that of the carnival.

For we should not allow such marks to baffle us, as though we were thus placed before some irremediable complexity. Such a reaction is to ignore history. The process is not unique, even if its ongoing outcome may be. Worse still, to dwell in such bafflement may result in erasing history entirely. 'Literature,' for example, may come to be read as an eternal questioning of dominant discursive structures (a process that simply reinscribes the permanence of the human at the level of the questioning instead of at that of the dominance—whereas the deconstruction of which I am speaking wishes to make a more radical critique). In our own time much literary criticism has argued itself into such a position, so that from Plato to Dante, from Ariosto to Milton, from Sterne to Diderot and Rousseau, from Hegel to Flaubert and Mallarmé, from Lauréamont to Nietzsche and Joyce, from Stevens to Genet, not to mention Athenian tragedy and the Homeric epics, the great literary texts (it is said) are those that put in question the dominant structures of order at the very level of their signifying practice: literature undoes or deconstructs the self-sufficient security of authority.[45]

The detail of one example is enough, and I use it out of respect, not scorn, for its source. But I also use it because this particular case does indeed seem ambiguous, the author in question having occupied a historical position perhaps analogous to our own. Donald

45. One could mention here writings by such critics as Paul de Man, Stanley Fish, Geoffrey Hartman, Philippe Lacoue-Labarthe, J. Hillis Miller, Jeffrey Mehlman, Jean-Luc Nancy, Patricia Parker, Pietro Pucci, and others (not to mention Derrida himself). Despite their manifold differences and disagreements, I would suggest that as a whole this critical enterprise has taken the logic of carnival, so to speak, "au bout de son calepin," as Montaigne wrote in a not-altogether different context. I have discussed both the status of literature and the position of such critics in "The Environment of Literature and the Imperatives of Criticism," *Europa*, 4 (1981), to appear. Among other things, I suggest such critics are in fact caught up in the same discursive space as the traditional critics whose practice they seek to "deconstruct." They are playing Gulliver to Crusoe.

Bouchard suggests that the final writings of Milton (*Samson Agonistes* and *Paradise Regained*) can be viewed as going beyond the progression suggested at the end of my Chapter 6. He sees them as overcoming a particular idea "of man as dreamed by Renaissance humanism," and as a recognition that what has been thus overcome was but "the product of a particular aesthetic and historical compulsion." He argues that in these late works Milton is not aggressively seeking to impose yet another version of man—his own—but rather to offer something else: "the undefined and the suspension of old beliefs and ways, and it is characterized by a waiting action in a space where God's ways replace images of human desire."[46] Milton as a seventeenth-century Derrida. The poet would offer a space of possible choice. He would even have composed a 'passing place' taut with expectation, himself unable to make the passage, and seeking to 'resolve' indefinition, indecision, and suspension through an appeal to millenarist urges: a temptation not unfamiliar to us in own time (and Thomas More's urge in the *Dialogue of Comfort*). Historically Milton may well have played such a role—the reading of history presented through the present work would suggest that *someone* is at least likely to have done so. But the role should not be ascribed indiscriminately to all so-called creative writers.

An understanding of the details of complexity is essential. Its achievement may require a momentary drawing back, a tensing and a collecting, but one cannot dwell in suspension, and such a gathering can only be so as to go beyond, with greater clarity and more usefully. The mark of its limits is of course fundamental in analytico-referential discourse. But the limits thus marked and their diverse consequences are now to a degree familiar. To dwell *in* them is to turn in circles. Once that is understood, we must look elsewhere: not so much, or only, in the contradictions of the dominant model, perhaps, as in the previously occulted dominant discourse practice.

I would suggest that just as Machiavelli had made a particular conflictual and contractual political practice into a meaningful and inescapable class of analysis, so, too, did Marx make an entirely analogous gesture. The practice that became meaningful analysis has been called the "socioeconomic fact of relations of production," but it is more than that; it is a particular interrelation of human productivity whose ramifications tend to have been placed so far at the service of a hegemony whose premises they actually put into serious

46. Donald F. Bouchard, *Milton: A Structural Reading* (London and Montreal, 1974), p. 176.

question. This is hardly the place to explore that question, but it is worth noting that just as it was impossible after Machiavelli not to take his kind of analysis into account (whether one agreed or disagreed with what seemed to be its implications), so too after Marx. What is in question, that is to say, is not a specific analysis or a specific proposition, but a particular order of conceptualization, a particular way of ascribing meaningfulness to human relations, and a particular way in which, in turn, those relations produce meaningfulness. What is also in question, of course, is a new order of society.

We thus find ourselves in a situation akin to what faced Machiavelli's successors, who, a century later, felt themselves confronted with a *crisis* in all forms of discursive practice. The immediate reaction had been the verbal outpouring of the humanist writers, the mixture of "magic" and "science" of the humanist philosophers, the political unbalance of civil and international war, the economic violence of extreme inflation and widespread poverty and 'unemployment.' This time of disequilibrium was resolved during the following century, by what Hiram Haydn and others have termed the "counter-Renaissance," by the imposition of what I am calling analytico-referential discourse. Once that situation of crisis had been 'identified' (sufficiently widely experienced), the achievement of consolidation and new dominance took another half-century. That is what we have been following in a particular type of discourse (the literary one of science fictions and utopias) that is perfectly characteristic of the analytico-referential. I would suggest that we now find ourselves in a moment precisely analogous to that occupied by Bacon and Descartes, Galileo, Milton, and Hobbes. They were preceded by the humanists. We are preceded perhaps by their analogue: from Peirce to Freud, from the existentialists to the "new philosophers," from Heidegger to Derrida. The response of the seventeenth-century scientists was not a marginalization, nor was it an attempt to take up questions the humanists had been unable to decide. The critical problems were not solved—'answered,' that is to say—but were simply rendered irrelevant by first understanding and then leaving behind the discourse that had earlier been dominant but whose internal contradictions and inescapable limits had now become insufficient to the development of human relations. A new class of discourse was already becoming available, one which was both productive of and produced by such development.

Bibliography

Before 1800

Abelard, Peter. *The Story of My Misfortunes: The Autobiography of Peter Abelard.* Trans. Henry Adams Bellows. 1922. Rpt. New York, 1972.

——, and Heloise. *Correspondance.* Trans. and ed. Paul Zumthor. Paris, 1979.

Agricola, Georgius. *De re metallica.* Trans. Herbert Hoover and Lou Henry Hoover. London, 1912.

Andreae, Johann Valentin. *Christianopolis* [*Reipublicae Christianopolitanae descriptio* (1619)]. Trans. and ed. Felix Emil Held. Urbana, Ill., 1914.

Anselm of Canterbury, St. *Basic Writings: Proslogium, Monologium, Cur Deus Homo and Gaunilon's In Behalf of the Fool.* Trans. S. N. Deane. Intro. Charles Hartshorne. 2d ed. La Salle, Ill., 1974.

Aquinas, St. Thomas. *Summa Theologica.* Trans. Fathers of the English Dominican Province. 3 vols. New York, 1947–48.

Aristotle. *The Basic Works.* Ed. Richard McKeon. New York, 1941.

——. *On Interpretation: Commentary by St. Thomas and Cajetan (Peri hermeneias).* Trans. Jean T. Oesterle. Milwaukee, 1962.

Arnauld, Antoine, and Claude Lancelot. *Grammaire générale et raisonnée . . .* Preface Michel Foucault. Paris, 1969.

——, and Pierre Nicole. *La logique ou l'art de penser.* Ed. Louis Marin. Paris, 1970.

Ascham, Roger. *English Works.* Ed. William Aldis Wright. Cambridge, 1970.

——. *The Scholemaster.* London, 1571.

Augustine of Hippo, St. *Concerning the City of God against the Pagans.* Trans. Henry Bettenson. Intro. David Knowles. Harmondsworth, 1972.

——. *The Confessions.* Trans. Edward B. Pusey. Intro. Fulton J. Sheen. New York, n.d.

——. *On Christian Doctrine.* Trans. and ed. D. W. Robertson, Jr. Indianapolis and New York, 1958.

——. *On Free Choice of the Will.* Trans. Anna S. Benjamin and L. H. Hackstaff. Intro. L. H. Hackstaff. Indianapolis and New York, 1964.

——. *On the Holy Trinity, Doctrinal Treatises, Moral Treatises.* In *A Select Library of the Nicene and Post-Nicene Fathers of the Christian Church.* Ed. Philip Schaff. Vol. 3. Grand Rapids, Mich., 1956.

——. *La Trinité* [with the Latin text of the *De Trinitate*]. In *Oeuvres de Saint-*

Augustin, vols. 15–16. Trans. and ed. M. Mellet, O.P., and Th. Camelot, O.P. [vol. 16 by P. Agaësse, S.J., with J. Moingt, S.J.]. Intro. E. Hendrikx, O.E.S.A. Paris, 1955.

———. *The Teacher [De magistro]*. In *The Greatness of the Soul; The Teacher.* Trans. and ed. Joseph M. Colleran, C.SS.R. 1950. Rpt. Westminster, Md., 1964.

Bacon, Francis, Lord Verulam. *The Works.* Ed. James Spedding, Robert Leslie Ellis, and Douglas Denon Heath. 15 vols. Boston, 1861–64.

———. *The Advancement of Learning and New Atlantis.* Ed. Arthur Johnston. Oxford, 1974.

———. *The New Organon and Related Writings.* Ed. Fulton H. Anderson. Indianapolis and New York, 1960.

Biringuccio, Vannoccio. *Pirotechnia.* Trans. Cyril Stanley Smith and Martha Teach Gnudi. 1942. Rpt. Cambridge, Mass., 1966.

Boccaccio, Giovanni. *Boccaccio on Poetry: Being the Preface and the Fourteenth and Fifteenth Books of Boccaccio's "Genealogia Deorum Gentilium."* Trans. and ed. Charles G. Osgood. Indianapolis and New York, 1930.

Bouhours, le père Dominique. *Les entretiens d'Ariste et d'Eugène.* Ed. Ferdinand Brunot. Paris, 1962.

Bruno, Giordano. *The Heroic Frenzies.* Trans. and ed. Paul Eugene Memmo. Chapel Hill, N.C., 1964.

———. *Opere di Giordano Bruno e di Tommaso Campanella.* Ed. Augusto Guzzo and Romano Amerio. Milan and Naples, 1956.

Cajetan, Tommaso. [See Aristotle]

Campanella, Tommaso. *Apologia pro Galileo.* Frankfurt, 1622. Translation: *The Defense of Galileo.* Trans. and ed. Grant McColley. Northampton, Mass., 1937.

———. *La città del sole.* In *Opere di Giordano Bruno e di Tommaso Campanella.* Ed. Augusto Guzzo and Romano Amerio. Milan and Naples, 1956.

———. *La cité du soleil.* Ed. Luigi Firpo. Trans. Arnaud Tripet. Geneva, 1972.

———. *Realis philosophiae epilogisticae partes quatuor . . .* Frankfurt, 1623.

Cassiodorus Senator. *An Introduction to Divine and Human Readings.* Trans. and ed. Leslie Webber Jones. 1946. Rpt. New York, 1969.

La Chanson de Roland. Ed. Frederick Whitehead. Oxford, 1962.

Chaucer, Geoffrey. *The Complete Works.* Ed. F. N. Robinson. Boston and New York, 1933.

Columbus, Christopher. *Four Voyages to the New World: Letters and Selected Documents.* Trans. and ed. R. H. Major. Intro. John E. Fagg. New York, 1961.

———. *The Four Voyages . . .* Ed. and trans. J. M. Cohen. Harmondsworth, 1969.

Copernicus, Nicolaus. *On the Revolutions of the Heavenly Spheres.* Trans. Charles Glenn Wallis. In *Great Books of the Western World*, vol. 16. Chicago, 1952.

Cyrano de Bergerac, Savinien. *Oeuvres complètes.* Ed. Jacques Prévot. Paris, 1977.

———. *L'autre monde ou les estats et empires de la lune.* Ed. Madeleine Alcover. Paris, 1977.

———. *Histoire comique des état et empire de la lune et du soleil.* Ed. Claude Mettra and Jean Suyeux. Paris, 1962.

———. *Voyage dans la lune (L'autre monde ou les états et empires de la lune)*. Ed. Maurice Laugaa. Paris, 1970.

———. *Other Worlds: The Comical History of the States and Empires of the Moon and Sun*. Trans. Geoffrey Strachan. London, 1965.

Dante Alighieri. *The Divine Comedy*. Trans. Louis Biancolli. 3 vols. New York, 1966.

———. *Literary Criticism of Dante Alighieri*. Trans. and ed. Robert S. Haller. Lincoln, Neb., 1973.

———. *Vita nuova*. Trans. and with an essay by Mark Musa. Bloomington, Ind., and London, 1973.

Defoe, Daniel. *The Life and Strange Surprizing Adventures of Robinson Crusoe, of York, Mariner*. Ed. J. Donald Crowley. London, 1972.

———. *The Farther Adventures of Robinson Crusoe*. In *Robinson Crusoe*. Ed. Guy N. Pocock. 1945. Rpt. London and New York, 1969.

———. *Serious Reflections during the Life and Surprising Adventures of Robinson Crusoe: with his Vision of the Angelick World, Written by Himself*. London, 1720.

Descartes, René. *Oeuvres philosophiques*. Ed. Ferdinand Alquié. 3 vols. Paris, 1963–73.

Drake, Sir Francis. *The World Encompassed, Being His Next Voyage to That to Nombre de Dios, Formerly Imprinted; Carefully collected out of the notes of Master Francis Fletcher* . . . London, 1628.

Drake, Stillman, ed. *Discoveries and Opinions of Galileo*. Garden City, N.Y., 1957.

———, and C. D. O'Malley, trans. and ed. *The Controversy of the Comets of 1618*. Philadelphia, 1960.

Estienne, Henri. *Conformité du langage français avec le grec*. Ed. Léon Feugère. Paris, 1853.

———. *La précellence du langage françois*. Ed. Edmond Huguet. Paris, 1896.

Galilei, Galileo. *Dialogue Concerning the Two Chief World Systems—Ptolemaic and Copernican*. Trans. Stillman Drake. Foreword Albert Einstein. 2d ed. Berkeley and Los Angeles, 1970.

———. *Two New Sciences, Including Centers of Gravity and Force of Percussion*. Trans. and ed. Stillman Drake. Madison and London, 1974.

Gilbert, William. *De magnete*. Trans. P. Fleury Mottelay. 1893. Rpt. New York, 1958.

Gildon, Charles. *The Life and Strange Surprizing Adventures of Mr. D—— D——, of London, Hosier*. London, 1719.

Godwin, Francis. *The Man in the Moone: or, A Discourse of a Voyage thither, by Domingo Gonsales, The Speedy Messenger*. London, 1638.

Harvey, William. *The Circulation of the Blood and Other Writings*. Trans. Kenneth J. Franklin. 1907. Rpt. London and New York, 1968.

———. *Lectures on the Whole of Anatomy*. Trans. C. D. O'Malley, F. N. L. Poynter, and K. F. Russell. Berkeley and Los Angeles, 1961.

Henry, Desmond Paul. *The De Grammatico of St. Anselm: The Theory of Paronymy* [text and commentary]. Notre Dame, Ind., 1964.

Hobbes, Thomas. *The Works*. Ed. Sir William Molesworth. 16 vols. London, 1839–45.

———. *Leviathan*. Ed. Crawford Brough Macpherson. Harmondsworth, 1968.

John of Salisbury. *The Metalogicon: A Twelfth-Century Defense of the Verbal and Logical Arts of the Trivium.* Trans. and ed. Daniel McGarry. 1955. Rpt. Berkeley and Los Angeles, 1962.

Kepler, Johannes. *Opera omnia.* Ed. Christian Frisch. 8 vols. Frankfurt, 1858–71.

——. *Somnium, seu opus posthumum de astronomia lunari.* Divulgatum à M. Ludovice Kepplero Filio. Frankfurt, 1634.

——. *Somnium: The Dream, or Posthumus Work on Lunar Astronomy.* Trans. and ed. Edward Rosen. Madison, Milwaukee, and London, 1967.

——. *Traum vom Mond.* Trans. and ed. Ludwig Günter. Leipzig, 1898.

Lachèvre, Frédéric, ed. *Les oeuvres libertines de Cyrano de Bergerac.* 2 vols. Paris, 1921.

——. *Les successeurs de Cyrano de Bergerac.* Paris, 1922.

La Mothe Le Vayer, François de. *Soliloques sceptiques.* 1670. Rpt. Paris, 1875.

Lavoisier, Antoine-Laurent. *Traité élémentaire de chimie . . .* 3d ed. Paris, 1801.

Lear, Edward. *Kepler's Dream,* with the full text and notes of *Somnium, sive astronomia lunaris, Joannis Kepleri.* Trans. Patricia Fruh Kirkwood. Berkeley and Los Angeles, 1965.

Locke, John. *An Essay Concerning Human Understanding.* Ed. Alexander Campbell Fraser. 2 vols. 1894. Rpt. New York, 1959.

Machiavelli, Niccolò. *The Discourses.* Ed. Bernard Crick. Trans. Leslie J. Walker, S.J. Rev. Brian Richardson. Harmondsworth, 1970.

——. *The Prince.* Trans. and ed. Robert M. Adams. New York, 1977.

Marsilius of Padua. *Defensor pacis.* Trans. and ed. Alan Gewirth. New York, 1956.

Milton, John. *The Prose.* Gen. ed. J. Max Patrick. Garden City, N.Y., 1967.

Molière, Jean-Baptiste Poquelin. *Théâtre complet.* Ed. Robert Jouanny. 2 vols. Paris, 1962.

Montaigne, Michel de. *Montaigne's Essays.* Trans. John Florio. Intro. L. C. Harmer. 3 vols. 1910. Rpt. London and New York, 1965.

Montesquieu, Charles-Louis de Secondat, baron de. *Oeuvres complètes.* Pref. Georges Vedel. Ed. Daniel Oster. Paris, 1964.

More, Thomas. *Utopia.* In *Complete Works,* vol. 4. Ed. Edward Surtz, S.J., and J. H. Hexter. New Haven and London, 1965.

——. *Utopia.* Ed. Edward Surtz, S.J. New Haven and London, 1964.

Morley, Henry, ed. *Ideal Commonwealths.* London and New York, 1901.

Newton, Sir Isaac. *Mathematical Principles of Natural Philosophy and His System of the World.* Trans. Andrew Motte. Rev. Florian Cajori. 2 vols. 1934. Rpt. Berkeley and Los Angeles, 1966.

——. *Opticks, or a Treatise of the Reflections, Refractions, Inflections & Colours of Light.* Based on the Fourth Edition, London, 1730. Foreword Albert Einstein. Intro. Sir Edmund Whittaker. Pref. I. Bernard Cohen. Analytical Table of Contents by Duane H. D. Roller. New York, 1952.

Nowell, Charles E., ed. *Magellan's Voyage around the World: Three Contemporary Accounts.* Evanston, 1962.

Palsgrave, John. *L'eclaircissement de la langue française.* Ed. F. Genin. Paris, 1852.

Paracelsus the Great (Aureolus Philippus Theophrastus Bombast von Hohenheim). *The Hermetic and Alchemical Writings.* Ed. Arthur Edward Waite. 2 vols. 1894. Rpt. Berkeley, 1976.

Pegis, Anton C., ed. *Introduction to St. Thomas Aquinas.* New York, 1948.

Petty, Sir William. *The Political Economy of Ireland.* London, 1691.

Plato. *The Collected Dialogues.* Ed. Edith Hamilton and Huntington Cairns. Princeton, 1961.

Porphyry the Phoenician. *Isagoge.* Trans. and ed. Edward W. Warren. Toronto, 1975.

Rabelais, François. *Gargantua and Pantagruel.* Trans. J. M. Cohen. Harmondsworth, 1955.

Ralegh, Sir Walter. *The Discoverie of the Large, Rich, and Bewtiful Empyre of Guiana, With a Relation of the Great and Golden Citie of Manoa (which the Spanyards call El Dorado)* . . . London, 1596.

Ramus, Petrus [Pierre de la Ramée]. *Dialectique (1555).* Ed. Michel Dassonville. Geneva, 1964.

———. *Scholarum physicarum libri octo, in totidem acroamaticos libros Aristotelis.* Paris, 1565.

———. *Traitté des meurs et façons des anciens Gavloys.* Trans. Michel de Castelnau. Paris, 1581.

———. "Une lettre de Ramus à Joachim Rheticus (1563)." Trans. and ed. Marie Delcourt. *Bulletin de l'Association Guillaume Budé,* 44 (July 1934), 3–15.

Rousseau, Jean-Jacques. *Du contrat social ou principes du droit politique* [and other political writings]. Paris, 1962.

———. *Emile, ou de l'éducation.* Ed. François and Pierre Richard. Paris, 1964.

———. *Emile.* Trans. Barbara Foxley. Intro. P. D. Jimack. London, 1974.

Rymer, Thomas. *The Critical Works.* Ed. Curt A. Zimansky. New Haven, 1956.

Shaftesbury, Anthony Ashley Cooper, 3rd Earl of. *Several Letters Written by a Noble Lord to a Young Man at the University.* London, 1716.

Sophocles. *Oedipus the King.* Trans. David Grene. *Oedipus at Colonus.* Trans. Robert Fitzgerald. In *The Complete Greek Tragedies: Sophocles I.* Ed. David Grene and Richmond Lattimore. Chicago, 1954.

Swift, Jonathan. *Gulliver's Travels, 1726.* Ed. Herbert Davis. Intro. Harold Williams. 1941. Rpt. Oxford, 1965.

Tesauro, Emanuale. *Il cannocchiale aristotelico.* Ed. August Buck. Bad Homburg, 1968.

Tory, Geoffroy. *Champ Fleury ou l'art et science de la proportion des lettres.* Ed. Gustave Cohen. Paris, 1931.

Valincour, J. B. H. du Trousset de. *Avis sur les occupations de l'Académie.* Paris, 1714.

Varro, Marcus Terrentius. *On the Latin Language.* Trans. and ed. Roland G. Kent. 2 vols. Cambridge, Mass., and London, 1938.

Vesalius, Andreas. *The Epitome.* Trans. and ed. L. R. Lind. Anatomical Notes by C. W. Asling. Foreword by Logan Clendening. 1949. Rpt. Cambridge, Mass., and London, 1969.

Vico, Giambattista. *The New Science.* Rev. trans. Thomas Goddard Bergin and Max Harold Fisch. Ithaca, 1968.

Wilkins, John. *A Discovery of a New World, or, A Discourse Tending to prove, that 'tis Probable there may be another Habitable World in the Moon.* 4th ed. London, 1684.

———. *An Essay Towards a Real Character and a Philosophical Language.* London, 1668.

William of Ockham. *Ockham's Theory of Terms: Part 1 of the Summa Logicae.* Trans. and ed. Michael J. Loux. Notre Dame, Ind., and London, 1974.
——. *Philosophical Writings: A Selection.* Trans. and ed. Philotheus Boehner, O.F.M. 1957. Rpt. Indianapolis and New York, 1964.

After 1800

Abraham, Karl. *Traum und Mythos: Eine Studie zur Völkerpsychologie.* Leipzig and Vienna, 1909. Translation: *Dreams and Myths: A Study in Race Psychology.* Trans. William A. White. New York, 1913.
Alcover, Madeleine. *La pensée philosophique et scientifique de Cyrano de Bergerac.* Geneva, 1970.
Anscombe, G. E. M. "Thought and Action in Aristotle: What Is 'Practical Reason'?" In *New Essays on Plato and Aristotle,* ed. Renford Bambrough, pp. 143–58. London, 1965.
Auerbach, Erich. *Mimesis: The Representation of Reality in Western Literature.* Trans. Willard R. Trask. Princeton, 1953.
Bachelard, Gaston. *L'eau et les rêves: Essai sur l'imagination de la matière.* Paris, 1942.
——. *La formation de l'esprit scientifique: Contribution à une psychanalyse de la connaissance objective.* 7th ed. Paris, 1970.
——. *Le nouvel esprit scientifique.* 1934. Rpt. Paris, 1968.
——. *La psychanalyse du feu.* 1949. Rpt. Paris, 1969.
Barthes, Roland. *Critique et vérité.* Paris, 1966.
——. *Le degré zéro de l'écriture.* Paris, 1953.
——. *Leçon.* Paris, 1978.
——. *Mythologies.* Paris, 1957.
——. *Roland Barthes par lui-même.* Paris, 1975.
Baumgardt, Carola. *Johannes Kepler: Life and Letters.* New York, 1951.
Beaujour, Michel. *Le jeu de Rabelais.* Paris, 1969.
Benveniste, Emile. *Problèmes de linguistique générale.* Paris, 1966.
Berdyaev, Nicholas. *Dostoevsky.* Trans. Donald Attwater. 1934. Rpt. New York, 1969.
Blanchet, Léon. *Campanella.* 1920. Rpt. New York, n.d.
Bloch, Marc. *La société féodale.* 1939. Rpt. Paris, 1970.
Bloomfield, Leonard. *Language.* 1933. Rpt. London, 1970.
Borgerhoff, E. B. O. *The Freedom of French Classicism.* Princeton, 1950.
Borges, Jorge Luis. *Obras completas.* 3 vols. Buenos Aires, 1954.
——. *Labyrinths: Selected Stories and Other Writings.* Trans. and ed. Donald A. Yates and James E. Irby. Harmondsworth, 1970.
Bouchard, Donald F. *Milton: A Structural Reading.* London and Montreal, 1974.
Brémond, Claude. "Le message narratif," *Communications,* no. 4 (1964), pp. 4–32.
Brody, Jules. *Boileau and Longinus.* Geneva, 1958.
Brown, Norman O. *Life against Death: The Psychoanalytical Meaning of History.* 1959. Rpt. New York, n.d.
Buck-Morss, Susan. *The Origin of Negative Dialectics: Theodor W. Adorno, Walter Benjamin, and the Frankfurt Institute.* New York and London, 1977.

Burckhardt, Jacob. *The Civilization of the Renaissance in Italy.* Trans. S. G. C. Middlemore. 2 vols. New York, 1958.

Burtt, Edwin Arthur. *The Metaphysical Foundations of Modern Physical Science.* 2d ed. 1932. Rpt. Garden City, N.Y., 1954.

Carroll, Lewis. *The Works.* Ed. Roger Lancelyn Green. Feltham, Middlesex, 1965.

——. *The Annotated Alice.* Ed. Martin Gardner. New York, 1960.

Caspar, Max. *Kepler.* Trans. and ed. C. Doris Hellman. London and New York, 1959.

Cassirer, Ernst. *The Philosophy of the Enlightenment.* Trans. Fritz C. A. Koelln and James P. Pettegrove. Princeton, 1951.

——. *The Philosophy of Symbolic Forms.* Trans. Ralph Manheim. Intro. Charles W. Hendel. 3 vols. New Haven, 1953–57.

——. "Mathematical Mysticism and Mathematical Science." Trans. E. W. Strong. In *Galileo, Man of Science,* ed. Ernan McMullin, pp. 338–51. New York, 1967.

Cave, Terence. *The Cornucopian Text: Problems of Writing in the French Renaissance.* Oxford, 1979.

Chevalier, Jean-Claude. *Histoire de la syntaxe: Naissance de la notion de complément dans la grammaire française (1530–1750).* Geneva, 1968.

Chomsky, Noam. *Cartesian Linguistics: A Chapter in the History of Rationalist Thought.* New York and London, 1966.

——. *For Reasons of State.* New York, 1973.

Cioranescu, Alexandre. *L'avenir du passé: Utopie et littérature.* Paris, 1972.

Colie, Rosalie L. "Cornelius Drebbel and Salomon de Caus: Two Jacobean Models for Salomon's House," *Huntington Library Quarterly,* 18 (1955), 245–60.

Colish, Marcia. *The Mirror of Language: A Study in Medieval Theory of Knowledge.* New Haven and London, 1968.

——. "The Stoic Theory of Verbal Signification and the Problem of Lies and False Statements from Antiquity to St. Anselm." In *L'archéologie du signe,* ed. Lucie Brind'amour and Eugene Vance. Toronto, 1982.

Collingwood, R. G. *The Idea of Nature.* Oxford, 1945.

Cornford, Francis Macdonald. *From Religion to Philosophy: A Study in the Origins of Western Speculation.* 1913. Rpt. New York, 1957.

Cranz, F. Edward. "1100 A.D.: A Crisis for Us?" In *De Litteris: Occasional Papers in the Humanities,* ed. Marijan Despalatović, pp. 84–108. New London, Conn., 1978.

——. "The Renaissance Reading of the *De anima.*" In *XVIe Colloque International de Tours: Platon et Aristote à la Renaissance,* pp. 359–76. Paris, 1976.

——. "The Eyes of the Mind: Antiquity and the Renaissance." Typescript, 1975.

——. "New Dimensions of Thought in Anselm and Abelard as against Augustine and Boethius." Typescript, 1971.

——. "Nicolaus Cusanus as a Paradigm of Renaissance and Reformation." Typescript, 1979.

——. "Petrarch's Transformation of St. Augustine." Typescript, 1971.

——. "Technology and Western Reason." Typescript, 1980.

——. "Two Debates about the Intellect: 1, Alexander of Aphrodisias and the Greeks; 2, Nifo and the Renaissance Philosophers." Typescript, 1979.

394 · *Bibliography*

Culler, Jonathan. *Structuralist Poetics: Structuralism, Linguistics, and the Study of Literature*. Ithaca, 1975.

Curtius, Ernst Robert. *European Literature and the Latin Middle Ages*. Trans. Willard R. Trask. 1953. Rpt. New York and Evanston, 1963.

De Jean, Joan. *Scarron's "Roman comique": A Comedy of the Novel, A Novel of Comedy*. Berne, Frankfurt, and Las Vegas, 1977.

De Santillana, Giorgio. *The Crime of Galileo*. Chicago, 1959.

Delaney, Paul. *British Autobiography in the Seventeenth Century*. London, 1969.

——. "*King Lear* and the Decline of Feudalism." *Publications of the Modern Language Association of America*, 92 (1977), 429–40.

Deleuze, Gilles. *Logique du sens*. Paris, 1969.

Derrida, Jacques. *La carte postale, de Socrate à Freud et au-delà*. Paris, 1980.

——. *De la grammatologie*. Paris, 1967.

——. *La dissémination*. Paris, 1972.

——. *L'ecriture et la différence*. Paris, 1967. Translation: *Writing and Difference*. Trans. and ed. Alan Bass. Chicago and London, 1978.

——. "L'archéologie du frivole." In *Essai sur l'origine des connaissances humaines*, by Etienne Bonnot de Condillac, ed. Charles Porset. Paris, 1973.

Dickens, Charles. *Hard Times*. Afterword Charles Shapiro. New York, 1961.

Dijksterhuis, E. J. *The Mechanization of the World Picture*. Trans. G. Dikshoorn. London, Oxford, and New York, 1961.

Dodds, E. R. *The Greeks and the Irrational*. 1951. Rpt. Berkeley, Los Angeles, and London, 1961.

Donzé, Roland. *La grammaire générale et raisonnée de Port-Royal: Contribution à l'histoire des idées grammaticales en France*. Berne, 1967.

Dostoevsky, Fyodor. *The Brothers Karamazov*. Trans. Constance Garnett. Intro. Marc Slonim. New York, 1950.

Drake, Stillman. *Galileo Studies: Personality, Tradition, and Revolution*. Ann Arbor, Mich., 1970.

Dubois, Claude-Gilbert. *Mythe et langage au seizième siècle*. Bordeaux, 1970.

Duby, Georges. *The Early Growth of the European Economy: Warriors and Peasants from the Seventh to the Twelfth Century*. Trans. Howard B. Clarke. Ithaca, 1974.

——. *L'economie rurale et la vie des campagnes dans l'occident médiéval (France, Angleterre, Empire, ixe–xve siècles): Essai de synthèse et perspectives de recherches*. 2 vols. 1962. Rpt. Paris, 1977.

——. *Les trois ordres, ou l'imaginaire du féodalisme*. Paris, 1978.

——. "Histoire sociale et idéologies des sociétés." In *Faire de l'histoire*. Ed. Jacques Le Goff and Pierre Nora, I.147–68. Paris, 1974.

Ducasse, Isidore, comte de Lautréamont. *Oeuvres complètes*. Ed. Maurice Saillet. Paris, 1963.

Dumézil, Georges. "Lecture de Tite-Live." *Cahiers pour l'analyse*, no. 7 (March–April 1967), *Du mythe au roman*, pp. 5–31.

Durkheim, Émile. *Les formes élémentaires de la vie religieuse: Le système totémique en Australie*. Paris, 1912.

Duveau, Georges. *Sociologie de l'utopie et autres "essais."* Paris, 1961.

Earle, Peter. *The World of Defoe*. London, 1976.

Eco, Umberto. *Opera aperta*. Milan, 1962.

——. *A Theory of Semiotics*. Bloomington and London, 1976.

Ehrmann, Jacques. "Le dedans et le dehors," *Poétique,* no. 9 (1972), pp. 31–40.

Elbaz, Robert. "From Confessions to Antimemoirs: A Study of Autobiography." Ph.D. dissertation, McGill University, Montreal, 1980.

Eliade, Mircea. *Le chamanisme et les techniques archaïques de l'extase.* 2d ed. Paris, 1968.

———. *Forgerons et alchimistes.* Paris, 1965.

———. *Images et symboles: Essais sur le symbolisme magico-religieux.* Paris, 1952.

———. *Myth and Reality.* Trans. Willard R. Trask. New York and Evanston, 1963.

———. *Mythes, rêves et mystères.* Paris, 1953. Translation: *Myths, Dreams and Mysteries: The Encounter between Contemporary Faiths and Archaic Realities.* Trans. Philip Mairet. London, 1960.

Elliott, Robert. *The Shape of Utopia: Studies in a Literary Genre.* Chicago and London, 1970.

Else, Gerald F. *Aristotle's Poetics: The Argument.* Cambridge, Mass., 1963.

Farrington, Benjamin. *The Philosophy of Francis Bacon.* 1964. Rpt. Chicago, 1966.

Fish, Stanley E. *Self-Consuming Artifacts: The Experience of Seventeenth-Century Literature.* Berkeley, Los Angeles, and London, 1972.

Foucault, Michel. *L'archéologie du savoir.* Paris, 1969. Translation: *The Archaeology of Knowledge.* Trans. A. M. Sheridan-Smith. 1972. Rpt. New York, 1976.

———. *Folie et déraison: Histoire de la folie à l'âge classique.* Paris, 1961.

———. *Les mots et les choses: Une archéologie des sciences humaines.* Paris, 1966. Translation: *The Order of Things.* New York, 1973.

———. *L'ordre du discours.* Paris, 1971. Translation: *The Discourse on Language,* printed as an appendix to *The Archaeology of Knowledge* (above).

———. *Surveiller et punir.* Paris, 1975.

———. "Le langage à l'infini." *Tel Quel,* 15 (1963), 44–53.

Frazer, Sir James George. *The Golden Bough: A Study in Magic and Religion.* 3d ed. London, 1911–18. Vols. 10 and 11: *Balder the Beautiful: Fire Festivals of Europe and the Doctrine of the External Soul.*

Frege, Gottlob. *The Foundations of Arithmetic: A Logico-Mathematical Enquiry into the Concept of Number.* Trans. John L. Austin. 2d ed. Oxford, 1953.

———. *Translations from the Philosophical Writings.* Ed. Max Black and Peter Geach. Oxford, 1952.

Freud, Sigmund. *The Standard Edition of the Complete Psychological Works.* Trans. and ed. James Strachey, in collaboration with Anna Freud, Alix Strachey, and Alan Tyson. 24 vols. 1953–66. Rpt. London, 1975.

———. *Die Traumdeutung.* In *Studienausgabe,* vol. 2. Frankfurt, 1972.

Ganshof, F. L. *Feudalism.* Trans. Philip Grierson. 3d English ed. New York, 1964.

Gilson, Etienne. *Etudes sur le rôle de la pensée médiévale dans la formation du système cartésien.* 3d ed. Paris, 1967.

———. *Reason and Revelation in the Middle Ages.* New York, 1938.

Gimpel, Jean. *The Medieval Machine: The Industrial Revolution of the Middle Ages.* 1976. Rpt. Harmondsworth, 1980.

Gravel, Pierre. *Pour une logique du sujet tragique: Sophocle.* Montreal, 1980.

Green, André. "De l'*Esquisse* à l'*Interprétation des rêves*: Coupure et clôture." *Nouvelle Revue de Psychanalyse,* 5 (Spring 1972), 155–80.

Gurwitsch, Aron. "Galileo's Physics in the Light of Husserl's Phenomenology." In *Galileo, Man of Science,* ed. Ernan McMullin, pp. 388–401. New York, 1967.

Hacking, Ian. *The Emergence of Probability: A Philosophical Study of Early Ideas about Probability, Induction, and Statistical Inference.* Cambridge, 1975.

———. *Why Does Language Matter to Philosophy?* Cambridge, 1975.

Haidu, Peter. *Aesthetic Distance in Chrétien de Troyes: Irony and Comedy in "Cligès" and "Perceval."* Geneva, 1968.

———. *Lion-queue-coupée: L'écart symbolique chez Chrétien de Troyes.* Geneva, 1972.

———. "Repetition: Modern Reflections on Medieval Aesthetics." *Modern Language Notes,* 92 (1977), 875–87.

———. "Semiotics and History." Typescript, 1980.

Hanson, Norwood. *Patterns of Discovery.* Cambridge, 1965.

Harries, Karsten. "Descartes, Perspective, and the Angelic Eye." *Yale French Studies,* no. 49 (1973), pp. 28–42.

Harth, Erica. *Cyrano de Bergerac and the Polemics of Modernity.* New York, 1970.

Haskins, Charles Homer. *The Renaissance of the Twelfth Century.* Cambridge, Mass., 1927.

Haydn, Hiram. *The Counter Renaissance.* New York, 1950.

Hill, Christopher. *The Century of Revolution, 1603–1714.* 1961. Rpt. London, 1978.

———. *Intellectual Origins of the English Revolution.* Oxford, 1965.

———. *Milton and the English Revolution.* London and Boston, 1977.

———. *Some Intellectual Consequences of the English Revolution.* Madison, 1980.

———. *The World Turned Upside Down: Radical Ideas during the English Revolution.* 1972. Rpt. Harmondsworth, 1975.

Holt, J. C. *Magna Carta.* Cambridge, 1965.

Horkheimer, Max, and Theodor W. Adorno. *Dialectic of Enlightenment.* Trans. John Cumming. New York, 1972.

Hunter, J. Paul. *The Reluctant Pilgrim: Defoe's Emblematic Method and Quest for Form.* Baltimore, 1966.

Husserl, Edmund. "Die Krisis des europäischen Menschentums und die Philosophie." In *Gesammelte Werke,* vol. 6. The Hague, 1954. Translation: In *Phenomenology and the Crisis of Philosophy.* Trans. Quentin Lauer. New York, 1965.

Imbert, Claude. "Pour une structure de la croyance: L'argument d'Anselme." *Nouvelle Revue de Psychanalyse,* 18 (Autumn 1978), 43–53.

———. "Stoic Logic and Alexandrian Poetics." In *Doubt and Dogmatism: Studies in Hellenistic Epistemology,* ed. Malcolm Schofield, Myles Burnyeat, and Jonathan Barnes, pp. 181–216. Oxford, 1980.

———. "Théorie de la représentation et doctrine logique dans le stoicisme ancien." In *Les Stoiciens et leur logique,* pp. 223–49. Paris, 1978.

Jardine, Lisa. *Francis Bacon: Discovery and the Art of Discourse.* Cambridge, 1974.

Jolivet, Jean. *Arts du langage et théologie chez Abelard.* Paris, 1969.

Jones, Richard Foster. *Ancients and Moderns: A Study of the Rise of the Scientific Movement in Seventeenth-Century England.* 2d ed. St. Louis, 1961.

———. "Science and Criticism in the Neo-Classical Age of English Literature" [1940]. In *The Seventeenth Century: Studies in English Thought and Literature from Bacon to Pope,* by Richard Foster Jones and Others Writing in His Honor, pp. 41–74. Stanford and London, 1951.

Jung, Carl Gustav. *Mysterium coniunctionis: An Enquiry into the Separation and Synthesis of Opposites in Alchemy.* Trans. R. F. C. Hull. In *Collected Works,* vol. 14. London, 1963.

———. *Symbols of Transformation: An Analysis of the Prelude to a Case of Schizophrenia.* Trans. R. F. C. Hull. In *Collected Works,* vol. 5. London, 1963.

Kahler, Erich. *The Inward Turn of Narrative.* Trans. Richard and Clara Winston. Princeton, 1973.

Kemeny, John J. *A Philosopher Looks at Science.* New York, 1959.

Kenny, Anthony. *The Anatomy of the Soul: Historical Essays in the Philosophy of Mind.* Oxford, 1973.

———. *Aristotle's Theory of the Will.* New Haven, 1979.

———. *Will, Freedom, and Power.* Oxford, 1975.

Knowles, David. *The Evolution of Medieval Thought.* 1962. Rpt. New York, n.d.

Koestler, Arthur. *The Sleepwalkers: A History of Man's Changing Vision of the Universe.* New York, 1963.

———. "Kepler." In *Encyclopedia of Philosophy,* ed. Paul Edwards, IV.329–33. New York, 1967.

Koyré, Alexandre. *From the Closed World to the Infinite Universe.* Baltimore, 1957.

———. [Review article on Panofsky on Galileo, q.v.]. *Critique,* 12 (1955), 835–47.

Kretzmann, Norman. "The Main Thesis of Locke's Semantic Theory." In *Locke on Human Understanding: Selected Essays,* ed. I. C. Tipton, pp. 123–40. Oxford, 1977.

Kristeller, Paul Oskar. *Renaissance Thought: The Classic, Scholastic, and Humanist Strains.* New York, 1961.

Kuhn, Thomas S. *The Copernican Revolution: Planetary Astronomy and the Development of Western Thought.* Cambridge, Mass., 1957.

Land, Stephen K. *From Signs to Propositions: The Concept of Form in Eighteenth-Century Semantic Theory.* London, 1974.

Laugaa, Maurice. "Lune, et l'autre." *Poétique,* no. 3 (1970), pp. 282–96.

Leff, Gordon. *William of Ockham: The Metamorphosis of Scholastic Discourse.* Manchester, 1975.

Lévi-Strauss, Claude. *Anthropologie structurale.* Paris, 1958. Translation: *Structural Anthropology.* Trans. Claire Jacobson and Brooke Grundfest Schoepf. New York and London, 1963.

———. *Anthropologie structurale deux.* Paris, 1973.

———. *Mythologiques.* 4 vols. Paris, 1964–71.

———. *La pensée sauvage.* Paris, 1963. Translation: *The Savage Mind.* Chicago, 1966.

———. *Totemism.* Trans. Rodney Needham. Intro. Roger Poole. Harmondsworth, 1969.

———. "Introduction à l'oeuvre de Marcel Mauss." In Mauss, Marcel, q.v.

Lopez, Robert S. *The Commercial Revolution of the Middle Ages, 950–1350.* 1971. Rpt. Cambridge, 1976.

Lovejoy, Arthur O. *The Great Chain of Being: A Study in the History of an Idea.* 1936. Rpt. New York, 1960.

Macaulay, Thomas Babington. *The Life and Letters of Lord Macaulay.* Ed. George Otto Trevelyan. 2 vols. London, 1876.

Mach, Ernst. *Space and Geometry in the Light of Physiological, Psychological, and Physical Inquiry.* Trans. Thomas J. McCormack. 1906. Rpt. La Salle, Ill., 1960.

Macherey, Pierre. *Pour une théorie de la production littéraire.* Paris, 1966.

Macpherson, Crawford Brough. *The Political Theory of Possessive Individualism: Hobbes to Locke.* Oxford, 1962.

Mannheim, Karl. *Ideology and Utopia: An Introduction to the Sociology of Knowledge.* Trans. Louis Wirth and Edward Shils. New York, 1936.

Manuel, Frank E., ed. *Utopias and Utopian Thought.* Boston, 1966.

Marin, Louis. *Critique du discours: Sur la "Logique de Port-Royal" et les "Pensées" de Pascal.* Paris, 1975.

———. *Utopiques, jeux d'espace.* Paris, 1973.

Marks, Emerson R. *The Poetics of Reason: English Neoclassical Criticism.* New York, 1968.

Marx, Karl. *Capital.* Trans. Samuel Moore and Edward Aveling. Ed. Friedrich Engels. 3 vols. New York, 1967.

———, and Frederick Engels. *Selected Works.* New York, 1968.

Matson, Floyd W. *The Broken Image: Man, Science, and Society.* New York, 1964.

Mauss, Marcel. *Sociologie et anthropologie.* Intro. Claude Lévi-Strauss. Paris, 1950.

Michelet, Jules. *Renaissance.* Ed. Robert Casanova. In *Oeuvres complètes,* ed. Paul Viallaneix, VII.47–259. Paris, 1978.

Mill, John Stuart. *Philosophy of Scientific Method.* Ed. Ernest Nagel. New York, 1950.

Monk, Samuel H. "The Pride of Lemuel Gulliver." *Sewanee Review,* 63 (1955), 48–71.

Moore, John Robert. *Daniel Defoe and Modern Economic Theory.* Bloomington, Ind., 1934.

Morris, Colin. *The Discovery of the Individual, 1050–1200.* New York, 1972.

Nicolson, Marjorie Hope. *The Breaking of the Circle: Studies in the Effect of the "New Science" on Seventeenth-Century Poetry.* Rev. ed. New York, 1962.

———. *Science and Imagination.* Ithaca, 1956.

———. *Voyages to the Moon.* New York, 1948.

Novak, Maximillian E. *Defoe and the Nature of Man.* Oxford, 1963.

———. *Economics and the Fiction of Daniel Defoe.* Berkeley and Los Angeles, 1962.

Ong, Walter J., S.J. *Ramus, Method, and the Decay of Dialogue.* Cambridge, Mass., 1958.

Ozment, Steven E. *The Age of Reform, 1250–1550: An Intellectual and Religious History of Late Medieval and Reformation Europe.* New Haven and London, 1980.

Panaccio, Claude. "La Métaphysique et les noms." In *Culture et langage,* ed. J. P. Brodeur, pp. 249–81. Montreal, 1973.

Panofsky, Erwin. *Galileo as a Critic of the Arts.* The Hague, 1954.

———. *Renaissance and Renascences in Western Art.* 1960. Rpt. New York and Evanston, 1969.

Paris, Jean. *Rabelais au futur.* Paris, 1970.

Parker, Patricia Anne. *Inescapable Romance: Studies in the Poetics of a Mode.* Princeton, 1979.

Pater, Walter. *The Renaissance: Studies in Art and Poetry.* Intro. Louis Kronenberger, New York, 1959.

Pauli, Wolfgang. "The Influence of Archetypal Ideas on the Scientific Theories of Kepler." In *The Interpretation of Nature and the Psyche,* by C. G. Jung and W. Pauli. New York, 1955.

Peirce, Charles Sanders. *Collected Papers.* Ed. Charles Hartshorne and Paul Weiss [and Arthur W. Burks for vols. 7 and 8]. 8 vols. Cambridge, Mass., 1931–58.

——. *Philosophical Writings.* Ed. Justus Buchler. 1940. Rpt. New York, 1955.

Pirenne, Henri. *Economic and Social History of Medieval Europe.* Trans. I. E. Clegg. 1936. Rpt. London, 1972.

Planck, Max. *Where Is Science Going?* Trans. and ed. James Murphy. London, 1933.

Pocock, J. G. A. *The Ancient Constitution and the Feudal Law: A Study of English Historical Thought in the Seventeenth Century.* 1957. Rpt. New York, 1967.

Popper, Karl Raimond. *The Poverty of Historicism.* 1957. Rpt. New York and Evanston, 1964.

Prévot, Jacques. *Cyrano de Bergerac poète et dramaturge.* Paris, 1977.

——. *Cyrano de Bergerac romancier.* Paris, 1977.

Raab, Felix. *The English Face of Machiavelli: A Changing Interpretation, 1500–1700.* London and Toronto, 1964.

Raimondi, Ezio. *Letteratura baroca: Studi sui seicento italiano.* Florence, 1961.

Reiss, Timothy J. *Toward Dramatic Illusion: Theatrical Technique and Meaning from Hardy to "Horace."* New Haven and London, 1971.

——. *Tragedy and Truth: Studies in the Development of a Renaissance and Neo-classical Discourse.* New Haven and London, 1980.

——. "Archéologie du discours et critique épistémique: Projet pour une critique discursive." In *Philosophie et littérature* [ed. Pierre Gravel], pp. 143–89. Montreal, Paris, and Tournai, 1979.

——. "Cartesian Discourse and Classical Ideology." *Diacritics,* 6 no. 4 (Winter 1976), 19–27.

——. "The *concevoir* Motif in Descartes." In *La cohérence intérieure: Etudes sur la littérature française du xviie siècle, présentées en hommage à Judd D. Hubert,* ed. J. Van Baelen and D. L. Rubin, pp. 203–22. Paris, 1977.

——. "Cosmic Discourse or, The Solution of Signing (Gombrowicz)." *Canadian Journal of Research in Semiotics,* 8, no. 1–2 (Fall–Winter 1979–80), pp. 123–45.

——. "La décision du classicisme: Savoir ou carnaval?" *Romanic Review,* 70 (1979), 33–44.

——. "Du système de la critique classique." *XVIIe Siècle,* 116 (1977), 3–16.

——. "The Environment of Literature and the Imperatives of Criticism." *Europa,* 4 (1981), to appear.

——. "Espaces de la pensée discursive: Le cas Galilée et la science classique." *Revue de synthèse,* no. 85–86 (Jan.–July 1977), pp. 5–47.

——. "Le non-lieu de la fête et le projet d'ordre." In *La fête en question,* ed. Karin Gürttler and Monique Serfati-Arnaud, pp. 92–108. Montreal, 1979.

——. "Peirce and Frege: In the Matter of Truth." *Canadian Journal of Research in Semiotics*, 4, no. 2 (Winter 1976–77), 5–39.

——. "Sailing to Byzantium: Classical Discourse and Its Self-Absorption." *Diacritics*, 8, no. 2 (Summer 1978), 34–46.

——. "Semiology and Its Discontents: Saussure and Greimas." *Canadian Journal of Research in Semiotics*, 5, no. 1 (Fall 1977), 65–101.

——. "The Trouble with Literary Criticism." *Europa*, 3 (1980), 223–40.

——. "Vers un système de la tragédie renaissante: Buchanan, Montaigne, et la difficulté de s'exprimer." *Canadian Review of Comparative Literature*, 4 (1977), 133–78.

——, and Roger H. Hinderliter. "Money and Value in the Sixteenth Century: The *Monete cudende ratio* of Nicholas Copernicus" [with a translation]. *Journal of the History of Ideas*, 40 (1979), 293–313.

Richards, I. A. *Principles of Literary Criticism.* London, 1925.

——, and C. K. Ogden. *The Meaning of Meaning: A Study of the Influence of Language upon Thought and of the Science of Symbolism.* 1923. Rpt. New York, n.d.

Rieff, Philip. *Freud: The Mind of the Moralist.* 1959. Rpt. New York, 1961.

Rihs, Charles. *Les philosophes utopistes: Le mythe de la cité communautaire en France au xviie siècle.* Paris, 1970.

Romanowski, Sylvie. *L'illusion chez Descartes: La structure du discours cartésien.* Paris, 1974.

Rosenfield, Leonora Cohen. *From Beast-Machine to Man-Machine: Animal Soul in French Letters from Descartes to La Mettrie.* New York, 1941.

Roy, Jean. *Hobbes et Freud.* Halifax, N.S., 1976.

Russell, Bertrand. *An Inquiry Into Meaning and Truth.* London, 1940.

——. *Logic and Knowledge: Essays, 1901–1950.* Ed. Robert Charles Marsh. 1956. Rpt. New York, 1971.

Saint-Jarre, Chantal. "Le concept d'inconscient chez Freud." M.A. thesis, Université du Québec à Montréal, Montreal, 1981.

Sapir, Edward. *Language: An Introduction to the Study of Speech.* 1921. Rpt. New York, 1964.

Saussure, Ferdinand de. *Cours de linguistique générale.* Ed. Tullio de Mauro. Paris, 1972.

Schwonke, Martin. *Vom Staatsroman zur Science Fiction: Eine Untersuchung über Geschichte und Funktion der naturwissenchaftlich-technischen Utopie.* Stuttgart, 1957.

Serres, Michel. *Hermès.* 5 vols. Paris, 1968–80.

——. *La naissance de la physique dans le texte de Lucrèce: Fleuves et turbulences.* Paris, 1977.

——. *Le parasite.* Paris, 1979.

——. "Les sciences." In *Faire de l'histoire,* ed. Jacques Le Goff and Pierre Nora, II.203–28. Paris, 1974.

Servier, Jean. *Histoire de l'utopie.* Paris, 1967.

Simon, Gérard. *Kepler astronome astrologue.* Paris, 1979.

Snell, Bruno. *The Discovery of the Mind: The Greek Origins of European Thought.* Trans. T. G. Rosenmeyer. 1953. Rpt. New York and Evanston, 1960.

Southern, R. W. *The Making of the Middle Ages.* 1953. Rpt. New Haven and London, 1980.

Stephens, James. *Francis Bacon and the Style of Science.* Chicago and London, 1971.

Strauss, Leo. *The Political Philosophy of Hobbes: Its Basis and Its Genesis.* Trans. Elsa M. Sinclair. 1936. Rpt. Chicago and London, 1968.
Struever, Nancy S. *The Language of History in the Renaissance: Rhetoric and Historical Consciousness in Florentine Humanism.* Princeton, 1970.
———. "Metaphoric Morals: Ethical Implications of Cusanus' Use of Figure." In *L'archéologie du signe,* ed. Lucie Brind'amour and Eugene Vance. Toronto, 1982.
Surtz, Edward, S.J. *The Praise of Pleasure: Philosophy, Education, and Communism in More's "Utopia."* Cambridge, Mass., 1957.
Tillyard, E. M. W. *The Elizabethan World Picture.* New York, n.d.
———. *The Epic Strain in the English Novel.* London, 1958.
Turgenev, Ivan. *Fathers and Sons.* Foreword Avraham Yarmolinsky. New York, 1962.
Ullmann, Walter. *The Individual and Society in the Middle Ages.* Baltimore, 1966.
———. *Medieval Political Thought.* 3d ed. Harmondsworth, 1975.
Uscatescu, George. *Utopía y plenitud histórica.* Madrid, 1963.
Vance, Eugene. *Reading the Song of Roland.* Englewood Cliffs, N.J., 1970.
———. "Augustine's *Confessions* and the Grammar of Selfhood." *Genre,* 6 (1973), 1–28.
———. "Augustine's *Confessions* and the Poetics of the Law." *Modern Language Notes,* 93 (1978), 618–34.
———. "Désir, rhétorique et texte—Semences de la différence: Brunet Latin chez Dante." *Poétique,* no. 42 (April 1980), pp. 137–55.
———. "Le Moi comme langage: Saint-Augustin et l'autobiographie." *Poétique,* no. 14 (1973), pp. 163–77.
———. "Love's Concordance: The Poetics of Desire and the Joy of the Text." *Diacritics,* 5, no. 1 (Spring 1975), 40–52.
———. "Mervelous Signals: Poetics, Sign Theory, and Politics in Chaucer's *Troilus."* *New Literary History,* 10 (1979), 293–337.
———. "Roland and the Poetics of Memory." In *Textual Strategies: Perspectives in Post Structural Criticism,* ed. Josué Harari, pp. 374–403. Ithaca, 1979.
———. "Roland, Charlemagne, and the Poetics of Illumination." *Oliphant,* 6 (1979), 213–25.
———. "St. Augustine and the Poetics of Dialogue." Typescript, 1975.
Vernant, Jean-Pierre. *Mythe et pensée chez les Grecs: Études de psychologie historique.* 2d ed. 2 vols. Paris, 1971.
———. *Mythe et société en Grèce ancienne.* Paris, 1974.
———. *Religions, histoires, raisons.* Paris, 1979.
———. "Introduction." In *Les jardins d'Adonis: La mythologie des aromates en Grèce,* by Marcel Detienne. Paris, 1973.
———, and Pierre Vidal-Nacquet. *Mythe et tragédie en Grèce ancienne.* Paris, 1972.
Vickers, Brian. *Francis Bacon and Renaissance Prose.* Cambridge, 1968.
———, ed. *The World of Jonathan Swift: Essays for the Tercentenary.* Cambridge, Mass., 1968.
Voelke, André-Jean. *L'idée de la volonté dans le stoïcisme.* Paris, 1973.
Vološinov, Valentin Nikolaevič [and Mikhail Bakhtin]. *Marxism and the Philosophy of Language.* Trans. Ladislav Matejka and I. R. Titunik. New York, 1973.

Vygotsky, Lev Semenovich. *Thought and Language*. Ed. and trans. Eugenia Hanfmann and Gertrude Vakar. Cambridge, Mass., 1962.

Walker, Judy Carol. "The Unity of Cyrano de Bergerac's Imaginary Voyages." Ph.D. dissertation, University of Kentucky, Lexington, 1974.

Watt, Ian. *The Rise of the Novel: Studies in Defoe, Richardson, and Fielding*. Berkeley and Los Angeles, 1957.

Webster, Charles. *The Great Instauration: Science, Medicine, and Reform, 1626–1660*. London, 1975.

White, Lynn T., Jr. *Medieval Religion and Technology: Collected Essays*. Berkeley, Los Angeles, and London, 1978.

——. *Medieval Technology and Social Change*. Oxford, 1962.

Whitehead, Alfred North. *Science and the Modern World*. 1925. Rpt. New York, 1967.

Whorf, Benjamin Lee. *Language, Thought, and Reality: Selected Writings*. Ed. John B. Carroll. Cambridge, Mass., 1956.

Williams, Kathleen. *Jonathan Swift and the Age of Compromise*. Lawrence, Kan., 1959.

Williams, Raymond. *The Country and the City*. London, 1973.

——. *Culture and Society, 1780–1950*. London, 1958.

——. *The Long Revolution*. London, 1961.

——. *Marxism and Literature*. Oxford, 1977.

Wittgenstein, Ludwig. *Philosophical Investigations*. Trans. G. E. M. Anscombe. 1953. Rpt. Oxford, 1972.

——. *Tractatus logico-philosophicus*. Trans. D. F. Pears and B. F. McGuinness. Intro. Bertrand Russell. London, 1961.

Wolff, Philippe. *Western Languages, A.D. 100–1500*. Trans. Frances Partridge. London, 1971.

Zamiatin, Eugene. *We*. Trans. Gregory Zilboorg. 1924. Rpt. New York, 1952.

Zumthor, Paul. *Essai de poétique médiévale*. Paris, 1972.

——. *Langue, texte, énigme*. Paris, 1975.

——. *Le masque et la lumière: La poétique des grands rhétoriqueurs*. Paris, 1978.

Index

The Discourse of Modernism

Designed by Richard E. Rosenbaum.
Composed by Eastern Graphics
in 10 point Linotron 202 Baskerville
with display lines in Baskerville.
Printed offset by Thomson/Shore, Inc. on
Warren's Number 66 Antique Offset, 50 pound basis.
Bound by John H. Dekker & Sons, Inc.
in Joanna book cloth
and stamped in Kurz-Hastings foil.

Library of Congress Cataloging in Publication Data

Reiss, Timothy J., 1942–
    The discourse of modernism.

    Bibliography: p.
    Includes index.
    1. Knowledge, Theory of. 2. Epistemics. I. Title.
BD161.R46   190   81-15212
ISBN 0-8014-1464-4   AACR2